LEUTHEN

GREAT BATTLES

LEUTHEN

T. G. OTTE

OXFORD
UNIVERSITY PRESS

OXFORD
UNIVERSITY PRESS

Great Clarendon Street, Oxford, OX2 6DP,
United Kingdom

Oxford University Press is a department of the University of Oxford.
It furthers the University's objective of excellence in research, scholarship,
and education by publishing worldwide. Oxford is a registered trade mark of
Oxford University Press in the UK and in certain other countries

© T. G. Otte 2024

The moral rights of the author have been asserted

Published in the United States of America by Oxford University Press
198 Madison Avenue, New York, NY 10016, United States of America

British Library Cataloguing in Publication Data
Data available

Library of Congress Control Number: 2024939732

ISBN 978–0–19–287049–0

Printed and bound by
CPI Group (UK) Ltd, Croydon, CR0 4YY

Links to third party websites are provided by Oxford in good faith and
for information only. Oxford disclaims any responsibility for the materials
contained in any third party website referenced in this work.

To the memory of A. A. O. (1941–2019)

FOREWORD

The phrase 'great battle' carries four immediate connotations. The first relates to time. The standard narrative, whether applied to Marathon or Waterloo, Salamis or Trafalgar, assumes that the events occurred on a single day—or at most over two or three days. Secondly, a battle has to be on a scale large enough not to be deemed a skirmish. Fighting may characterise war but fighting itself does not constitute a battle. If the forces involved are too small or the commitment to engage by one or both sides too slight, then what happens is not a great battle. At least one side, and possibly both, must want to fight. Third, a battle occurs in a defined, and in some cases a confined, space. On land it is sometimes so geographically limited that it takes its name from an otherwise little-known geographical feature, such as Bunker Hill, or an obscure village or hamlet. At sea, its name may be more capacious but as often it gains precision by adopting the name of the nearest landfall. Lastly, a 'great battle' implies that the consequences are commensurate with the commitment; in other words, that the result proves decisive.

The infrequency with which all these four conditions have been met helps explain why 'great battles' have been rare. Great battles need to be infrequent or they lose their cachet Calling some forms of combat battles may be no more than a rhetorical device, coined for effect, or, more pragmatically, to give shape to otherwise seemingly inchoate episodes. Since the nineteenth century the word battle has been applied to events that are not concentrated in time and space. Persistent fighting in all seasons and all weathers combined with technological innovation and full social and economic mobilisation to make outcomes more cumulative than singular. In the Second World War, the 'battle' of the Atlantic was decisive, both in the economic war and in enabling the D Day landings, but it was not clearly defined in time or space. It lasted nearly four years and, although largely restricted to the North Atlantic, still embraced an expanse of sea larger than any major continent.

At sea especially, battle in a traditional sense was rarely decisive. As the British naval theorist. Julian Corbett, observed in 1911, man lives upon the land, and so 'it scarcely needs saying that it is almost impossible that a war can be decided by naval action alone'. The Greeks may have checked the Persians at Salamis in 480 BC but they did not topple the Persian empire. The Christian victory over the Turks at Lepanto in 1572 was similarly a great defensive success, which checked the Ottoman advance into the Mediterranean but not into continental Europe. On 21 October 1805 Nelson 'decisively' defeated the French and Spanish fleets at Trafalgar but war with France continued for another decade. In the short term too, while Nelson's victory ended the danger of a French invasion of Britain, it did not end Napoleon's freedom of manoeuvre within Europe. Just over six weeks after Trafalgar the French emperor won possibly his greatest victory, defeating the armies of Austria and Russia at Austerlitz on 2 December 1805. However, even in land warfare 'decisiveness' can be a relative, rather than an absolute, term. At Austerlitz Napoleon smashed the continental alliance which threatened him in the short term but he did not prevent its resuscitation in 1813. Nor did he win the economic and commercial war waged by Britain and underpinned by its maritime power.

In Corbett's day, the ability of warships to cope with adverse weather conditions enabled by the invention of steam power and the end of sail ought to have made naval battle more possible, but it did not necessarily do so, partly because improved navigation and advanced technology opened up more of the world's oceans and so created greater space in which an opponent could hide. Since the beginning of the twentieth century, war at sea has been increasingly fought under and over the surface, as well as on it. In the Second

World War 'great battles' were fought in the Pacific simultaneously at sea and in the air with devastating effects—at Pearl Harbor in December 1941, the Coral Sea in May 1942 and Midway in the following month. Each was conducted at scale and was limited in time, if less so in space. Each was more clearly a 'great battle' in the classical definition than the whole of the battle of the Atlantic, but the war against Japan was also won by sustained economic warfare conducted by submarines and by island-hopping amphibious assaults. The Second World War did not end in a climactic battle like Waterloo in 1815. That final defeat of Napoleon, for many then and since, embodies the concept of decisiveness, not least because it introduced nearly a century of comparative European peace, but its outcome too rested as much on the exhaustion of France, and of its enemies, after two decades of conflict as it did on the results of a single day on a confined battlefield, however sanguinary the fighting.

For those who practise war in the twenty-first century the idea of a 'great battle' can seem no more than the echo of a remote past. The names on regimental colours or the events commemorated at mess dinners bear little relationship to patrolling in dusty villages or waging 'wars amongst the people'. Contemporary military doctrine downplays the idea of victory, arguing that wars end by negotiation not by the smashing of an enemy army or navy. Indeed it erodes the very division between war and peace, and with it the aspiration to fight a culminating 'great battle'.

And yet to take battle out of war is to redefine war, possibly to the point where some would argue that it ceases to be war. Carl von Clausewitz, who experienced two 'great battles' at first hand—Jena–Auerstedt in 1806 and Borodino in 1812 wrote in *On War* that major battle is 'concentrated war', and 'the centre of gravity of the entire campaign'. Clausewitz's remarks related to the theory of strategy. He recognized that in practice armies might avoid battles, but even then the efficacy of their actions relied on the latent threat of fighting. Winston Churchill saw the importance of battles in different terms, not for their place within war but for their impact on historical and national narratives. His forebear, the Duke of Marlborough, fought four major battles and named his palace after the most famous of them, Blenheim, fought in 1704. Battles, Churchill wrote in his life of Marlborough, are 'the principal milestones in secular history'. For him, 'Great battles, won or lost, change the entire course of events, create new standards of values, new moods, new atmospheres, in armies and nations, to which all must conform'.

Clausewitz's experience of war was shaped by Napoleon. Like Marlborough, the French emperor sought to bring his enemies to battle. However, each lived within a century of the other, and they fought their wars in the same continent and even on occasion on adjacent ground. Winston Churchill's own experience of war, which spanned the late nineteenth-century colonial conflicts of the British Empire as well as two world wars, became increasingly distanced from the sorts of battle he and Clausewitz described. In 1898 Churchill rode in a cavalry charge in a battle which crushed the Madhist forces of the Sudan in a single day. Four years later the British commander at Omdurman, Lord Kitchener, brought the South African War to a conclusion after a two-year guerrilla conflict in which no climactic battle occurred. Both Churchill and Kitchener served as British Cabinet ministers in the First World War, a conflict in which battles lasted weeks, and even months, and which, despite their scale and duration, did not produce clear-cut outcomes. The 'battle' of Verdun ran for all but one month of 1916 and that of the Somme for five months. The potentially decisive naval action at Jutland spanned a more traditional twenty-four-hour timetable but was not conclusive and was not replicated during the war.

Clausewitz would have called these twentieth-century 'battles' campaigns, or even seen them as wars in their own right. The determination to seek battle and to venerate its effects may therefore be culturally determined, the product of time and place, rather than an inherent attribute of war. The ancient historian Victor Davis Hanson has argued that seeking battle is a 'western way of war' derived from classical Greece. Seemingly supportive of his argument are the writings of Sun Tzu, who flourished in the warring states period in China between two and five centuries before the birth of Christ, and who pointed out that the most effective way of waging war was to avoid the risks and dangers of actual fighting. Hanson has provoked strong criticism: those who argue that wars can be won without battles are not only to be found in Asia. Eighteenth-century European commanders, deploying armies in close-order formations in order to deliver concentrated fires, realized that the destructive consequences of battle for their own troops could be self-defeating. After the First World War, Basil Liddell Hart developed a theory of strategy which he called 'the indirect approach', and suggested that manoeuvre might substitute for hard fighting, even if its success still relied on the inherent threat of battle.

The winners of battles have been celebrated as heroes, and nations have used their triumphs to establish their founding myths. It is precisely for these reasons that their legacies have outlived their direct political consequences. Commemorated in painting, verse, and music, marked by monumental memorials, and used as the way points for the periodization of history, they have enjoyed cultural afterlives. These are evident in many capitals, in place names and statues, not least in Paris and London. The French tourist who finds himself in a London taxi travelling from Trafalgar Square to Waterloo Station should reflect on his or her own domestic peregrinations from the Rue de Rivoli to the Gare d'Austerlitz. Today's Mongolia venerates the memory of Genghis Khan while Greece and Macedonia scrap over the rights to Alexander the Great.

This series of books on 'great battles' tips its hat to both Clausewitz and Churchill. Each of its volumes situates the battle which it discusses in the context of the war in which it occurred, but each then goes on to discuss its legacy, its historical interpretation and reinterpretation, its place in national memory and commemoration, and its manifestations in art and culture. These are not easy books to write. The victors were more often celebrated than the defeated; the effect of loss on the battlefield could be cultural oblivion. However, that point is not universally true: the British have done more over time to mark their defeats at Gallipoli in 1915 and Dunkirk in 1940 than their conquerors on both occasions. For the history of war to thrive and be productive it needs to embrace the view from 'the other side of the hill', to use the Duke of Wellington's words. The battle the British call Omdurman is for the Sudanese the battle of Kerreri; the Germans called Waterloo 'la Belle Alliance' and Jutland Skagerrak. Indeed, the naming of battles could itself be a sign not only of geographical precision or imprecision (Kerreri is more accurate but as a hill, rather than a town, it is harder to find on a small-scale map), but also of cultural choice. In 1914 the German general staff opted to name their defeat of the Russians in East Prussia not Allenstein (as geography suggested) but Tannenberg, in order to claim revenge for the defeat of the Teutonic Knights in 1410.

Military history, more than many other forms of history, is bound up with national stories. All too frequently it fails to be comparative, to recognize that war is a 'clash of wills' (to quote Clausewitz once more), and so omits to address both parties to the fight. Cultural difference and even more linguistic ignorance can prevent the historian considering a battle in the round; so too can the availability of sources. Levels of literacy matter here, but so does cultural survival. Often these pressures can be congruent but they can also be divergent. Britain enjoys much higher levels of literacy than Afghanistan, but in 2002 the memory of the two countries' three wars flourished in the latter, thanks to an oral tradition, much more robustly than in the former, for whom literacy had created distance. And the historian who addresses cultural legacy is likely to face a much more challenging task the further in the past the battle occurred. The opportunity for invention and reinvention is simply greater the longer the lapse of time since the key event.

All historians of war must, nonetheless, never forget that, however rich and splendid the cultural legacy of a great battle, it was won and lost by fighting, by killing and being killed. The battle of Waterloo has left as abundant a footprint as any, but the general who harvested most of its glory reflected on it in terms which have general applicability and carry across time in their capacity to capture a universal truth. Wellington wrote to Lady Shelley in its immediate aftermath: 'I hope to God I have fought my last battle. It is a bad thing to be always fighting. While in the thick of it I am much too occupied to feel anything; but it is wretched just after. It is quite impossible to think of glory. Both mind and feelings are exhausted. I am wretched even at the moment of victory, and I always say that, next to a battle lost, the greatest misery is a battle gained.'

Readers of this series should never forget the immediate suffering caused by battle, as well as the courage required to engage in it: the physical courage of the warrior, the soldier, sailor or airman, and the moral courage of the commander, ready to hazard all on its uncertain outcomes.

HEW STRACHAN

PREFACE AND ACKNOWLEDGEMENTS

The village of Leuthen, which today bears the Polish name of Lutynia, lies some 17 km (11 miles) from Breslau (now Wrocław), the regional capital of Silesia, once one of Germany's eastern provinces and now a region in Western Poland. Here, on 5 December 1757, a Prussian army attacked and routed an Austrian force almost twice its size in a daring flanking operation. It was a textbook example of the so-called 'oblique order', in which one wing of the army was declined and the bulk of the force deployed in an echelon, thereby allowing it to achieve local superiority in numbers and to concentrate its fire on one point of the enemy's flank, which was then dislodged.

Leuthen was not the largest or the bloodiest battle of the Seven Years' War (1756–63), arguably the most significant conflict in Europe between the Thirty Years' War (1618–48) and the wars against Revolutionary and then Napoleonic France (1792–1815). But it marked a crucial turning point in this, the third round of fighting for mastery of Silesia and power in Germany between Frederick II ('the Great') of Prussia and his principal adversary, Maria Theresa, Holy Roman Empress, Queen of Bohemia, Hungary, and Croatia, Archduchess of Austria, and Lady of the Netherlands. Leuthen was the encounter remembered more than any other of Frederick's battles, including even Rossbach (5 November 1757). This applied in equal measure to the events on the field of battle as to the event that seemed to crystallize the wider meaning of Leuthen for later generations, the seemingly spontaneous intonation of a church hymn by Frederick's exhausted but victorious grenadiers after the battle as night fell. For more than two centuries the 'Chorale of Leuthen' was to reverberate through German public life. This book aims to explain Leuthen's wider significance. To do so it is necessary, in the first instance, to situate the battle in its specific, contemporary military and political context. But Leuthen left a larger military, political, and cultural legacy which also needs to be explored.

Studying battles poses conceptual and practical challenges. The notion of their 'decisive' nature may be seen as somewhat problematic, not least because it was shaped by nineteenth-century understandings that, in turn, were conditioned by contemporary attempts to grapple with the experience of the phenomenon of Napoleonic-style warfare.[1] The insight of one nineteenth-century writer, Carl von Clausewitz, nevertheless bears closer inspection. Battles, he noted, are 'the bloodiest means of solution' of a conflict. They are never a case of simple 'mutual murdering … yet the price is always paid in blood and slaughter is its character'. As a human being any commander would recoil from this prospect, Clausewitz suggested. But even more does 'the human spirit shudder at the thought of a decision brought about with a single stroke. All action is condensed here *in one point* in space and time'.[2]

Clausewitz's observation about the extreme pressures that come to bear on those engaged in battle has implications for anyone exploring this aspect of war. If politics are saturated with contingency, then battles are dripping with it. The outcome on the day is not preordained. Often it hinges less on the brilliance of one commander than on the decisions of his adversary or on the conditions under which they join battle. Nor are longer-term consequences of a battle inevitable. It is important, then, to reconstruct the course of events as much as possible from the perspective of those who fought it, whether from their command post or in the midst of the mêlée; and in what follows here it will become plain that Leuthen was a little different, altogether more ambiguous and complex, than later reconstructions suggested.

In recent times, it has become fashionable to write battles out of history. In their place, broader questions of war and its relation to the society that gave rise to it, and that produced the means for its conduct, have gained prominence. Such studies frequently focus on social groups that played a role on the domestic front, especially in the two world wars, or they explore the societal background of those who found themselves, whether voluntarily or by compulsion, in the ranks of the armed forces. Such an approach can be fruitful. It can develop new perspectives and so help to elucidate broader contexts; and it can help to sharpen our understanding of the wider significance of war. But it is not without problems of its own. Chief amongst them is a tendency to demilitarize military history by leaving out the fighting, which after all was—and is—the purpose of armies and navies. *Leuthen* follows a different path. Whilst acknowledging these 'war and society' aspects, which are given due consideration in Chapter 1, its principal interest lies in the great power dimension of the Seven Years' War and the conduct of operations in the conflict and at Leuthen. Tracing Leuthen's legacy in nineteenth- and twentieth-century Germany will round off the discussions.

Writing is a solitary business, but scholars never work entirely in monkish isolation from the outside world. I have been fortunate to have been able to draw on the support and expertise of numerous people during the work on this book, and it is a pleasant duty to acknowledge their help. In the first place I must thank Hew Strachan for accepting the idea for this book so enthusiastically and then supporting the project afterwards. I am grateful to Jeremy Black for stimulating conversations over the years and unfailing support for this book, which falls into his particular area of expertise, and for much else besides. I am also grateful to the, alas now late, Hamish Scott, whose work I have always greatly admired, and who gave advice at an early stage. Peter Wilson pointed me in the direction of material which otherwise would have escaped my notice, and for that I am thankful. At Vienna, Michael Hochedlinger and Lothar Höbelt were unfailingly helpful. Amongst my colleagues at the University of East Anglia, I owe a debt of gratitude once more to Jan Vermeiren, who readily procured copies of obscure periodical literature from the Berlin state library.

I am also grateful to Rob Liddiard with whom I taught eighteenth-century wars, though mostly those featuring redcoats rather than bluecoats. My old friend Sven Bergmann likewise gave me the benefit of his observations and placed material at my disposal.

All historians have 'their' periods, sections of the past in the study of which they specialize. My first love has always been the eighteenth century, though I have often abandoned it since. The seeds of my fascination with this era were planted at an early stage by my late father. Though no historian himself, he had a love for the subject, which he passed on to me and which he fostered, even if he may not have known it. It is to his memory that I dedicate this book.

TGO
North Norfolk
January 2023

CONTENTS

LIST OF FIGURES

LIST OF MAPS

ABBREVIATIONS

AFA	Alte Feldakten
AÖG	*Archiv für Österreichische Geschichte*
AHVN	*Annalen des Historischen Vereins für den Niederrhein*
BL	British Library
BMW	*Beiheft zum Militär-Wochenblatt*
CEH	*Central European History*
DJ	*Düsseldorfer Jahrbuch*
DR	*Duquesne Review*
EHR	*English Historical Review*
FBPG	*Forschungen zur Brandenburgisch-Preussischen Geschichte*
GH	*German History*
HHStA	Haus-, Hof- und Staatsarchiv
HJ	*Historical Journal*
HJWG	*Hamburger Jahrbuch für Wirtschafts- und Gesellschaftspolitik*
HZ	*Historische Zeitschrift*
IHR	*International History Review*
JbfGO	*Jahrbuch für die Geschichte Osteuropas*
JBS	*Journal of British Studies*
JMH	*Journal of Modern History*
JSYWA	*Journal of the Seven Years' War Association*
KA	Kriegsarchiv
LANRW	Landesarchiv Nordrhein-Westfalen
MA	*Military Affairs*
MGM	*Militärgeschichtliche Mitteilungen*
MIÖG	*Mitteilungen des Instituts für Österreichische Geschichte*
MÖSA	*Mitteilungen des Österreichischen Staatsarchivs*
NJbfLG	*Niedersächsisches Jahrbuch für Landesgeschichte*

PC	Politische Correspondenz Friedrich des Grossen
PJ	Preussische Jahrbücher
P&P	Past & Present
SCJ	Sixteenth Century Journal
SJH	Scandinavian Journal of History
SP	State Papers
TNA	The National Archives (Public Record Office)
VSWG	Vierteljahresschrift für Sozial- und Wirtschaftsgeschichte
VfTH	Vierteljahresheft für Truppenführung und Heereskunde
VjfZG	Vierteljahresheft für Zeitgeschichte
ZHF	Zeitschrift für Historische Forschung
ZfPGL	Zeitschrift für preussische Geschichte und Landeskunde

NOTE ON NAMES

In line with scholarly practice, I decided to anglicize the first names of rulers rather than use their native name, i.e. Frederick rather than Friedrich, Maria Theresa as opposed to Maria Theresia and Elizabeth in place of Elizaveta. In all other cases I have retained the original first names. The end result is not entirely satisfactory, but it does at least have the benefit of agreeing with custom.

The principal theatres of the three Silesian wars now lie in Poland and the Czech Republic. Battles are referred to here by their contemporary German place names throughout. Their modern Polish or Czech variant is given at first mention to facilitate orientation.

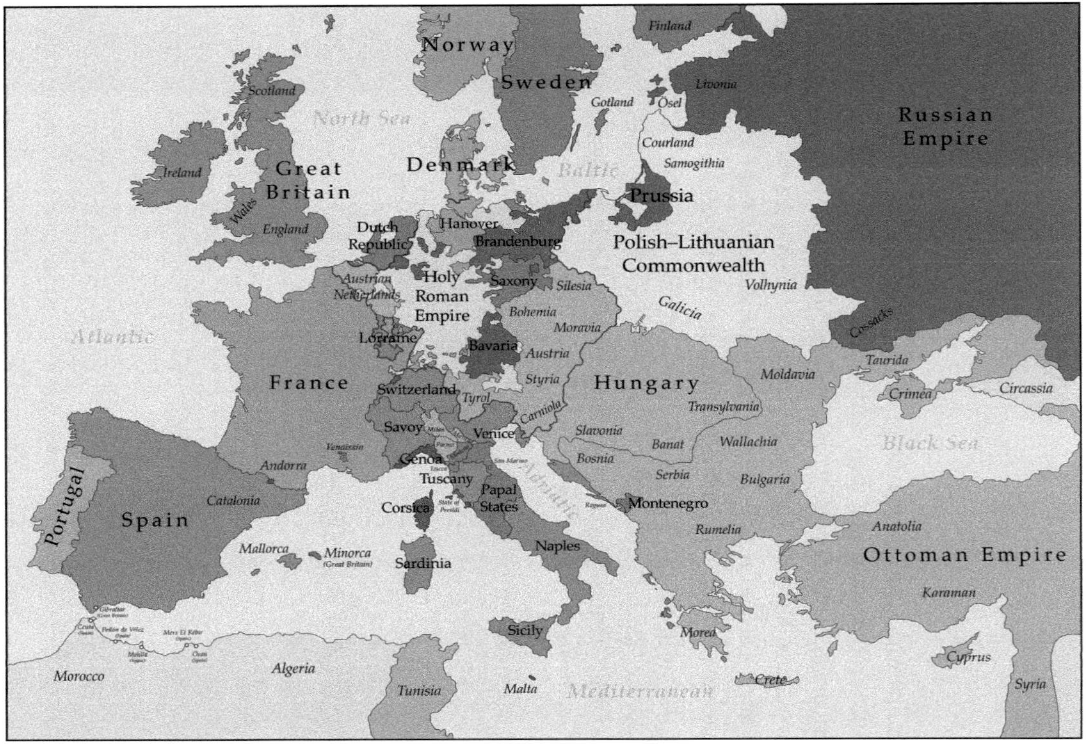
Norway
Sweden
Finland
Livonia
Gotland
Ösel
Russian Empire
Scotland
North Sea
Courland
Samogithia
Ireland
Great Britain
Denmark
Baltic
Prussia
Wales
England
Dutch Republic
Hanover
Brandenburg
Polish–Lithuanian Commonwealth
Austrian Netherlands
Holy Roman Empire
Saxony
Silesia
Volhynia
Bohemia
Galicia
Moravia
Cossacks
Atlantic
Lorraine
Bavaria
Austria
Taurida
Moldavia
France
Switzerland
Styria
Hungary
Tyrol
Crimea
Circassia
Carniola
Transylvania
Savoy
Venice
Slavonia
Wallachia
Black Sea
Venaissin
Banat
Genoa
Andorra
Bosnia
Tuscany
Serbia
Bulgaria
Portugal
Adriatic
Catalonia
Papal States
Corsica
Montenegro
Spain
Rumelia
Anatolia
Mallorca
Minorca
(Great Britain)
Naples
Sardinia
Ottoman Empire
Karaman
Sicily
Morea
Algeria
Cyprus
Morocco
Crete
Tunisia
Malta
Mediterranean
Syria

Map 1 Europe 1740.

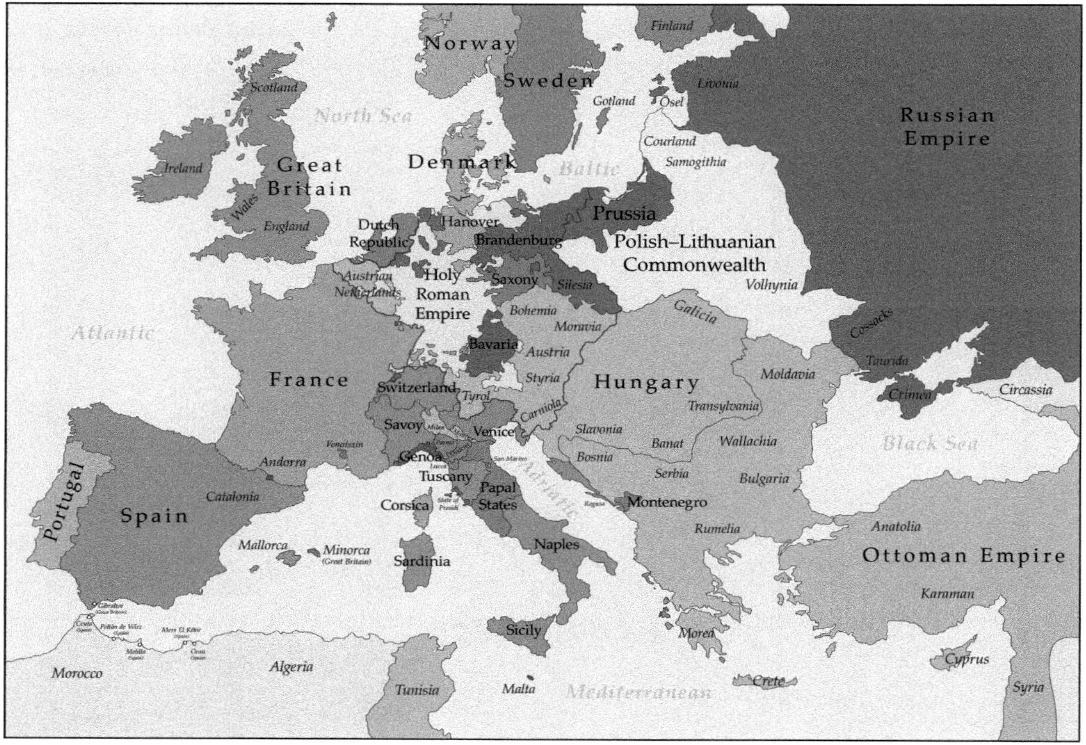
Norway
Sweden
Finland
Livonia
Gotland
Ösel
Russian Empire
Scotland
North Sea
Ireland
Great Britain
Denmark
Baltic
Courland
Samogithia
Wales
England
Dutch Republic
Hanover
Prussia
Brandenburg
Polish–Lithuanian Commonwealth
Austrian Netherlands
Holy Roman Empire
Saxony
Silesia
Volhynia
Bohemia
Moravia
Galicia
Atlantic
Bavaria
Austria
Cossacks
Taurida
France
Switzerland
Tyrol
Styria
Hungary
Moldavia
Crimea
Circassia
Carniola
Transylvania
Savoy
Venice
Slavonia
Banat
Wallachia
Black Sea
Venaissin
Andorra
Genoa
San Marino
Bosnia
Serbia
Bulgaria
Tuscany
Papal States
Adriatic
Catalonia
Corsica
Montenegro
Portugal
Spain
Rumelia
Anatolia
Mallorca
Minorca
(Great Britain)
Sardinia
Naples
Ottoman Empire
Karaman
Sicily
Morea
Morocco
Algeria
Cyprus
Tunisia
Malta
Mediterranean
Crete
Syria

Map 2 Europe 1786.

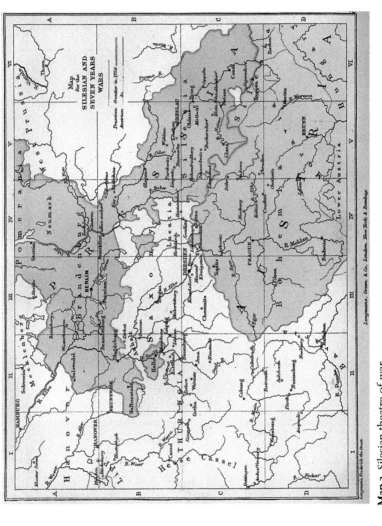

Map 3 Silesian theatre of war.

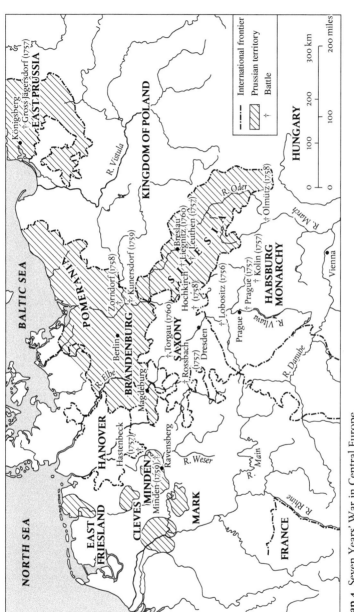

Map 4 Seven Years' War in Central Europe.

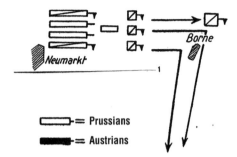

Map 5 Schematic map showing the Prussian advance.

Map 6 Schematic map showing the Prussian deployment in oblique order.

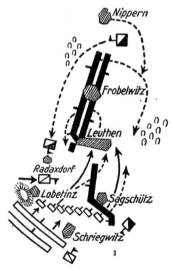

Map 7 Schematic map showing the final phase.

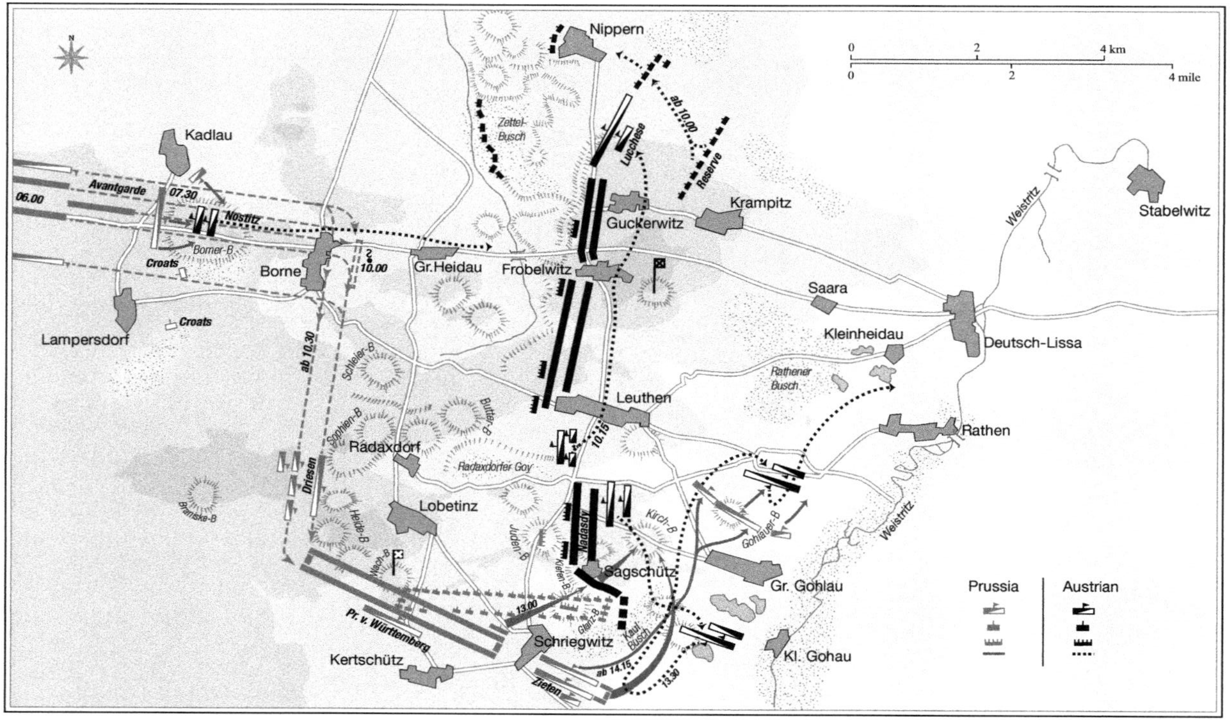
N
0
2
4 km
0
2
4 mile
Nippern
Zettel-Busch
Lucchese
ab 10.00
Reserve
Kadlau
Avantgarde
06.00
07.30
Nostitz
Bornе-B
Croats
Borne
10.00
Gr.Heidau
Frobelwitz
Guckerwitz
Krampitz
Stabelwitz
Weistritz
Croats
Lampersdorf
ab 10.30
Schleier-B
Saara
Kleinheidau
Deutsch-Lissa
Rathener Busch
Leuthen
Butter-B
Sophien-B
Radaxdorf
10.15
Radaxdorfer Goy
Rathen
Driesen
Branske-B
Heide-B
Lobetinz
Juden-B
Nadasdy
Kirch-B
Gohlauer-B
Weistritz
Wach-B
Kiefen-B
Sagschütz
Gr. Gohlau
13.00
Glanz-B
Kaul Busch
Pr. v. Württemberg
Schriegwitz
Kertschütz
ab 14.15
13.30
Zieten
Kl. Gohau
Prussia
Austrian

Map 8 The battle, phase 1.

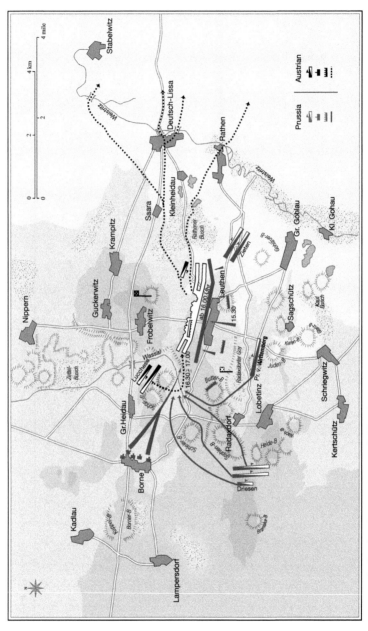

Map 9 The battle, phase 2 (the parallel battle).

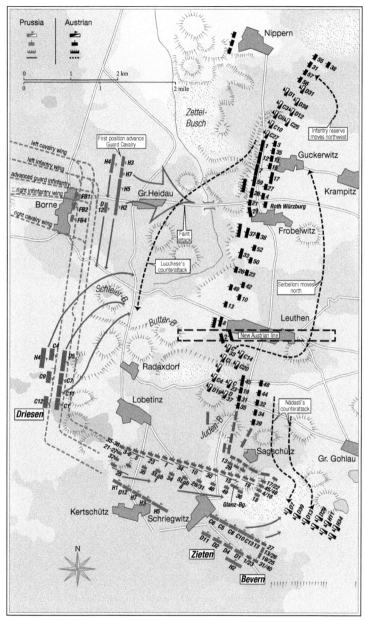

Map 10 The battle (both phases).

1

War in the Holy Roman Empire

The battle of Leuthen was scarcely over when the victor composed a lengthy report, for public dissemination, on the recent campaign that had led to the encounter on 5 December 1757. Frederick II set out in some detail how his troops 'outflanked' the enemy and then drove him off the battlefield: 'The fight commenced at 1 pm and ended at 4 pm. If we had had one more hour of daylight, the defeat of the enemy would have been greater yet.' The Prussians had taken 21,500 prisoners, he enumerated, and captured 116 cannon, fifty-one regimental flags and standards, and 4,000 forage and ammunition carts. 'It is unnecessary', he concluded, 'to reiterate that our entire army, from the officers to the common soldier, performed marvels of bravery in the *bataille*. Let the deed speak for itself.'[1] The deed did not speak for itself, of course. The king's report saw to that. Indeed, it established the parameters of later perceptions of Leuthen. To appreciate these, it is necessary to place the battle in its contemporary contexts first.

Historians have frequently commented upon the bellicosity of the seventeenth and eighteenth centuries.[2] To no small degree, the higher incidence of wars was rooted in the rise of the modern state. Whether changes in military technology unleashed a 'military revolution', in which such advances and the growth of government bureaucracies reinforced each other, has been the subject of considerable discussion amongst scholars of the early modern period.[3] This interpretation has proved remarkably appealing, seductive even. Whatever its flaws, few would deny that the desire to enhance their war-making capabilities encouraged princes and their ministers to interfere in the administration, constitution, and society of the territories they ruled to an unprecedented degree. War determined the position of a state relative to others. Success in war, or by making themselves militarily useful to the major powers, allowed states to establish or maintain themselves as greater powers.

War also mattered domestically. In the trenchant observation by the Prusso-German historian Otto Hintze, war had become 'the great fly-wheel for the whole operation of the modern state'.[4] Standing armies emerged, navies, armaments factories, followed by modern systems of taxation that grew up around a range of war levies. Tax inspectors sprang forth from central treasuries as from the head of Bellona, and the new state bureaucracy devised methods of servicing government debts. There were, however, exceptions, the most significant being the Holy Roman Empire of the German Nation which, as such, was left untouched by this development. Neither empire nor state, nor especially German or, for that matter, holy, it was, as one seventeenth-century legal scholar noted resignedly, '*irregulare aliquod corpus et monstro quasi simile*'.[5] However monstrous in appearance, in essence, it was a pacified area in Central Europe, a loose confederation of princes and cities, a complex network of ties and relationships, based on a vast body of feudal law and the public order arrangements of the *Landfriedensordnung* of 1495, with the emperor as its elected head.[6] The constitutional arrangements did not permit member states, the *Reichsstände* or Imperial Estates, the component principalities and free cities of the Empire, to resort to military force in pursuit of their interests. The Peace of Westphalia of 1648, one of the pillars on which the constitution of the Empire came to rest after the end of the Thirty Years' War (1618–48) granted individual states the right to conclude alliances amongst themselves and with foreign powers, but with the proviso that they were not to take a position against the Empire and the emperor, the *Landfrieden*, and the peace settlement itself.[7] Conversely, princes now guarded their right to enter into alliances ('*Gutte Alliancen … so woll in als ausser dem Romischen Reich zu machen*') all the more jealously.[8]

Intra-imperial disputes were to be settled by means of arbitration or at the *Reichskammergericht* (Imperial Chamber Court) at Wetzlar, an institution more effective than its reputation for legal prolixity and proceedings dragging on for centuries suggested.[9] In the event of extra-imperial complications, the *Reichskriegsverfassung* (imperial war constitution) was supposed to come into effect. In practice, it tended to involve often cumbersome exchanges between the Estates until a *Reichsarmee* (imperial army) could take to the field, formed by contingents furnished by the individual states which were organized in ten *Kreise* or Circles.[10] Attempts at centralizing imperial defence, such as the efforts of the Emperor Leopold I, in 1681, to ward off imminent threats to his possessions in the east and west by establishing a permanent *Reichsarmatur*, a defensive force of some 40,000–60,000 troops, ultimately failed.[11]

Whatever the shortcomings of this pre-modern entity, the rudiments of a Central European political order existed. The Empire functioned quite effectively and was still capable of significant military efforts until its very end. Some scholars, in fact, have suggested that, had the constitutional arrangements of the Empire been allowed to mature properly, the German lands might well have developed into something akin to the Swiss confederation.[12] Germany's geopolitical position, however, vitiated against an existence in the lee of great power politics. In an age in which dynastic interests, based on far-flung, often pan-European, familial ties, were inextricably interwoven with state interests such isolation was impossible—and the German lands were the theatre or the object of many of the wars of the period.

Each war is the product of specific contexts and circumstances.[13] If wars of religion tended to dominate in the sixteenth and early seventeenth centuries, wars of succession were characteristic of the later seventeenth and early eighteenth centuries, so much so that they formed something like the *basso continuo* of great power politics in the baroque period.[14] The reasons for this were manifold. But in an age in which political life was focused largely on the person of the monarch, dynastic considerations and interests played an inordinate role, especially so since the ruling houses formed a pan-European monarchical cousinhood. Family pacts, marriage contracts, and house treaties brought a never-ending stream of employment opportunities for windy advocates but rarely produced the desired legal or political clarity. More often, such compacts produced grounds for fresh disputes. Given the prominence of dynastic aspects in great power politics, inheritance claims offered at least a semblance of legitimacy. Louis XIV's Wars of Reunion (1679–81) to round off France at the expense of the Empire and the Low Countries were based ostensibly on legal claims to the coveted territories, even though these were spurious at best.[15]

Frequently, inheritance claims cloaked motivations of a different kind. Frederick II's invasion of Silesia in 1740 was a case in point. In a series of pamphlets the king sought to convince the political public in the Empire and in Europe of the justice of his claims to the province, but at the root of his expansionist designs was an amalgam of sober calculations of strategic and commercial state interests and personal ambitions: 'I love war for the sake of it.'[16] The striving for *la gloire* and the ideal of the warrior-king had already something backward-looking about it at a time when few princes took to the field themselves. Charles XII of Sweden was an obvious exception, though his ultimate failure also served as warning example. Even George II of Britain thought better of it after the battle of Dettingen in 1743. Louis XIV was more typical of the age. His appearances on the Rhine and in the Low Countries in 1672 and 1673 were carefully stage-managed, and the numerous commemorative medals and portraits of the king commanding sieges, commissioned subsequently, presented an idealized picture of a monarch at war.[17] *Gloire* was thus an important factor in the origins and conduct of wars, in establishing military objectives and in memorializing success on the battlefield to affirm established crown-elite hierarchies.[18] Although military command was frequently separated from kingship—the names of Prince Eugene of Savoy, the Duke of Marlborough, or Maurice de Saxe spring to mind—it was an important aspect of princely rule. Most West European monarchs wore military uniform, and even lesser princes held military reviews and staged mock campaigns.[19]

State interests, the *raison d'état*, were no less significant, however, if not indeed more so. War was the principal means of enhancing a state's dynastic position. As Frederick II reflected in later years, until 1740 Brandenburg-Prussia's rulers had been treated more as electors than as real kings. With his Silesian landgrab he 'put an end to this Hermaphrodite status'.[20] But already his three Silesian wars contained within them elements of, and so presaged, a new type of war, the national wars that were to define the long nineteenth century. In their course larger resources, both material and manpower, were mobilized, and so was the energy of popular patriotism.[21]

In another respect, however, Frederick's wars were distinctly of their time. The origins of later nineteenth- and twentieth-century conflicts tended to be complex, the fuse often primed by a sequence of pre-war crises and considerations of external and internal aspects shaping decision-making. The post-Westphalian wars, by contrast, were still rooted in calculated aggression. With wars prepared, conducted, and terminated by cabinets, monarchs and their ministers had considerable latitude in their actions. Not only was the resort to military violence permissible as the *ultima ratio regis*, but reversing alliances, reneging on previous treaties and concluding separate peace agreements were all part of the spectrum of contemporary diplomacy. In consequence, though they could start wars, rulers had far less control over how conflicts evolved diplomatically and politically.

Great power politics were thus fraught with considerable risks. To contain the threat of war, post-1648 European diplomacy developed a range of techniques and instruments, habits and institutions. Amongst them was a more sophisticated understanding of international law. Combining elements of Christian theology and natural law precepts, it sought to establish rules for acceptable state conduct, not least by refining further the idea of the '*bellum iustum*' ('just war'). By establishing the parameters within which the resort to force was morally and legally justified, diplomats, philosophers, and jurists hoped to reduce the frequency of wars and the number of belligerents. Warfare itself was likewise to be made subject to a certain, if still somewhat loose, framework of rules; and envoys and lawyers compiled manuals on the art of diplomacy and treaty-making.[22]

Law was a weak reed to lean on, and lawyers were as likely to be found to be arguing abstruse points of feudal law in support of their prince's aggressive intentions as to be compiling weighty treatises against them. Diplomatic practice relied on other means to make great power politics more calculable. The notions of *convénance* and equilibrium were central to contemporary political thought. Both served to place certain limitations on the ability of states to act in pursuit of narrow, egotistical aims, and so helped to limit any wars that did erupt. In response to Louis XIV's wars, Anglo-Dutch diplomacy popularized the idea of a 'balance of power'. Significantly, a European equilibrium was as much a guarantee of relative stability as war was an instrument to maintain that balance. As the Scottish enlightenment historian William Robertson reflected, Europe had been taught:

> that great secret in modern policy, the preservation of a proper distribu-
> tion of power among all the members of the system.... [T]he mainten-
> ance of a proper balance of power became the great object of attention to
> the statesmen of Italy.... Self-preservation taught other powers to adopt
> it. It grew to be fashionable and universal. From the aera we can trace the
> progress of that intercourse between nations...; and we can discern the
> operations of that provident policy, which during peace, guards against
> remote and contingent dangers; and, in war, had prevented rapid and
> destructive conquests.[23]

In the Peace of Utrecht (1713) at the end of the War of the Spanish Succession, the maritime powers succeeded in enshrining the principle of a balance of power between the Habsburgs and Bourbons in international law.[24] From now on, the equilibrium of Europe was an important element of great power politics, although it could not guarantee international stability. Other powers rose, the circle of the great powers expanded, and this added to the intricacies of international diplomacy, especially so in the east. The Peace of Nystad (1721) confirmed Russia's growing dominance in the Baltic and in Eastern Central Europe, largely at the expense of defeated Sweden, now but a shadow of its former self and for much of the eighteenth century little more than a French satellite.[25] Two decades later, Frederick's irruption onto the European scene disrupted both the great power system and the internal balance of the Holy Roman Empire. Over the next quarter of a century, and in the course of three wars, the *arriviste* king defended his conquests and compelled Europe to recognize Prussia as the fifth great power.

The new pentarchy, the cartel of the five dominant powers, was no proper guarantee of stability either. For with the rise of Prussia a new element entered great power politics, the intra-German Austro-Prussian dualism. From now on Hohenzollern–Habsburg rivalry was the source of often latent, sometimes dormant, but never extinct friction in European and German politics until Austria's extrusion from Germany in 1866.[26]

The equilibrist principle on its own was not sufficient to rein in state behaviour. If taken to its logical conclusion, it would have compelled the powers to operate strictly within the confines of the status quo. This, however, ran contrary to the accepted understandings of state sovereignty and the sovereignty of princes. To allow them greater room for manoeuvre international diplomacy was guided by the notion of *convénance*.[27] Its practical advantage lay in its flexibility, but the lesser powers could secure their interests only in so far as they were aligned with those of one or several of the greater powers. Even so, their presence at peace congresses was now deemed necessary to maintain the notion of the comity of states.

If the ability to wage war was a matter of sovereign right, the Holy Roman Empire was again something of an exception. Its constitutional set-up and the close connection between Austrian and imperial interests made it resistant to attempts at modifying the rights of the individual states.[28] From time to time the estates of the Empire might agree to a *Reichsexekution*, a military expedition to enforce decisions by the *Reichstag*, the imperial diet at Ratisbon (Regensburg), a permanent assembly of the diplomatic representatives of the German states. The Seven Years' War, in fact, involved one of the largest imperial executions of the period. Even so, it is a remarkable fact that the Empire waged a *Reichskrieg*, a war officially declared by and in the name of the Empire, very rarely, and always on its western borders. On only five occasions, invariably following protracted deliberations at Ratisbon, did the emperor declare an imperial war: in 1689 during the Nine Years' War (also called the War of the Palatine Succession) (1689–97), in 1702 and 1734 during the Spanish and Polish succession wars (1701–13 and 1733–6), in 1793 during the First Coalition War (1792–7), and, for the final time, in 1799, one year into the Second Coalition War (1798–1801). During the wars in the Low Countries in the 1660s and 1670s, the *Reich* played a marginal role; and in the Wars of Reunion at the end of the latter decade, French encroachments notwithstanding, the emperor exhausted himself in political and diplomatic manoeuvres to thwart his Bourbon enemy but did not oppose him militarily.[29]

A growing divergence of interests between the emperor and the princes contributed to the steady weakening of the Empire. Leopold I sought to strengthen the imperial position within the *Reich*, after 1681, but made no real progress.[30] He also had to keep a weather eye on the renewed Turkish threat, which led to the siege of Vienna two years later. Yet the conflict with France and the Turkish war strengthened the emperor's position, in practice if not as a matter of constitutional arrangements. The hegemonic ambitions of the French king in the west turned one of the guaranteeing powers of the Treaty of Westphalia into a near-permanent threat to the status quo. Many, though not all, German princes therefore began to look to Vienna for protection, with the most obvious exception of the Wittelsbach rulers in Bavaria and their ecclesiastical secundogeniture on the Rhine.[31] The struggle with the Ottomans, meanwhile, had a unifying effect in Germany.[32] There was a curious dynamic at work. In the west, Leopold acted as the protector of the *Reich* and the peace settlement of 1648. But in the east he drew on the resources of the Empire increasingly to extend Habsburg territorial interests in Hungary and beyond, a pattern his successors continued well into the eighteenth century.[33] And yet, although the emperor required the military assistance of other German states, efforts by the latter to turn the campaigns in southeastern Europe into regular *Reichskriege* failed. Too strong was Vienna's resistance to strengthening the war constitution of the Empire, which could only come at the expense of the House of Habsburg. The stand-off with the princes nevertheless produced one significant constitutional innovation. Already in 1663 negotiations between the two sides resulted in the transformation of the diet into the '*immerwährende Reichstag*', permanently in session until the dissolution of the *Reich* in 1806.[34]

The wars against the Turks also stood in sharp contrast to the politico-military practice in the west in that the treaties of 1648 had tied the hands of the emperor. In that role, though not as ruler of the Austrian territories, he could make war only with the consent of the *Reichstag*; nor was he permitted to take offensive actions. The Empire was structurally a defensive organization, incapable of initiating the use of military violence. This was unique, and it made imperial proceedings prolix. It was not uncommon for a whole year to pass between the opening of hostilities and the formal declaration of war, and before an imperial army lumbered into being. During the War of the Polish Succession, which broke out in 1733, the *Reichsarmee* did not take to the field on the Upper Rhine until 1734.[35] Once war had been declared, the *Reichskriegsverfassung* came into effect. Yet this, too, did not necessarily facilitate swift action since the burden of the war effort rested on the shoulders of the *Reichskreise* or Circles, quasi-federal associations of the German states on a broadly regional basis. The interests of the Circles often ran contrary to those of the larger states. More often still, there was a yawning gap between the Circles' commitments and their capabilities. Petty squabbles between the smaller princes further diminished the military effectiveness of the Empire. At the outbreak of the Seven Years' War, for example, the Duke of Saxe-Hildburghausen disputed the right of the Elector of Cologne to appoint the commander of the infantry companies furnished by the

Westphalian Circle to which both contributed; the dispute was still not settled in 1792.[36]

The Holy Roman Empire was in effect divided into two quite unequal groups. On the one side stood the greater German powers, whose separate interests never entirely aligned with those of the Empire, on the other stood the smaller and medium-sized principalities on whom the *Reich* relied for its military organization and who, in turn, looked to it for protection. With the exception of Hanover, whose army remained sizeable at around 20,000 men, even some of the larger amongst this group, such as Saxony and Bavaria, steadily reduced their armies. Financial support for imperial military efforts— the so-called *Römermonat*, a monthly levy to pay for the imperial army—also declined.[37]

There were exceptions. The landgraves of Hesse-Kassel, for instance, maintained a regular army of 12,000 well-drilled and well-equipped troops, augmented by anyone who fell into the hands of their recruiting officers, whom they hired out to fellow-Protestant powers, notably Great Britain, for campaigns in Europe and overseas. In turn, the force became yet more experienced and battle-hardened and thus an even more valuable 'commodity', so much so that around half of the landgravate's revenues were earned through its 'trade' in soldiers.[38]

These two contrasting trajectories, along which the German states developed, began to emerge after the Thirty Years' War. The experiences of that conflict, the devastations it had wrought on ill-defended lands, induced the rulers of Brandenburg-Prussia and—with some delay—of Austria to establish standing armies under their own exclusive command.[39] As elsewhere in early modern Europe, a feudal aristocracy and nobility, whose loyalty could be relied upon, officered the army. It was a *noblesse d'épée* in the fullest sense of the term. Its history was that of military service as its principal and proper occupation; its rewards were the honours and perquisites that came with victory in the field.[40] As elsewhere, the Habsburg and Hohenzollern armies often lacked homogeneity. Between a quarter and two-thirds of the armed forces were comprised of 'foreigners' recruited outside the state's borders. Brandenburg-Prussia and Austria were no exception, at any rate up to a certain point. They showed, however, also quite distinctive features. The institutions, organizations, and practices in the two largest German states evolved along rather different patterns, different from each other and different also from other European states. In Prussia the fiscal and military authorities were merged in one body, the *General-Kriegs-Kommissariat*, which raised and administered all state revenues. In the far-flung Habsburg territories, which never grew into a unitary state, no such centralized authorities existed prior to the reforms instituted by the Empress Maria Theresa in the 1750s. Until then, the estates retained responsibility for raising taxes and troops. Brandenburg-Prussia developed into an exceptional military state, while Austria retained the essential character of a 'composite monarchy'.[41]

There was a kernel of truth in one of Mirabeau's less well-known witticisms that Prussia 'only constituted a vast and formidable camp'. By the time the French visitor ventured his observation in 1788, the country had become steadily more centralized and militarized.[42] A kingdom since 1701, Brandenburg-Prussia slowly rose from one of the many smaller 'composite' territories that constituted the Holy Roman Empire. It is important to note that only in the language of diplomacy was the whole state referred to as '*la Prusse*'. Strictly speaking, the Kingdom of Prussia was confined to the northeastern province of East Prussia on the Baltic coast, whose capital Königsberg, rather than Berlin, served as the place of coronation for the kings, and its ruler was king 'in' rather than 'of' Prussia. The province itself lay outside the boundaries of the *Reich*, and until the middle of the seventeenth century it had been under the suzerainty of the Polish kings.[43] In the Brandenburg core area, and for the purposes of imperial politics, the Prussian king remained the 'Elector of Brandenburg' even after 1701. In the provinces of Cleves, Magdeburg, and Pomerania he was 'the Duke', in Mark, Moers, and Ravensberg he was 'the Count', and in Halberstadt and Minden 'the Prince'. This practice reflected the gradual growth of the state, a process that owed more to inherited accessions and diplomacy than to war.

In this respect, the Prussian monarch did not differ from other German princes, whose authority was based on different legal titles. The more important dynasties had long sought to emulate the greater powers by establishing a strong central government with control over the whole of their territories. Brandenburg was no exception. In 1653, with his *General-Rezess* Frederick William, the 'Great Elector' (Fig. 1.1), forced the hitherto powerful estates—the land-owning nobility and

Fig. 1.1 Frederick William, Elector of Brandenburg ('the Great Elector'). Wikimedia Commons.

the town corporations—to agree to a *Heeressteuer*, a hypothecated tax designed to raise funds for a permanent military force. Seven years later, the recalcitrant nobles of Cleves and, in 1661 and 1663, the no less independent-minded East Prussian estates, also ceded control over state revenues to him.[44] Through improvements in the administration of the domain lands and the introduction of a system of indirect taxations, the *Akzise* (or Excise), as well as by accepting French subsidies, he made central government well-nigh financially independent of the estates. Soon the tentacles of the *General-Kriegs-Kommissariat* stretched into every nook and cranny of the Brandenburg possessions, where *Kriegs- und Steuerräte* (war and tax councillors) represented the central authorities in the towns and rural districts. From 1693 onwards the estates were obliged to raise a specific number of local recruits.[45]

Centralization was, in part, designed to overcome Brandenburg's disadvantageous, for dispersed, geographical position. There were no good seaports until 1720, when Stettin was acquired. None of the territories had defensible borders, and all were vulnerable to the depredations of covetous neighbours. Centralizing power made possible the establishment of a serviceable standing army, and with it the pursuit of an ambitious foreign policy, notably against Sweden and Poland. Not without reason did Frederick II later suggest that his great grandfather had laid the foundations of Prussia's later rise. In this manner, the elector succeeded in raising the size of his army from 4,000 in 1644 and *c.*8,200 in 1667 to a fixed peacetime strength of 30,000 in 1688—in wartime, for instance in 1678, it swelled to 45,000 men. Electoral Brandenburg was now the dominant political and military force in northern Germany.[46]

Centralization and militarization reached their zenith under Frederick William I, the second King of Prussia.[47] Already in his own time he was known as the 'soldier king', and that not simply because of his penchant, bordering on the obsessional, for uniforms and anything connected with army life. In 1723, this '*roi militaire et pacifique*'[48] established the General Directorate (*General-Direktorium*). Headed by four ministers, but under the control of the king, and each responsible for a particular province or group of territories and supported by a growing number of privy councillors, the Directory was supervised state finances and commerce in the interest of increasing general prosperity and, thus, government revenues.[49] In practice, the new body made Prussia's administrative apparatus subservient to the needs of the army, which remained the primary concern of government. Its set-up was by no means flawless, but it worked with, for the period, remarkable efficiency, generating around 7 million *Thalers* in central government revenues. Of this sum, about 70 per cent, some 5 million *Thalers*, could be devoted to military purposes. From the remainder, all other government expenditure was be paid and an annual contribution to the *Kriegskasse* (war chest). By the time of Frederick II's accession to the throne, the treasure amounted to around 8.7 million *Thalers*, neatly packed away in casks in the cellars of the royal residence.[50]

The militarization implicit in the Directory's tight control over the internal administration of the country was reinforced a decade later, in May and September 1733, with the *Kantonsreglement*. It enshrined in law the duty of the rural male population to serve in the army. To that effect the new law divided the whole kingdom into recruiting districts, so-called cantons, each responsible for a regiment and large enough to recruit three times over. Male children were 'enrolled', that is reported to the local authority by the baptizing minister and their names entered into the regimental lists of their canton. From the age of fourteen the '*Enrollierte*' had to sport the regimental bobble on their hats as an outward sign of their status. In practice, however, this did not constitute universal conscription. Town dwellers were exempted from the new obligations, as were large parts of the rural population, for instance, village mayors, only sons, master artisans, students of theology, peasants on isolated farms or with very large families, and certain pacifist religious communities, such as the Pietists.[51] It is also worth noting that alongside this compulsory element the *Reglement* also suppressed for good the pressing of recruits which, though banned since 1721, was still common in isolated rural spots. Those drafted spent large parts of the year on leave, working the fields in their home villages. The majority of soldiers was still recruited outside Prussia's borders in 1740, though the proportion of *Ausländer* from outside the Empire was relatively small (around 11.5 per cent). The number of non-native Prussians declined steadily, moreover. In 1742, two years into Frederick II's reign, one-third of his army was native. By 1750 it had risen to half, and by the end of the Seven Years' War it had reached two-thirds. Around 15 per cent of the soldiers were Prussian subjects exempt from the *Reglement* who volunteered to serve or who came from military families.[52]

Prussia had developed a highly efficient recruiting system and was able to maintain an army that was, in proportion, larger than those of others. With a population twelfth in size in Europe, around 2.34 million, its peacetime field army was 72,000 strong—83,000 at the time of Frederick William I's death in 1740, if the garrison forces were included. France, Russia, and Austria had armies of 160,000, 130,000, and 80,000–100,000 men, respectively, but their populations were ten times greater than that of Prussia. The whole Prussian army in 1761 comprised 4.4 per cent of the country's population, as compared with 1.2 per cent in France. At the end of Frederick II's reign, in 1786, the army had grown to 195,000 men, or 3.3 per cent of Prussia's population of 5.8 million.[53] Its army made the kingdom a power with which others had to reckon.

The *Kantonsreglement* complemented the privileged position of the landed nobility, the *Junkers*, who had their rights confirmed in return for serving in the king's army. Frederick II and his predecessors were intent on preserving the rigid balance between the social groups and classes, and between economic production and the power of the state. This was essential to both army and state. To preserve their privileged position nobles were prohibited from selling their estates to peasants or townspeople. The *Reglement* and attendant practices thus reinforced the process of 'social militarization'. The peasantry encountered in the nobleman the king's representative, who dispensed justice in the local magistrates' courts. But he was also their feudal landlord, to whom they were tied, and the officer commanding their local regiment.[54] At the same time, the *Kantonsreglement* protected the peasantry against arbitrary excesses at the hands of their local magnate. For the *Junkers* were now responsible for the well-being of the peasantry, and they were answerable to the king.[55] In the king's understanding, kingship was a sacred duty held in trust for the benefit of his subjects, and this form of authoritarianism was the only rational form of government. The power of the state thus increased in all directions. And yet, as Hintze noted, the power of the state was the primary concern of Prussia's kings: 'Alongside [state] power there certainly appeared as the aim of all administration the welfare of the country, the happiness of the subjects.... Power and welfare of the whole are closely entwined; the one conditions the other; neither can exist for long without the other. But it is not the spirit of the welfare state that pervades the whole system but the spirit of power politics.'[56]

In Prussia the relationship between monarch and soldiers was very different from that in other states in the eighteenth century, and this also extended to the military sphere. In the 1680s the 'Great Elector' abolished the system of capitulations under which he had to enter into contracts with regimental colonels for the raising and drilling of soldiers on his behalf. Government now took the place of these military enterprisers, and financed and controlled the troops itself. In this, the Brandenburg ruler emulated the more advanced states of Western Europe, France and especially the Netherlands, the latter being the source of much inspiration for this fellow-Calvinist ruler.[57] From now on, the regiment was the basic unit of the army, which operated, in war and peace alike, as an autonomous administrative, disciplinary, financial, and tactical body. As it was also under the direct control of the elector, it—on its own and as part of the army as a whole—came to represent the absolutist regime, or at any rate what the regime pretended to be.[58] Frederick William I went a step further still. From 1725 on, he invariably wore the uniform of an army officer. It was a highly symbolic act. For the monarch himself to don the 'king's coat' signalled to his subjects that he considered himself to be subject to the law and bound by the military code of behaviour with its stern emphasis on duty and service to the state.[59]

The Habsburg dominions never entirely followed the Prussian model, except in the matter of recruitment, which was centralized—although only after a delay of nearly eight decades—in 1753, in response to the military reverses of the 1730s and 1740s. The slowness of this process was telling. For one thing, at 110,000 men at the death of the emperor Leopold I in 1705, the Austrian army was already of considerable size.[60] For another, the composite nature of the 'Monarchia Austriaca', the bureaucracy entrenched in its sprawling provinces, and the lack of a compact territorial mass complicated any efforts towards full centralization.[61] In Bohemia and the Austrian *Erblande* (hereditary possessions) the estates were in no position to challenge the king-emperor, nor did they wish to do so. He was free to determine the direction of central policy, and the main administrative functions in the various provinces were in the hands of his governors.[62]

The monarch's position in Hungary was rather different. Although the kingdom was linked 'indivisibly and inseparably' to the other Habsburg dominions, that union respected Hungary's separate laws and institutions, especially the extensive privileges of the Magyar magnates, which included exemption from taxation and the convocation of a regular diet at Pressburg (Bratislava/Pozsony), where also the king's government under his representative, the Palatine, resided. The Hungarian court chancellery in Vienna was independent of any other institutions there and answerable only to head of the dynasty as King of Hungary. The Hungarian nobles were exempted from any obligation to serve their ruler, except in the event of attack by an external enemy. The king could employ his standing army according to his discretion, inside Hungary and without, and for defensive and offensive purposes, but there was always the fear of insurrection.[63]

Across the Habsburg dominions local bureaucracy reflected historically grown practices and its apparatus was left largely untouched by the reforms of the 1750s and 1760s, but neither a *Junker*-type class nor the person of the monarch was central to the Habsburg military system.[64] The fate of reform efforts by Prince Eugene of Savoy, the celebrated general and military supremo, underscored this fact. The prince had done much to improve and expand the Austrian standing army in the aftermath of the Spanish war, but the debacles that followed his death in 1736, first against the Ottomans and then in the contests with Prussia, showed that his reforms lacked the necessary political and financial underpinnings. Military matters remained in the hands of the *Hofkriegsrat* (court war council), which, as its name suggested, operated along bureaucratic lines, and which retained complete control over all aspects of the military sphere in both war and peace. Only the Emperor Joseph II, in the 1780s, occasionally sought to circumvent this body, albeit with mixed success.[65]

While the foundations of Austrian power were fragile and the Monarchy's administrative structures cumbersome, its army was not noticeably worse than the Prussian. It emerged mostly, though not always, victorious from the wars against the Ottomans in the Balkans. If the Italian campaign of 1718–19, especially the operations in Sicily, ended in disorder and ignominy, in the various *Reichskriege* in the west Habsburg armies usually held their own against their French adversary. Only in the three Silesian conflicts with Prussia did Austria come off worse, albeit by narrow margins. In these wars, the bureaucratic nature of the Habsburg state was as much a hindrance as an element of strength. It did not prevent the significant increase in troop numbers—by 1756, for instance, the army had grown to *c*.165,000 men, though only *c*.69,000 were ready and deployed in Bohemia.[66] Further, if decision-making was tardy, it also made the Monarchy more resilient in times of adversity. Prussia's fortunes waxed and waned with Frederick's successes on the battlefield; Austria's remained largely unaffected by military reverses. The essential truth of this was underscored during the Napoleonic wars. As Prussian and Austrian forces were swept aside by new model French armies, Prussia teetered on the brink of total collapse, its very existence dependent on the whim of Napoleon Bonaparte. Austria weathered the shock of repeated defeats much better, its survival never in doubt.[67]

As for Prussia and Austria, so for the smaller and medium-sized German states. Their armies were no mere playthings of dissolute princes. They served wider purposes. Given the need for the effective administration of the military and its requirements, centralization was one aspect of the development of more systematic, rationalized state structures. This usually meant strengthening the powers of the monarch, even though his rule was never as absolute and arbitrary as nineteenth- and twentieth-centuries mythology might suggest. Standing armies and absolutism were two sides of the same coin.[68] Maintaining an army yielded diplomatic and financial benefits, too. Most of the smaller states entered into subsidies treaties with foreign great powers, contractual arrangements which obliged them, in return for an annual subsidy, to place a portion of their troops at the disposal of the subsidizing power in the event of war. This was not only lucrative for small princes; it also offered the perspective of concluding such arrangements with competing powers or groups of powers, which in turn enhanced the strategic significance of smaller states, so helped to protect their possessions and might even enable them to enhance their status and positions. The electors of Cologne, for instance, received subsidies from France but also from the maritime powers.[69] Even Fredrick William I of Prussia, during the early years of his reign, was content to let great powers subsidize his growing army. The interplay between expanding military prowess and frequent changes of diplomatic alliances, in fact, fuelled the rise of his kingdom.[70]

The utility of soldiers was not confined to battle. An encounter on the battlefield was only one aspect of war, the final resort in a complex and multifaceted contest between states and their armies. Few contemporaries would have questioned the validity of the maxim, attributed to the Duke of Alva, the Spanish commander of the 1570s, that: '[i]t is the business of a great general always to get the better of his enemy, but not always to fight; and if he can do his business without fighting, so much the better.'[71] Soldiers were a valuable commodity, so precious that, as a rule, a commander wished to avoid exposing them to the uncertainties of battle. Special vigilance was required to prevent desertion when troops were on the move;[72] and in the pell-mell of battle, and in its immediate aftermath, the danger was at its greatest.[73] Even Frederick William I, despite his militaristic reputation, was loath to risk his army in combat. During his reign Prussia took part in only one campaign, that of 1734–5 on the Upper Rhine—and yet, over the twenty-seven years of his rule, he lost some 30,000 soldiers through desertion, the equivalent of 36 per cent of the Prussian army at the time of his death.[74]

To eliminate, or at least to reduce, the risk of desertion was also the aim of the linear fighting tactics that dominated contemporary doctrine. Fighting in such formations ensured a high degree of control over the troops in battle and already before then, in camp and on the march. Such control, however, came at the price of increased numbers of combat casualties, which the inflexibility of steadily advanced lines made well-nigh unavoidable. This was yet more reason for the skilled commander to avoid battle as much as he could, and instead to seek to wear down the enemy and his resources by constant manoeuvring which would overstretch his supply lines and so force him either to fight under adverse circumstances or to vacate territory without making a stand. The armed forces represented a significant investment in both time and money for the governments of the *ancien régime*, who could draw on only limited resources. If depleted in combat, regiments, let alone whole armies, could not easily or swiftly be replaced.[75] Contemporary warfighting concepts, the 'art of war', reflected this basic fact.[76] Precedent and convention were the hallmarks of eighteenth-century warfare, often accompanied by pedantry and an excessive regard for the rigid rules and conventions of generalship. The armies of the period steadily grew in size as population increased. Means of transport and communication also gradually improved. The fundamental assumptions about strategy and tactics, however, remained barely altered until the end of the century. Conventional manoeuvring was preferable to seeking a decision by battle. Fortresses and siegecraft occupied a more prominent place in most wars on land than offensive action.[77]

Wars were conducted with a view to economy. Caution was valued more highly than audacity; observation of the enemy prevailed over seeking the offensive. At Hastenbeck, in July 1757, the Duke of Cumberland, commanding the Allied Army of Observation, adopted a plan that could barely be faulted in its adherence to the conventions of the age; and yet in its very correctness lay its weakness, and his force was pinned down with ease by the French.[78] The dominance of the defence reflected the nature of dynastic wars that dominated the seventeenth and eighteenth centuries. As seen earlier, this type of war was fought for specific objects, often conflicting inheritance claims, rather than the moral or ideological purposes implicit in the earlier wars of religion. War in the eighteenth century was a matter of limited liability, dynastic states fighting limited wars for limited objectives. These tended to end in a negotiated settlement in which limited changes were agreed to the status quo. Revulsion at the carnage wrought by the religious fanaticism in the wars of the sixteenth and early seventeenth centuries acted as a further limiting factor. Wars, even major ones, of course, still occurred, but unnecessary bloodshed and devastation were reduced by the customs of eighteenth-century warfare. War was a matter of reason; it could be planned and tamed, risks minimized and opportunities maximized, hence the elaborate rules of strategy, sieges, and surrender, of military honours, the treatment of prisoners and the protection of civilians that guided princes and generals from the inception of war to its termination.[79]

Wars thus became formalized. Just as the principle of a European equilibrium guided international diplomacy, so 'balance' was the most notable feature of eighteenth-century warfare. Open field battles were destructive, so might disrupt the overall balance, and were therefore not sought. Positional warfare, punctuated by complex manoeuvrings, prevailed over war of movement. The object of all strategy was to secure successive, cumulative advantages rather than the complete destruction of the enemy's forces. Wars might be long, but they were seldom intense. This circumstance reflected the concerns of governments and the contemporary intellectual context. War and diplomacy were concerned with the balance between dynastic states. Royal war and monarchical marriage diplomacy were the two means by which dynastic interests and the equilibrium could be adjusted. It is instructive to note that the three great wars of the age—those of the Spanish (1701–14), Polish (1735–8) and Austrian Successions (1740–8)— were about the transfer of claims and estates of defunct (or near-defunct) dynasties, and that they broke out after diplomatic arrangements had collapsed or the points at issue had become so involved as to be beyond the finesse of envoys and lawyers.[80] Defensive manoeuvres dominated, and defeat rarely resulted in complete annihilation. Operations were precise and mechanical. This was not merely a matter of enlightenment ideas, though these reinforced contemporary habits. There were also practical reasons for it. Roads were poor, few could accommodate an army on the move, and fewer still were serviceable in autumn and winter. Water-logged or frost-bound roads put a stop to the movement of guns and heavy supply trains, and supply lines could no longer be maintained. As soon as the cold season was upon them, armies went into their winter quarters, and campaigns ground to a halt. Communication by despatch riders was slow; and then there was the constant problem of maintaining supply lines when operating in enemy territory. All of these attendant factors reduced the mobility of eighteenth-century armies. But lack of mobility also meant that smaller states could survive against greater powers. Limited wars were always liable to end in a compromise settlement, and sides could always be switched to improve one's negotiating position, even in the midst of a war. Frederick II, for example, executed such a manoeuvre in 1742 when he defected from the anti-Austrian coalition.[81]

Given the defensive bent of eighteenth-century warfighting doctrines, the number of sieges tended to exceed that of battles. Fortresses of considerable size and sophistication studded many of the historically contentious borders of Europe, such as the Low Countries, the Upper Rhine valley, or the North Italian plain. They were also built along well-defined invasion routes. Belgrade and Adrianople were notable examples in southeastern Europe. Equally important, as will be seen, was the Silesian fortress belt with the strong points of Breslau (Wrocław), Glatz (Kłodzko), Glogau (Głogów), Kosel (Koźle), Neisse (Nysa), and Schweidnitz (Świdnica) between the river Oder and the Sudeten mountains, each controlling key access routes in and out of, and across, that province. Fortresses impeded the advance of the enemy. Conversely, possession of a hostile fortified strongpoint gave control over the surrounding territory and its resources. Such tactical advantages aside, it also served as a useful bargaining counter during any peace negotiations. Capturing a fortress, then, yielded more positive value than victory in a field battle; and as with all aspects of war, the conduct of sieges was subject to elaborate rules. It was taken as axiomatic that a fortress be taken by siege rather than a surprise coup. But equally, it was inconceivable that any general commanding an army in the field could ignore fortified enemy places by sweeping around them.[82]

Another constraining factor was the nature of feudal society, from which the armed forces were recruited. To maintain discipline amongst the rank and file regular and adequate supplies were needed. Well-fed troops, properly supplied with all necessary equipment, were less prone to ill-discipline. This, too, required organization. Allowing soldiers to feed off the enemy's land in wartime increased the risk of popular resistance to the occupying army. Worse, it invited wholesale desertion. To that end, governments built large magazines to store equipment and foodstuffs. In preparation for war, forward food and ammunition dumps were readied, from which the armies in the field were supplied and where field bakeries were set up. Necessary as they were, such arrangements further restricted the mobility of the armies of the period. For as long as they remained chained to a system of magazines and forward distribution depots they could not venture far or fast, as Leuthen would demonstrate. No army could move further than five days' distance from its nearest magazines, unless it had secure access to a navigable river in its back. For the same reason, the swift pursuit of a routed and retreating enemy, perhaps in separate columns, was scarcely possible. Any such attempt would disrupt the order of the pursuing army, and it would have offered plenty of opportunity for desertion.

The same relative lack of mobility and the same adherence to certain formalities also characterized the experience of battle. It also explains the harsh discipline and constant drill in the armies of the period. Only savage discipline, it was thought, could hold together men who fought for no great common cause, but who had enlisted either to make a living or because their lowly social position made it impossible for them to evade conscription. As Frederick II reflected after his first two Silesian campaigns, the bulk of any army 'consists of indolent men; if the general does not keep constantly at them, this artificial and perfect machine will soon be in disarray.... One will, therefore, have to grow accustomed unceasingly to work at this.'[83] Order and purpose had to be imposed from outside and above to turn this motley crew into an effective fighting force. Drill inculcated a sense of discipline, instilled the necessary moves and numbed soldiers' senses through incessant repetition until the moves become automatic, until this lumbering machine had become an effective fighting force. The columns, lines, and other close formations exercised on the parade ground were the actual tactical formations and movements employed in battle. Discipline, it was thought, was the essence of the army. It made small forces formidable, and on it alone rested the prestige and glory of the entire army. Thinking was no part of the common soldier's duty. Neither could there be reasoning with these uneducated men nor could the carrying out of orders be left to their judgement.[84]

Discipline was a paramount concern in the Prussian army. Its camp, noted a British diplomat, was 'no Place of Pleasantries; neither convenience nor Luxury dwell here; you are well provided with everything, if you bring it along with you'.[85] Still, discipline was a two-way process. If wearing the king's coat subjected the ordinary soldier to harsh discipline, that same garment made equally stringent demands on the monarch himself, another British visitor observed in 1758.

Frederick's 'dress is that of his whole army', his 'table is a very neat and frugal one.... His equipage is a moderate one, if considered as that of a King.' He was 'very attentive to have his soldiers well furnished with everything necessary and I really think, the whole considered, that they are better in that service than in any other'. The supply system was sufficiently robust to ensure that 'the army never wanted bread for a moment'. In fine weather the troops were given beef twice and in inclement weather four times a week: 'Besides these attentions and many others for the men, he never fatigues them unnecessarily, so that, when they have once learned their exercise, which they do quicker there than anywhere else, they have nothing to do but their ordinary duty.' Punishment, 'except the ordinary one with the cane', was light, the death penalty being rarely administered even for plunder. Frederick used more subtle techniques. Regiments upbraided for not having done well before the enemy were ordered to cut off their *aiguillettes* or other decorative parts of their uniform. So dreaded was this 'mark of infamy' that regiments thus treated performed 'next to impossibilities to recover their reputation'. The king could rely on the loyalty of his troops, 'for they are sure to see him always with them; and upon a march he mixes in the ranks and converses freely with the men'. In short, 'the machine is created, subsists and is put in motion solely by the genius of the Prince that presides over it'.[86]

The Prussian *Exercierreglement* of 1714, drafted largely by Frederick William I himself and revised by his son in 1743, epitomized the nature of eighteenth-century infantry drill. It created, as Frederick later commented, 'that discipline, that order and that astonishing precision which made these troops resemble clockworks, which, through careful gearing, produce exact and regular movement'.[87] Its main emphasis was nevertheless on the defence. In this it underlined the specific character of warfare between c.1660 and the 1780s. Before then, commanding officers had little control over their charges once battle had been joined; thereafter, during the early stages of the French revolutionary wars, the first battles of envelopment and expanding war aims offered a glimpse of an altogether new type of war. By then the dynastic wars were giving way to the wars of nations. In many ways, the Seven Years' War was a point of inflection in that process. The Prussian *Reglement* was an attempt at finding the forms and evolutions best suited to the effective use of flintlock muskets and bayonets, the principal problem of infantry combat in that period. In order to fire, the soldiers had to stand side by side. This also helped to multiply the effect of their fire. Their muzzle-loading muskets, however, were anything but accurate except at short range (around two hundred paces). Above all, it took time to load them. If a line was always to be ready to fire, or to be able to maintain a continuous fire, it had to have several ranks. In that way, when one rank was discharging its firearms, the others reloaded. The Prussian army was the first to introduce lines three ranks deep, dispensing with the previously usual fourth row. This formation remained the norm until the end of the eighteenth century. It enabled a given number of foot soldiers to produce the greatest volume of fire with what was an unreliable weapon.[88]

The formation of such a line required precise movements, but it was also slow. Drill was meant to remedy this by training the men, marching in open columns of eight platoons of up to eighty men in three files, to form the line with promptitude and precision, flanked by field guns and usually backed up by a second line two hundred paces behind to allow for any gaps to plugged. It also aimed at increasing the rate of fire. At their peak, Prussian infantrymen managed around three rounds per minute. The greater length of Prussian infantry musket (155 cm) also made them a more accurate weapon than the average firearm of other armies (140 cm). Speed and accuracy of fire kept most approaching enemy formations at bay, and conversely turned the Prussian infantry into a formidable force in attack.[89] Speed and accuracy in falling into line, the so-called '*rangieren*' to form the battle order, and firing were also necessary to mitigate the principal weakness of line formations. While the line was being formed, the troops were defenceless. The sooner it was formed, the less the men were exposed to danger. Once formed, however, there were other risks. The flanks were the weak spots, offering little or no resistance to an attack. To obviate that danger, commanders sought to exploit the battlefield terrain to their advantage by resting their flanks on physical obstacles, such as ridges or marshes that were difficult to cross. Nevertheless, the formations remained vulnerable in general and on their flanks in particular. Line tactics, in fact, were the principal reason for the heavy casualties of the wars of this period. Frontal attacks were best avoided, and generals sought to attack the enemy on his flank, or even in his rear. To defend against such attacks, a further line facing the flank, or the rear, became necessary—and ultimately the square, a line facing in every direction, though this only rarely happened in the eighteenth century, most notably at Zorndorf (1758) and Kunersdorf (1759).[90] Were flanks and rear protected by natural obstacles, little was to be feared even from a numerically superior enemy force. This explains the insistence on good geographical knowledge and man-oeuvring skills, to find a position which the opponent could not assail without incalculable risk.

All major European armies of the eighteenth century conformed to the same model. The warfare for which they were drilled was highly formalized; shock, provided by the cavalry, and the fire of the infantry were fairly well balanced. Campaigns were conducted with moder-ation. Now that the fire of religious fanaticism had been extinguished, war had been tamed to an absolute minimum never attained before or since. Artillery was brought into greater use by the middle of the eighteenth century, but otherwise military technology scarcely advanced, if at all. One of the few innovations in this period was the introduction of the iron ramrod in place of the wooden one by Prince Leopold of Anhalt-Dessau, the long-serving Prussian general. Armies were still limited in size, and continued to operate as a single unit, forming an unbroken line in battle. No subdivision, in fact, emerged until much later in the century. Success in war depended on superior skill rather than force of arms. Quantity mattered more than quality; and the outcome of battles was determined more by outmanoeuvring the opponent's forces than by destroying them. Wars were limited also in that they were conducted by professionalized bodies of men rather than fought between peoples. It was the sport of princes; and the princes kept their sport within tolerable bounds. Their armies were not conscript armies; they did not forage over the countryside they occupied; and, mostly, they did not lay waste to enemy territory, the devastation wrought by Louis XIV's armies in the Palatinate and the Upper Rhine region in 1689 being an obvious exception.[91] They observed the formalized rules of their profession; and they pursued limited aims, eschewing crippling peace terms in victory, conscious that they, too, might be defeated in the next war. In all this, the art of war reflected the belief in mechanical solutions, so common to this period.

Frederick II's wars were to challenge some of the basic tenets of that thinking.

2

The Silesian Wars

The Seven Years' War tested the military system created by Frederick II and his predecessors to near-destruction. It survived, and in doing so it confirmed a new continental, indeed global, dynamic in great power politics.

Five trajectories, in motion since the middle of the previous century, converged in this conflict. There was, first and foremost, concern about the European 'balance' in the face of French pretensions on the continent and overseas. This was complemented by the emergence of a new factor in European politics, the growth of Russia, recognized as a European great power since 1709/21. Its focus was on the 'North' (Scandinavia and the Baltic) but increasingly also on the Ottoman Empire.[1] The emergence of Austria as a major Central European power, the third line of development, began in the middle of the sixteenth century, fuelled by a succession of initially defensive wars with the Turks. A deep antagonism towards France and Russia marked Austrian policy until the eighteenth century. The fourth trajectory was Britain's ascent as the leading naval and increasingly financial power in Europe, and this, too, led to antagonistic relations with France. And then there was the slow rise of Prussia.

These five lines framed the constellation of the great powers, but they also diverged in new directions just prior to outbreak of the war. It will suffice to focus on the more immediate origins of the war. By the end of the 1730s Europe was engulfed in a sequence of international crises. The War of the Polish Succession (1733–5) had eventually been brought to a formal end in the Treaty of Vienna in

November 1738, which secured the succession to the Polish throne of the Austro-Russian candidate, the Saxon Elector Frederick Augustus II, over the pretender favoured by French diplomacy. But this was purchased at the price of compensating the latter with the duchy of Lorraine, which still remained under the suzerainty of the Empire. There were territorial gains for the Spanish Bourbons in Italy, largely at Habsburg expense, as a reward for their support for France.[2]

The settlement was an awkward compromise that satisfied no one, left many grievances untreated, and so gave scope for new ones. What lent wider European significance to the Polish war was the appearance, for the first time, of a Russian army deep in the heart of Europe, operating alongside the Austrians in southwestern Germany. While the envoys of the great powers were bartering over the future of Poland, Austria and Russia were also involved in a war with the Ottomans (1735–9). The Turks proved more resilient than expected, and the treaties of Belgrade of September 1739, brought about with French mediation, marked a stalemate in the ongoing struggle between the three empires.[3] The relative decline of Habsburg power in the Balkans was palpable, however, and so was the growth of Russian power.

No sooner had the Austro- and Russo-Turkish treaties been signed than another war broke out, this time between Britain and Spain. A dispute over British ships captured by Spanish colonial authorities in the West Indies, the loud clamour for war in commercial circles in London, and stiff anti-English sentiments at the Madrid court propelled the two sides towards war which broke out in October 1739. Its leaning towards the fellow-Bourbon power notwithstanding, French diplomacy refused to enter into a closer alliance with Spain without commercial concessions in the Americas, but a French fleet had been ordered to the Caribbean as a check on British aggression.[4]

But for the death, in October 1740, of Emperor Charles VI, France might well have kept out of the war in the Mediterranean. The emperor's demise transformed the political landscape of Europe; and the Anglo-Spanish war was soon caught up in the struggle for the

Fig. 2.1 Friedrich der Große by Johann Georg Ziesenis. Wikimedia Commons.

Habsburg succession in which the two Bourbon powers were to fight against Austria. The further spread of the war, however, was caused by the actions of Prussia, where Frederick II had succeeded his father in May 1740 (Fig. 2.1). Since then British diplomacy had sought to cajole him into an alliance in the hope of thus securing a potential counterweight to France on the continent to protect the Hanoverian dynasty's ancestral possessions in northern Germany in the event of a war with France. Frederick was too astute to be made into a catspaw of British continental policy. He was certain that France would exploit the death of the emperor, and this opened up altogether new prospects for the ambitious young monarch.[5] For in the Empire there was a rival claimant to the imperial title, the Elector of Bavaria, Charles Albert, and in Italy Sardinia and Spain were ready to take advantage of any signs of Habsburg weakness. Both France and Britain hesitated which course to take in the ensuing disputes, but both became embroiled in the European war that now broke out.[6]

That Charles VI's sudden death should lead to war was anything but unexpected. But the manner in which it came about, perhaps, was surprising. The twin objectives of the late emperor's activities since the middle of the 1720s had been to strengthen his powers in the Empire and to secure international recognition of the Pragmatic Sanction, a declaration regulating the formal succession to the Habsburg possessions in the female line in favour of his daughter Maria Theresa (Fig. 2.2). This planted another bramble into the thorn hedge of conflicting dynastic claims and wider ambitions and interests of the European powers. Charles' dogged pursuit of his scheme initially placed him at odds with the maritime powers (Britain and the Dutch Republic) as well as France and Spain, all of whom felt threatened by his Ostend Company, a privileged trading company that was meant to establish itself as a major force in the East and West Indian trades. Single-mindedness and skill enabled Charles to exploit existing rivalries and suspicions between the major powers, and to persuade them, singly or in groups, to guarantee the Pragmatic Sanction.[7] He had to make concessions, including the suspension of his Belgian trading company and territorial gains for Spain in central Italy (Parma and Piacenza). Amongst the German princes, Frederick William I of Prussia was one of the first, in 1726, to offer the desired guarantee. He also undertook to support the candidature of Maria Theresa's future husband for the imperial crown, provided she married a German. The Empire as such followed in 1732.[8] Significantly, the Electors of Bavaria and Saxony, and the three branches of the Palatinate dynasty dissented, though the Saxon ruler was won over the following year when Austria joined Russia and Prussia in supporting his candidature for the Polish throne.[9]

This latest twist underscored the complex nature of eighteenth-century international relations, with their conflicting yet inseparably entwined dynastic claims and strategic interests. During the War of the Polish Succession, the emperor fought against a new combination of

Fig. 2.2 Maria Theresia, Roman-German Empress. Copper engraving by Gustav Adolf Müller after drawing by Martino Altomonte (after paintings by Martin van Meyten). Alamy, 2F95WJY.

powers, led by France, supported in Germany by the Wittelsbach princes of Bavaria and Cologne and the Palatinate, and by Spain and Sardinia in Italy. In the east, Russia, as Charles' ally, took to the field in Poland. The preliminary peace of 1735 and the final treaty three years later, which settled the Polish succession in favour of the Saxon candidate, also introduced yet another factor into European politics. Francis Stephen, the Duke of Lorraine and Bar, had been brought up at the imperial court in Vienna and, in February 1736, married the emperor's heiress. Unusually for the period, it was really Maria Theresa who had the last word in the matter of her nuptials, and who would not countenance anyone but the Lorrainer.[10] The preliminary peace treaty had made provisions for this union, and the Treaty of Vienna of November 1738 confirmed it. As part of this settlement, the contested Italian territories were divided between the emperor, Sardinia, and Spain. Tuscany was allotted to Francis Stephen, who, in turn, had to relinquish his ancestral possessions in Lorraine to the defeated French candidate to the Polish throne, Stanislas Leszczyński, upon whose death the duchy was to pass to the French crown—a rather complex diplomatic minuet, typical of the period.[11]

It was an undoubted diplomatic success; and, as with many diplomatic successes, its outward appearance belied more conflicted and complex realities. It was little more than a paper construction that folded with the emperor's death in October 1740. The sanctity of treaties proved insufficient protection for the Habsburg Monarchy, which was in no position materially to resist aggression. Vienna's coffers were empty, and the recent reverses in the wars against the Turks, culminating in the cession of Belgrade to the Sultan in 1739, had left the army exhausted and demoralized.[12] There was also a leadership vacuum of sorts. The heiress, Maria Theresa, was politically untried and untrained, her husband a nullity with little political sense, and her ministers were mostly superannuated placemen, who had outlived their usefulness and who were scarcely able to rise to the challenges that now bore down on the young monarch. Her difficulties were compounded by the fact that she could not be certain of the loyalty of her subjects. In Hungary, Habsburg authority remained fragile; and the Magyar magnates appeared readier to weaken it further rather than to defend their queen.[13] In the dynasty's core areas in Austria and Bohemia many nobles were willing to support her Bavarian rival whose claims rested on his marriage to a sister of the late emperor, which he argued constituted 'un patto di famiglia'.[14] The claim itself was not, perhaps, a particularly strong one. Nor was the Bavarian ruler in any position to enforce it; his army was small— some 10,000 troops—and his debts were enormous—around seven times his electorate's annual revenues.[15] He could, however, expect support from other German princes and, above all, from France.

The French position was ambiguous. Whilst this made for some uncertainty in the international manoeuvres surrounding the question, Austrian complacency also played a role. Vienna chose to rely on the French guarantee of the Pragmatic Sanction, secured in 1735 as part of the Polish settlement, even though this did not cover the eventuality of another party laying claim to the imperial succession. Eight years earlier, in fact, in a Franco-Bavarian treaty of 13 October 1728, Versailles agreed to support any legitimate claims the elector might have to any of the Habsburg possessions on the death of the emperor without male heirs.[16] That the apparent guarantee of 1735 did not supersede any obligations under the earlier treaty should have been obvious to the Austrians since French diplomacy repeatedly offered to mediate between Vienna and Munich. Still, French support for the latter after 1740 was not inevitable. Fleury, the cardinal-statesman in charge of foreign policy, was risk-averse and shied away from pursuing several objectives simultaneously. Just then, he was preparing for intervention in the Anglo-Spanish conflict on the side of the Spaniards. To take up the case of Charles Albert as well meant accepting a wider European war not only with Maria Theresa and whatever allies she could muster in the Habsburg dominions and the Empire but also with the maritime powers.[17] For it was generally understood that Austria was central to the continental strategies of Britain and the Dutch Republic, and that neither London nor The Hague would countenance its diminution. French calculations were further complicated by the insufficient resources the Wittelsbach pretender could command. Even if his candidature were to be successful, an emperor required ample means to maintain his dignity, means with which the Wittelsbach dominions could not furnish him. For France, then, simply supporting the Bavarian's claims to the imperial title without also securing for him an enlarged territorial base had no practical value. If it were to be done, it meant robbing Maria Theresa of title and land. However prudent his diplomacy, Fleury's influence at the court of Versailles was on the wane. Louis XV had begun to lean towards those who urged him to seize the opportunity presented by the emperor's death to destroy Habsburg power for good and place Charlemagne's crown on the brow of a French satellite prince.[18] All the cardinal could do was delay matters as French policy drifted towards a policy of dismembering Austria. The key decision, however, was not made in the council chambers of Versailles. It was made in Potsdam.

In so far as any single person can be said to be responsible for the War of the Austrian Succession, it is Frederick II. The young king grasped that '[c']est le moment du changement total de l'ancien système politique'.[19] He controlled Prussian policy; he willed war; and his decision, in December 1740, to invade Silesia propelled the powers along the path towards a European conflict. Prussia had claims to certain parts of that prosperous province, but previous rulers of Brandenburg-Prussia had pursued these only haphazardly and without much conviction or success.[20] Frederick's father, during the last years of his reign, had placed greater importance on securing the remainder of the Jülich-Berg inheritance, only to be duped in this matter by the late emperor. For Frederick these distant western territories were of little value.[21] Silesia, the economically most advanced of the Habsburg possessions, by contrast, was an evidently desirable acquisition. Disarray at Vienna following the emperor's death aside, the situation in Silesia was also promising. Lower Silesia was strongly Protestant and leaning towards Prussia, and Breslau, the provincial capital, was even more pro-Prussian.[22] Whether the king expected to be able to secure the whole of the province, he certainly thought he had a good chance of obtaining at least Lower Silesia. Strategic calculations mingled with a desire to acquire personal glory, for both of which older legal claims served as a very small fig leaf.[23]

Frederick hoped to secure Silesia without a real war by striking swiftly. But, if necessary, he was willing to fight. The Austrian troops in the province were weak and scattered across the main fortresses of Breslau, Glatz, and Liegnitz (Legnica). At most, they might hold these; but they were in no position to offer meaningful resistance to an invading army. At dawn on 16 December 1740, the Prussian army entered Silesia; the king had 'crossed the Rubicon with flying colours and drums beating'.[24] It was a small step, but it would shape his policy for the remainder of his reign. After the invasion had begun, Frederick proposed a settlement: in return for the cession of Silesia, he offered financial compensation, coupled with a promise to aid Maria Theresa in the defence of her other possessions and to use his vote for her husband in the forthcoming imperial election. To his consternation, she refused.[25] It was the beginning of a deep, and deeply personal, feud between the two monarchs, unusual at a time when cold calculations of relative advantage were expected to guide political decision-making.

Whatever affront Maria Theresa felt, her actions were not guided entirely by personal pique. There were sound practical reasons for resisting, even if these were not always fully grasped at Vienna.[26] Yielding to the Prussian upstart's demands meant she would have to violate the Pragmatic Sanction herself, and this might well weaken her title to the remainder of her inheritance. Frederick's assurances of future support counted for little. If anything, his attempted robbery threatened to unsettle the delicate balances of Central Europe and with them the foundations of Habsburg rule. Energetic action against the aggressor, by contrast, might deter others and coax some of the guarantors of the Pragmatic Sanction out of their present reserve. After all, the military value of the Prussian army, not really tested in combat since 1713, was unknown.

Swift action, let alone success in the field, however, proved unattainable. The inclement weather and more so 'the present scarcity of corn and all other provisions' necessitated delay, reported Britain's envoy at Vienna.[27] It took several months before the Austrians had mustered sufficient numbers to take the fight to Frederick in Silesia. But Maria Theresa had high hopes of assistance from Britain, whose king, George II, tended to prioritize the interests of his hereditary German dominions. Prussian expansionism threatened their security, and the electors of Hanover tended to look towards the emperor to keep Brandenburg-Prussia in check in the North. After their succession to the English throne, the imperial connection became significant also as a deterrent against any attempt by France to seize the king's German homelands in any Anglo-French war to extract concessions from London during peace talks. British—as opposed to Hanoverian— opinion was not hostile to Frederick's ambitions, however.[28] In Whitehall there was far greater concern about France joining Spain in a renewed conflict in the Mediterranean. It seemed sensible, then, to extend Britain's traditional alliance with Austria by bringing Prussia into the fold. Hanoverian and British interests thus pulled in different directions, and this acted as a restraint on the king. In Hanover he was absolute; in Britain he was dependent on the whims of Westminster parliamentarians; and in consequence, British policy was left hobbled. The Habsburg heiress never understood George's domestic constraints, and so expected more from him than he was in a position to give.

In a similar manner, she misread Russian and Saxon policy, confident that both could be induced to join an anti-Frederician coalition. Russia's support was particularly important, for there was no other power that the Prussian king feared more.[29] Yet Russian aid was not to be had. Internal instability following the death of the Tsarina Anna in October 1740 and another war with France's Nordic satellite Sweden (1741–3) prevented an active Russian policy in Central Europe. Russian support, Austrian diplomats calculated, would also bring the Saxon elector into the imperial camp. As King of Poland, Augustus III owed his throne to Austro-Russian support after all. But with Russia remaining largely passive, the king-elector at Dresden also stayed his hand. The longer he held aloof, the better his prospects of extracting concessions from the beleaguered Queen of Bohemia and Hungary. What he coveted most was the acquisition of territory to make his Saxon electorate contiguous with his Polish kingdom. This could only be done at the expense of Prussia or by Austria ceding part of lower Silesia to Saxony. Augustus inclined towards Austria—Prussia's invasion of Silesia, after all, threatened to block any plans of linking the Saxo-Polish halves. But Maria Theresa was as dogged in her refusal to purchase Saxon support with even a sliver of Silesia as she was in opposing Frederick. All she would consent to offer was money—expected to come from Britain or Holland—and a part of any conquests made at Prussia's expense. She was also reluctant to allow her husband, if elected emperor with Saxon support, to elevate Saxony to a kingdom. An Austro-Saxon alliance was signed in April 1741, but Maria Theresa delayed ratification because it committed her to such a step.[30]

By then, the Austrian position was precarious. Not until the autumn of 1918, in fact, was Habsburg power so close to collapse. A Russian alliance remained elusive, and British support was not forthcoming either. Westminster granted her subsidy, and also confirmed that Britain would supply her with 12,000 troops, as stipulated by the Anglo-Austrian treaty of 1732, to defend the Pragmatic Sanction, but this did not commit Britain to war. If matters escalated, Britain would act as an Austrian auxiliary but not as a principal belligerent. Nevertheless, for Maria Theresa the subsidy held out the prospect of further aid.[31] While Austrian diplomats plotted these moves, France at last intervened, dispatching, in March 1741, a special envoy to those German princes who might be induced to support Charles Albert. The Elector Palatine was easily won. Of the three ecclesiastical electors, the Archbishop of Cologne was the younger brother of the Wittelsbach pretender, and the other two episcopal rulers at Trier and Mainz were susceptible to French bribes and threats and fell into line. The Palatinate and the three bishops pledged to vote for the Bavarian and aid

French intervention in support of his territorial claims. France was now embarked on an attempt to partition the Habsburg possessions.[32]

This left Frederick, whose 80,000-strong army was now the most important factor in Central European politics. Francophile by inclination, he nevertheless refused to commit himself. Victory in battle could only strengthen his bargaining position. In April, the Austrians at last took the offensive against him in Silesia. They advanced only slowly, and the two armies eventually met at Mollwitz (Małujowice) near Brieg (Brzeg) on the Oder on the 10th. Their encounter very nearly ended in a rout. The Austrian heavy cavalry, experienced and by far outnumbering their opponent, threw the Prussian horse, and Frederick, believing that all was lost, was persuaded by his generals to flee the field. One of them was Prince Leopold of Anhalt-Dessau, the 'old Dessauer', one of the brains behind the Prussian *Exercierreglement* of 1714, with its emphasis on infantry fire power.[33] At Mollwitz it proved its worth. The foot regiments remained steady under fire, advanced, and then drove back the Austrian cavalry and infantry. The Prussian infantry established its reputation as one of the principal fighting forces in Europe. Frederick, moreover, was swift to learn the lessons of Mollwitz and took prompt measures to improve his cavalry.[34]

Defeat was not enough to force Maria Theresa to treat, but it had the effect of hardening France's stance. The resulting Treaty of Nymphenburg (18 May 1741) left no doubt as to who the dominant partner in the Franco-Bavarian combination was. The French promised financial and military support for Charles Albert, but little beyond that. According to a plan drawn up by the special envoy, a Franco-Bavarian force was to occupy Passau and parts of Upper Austria before moving into Bohemia with the aim of capturing Prague. But French ministers refused to guarantee Charles Albert any portion of the Habsburg territories.[35] Much would depend on the talks that were expected to commence once Prague had been taken. It was also expected that Prussia and Saxony would follow the French lead and join the anti-Austrian alliance. That hope was strengthened in June, when

Frederick, having failed to make Maria Theresa negotiate, concluded an alliance with France. He pledged his support for the Wittelsbach candidate and guaranteed French territory in Europe in return for a French guarantee of his possessions, including Lower Silesia. For Frederick the treaty was a form of reinsurance. At a minimum, he would obtain part of the rich province of Silesia. But the treaty also left him free to make peace with Vienna on any terms he could secure. His chances of securing more than just Lower Silesia would rise, the harder and the more quickly the Franco-Bavarians allies struck—and the treaty of June allowed Frederick repeatedly to urge them to act expeditiously and energetically.[36]

The execution of French plans proceeded too slowly for Frederick's liking, but it proceeded. Maria Theresa's hopes for military assistance from other powers, by contrast, were frustrated. Faced with the prospect of a potential Franco-Prussian pincer movement, George II refused to move any of his 25,000 Hanoverian troops, and instead sought to secure his possessions by mediating between Vienna and its enemies. Saxony also succumbed to French blandishments and broke off talks with the Austrians. By the end of July, Charles Albert had seized Passau and, joined by a powerful French army, broke into Upper Austria which was swiftly overrun. At this point, the survival of the Habsburg state was at risk. Yet differences emerged between the anti-Austrian allies. Frederick encouraged the Franco-Bavarian army to advance to Vienna, which was practically undefended. France, in fact, came closer to securing dominance on the continent now than at any other point prior to Napoleon's rule.[37] His advice was not disinterested. The Austrian main army had taken up a strong position in Upper Silesia covering the fortress of Neisse, one of the main fortified points in Silesia, guarding the road into Bohemia. To make his own position in Silesia well-nigh unassailable, Frederick had to take Neisse and the withdrawal of the Austrian force to cover Vienna would have made this an easier undertaking.

If self-serving, the king's counsel was nevertheless sound. With the Prussians threatening Bohemia and a Franco-Bavarian army in possession of the Habsburg capital, Maria Theresa would have had to make terms. As it was, the French commander, the aged François-Marie, duc de Broglie, refused to act. It was a matter of personal dislike of the young king more than military judgment. Instead, Broglie insisted on advancing on Prague, and the Elector of Bavaria had to do as he was told. Progress was slow, however, and the invasion of Bohemia did not commence until October.[38]

The possible threat to Vienna and London's urging to settle nevertheless weakened Maria Theresa's resolve to resist further. She had already tried to buy off her three enemies with promises of territorial concessions in the Austrian Low Countries, only for such tentative offers to be rejected by all three. By late September, she turned once more to Frederick. The Franco-Bavarian threat was the more pressing, and to deal with it she needed her army in Silesia. Concessions to Prussia would be painful, but they would be less severe than those she would have to make to all three enemies in the event of Austria's near-certain defeat. The result was the Convention of Klein-Schnellendorf (Przydroże Małe) of 9 October.[39] It was a curious arrangement, curious because nothing was formally signed, the two sides accepting terms suggested by the British minister to Prussia. The Prussian king agreed to let the Austrian main army withdraw unmolested, and in return Maria Theresa agreed to let him take Neisse after a sham siege (to satisfy contemporary norms). She further promised not to contest his possession of that fortress and of all of Lower Silesia. The convention also stipulated that negotiations for a peace settlement commence before the end of the year. In the meantime, the understanding was to be kept secret; if news of it got abroad, the king was freed from his obligations. The clause was an obvious device to allow Frederick to resume hostilities if he so wished, for secrecy was impossible to guarantee. Neither he nor his Habsburg opponent was yet ready to commit to a final settlement, but the convention had far-reaching consequences: it saved the Habsburg Monarchy.[40]

Just how fluid the situation remained was underlined by the events of the next few months. The immediate result of Klein-Schnellendorf was that Frederick took Neisse. But the Austrian army in Silesia was too slow to halt the Franco-Bavarian advance into Bohemia. Augustus III of Poland/Saxony had been lured to their side with the promise of Moravia and parts of Lower Austria. It was not the territorial link between Saxony and Poland which he had hoped for, but the new territories were to be made a kingdom, which would raise his position in the Empire and in Europe. With the aid of a Saxon contingent, Prague was taken on 26 November. Shortly afterwards, Frederick resumed hostilities against Austria by taking the fortress of Glatz before pushing into Moravia.[41]

At the beginning of 1742 Maria Theresa thus found herself in a curious position. In January, all eight votes of the Electoral College were cast for the Wittelsbach claimant; even George II as Elector of Hanover supported him.[42] Charles Albert was now emperor, styling himself Charles VII. There was, however, a fly in the coronation ointment, the contested status of Bohemia. The other electors refused to allow Maria Theresa to cast the Bohemian vote through her husband as her co-regent, but at the same time they also refused to recognize Charles VII as King of Bohemia. To do so would have meant committing the whole of the *Reich* to war. Nor did the Bavarian secure the support of the other princes for his territorial claims. French backing and the Prussian alliance had won him the imperial title but little else. The combination with France might yet help him to more territory, but this would have to be decided on the battlefield.[43]

Charles' election was a political setback for the Habsburg heiress, but it had no influence on the course of the war. Militarily, Maria Theresa was on the up, and her army operated with renewed energy. In the late summer of 1741, on 11 September, she had appealed in person to the Magyar nobles assembled in the Hungarian diet, an encounter much romanticized in later years. There was, in fact, a good deal of haggling, and the queen was forced to make concessions to the magnates to secure their assent to the dispatch of a Hungarian army, paid for by the Hungarian estates.[44] The practical value of that contribution was more limited than expected, but it did at least preserve the appearance of unity amongst the Habsburg dominions. This mattered also because the Austrian army made steady progress in Upper Austria and Bohemia, where the position of the Franco-Bavarian force became precarious. Poor leadership compounded its problems; reinforcements were not sent; and Broglie would not engage the enemy. The marshal also failed to support Frederick's Moravian offensive, for which Saxon and French units had been promised.

Frustrated by the stalemate and wary of his allies, Frederick sought a way out of the war. However French in his tastes and habits, he viewed Versailles with some suspicion. He had not forgotten that France had deserted its allies during the Polish succession struggle; and he could not dismiss rumours, swirling around the capitals of Europe, that French diplomacy sought to mediate a settlement between the Wittelsbach emperor and the Habsburg heiress. His troops also needed a rest, and his cavalry still had to be reformed. Prussia's financial reserves were nearly exhausted, and, while the war with Austria lasted, the important Amsterdam and London money markets were closed to Frederick.

The Dutch factor, meanwhile, weighed on Maria Theresa's mind. She hoped that the Dutch Republic, which since 1714 garrisoned the so-called barrier fortresses along the frontier between France and the Austrian Netherlands, might be enticed to join an invasion of France.[45] To facilitate this, it was necessary to free resources by terminating the conflict with Prussia. A Prussian victory over Austrian forces at Chotusitz (Chotusice) on 17 May convinced her that nothing was to be gained by continuing it.[46] Frederick, too, was ready to settle terms with her. Better to secure what he held than to emerge as 'the Destroyer of Germany', entirely dependent on a jealous France.[47] After Chotusitz he was in a reasonably strong position. Delay could only diminish it. British mediation eased the path towards the preliminary peace treaty of Breslau of 11 June 1742. The terms were very favourable for Frederick, who benefitted from the fact that British diplomacy prioritized concluding an arrangement over securing equitable terms its ally. Prussia thus gained Lower Silesia, the county of Glatz and most of Upper Silesia with the exception of Jägerndorf (Krnov) and Troppau (Opava).[48]

The Austro-Prussian war was over, and Frederick's defection also encouraged the Elector of Saxony to accede to the Breslau preliminaries, though there were no territorial gains for him. The War of the Austrian Succession nevertheless continued, and as Vienna was by no means reconciled to the permanent loss of Silesia, the peace was little more than a temporary arrangement. Meanwhile, the Austrians recovered Bohemia and could expect to make advances in Germany and, perhaps, the Low Countries in the following year. The conflict, however, had spilled over into Italy, where the Spanish Bourbons laid renewed claim to the Habsburg inheritance. Neither there nor in the other two theatres of war could either side make much progress. On the other hand, Britain, the Netherlands, and also Sardinia were now committed to the expanding war, and the various diplomatic manoeuvres in 1743 contributed to Prussia's re-entering the conflict. Frederick was alarmed at the Treaty of Worms of 13 September, which confirmed the alliance between Austria, Britain and Sardinia.[49] In early 1744, he discovered that its terms included a guarantee of the Pragmatic Sanction without excepting the Silesian territories recently ceded to Prussia. This did not bode well for Prussia when it came to the final peace treaty. He had also come to the view, quite correctly, that Maria Theresa intended to annex all or much of Bavaria. Efforts on his part to rally the other German princes in defence of the imperial constitution and the emperor—a forerunner of his *Fürstenbund* ('League of Princes') scheme four decades later—came to nothing, too deep were the suspicions of Prussia's own ambitions.

Frederick, therefore, began to prepare for a pre-emptive strike against Austria before it became too strong. As in 1740, so now the king tended to think in extremes, in the categories of victory or utter defeat.[50] His decision was aided by the escalation of the war in north-western Europe. In March 1744, the French, fulfilling earlier pledges to Spain, declared war on Britain and Hanover, and in May on Maria Theresa. The focus of attention thus shifted to the Low Countries and the Upper Rhine. The French made rapid progress in Flanders against numerically inferior Anglo-Dutch and Austrian forces; in early June a large Austrian army under Maria Theresa's brother-in-law, Charles V Alexander of Lorraine, crossed the Rhine and invaded Alsace. This was Prussia's opportunity, for the move left Austria exposed in Bohemia. Frederick's preparations for another contest with Austria were not confined to readying his own army. He won the support of Hesse-Kassel and the Palatinate—the so-called League of Frankfurt—ostensibly to defend the interests of the emperor, and he had entered into a renewed compact with France. It was an alliance for war, and the joint plan was promising. When the Austrians marched into Alsace, Frederick would invade Bohemia. It was only to be expected that Charles' army would be recalled; and the French would then harry the retreating forces, possibly even destroy them. French subsidies, moreover, were to enable Charles VII to raise a large army in the Empire. Only the first part of the plan was executed successfully. Frederick marched into Bohemia and by mid-September had captured Prague and other fortresses. As anticipated, Charles retreated, but was left largely unmolested, the French following him at a leisurely pace and then diverting their attention to besieging Freiburg. It eventually fell, but it mattered neither to Maria Theresa nor to Frederick, who was left to fend for himself in Bohemia.[51] Nor was Charles VII able to help him. What troops he could raise fell well short of expectations. Aided by a small French contingent, itself only a fraction of the promised 60,000 mean, he still recaptured Bavaria. But it was his last move—he died on 20 January 1745.[52]

Already before then, in November 1744, with the Austrian main army under Field Marshal Otto Ferdinand Count von Abensperg und Traun now threatening his lines of communications and with dysentery and desertion having decimated his army, Frederick left Bohemia.[53] At the beginning of the new campaigning season he was in some danger. He was on his own. Military assistance from his French ally was not to be expected, and even his repeated requests for financial aid had met with evasive replies. To compound his difficulties, Saxony had re-entered the war now as an Austrian auxiliary, paid for by the maritime powers; and there was no doubt that Maria Theresa's immediate focus was on the recovery of all of Silesia. She brought the conflict with the Wittelsbachs to an end on the basis of the status quo ante bellum. In the Peace of Füssen of 22 April 1745, the new Bavarian elector, Maximillian III Joseph, regained his homeland but had to renounce his father's claims to Bohemia and the imperial title. But however short the Wittelsbach interlude, it had inflicted considerable damage to imperial authority.[54]

Frederick, meanwhile, although tempted to strike again before 19,000 Saxon troops joined the fighting, feared that a Prussian invasion of Saxony might bring Russia into the war, now that the conflict with Sweden was over. From now on, until the end of his reign, the Russian threat was the constant in all his strategic calculations. Under the circumstances, he decided to remain passive in Silesia rather than to pre-empt the onslaught of the combined Austro-Saxon army.[55] But he seized the initiative by attacking the Austrians before they could gain the Oder plain. His victory at Hohenfriedberg (Dobromierz) in the foothills of the *Riesengebirge* mountain range on 4 June 1745 was a remarkable feat that showed many of the hallmarks of Frederick's generalship, superior use of the terrain and the willingness to act decisively and energetically. It was a personal triumph for Frederick and established his reputation as an exceptional military commander. The key role of the cavalry, spearheaded by the 5th (or Ansbach-Bayreuth) Dragoons, in routing the enemy also affirmed his reforms of that branch of the army after the near-catastrophe of Mollwitz in 1740.[56]

After Hohenfriedberg Frederick was willing to make terms, ratcheting up the pressure by invading Bohemia once more, and although Prince Charles manoeuvred him out of the province again, his retreat was covered by another victory at Soor (Hajnice) on 30 September, based on a flanking movement.[57] Maria Theresa still resisted pressure to treat. But Frederick seized the offensive late in the year by invading Saxony with two armies, winter banishing the prospect of immediate

Russian intervention. The Saxons were defeated at Kesselsdorf on 15 December, and Dresden fell to the advancing Prussians.[58] The Elector of Saxony had no choice but to seek terms, and even Maria Theresa, her earlier attempts to agree a peace with France having been rebuffed, agreed to enter into talks. The French court had given little support to its Prussian ally, but the Frederick and his army were still regarded as a useful counterweight to Habsburg influence in the Empire, itself strengthened by Maria Theresa's procuring her husband's election as emperor in September. As for Frederick, he was content to settle on the basis of the terms agreed at Breslau. The state of his depleted finances counselled against another campaign in 1746; and there was also the fear of Russia's eventual intervention, a fear kindled by military movements in Livonia. Talks were swiftly concluded, and before the year was out Prussia and Austria had signed a peace treaty at Dresden, which reaffirmed the return to the Breslau preliminaries. The Second Silesian War had come to an end; the struggle for power in Germany, hitherto the dominant theme of the war, subsided.[59]

The larger war was not over, however, and the belligerents continued their operations in Italy and the Low Countries until, exhausted by nearly eight years of fighting, they agreed to treat in early 1748, previous talks at Breda having collapsed at the turn of 1746–7. At the peace conference at Aix-la-Chapelle (Aachen), Austrian envoys sought to revive the Silesian question by offering the cession of part of the Austrian Netherlands to France in return for a French undertaking not to oppose any attempt to reverse Frederick's landgrab. But it was not in the interest of French diplomacy to allow the Habsburg state to revive its influence in the *Reich*, nor did it serve British interests to weaken the Empire by entrenching the antagonism between Potsdam and Vienna. The decisive negotiations at the conference were between Britain and France, and once they agreed on a final draft, the other belligerents had no choice but to follow their lead.

The Treaty of Aix-la-Chapelle of 18 October 1748 marked a return to very nearly the status quo ante bellum, with only some minor alterations to the territorial arrangements in Italy and to the barrier regime in Belgium. Although Prussia, having left the war in 1745, was not party to the negotiations at the Aix-la-Chapelle, the treaty guaranteed its possession of Silesia.[60] There was, however, a catch. In contrast to earlier major peace settlements, usually a series of separate treaties, this one consisted of one single document. The stipulations regarding Frederick's Silesian possessions were such as to suggest that the guarantee would only come into effect if the Prussian king pledged himself to guarantee the treaty as a whole—and this he would not do.

By inserting the stipulation British and French ministers had meant to court Frederick, whose support either side needed in the event of another European war. No one believed that the treaty would usher in a period of prolonged peace. Whatever the specific details of the settlement, its principal aspect was the survival and, certain losses notwithstanding, the relative strengthening of the Habsburg Monarchy in the Empire and in Europe. Maria Theresa had every prospect of a period of tranquillity during which the necessary reforms of Austria's bureaucracy and army could be carried out. One might well speculate that her Franco-Prussian enemies had an opportunity of destroying the Habsburg state in 1741–2 and, perhaps, again in 1744. But the French never pursued it with any real vigour or sense of direction.

Frederick also did not strain himself to bring about the collapse of Austrian power. After the setbacks of the campaign in 1744, he moderated his aims. The campaign of the following year, especially his victory at Hohenfriedberg, earned him great prestige, and already now his subjects began to refer to him as 'the Great'.[61] And yet, his possession of Silesia was by no means secure. What Dresden had conferred, another bout of fighting with Austria could undo. Neither the 1745 treaty nor the peace settlement of 1748 established a viable intra-German equilibrium which would have provided for greater security. Both, in fact, left the Habsburg state strong enough to contemplate just such a contest. The treaties of 1745 and 1748 marked the beginning of an armistice, and thus a point of transition in the evolving Austro-Prussian 'cold war' that began to shape Central European politics for the next hundred years and more.

Just under eight years after they had made peace, the European great powers and the German lands were plunged into war once more.[62] The conflict was to last for seven years before the peace treaties of 1763 (Paris and Hubertusburg) restored order for the remainder of the *ancien régime*.

The term Seven Years' War is a convenient envelope which, in fact, contains several sheaves, each headed with the name of a different conflict. For Prussia and Austria this was the Third Silesian War.[63] Frederick started it, but this was Maria Theresa's war. At Vienna, the Prussian king's landgrab of 1740 had not been forgotten, let alone forgiven. The empress-queen had carefully cultivated a personal grudge against '*der böse Mann*', the philosophizing and flute-playing robber-king at Potsdam. She was encouraged, perhaps misled, in this by her principal advisers, most notably by Prince Anton Wenzel von Kaunitz-Rietberg (Fig. 2.3).[64]

Frederick had no illusions about the empress's persistence. He had reckoned with another round of fighting ever since the Second Silesian War had ended in 1745.[65] But for the Prussian king there was more at stake than the possession of the duchies of Jägerndorf, Liegnitz, Brieg, and Wohlau and the county of Glatz. What was at risk was Prussia's continued existence as a great power. The likely alternative was partition and survival at the sufferance of its enemies, reduced to little more than the margravate of Brandenburg, from which position the state had slowly risen over the previous century. At Vienna, indeed, the king was condescendingly referred to as the '*marquis de Brandenbourg*'. His most implacable enemies at the imperial court and elsewhere in the Empire even envisaged '*une déstruction totale*'.[66] Such a plan sharply diverged from the contemporary norms of international affairs. Competing claims and interests were contested by means of diplomacy or war, but the existence or non-existence of major dynastic states was not called into question.[67] Even in the event of total defeat the plans were unlikely to be executed in full. And yet, the enemy coalition that was emerging against him was committed 'to weaken Prussian power...by taking so many territories as general

Fig. 2.3 Prince Kaunitz. Image from the author's own collection.

tranquillity demanded, so that it [Prussia] must, against its will, remain quiet and stop the burdensome plagues of war'.[68] The stakes, then, were high for Frederick. Prussia would be a great power or no power at all.

There was less at stake for Vienna. The Habsburg Monarchy was no longer in danger, the peace of 1748 having confirmed its position as a European great power; Maria Theresa's rule in the 'Erblande' and Hungary was undisputed; and her husband was installed as emperor, while the *mater familias* pulled the levers of power. Habsburg policy was driven by defensive as much as by offensive considerations. Fear of further Prussian aggression, fuelled by the full military integration of Silesia in the Prussian state, was one factor.[69] Austrian ambitions in this war revolved around two objects. The recovery of Silesia, Kaunitz argued, was imperative if the shift in the balance of power since 1740 was to be reversed.[70] Reasserting Habsburg leadership in the Empire was the other aim. The alternative was to accept an uneasy Austro-Prussian condominium in Germany, and, perhaps, decline. Restoring Habsburg ascendancy did not imply a return to the mediaeval imperial tradition or even the seventeenth-century ideas of a centralized *Kaiserstaat*. But it did entail a revision of the European great power system in Central Europe based on Habsburg dominance. As Kaunitz reflected a decade and a half after the Seven Years' War, his policy had aimed at reducing Prussia to an '*état primitive de petite très secondaire*'.[71] Any war with Prussia was therefore likely to turn into a wider European conflict.

Viennese policy had more far-reaching aims still that combined religious aspects with raw power politics. Religion as a force in the affairs of Germany had declined in significance since the bloody wars of the sixteenth and seventeenth centuries. But it had not disappeared altogether. The Protestant states of northern Germany tended to lean towards Prussia, even if they remained wary of their co-religionist's ambitions. They had to be weakened to reaffirm the Catholicity of the Holy Roman Empire. The Protestant *pestis Germaniae* was to be extirpated and the *pietas Germaniae* be restored as the dominant denomination, protected by and in turn buttressing the Habsburg Monarchy as the dominant power on the continent. Nearly two and a half centuries after the Reformation, then, political and cultural aims, with a strong religious undercurrent, were entwined in Austrian foreign policy.

The Seven Years' War was only in part an intra-German, Central European conflict. It was embedded in a wider European, indeed global, competition between the great powers.[72] By the middle of the eighteenth century a new balance of power had emerged. The emergence of Prussia as the second German great power therefore also affected Anglo-Austrian relations. There was no decisive change in British policy, but the rise of Prussia and the evolving dualism within the Empire gave it what it had previously lacked—a viable alternative ally against France. Already during the War of the Austrian Succession powerful voices at Westminster had called for such a combination.[73] Nothing came of it then, not least because the Prime Minister, the strongly Francophobe Thomas Pelham-Holles, 1st Duke of Newcastle, reverted to the idea of Austria as the cornerstone of any continental system against France. The British government even concluded sub-sidy treaties with Bavaria and Saxony, previously clients of either Vienna or Versailles.[74] Resurrecting the Austrian alliance was an altogether unrealistic ambition, as was the duke's hope of including Prussia in a pact. But whatever Newcastle's failings, Britain's contin-ental policy now had a potential alternative option at a time when disputes in North America complicated Anglo-French relations; and this circumstance was to play a role in the events prior to the outbreak of the Seven Years' War.

Victory in the two previous Silesian wars had enhanced Prussia's military reputation as well as the standing of its king. More important still, Silesia, rich and populous, furnished the necessary material under-pinning for the young kingdom's great power status.[75] The Austro-Prussian dualism was now a factor in European politics, and Berlin's efforts to preserve Prussia's great power position influenced the calcu-lations and interests of the established European powers. It was no surprise, then, that Russia, France, and Great Britain entered the next war. For it was framed by a series of other European and overseas power struggles. The most significant of these was the Anglo-French antagonism, a largely maritime struggle for mastery over the oceanic highways and colonial possessions in the West and East Indies.

The trigger event that started the Seven Years' War, the Prussian invasion of Saxony on 29 August 1756, brought all these political and psychological aspects together. At the court of Versailles, since about 1752, Louis XV and his closest advisers had been casting about for new diplomatic combinations to strengthen France's position against Britain. They were ready to contemplate the hitherto unthinkable and set aside the age-old Bourbon-Habsburg *animosité*. Hostility towards Austria had become an instinctive habit,[76] war against it a tradition, and absorbing Flanders an obsession. The French could ill afford any of this now; nor was any of it necessary anymore. The spectre of Habsburg encirclement had long been banished. In Spain a Bourbon scion had been on the throne for a generation, likewise at Naples, where a great-grandson of Louis XIV was king following one of the convoluted and intricate gavottes of contemporary diplomacy that had helped to settle the Polish succession in 1735/8. The consolidation of Austrian power elsewhere, in Northern Italy and the Southern Netherlands, meanwhile, made impossible the incremental expansionism that had characterized French foreign policy under the Sun King. France's principal opponent in the Mediterranean was no longer Austria, however, but Britain. The main object was to secure French interests against Britain in the region and overseas, in Canada, in the Ohio valley, and in India where the decline of the Mughal Empire was attracting European powers.[77] Relations between London and Paris had hardened into near-permanent hostility just below the threshold of actual war. It was a condition that was not likely to last for much longer. In the late autumn of 1754, the British decided to reinforce their position in the Ohio valley.[78] Real war was now a real possibility. The Bourbons had to look elsewhere for allies in Europe, and the timeworn hostility towards the Habsburgs was a luxury they could ill afford.

There was a corresponding shift in Viennese thinking. This was very much the work of Kaunitz, whose political influence had been growing from the late 1740s onwards. He had headed the Austrian delegation at the peace congress of Aix-la-Chapelle, and before then he had been the Habsburg envoy at Turin and at Brussels, both important

European missions. His Belgian sojourn—he was in all but name head of the local Habsburg administration—impressed upon him the weakness of Austria's position there. The Low Countries could not be defended against a determined French attack; and the various restrictions on Habsburg sovereignty in the Southern Netherlands imposed by the Utrecht peace settlement of 1713/14, and upheld since by the maritime powers, reduced the province's strategic value for the Monarchy.[79] Further, the proceedings at Aix-la-Chapelle confirmed him in his view that Britain would not assist in the recovery of Silesia. Efforts to win a French commitment to support it in return for territorial cessions in the Netherlands came to nothing.[80] But French diplomacy had not rejected Kaunitz's scheme. In March of the following year, he submitted a new plan to Maria Theresa for the recovery of Silesia. Russia was a potential ally, Prussia 'the greatest, most dangerous and most irreconcilable enemy of the Serene Dynasty', not France whose king, Louis XV, though intelligent, found the business of government distasteful and the need to make decisions irksome. Austria, then, should abandon '*das alte Systema*' of its foreign policy, persuade France of its pacific inclinations and, playing on Prussia's abandoning its French ally during the recent war, wean Versailles off its preference for a Prussian alliance.[81]

The queen-empress accepted the plan. By presenting power politics—the struggle for mastery in Germany—as a moral crusade in defence of the *Reich*, its constitution and Catholicism against the cynical, unprincipled and unbelieving ruler in Potsdam, Kaunitz won Maria Theresa's unwavering support. She saw the object of Habsburg policy, as she affirmed in 1759, 'not merely in the reconquest of Silesia and Glatz, but in the happiness of the human race and in the defence of Our holy religion'.[82] Conversely, the Lutherans now had in Frederick, for the first time since the days of Gustavus Adolphus of Sweden, a Protestant prince playing an active role in the affairs of the *Reich*.[83]

In the late autumn of 1750, the Empress sent Kaunitz on a special mission to Versailles. Whatever expectations he and his monarch may have had, he made little progress during his embassy, which ended in

1753 with his recall to Vienna to take up the position of chancellor. But conditions were not yet ripe for executing his plan, not least because Anglo-French relations had not deteriorated sufficiently. Besides, it did not take much diplomatic nous to detect an obvious incongruity at the heart of Kaunitz's scheme: while dressed in the ornate language of pacific intentions, it scarcely concealed an ambition to reduce and render harmless, by force, the Prussian king, the undisputed leader of the pro-French party amongst German princes. At the same time, Austrian diplomacy was playing along with Newcastle's attempt to revive the Anglo-Austrian alliance. Kaunitz did not anticipate becoming embroiled in any Anglo-French quarrels as long as these remained confined to the Americas or Indies. If anything, Vienna might even act as an 'honest broker', offering its mediation to the courts of St. James and Versailles.[84]

Kaunitz's Paris embassy was nevertheless a direct prelude to the great rapprochement three years later. Conditions were more propitious then, and the Austrian chancellor succeeded in engineering a *renversement des alliances*, the 'diplomatic revolution' of an Austro-French alliance. Such flexibility and willingness to sacrifice sentiment, that had hardened into dogma, to state interests astounded and alarmed the European chancelleries. Kaunitz later suggested, in a somewhat exaggerated reflection on the origins of this new combination, that the recent increase in Prussia's power had shaken the balance of power in Europe. For this disruption he blamed the rigidity of the old alliances, which Frederick had been able to exploit:

In this extreme emergency we could not waste a moment's time to save the Monarchy, and there remained no other means but to interest the rival [France] in its preservation.... To persuade a great power that the system on which its entire policy was built, contradicted its interests; to show that it was useless; to convince it that with its support for... Prussia... it was on the wrong path; in one word, to uproot its ancient rivalry with the House of Habsburg, indeed finally to transform the native habits of an entire ministry: this was an enterprise which alone Providence could inspire, conduct and bring to fruition.[85]

Whatever the role of divine intervention, a number of developments came together to facilitate a rapprochement. The brewing Anglo-French conflict in North America was one, and so were the actions of the Prussian king. In retrospect, it seems obvious that Britain and Austria had begun to drift apart after 1748. To some extent, Britain's growing preoccupation with the colonial rivalries with the two Bourbon powers accounted for this. London's habit of ignoring the steady decline of the Dutch Republic, the third party to the old anti-French alliance further fuelled the estrangement.[86] The Austrians, by contrast, had formed a much more realistic appraisal of the United Provinces, but their fate was of far less concern to them than Central and Eastern Europe, and Maria Theresa was unwilling to take on the heavy burden of defending the near-worthless Dutch ally. The relative positions of Britain and Austria, moreover, had been reversed. In previous crises Vienna had been the supplicant. Now, with a Franco-British war in the offing, it could ask a stiff price for an alliance. The two sides remained far apart. Kaunitz demanded a British guarantee for Austrian interests in Italy and a British subsidy treaty with Russia as part of a raft of measures to prevent France and Prussia from dominating the Empire, which also included financial support for various German princes so that a large army could be raised for use in Germany and the Netherlands. London was ready to accept much of this but expected that up to 30,000 Austrian troops be sent to the Low Countries and another force be held in readiness for the defence of Hanover or for a diversionary attack on France. The gap could not be bridged.[87] From Kaunitz's perspective, in return for an altogether insufficient offer of support, combined with the passivity of the Dutch, Austria was expected to bear the brunt of any continental war. Clearly, the interests of Britain and Austria were too disparate. A rapprochement with France appeared an even more attractive prospect now.[88]

When his renewed demands for a more substantial military and financial assistance in Europe went unanswered, the chancellor reverted to his old idea of an anti-Prussian alliance with France. He knew that, as French troops were being drawn up along the frontiers of Flanders, he had to move swiftly: 'The fact is, Prussia has to be knocked over if...the House [of Habsburg] is to stand upright.' The Hague would offer no help, and London not enough, but might be induced '*die preussische Allianz zu abandoniren*'.[89] Tentative feelers were stretched out towards Louis XV, using his mistress, Madame de Pompadour, as a conduit. The Austrians played on the king's resentment at the upstart Prussian ruler's pretence to be his equal and on his religious bigotry—he had always bridled at having to ally with a heretic and infidel whom he once compared to Julian the Apostate. French diplomacy was by no means passive itself.[90] Louis favoured a rapprochement with Austria, but by the end of 1755 the secret talks had reached a stalemate.[91]

The next moves by Britain and Prussia helped to break the impasse. Relations between them were rather strained after the recent war, calls by some in London for a Prussian alliance notwithstanding. A series of quarrels complicated matters: Hanover's contesting Frederick's claims to East Friesland, acquired by Prussia in 1744; the seizure of Prussian merchant vessels; Berlin's refusal, in retaliation, to repay a loan which the Austrian authorities in Silesia had raised in London before 1740; Britain's pursuit of a subsidies treaty with Russia, which Frederick feared was aimed against him; and the Prussian king's harbouring of former Jacobite rebels.[92]

This was much bickering about trifles. Once a common interest drew the two sides together, these quarrels dissipated. Frederick's policy was essentially defensive, out of fear more than genuine pacific inclination. Prussia was by no means a saturated state. The kingdom's scattered and disjointed possessions were a source of strategic weakness, as Frederick reflected in his political testament of 1752, and further acquisitions were desirable. The Silesian landgrab, necessary though it had been, had also put the other powers on their guard: '[T]hrough this geographical position we are neighbours of the greatest European princes; all these neighbours are envious, or else secret enemies of our power. The position of their territories, their ambitions, their interests, all these varying factors determine the principles of their policies, more or less hidden, depending on times and circumstances.'

Frederick had cast an eye on Saxony and West Prussia as useful for rounding off Prussian territory, but he understood that any further expansion depended entirely on favourable circumstances. And they were not encouraging. Maria Theresa, 'the cleverest and politically the most significant' amongst the European rulers, exploited the interests of others for her own ends: 'She hides her ambition and even her hatred and will not reveal her plan, except under auspicious circumstances.' George II, 'more Hanoverian than English', was speculating on cheap gains, 'but he calculates neither as well nor as far ahead as the Queen of Hungary'. Elizabeth of Russia was dominated by her foreign minister, Aleksei Bestuzhev-Ryumin, a particular enemy of Prussia. Saxony gave the appearance of 'a ship without a compass . . . exposed to wind and waves', as if the electorate 'were governed but its most brutal enemy', while Dutch politics were dominated by 'a mixture of foolishness and weakness'. Amongst the smaller powers in Northern or Southern Europe, few were reliable; the Empire was disunited; and Turkey too weak and disorganized to act as a possible counterpoise to Austria. France was Prussia's most likely ally. Interest bound the two states together: 'Silesia and Lorraine are like two sisters, of whom the older has married Prussia and the younger France.' The two powers therefore had to pursue the same policy: 'Prussia must not look on if Alsace and Lorraine were taken from France, and French moves would be effective because they would take the war into the centre of the [Habsburg] hereditary possessions.' And yet, this ally had to be treated with caution. Louis XV was 'a weak prince', bullied by his mistress and his ministers, all of whom cheated him and plundered the state coffers. Even so, France wished to have 'a hand in all of Europe's affairs', and it pursued the aim of securing the Rhine frontier at the expense of the Low Countries and the Empire. The basic axiom of French policy was 'to let the allies carry the full burden of war . . . Therefore one has to be on guard against this power in any negotiations so that one is not defrauded.'[93]

The growing threat of an Anglo-French maritime conflict, following clashes in the Ohio valley in October 1754, brought movement into European politics. Negotiations between Britain and Prussia began in the summer of the following year with Charles I, Duke of Brunswick-Wolfenbüttel, a cousin of George II and Frederick's brother-in-law, acting as a go-between. An arrangement suited both sides. George was fearful lest, in the event of an Anglo-French overseas war, the French, or their Prussian ally, occupy all or part of his Hanoverian homeland for use as a bargaining counter in any peace negotiations. Frederick, although not contemplating a break with France, had no intention of acting as his erstwhile ally's subsidiary. He hoped to act as mediator between the two powers, and, if possible, secure some advantage for himself as a reward for his services. It was not difficult to divine that London's approach was the result of a cooling in Anglo-Austrian relations. At the same time, he reasoned that France was determined to stay out of any European complications, mindful of the need to concentrate all resources on the looming naval war with Britain.[94] Frederick had also concluded, correctly, that Franco-Austrian talks of some kind were in train. He therefore had to take steps to secure his position. An Anglo-Prussian understanding, which would commit Britain not to assist Austria in a continental conflict in return for a Prussian guarantee not to attack Hanover during a Franco-British war, would provide for this. Anglo-Hanoverian and Prussian interests clearly coalesced, and the arrangement would parallel what Frederick anticipated France and Austria to agree between them. Above all, he considered it to be compatible with his alliance with France, which was defensive and confined to Europe.

Frederick's attention remained focused on Habsburg revisionism, but he was no less actuated by a fear of his eastern neighbour: 'Prussia can only be kept in awe by Russia.'[95] Austro-Russian hostility to Prussia was nothing new. The two powers tended to cooperate in the affairs of the East ever since their alliance of 1726, most notably during the Polish succession and then in the war against Turkey (1738–9); and the treaty which the two empresses signed in 1746 left little doubt about their animosity towards the upstart at Potsdam.[96] Frederick's calculations were complicated by news of the conclusion of a preliminary Anglo-Russian convention in late September 1755. On this point, British and Prussian interests appeared to diverge. Neither party read the other correctly, in fact, and both miscalculated. British diplomacy had sought to conclude a subsidies treaty with Russia for the better part of a decade, primarily to procure Russian troops for the defence of Hanover. With the end of the Austrian succession war the need for such an arrangement had become less pressing, but the American quarrel with France had revived concerns for the king's electoral homeland. Undoubtedly, George's Hanoverian instincts gave a fillip to his ministers in London, but it was also in Britain's interest to strengthen its continental system. Whatever the precise nature of Russia's military contribution, the prospect of its intervention was also calculated to act as a deterrent against Prussia siding with France after all.[97]

Fear of encirclement by a powerful combination of enemies shaped Frederick's thinking. He saw himself caught on the horns of a dilemma. Since France evidently wished to avoid any entanglement in a continental war, a French alliance entailed considerable risk. Refusing to aid France in the event of an Anglo-French war, on the other hand, would mark the final breach of an alliance that had served Prussia well enough. It would leave it exposed, for it removed the one obstacle that, until now, had held Austria and Russia in check. Under these circumstances, Frederick the adventurer of 1740 gave way to Frederick the preserver of peace. The only way out of his dilemma was to take up London's offer of an understanding. Britain and Prussia now shared a common interest in maintaining peace in Germany. That way Hanover was protected, while Frederick could keep the threat of a Russian attack at bay. In December, British ministers communicated to him the text of the as yet unratified treaty with Russia and the draft of an Anglo-Prussian convention to neutralize the Empire. The Prussian king accepted it with one significant modification—the area to be neutralized was to exclude the Low Countries. Frederick could point to the Treaty of Dresden of 1745 as a precedent, in which he had guaranteed only Austria's German possessions. But by leaving France thus free to operate in the Netherlands, should it wish to fight Britain on land as well as at sea, the king hoped to preserve his alliance with France. Neither he nor the British ministers thought it likely that the French would do so. The exclusion of the Netherlands from the treaty's provisions, then, seemed an insignificant concession, and so Frederick's envoy in London duly signed the text on 16 January 1756.[98]

In the Convention of Westminster the two parties affirmed their commitment to European peace and to peace in Germany in particular. They guaranteed each other's possessions, and promised that, in the event of foreign forces setting foot on the soil of the Empire, they would combine their forces to restore the 'tranquillity of Germany'.[99] The compact fell well short of an alliance. It was, in fact, little more than an ad hoc expedient to preserve the neutrality of the Empire. But it affected the delicate workings of European diplomacy in a way that neither party had anticipated. Newcastle clung to the wholly unrealistic notion that the understanding was a first step towards including Prussia in an Anglo-Austrian alliance. He even assured the Austrian envoy that the conventions with Prussia and Russia gave Austria complete security, so that Vienna could deploy a large army to the Southern Netherlands. Frederick was less naive than the prime minister nor as cavalier towards the interests of his ally. He, too, however, misjudged the situation. Not only did the prospect of British guineas have far less sway over the Russian court, he also 'did not foresee that France would have broke[n] with Him'.[100]

At Versailles news of the Anglo-Prussian compact was viewed with dismay and suspicion. Frederick fuelled French fears further. Not only had he kept his old ally in the dark until quite late in the day. He also responded rather heavy-handedly to French complaints about his consorting with *l'ennemi héréditaire*. The Prussian envoy at Paris was to remind the French foreign minister, that a crowned head had the right to conclude treaties and was no obliged '*d'en solliciter la permission auprès d'un autre puissance*'.[101] True, he did not have to seek permission from others, but Frederick's acerbic tone played into the hands of the pro-Austrian party at Versailles. There was an ironic twist to this. Just before news of the Anglo-Prussian understanding reached Versailles and Vienna, Kaunitz had reluctantly decided to abandon his offensive plans. The convention helped to close that gulf, but problems remained. François-Joachim de Pierre de Bernis, the latest in a line of cardinal-statesmen to control French diplomacy, had already decided against renewing the alliance with Prussia, which was to expire in June 1756. There was, however, still the triple alliance with Prussia and Sweden, which ran until May of the following year. Kaunitz's plans against Prussia, then, had to be delayed until at least the summer of 1757. Further, Bernis insisted on complete reciprocity. If France was to break with Prussia, Austria had to abandon the alliance with Britain. The Westminster convention, then, brought Versailles and Vienna back to the negotiating table on the basis of the original Austrian plan, but it did not guarantee the successful conclusion of the talks. Patience was still required: 'We know from our own experience how many and important reservations afflict the decision to abandon an old state system, to overcome deeply rooted prejudices and to pursue a new course.'[102] Kaunitz was patient, and, no matter how alarmed French ministers were at his plans, they had gone too far to abandon the negotiations. An arrangement with Austria would allow France to concentrate all her resources on the war with Britain; it might also make Frederick more pliable than in the recent past.[103]

By mid-April, matters had been settled, and on 1 May the Austrian ambassador and the French plenipotentiaries signed the first Treaty of Versailles. It actually consisted of two conventions, one of neutrality, loosely modelled on the Westminster understanding, and the other a defensive alliance. Under the terms of the former, Austria promised to remain neutral in the war with Britain that had now begun in return for a French undertaking not to endanger any Habsburg possessions in the Low Countries or elsewhere. The alliance treaty—the second convention—was confined to Europe and the Franco-British maritime conflict expressly excluded from its stipulations. But the Austrians secured recognition of the Pragmatic Sanction in return for guaranteeing

French rights in the Empire under the Westphalian peace treaty. Five secret articles added further substance to it. They established that, were a British ally to become involved in the Franco-British war or Prussia, as an ally of Britain, to attack Austria, the mutual assistance clause of the alliance came into effect. The secret articles also set out the ambition of the two courts to settle the affairs of Italy and any territorial and other disputes left unresolved by the Peace of Aix-la-Chapelle to secure a stable European peace. Under article IV they also promised, for the duration of the present war, not to make or renew treaties without consulting with the other—suspicions clearly still lingered between the new allies.[104]

By casting aside a century and more of animosity France and Austria upset the established pattern of European politics, not least because it also implied the further elevation of Russia as a factor in great power politics. But the 'diplomatic revolution' was not yet complete. Nor had Kaunitz won French support for his scheme to annihilate Prussia. After all, the explicit reference in the third secret article to the 1748 peace treaty confirmed Prussia's possession of Silesia, which it was still Austria's aspiration to recover. The treaty, then, lacked inner coherence. For the moment, Kaunitz had failed to enlist active French support for his grand scheme. The leading French ministers and, what was more important still, Louis XV's political brain, *la* Pompadour, regarded the Franco-Austrian treaty as an end in itself. European peace thus secured, France would be free to concentrate on the maritime war with Britain; and if the Austrians offered a high enough price, France might well observe benevolent neutrality in any conflict between Habsburgs and Hohenzollerns. By contrast, to Kaunitz and his queen-empress the treaty was a step along the road towards a general European war in alliance with France and Russia.[105] But the chancellor was patient. An able diplomat, he knew that he need not necessarily take the offensive. There was quiet confidence in Austrian diplomatic circles that, having secured a defensive alliance with France, the Prussian king himself might take steps that would tighten that compact yet further. As the ambassador wrote from Paris,

Habsburg diplomacy would eventually secure *'notre grand projet'*, and that Prussia might even furnish it with *'les meilleurs moyen'*.[106]

The comment was prescient. Ultimately, it was Frederick whose action provided the means for completing the 'revolution' rather than Kaunitz's cunning. But the most immediate effect of the Versailles treaty was on the maritime powers. Alarmed by the prospect of renewed war in the Low Countries, the United Provinces agreed to remain neutral in return for a French promise not to attack them or the barrier fortresses. The *'renversement des alliances'* was thus gathering pace. Not only had the Franco-Prussian and Anglo-Austrian alliances been broken, the close union between the maritime powers had also ended.[107]

Prussian diplomacy was the principal loser of this reversal. The Bourbon-Habsburg antagonism had been the bedrock of Frederick's calculations. He assumed that Prussia could take the initiative without running the risk of diplomatic isolation. The Westminster convention was meant to give him scope to pursue fresh political options in the East, where Prussia had come under considerable Russian pressure. Given the previous Franco-Prussian alliance, Russian diplomacy had worked towards isolating and weakening Frederick with a view to undermining French influence in the Baltic and Eastern Central Europe.[108] Its aim was to check France's policy of a *barrière de l'Est* to contain Russia in Eastern Europe. In turn, breaking that barrier meant reducing Prussia territorially and making her dependent on Austria. All of this was well understood at Berlin. Russian diplomacy was working more or less openly towards war. The alliances with Saxony (1744) and Austria (1746) and the two subsidy treaties with Britain of 1747 and 1755 were all pointers in that direction. The Westminster convention was meant to force Russia to change course either by joining the two powers or else by holding aloof from international complications. Frederick needed Eastern Europe to be calm if he wanted to defend his kingdom against Austrian covetousness.

The king underestimated the determination and intent of Russian diplomacy. The tsarina and her chief minister were as resolved to reduce Prussian power as the *Kaiserin* at Vienna. Her chancellor Kaunitz, moreover, was as skilled in his handling of Russia as he had been in his dealings with the French court. The success of his anti-Prussian plans depended on Russia's cooperation. At the same time, the erratic, yet always aggressive, nature of Elizabeth's policy—in 1753 she sought to bully Prussia, in 1754 she threatened to go to war against Turkey—made him tread warily. News of the Westminster convention gave him an opening to play on common grievances against Britain. The tsarina felt affronted, and complained to the Austrian ambassador that his British colleague was 'a comedian, a deceiver, a traitor, an intrigue maker etc. etc.'[109] In March and April Kaunitz let the Russians into the secret of the Austro-French talks. Whatever their doubts about the need for active French cooperation, the proposed diplomatic realignment reinforced the decisions already taken by the tsarina and her ministers to act against the King of Prussia. In April, before the terms of the Versailles treaty had been agreed, Elizabeth offered Maria Theresa an offensive alliance. Russia would attack Prussia in the course of 1756, if Austria undertook to do likewise, and to fight the war until Austria had recovery Silesia and Glatz.[110]

There were still hurdles to be cleared, not least between Russia and France—the French refused to pay a subsidy directly to St. Petersburg and wished to preserve the alliances with Turkey and Sweden[111]— there could be no doubt in the summer of 1756 that Russian diplomacy was following in Austria's wake. The *'renversement'* was nearing completion. The incompetence of British diplomacy had played a role in this. In his attempt to combine the Anglo-Russian subsidies treaty with the understanding with Prussia, Newcastle destroyed completely the system of alliances on which British policy had rested until then. His pacific intent cannot be doubted, but it never seems to have occurred to him that the imperial court might look askance at two electors making arrangements for the 'tranquillity of Germany' without consulting the emperor. Nor had it struck him that news of the convention would hand Kaunitz the card he needed to overcome any residual French doubts about an alliance. And with Britain already on the defensive following General Braddock's defeat in the Ohio valley and Admiral Byng's ignominious surrender at Minorca in April, there was little chance of persuading Russia to change course. If anything, Newcastle was ready to abandon the European continent altogether.

The only one to appreciate that in the relative isolation of Britain and Prussia lay an opportunity for combined action was the King of Prussia. The 'diplomatic revolution' did not make a European war inevitable. The French after all had not signed up to an offensive war yet, though they agreed that one might take place in the spring of 1757. However passive he had been earlier, Frederick would not now wait. While the cabinets at Vienna, Versailles, and St. Petersburg were busy extending and refining their diplomatic *instrumentaria* in preparation for war in the spring of 1757, he decided to strike. He informed his foreign minister, the seasoned Count Heinrich von Podewils, that reliable information had reached him of his enemies' aggressive plans against him—the Prussians had cultivated an informant in the Saxon chancellery at Dresden.[112] The intelligence was suggestive rather than conclusive, but Frederick also knew that Austria was not prepared for warlike operations in the current year.[113] This insight explains his decision now to launch a preventive strike: '*Il ne me reste plus que praevenire quam praeveniri.*'[114] In this manner, Frederick laid the foundations of the notion that Prussia's *Mittellage* (encircled position) necessitated and so legitimated preventive war as a tool of statecraft, a notion that was to exercise considerable influence on the thinking of German leaders up to the middle of the twentieth century.[115]

There was by now an air of unreality about the Austro-French-Russian wrangling over plans for a spring offensive. Reports of troop concentrations along the Saxon frontier left little doubt that the Prussian king would seek to '*prevenir ce qu'il croit a craindre dans la Suitte*'.[116] The war Kaunitz desired, but could not engineer, would be triggered by Frederick. To prepare the ground—and to maintain the appearance of diplomatic rectitude—he sent a sharply worded note to Vienna, accusing the Habsburg and Romanov empresses of planning a war and demanding a formal non-aggression promise. The Hofburg's reply was frosty, formally denying the existence of any offensive alliance but ignoring the king's demand for an undertaking not to resort to force. It was enough to furnish Frederick with the desired pretext to launch a preventive strike to avert 'les complots des mes ennemis'.[117]

The invasion caught Vienna by surprise.[118] There is no denying, however, that Frederick's political strategy had ended in failure. He had lost his French ally without winning a new one. He had done nothing to ease Russian pressure. If anything, it had increased, and he was now surrounded by hostile states. He had to confront the loss of the strategic initiative on which both military success and diplomatic effectiveness rested.[119] He had walked into a trap set for him by the wily Austrian chancellor. London, meanwhile, offered little more than vague promises of unspecified support, which, moreover, was predicated on him fighting a defensive war, not starting one. Once the war commenced, Britain faced the customary quandary of whether to concentrate on the transoceanic war with France or force France into dissipating its resources by forging a continental coalition. The former meant surrendering Hanover to the enemy, trusting to Providence, that staunch ally of Protestant Britain, and to superior naval power to regain the king's German possessions at the making of peace. The latter entailed a military alliance with Prussia, and it meant straining the sinews of Britain's financial power to subsidize the armies of Hanover, Hesse, and Brunswick and other smaller northern German states to provide the manpower needed.[120] In the end, British policy was a compromise of the two as George would not abandon Hanover. To do so would have meant redeeming it later by sacrificing overseas acquisitions at the peace conference.[121]

As for Frederick, his prospects appeared bleak. Lacking in diplomatic imagination to devise a political solution, he had sought refuge in war. And yet, he had a case for doing so. His enemies' defensive moves and their lack of unity could not entirely disguise their offensive intent. If Frederick was aggressive, it was because he saw himself forced to act. That renewed war was not his preferred course is apparent from the advice he laid down for his successor in 1752. Prussia's principal aim was the preservation of peace. To repeat the lightning strike of 1740, he thought, was 'comparable to the books, the original versions of which succeed, but whose imitations fall short'.[122] Exactly four years later he saw no other option but to improvise a variation on his Silesian theme of 1740. Back then he had opined that '[p]rudence is very suitable for preserving what one already possesses, but only boldness can make acquisitions'.[123] Now, it seemed that prudence would invite defeat, and only boldness could help him to preserve his possessions. To leave the initiative to the enemy coalition was to risk '*l'Existance de Ma Maison*'.[124]

Outnumbered—Prussia's population of four million was about a third of that of Austria and a fifth of that of France—and with scarcely defensible possessions—East Prussia was entirely isolated and Silesia attached to the core area of the Mark by a narrow corridor of only 50 km in width—he could not afford to await their onslaught. Operating on three fronts and with the aim of converging on him, they would overwhelm him. His only hope lay in seizing the initiative by moving against each enemy in turn and, above all, to prevent the Austrian and Russian main armies from combining. Only thus could he exploit what advantages he had, the superior drill and firepower of his troops, the ability of the Prussians to operate on the internal line, his own generalship and, indeed, the fact that he was acting a *roi connétable*, commanding his armies himself.[125] He decided on a move against Saxony, Austria's ally, calculating correctly that, given the depleted state of the Saxon military, he could expect the least resistance there. Controlling Saxony would also open the road to Bohemia, the main base from which the Austrian armies would operate against Silesia and the core area around Berlin. Moving across the range of the Sudeten mountains that separated the two provinces was near impossible until the following century.[126]

Podewils, the seasoned and cautious diplomat who had been responsible for Prussia's foreign policy since the 1740s, warned of the inevitable '*Inconvenienzen und terriblen Suiten*' (inconveniences and terrible consequences) that would follow a preventive strike. But Frederick poured scorn on his representations, dismissed him with an '*Adieu, Monsieur de la timide politique*', and replaced him with a close confidant.[127]

The timid diplomat had been right. The lightning strike of 1740 could not be replicated. Prussia was no longer a medium-sized regional power whose further growth the great powers and neighbouring German princes might tolerate. Perhaps, the lonely monarch at Sanssouci had also failed to grasp the psychological moments that influenced Austrian and Russian policy. However unreasonable Maria Theresa might have been in refusing to accept the loss of Silesia, both she and Tsarina Elizabeth were offended by Frederick's undisguised misogyny when treating with them or speaking about them in court and other circles, crudities that swiftly found their way to Vienna and St. Petersburg.[128] As Podewils had predicted, Frederick appeared the aggressor. The initially defensive Austro-French alliance was converted immediately into an offensive pact. Already before then, from May 1756 onwards, French policy was inching towards such a destination.[129] In January of the following year, Russia joined the anti-Prussian combination, followed by Sweden and most of the German states, with the exception of Brunswick, Hesse-Cassel, and Saxe-Gotha, all of whom were related or otherwise friendly with Prussia—and, of course, Hanover. A powerful European coalition was taking shape against Frederick, and the ambitions of its principal members were far-reaching. Recovering Silesia and reducing Prussia to the position of a minor principality remained Austria's object. Russia shared this aim, and hoped to obtain Eastern (Ducal) Prussia in the process. France had cast an eye on the duchy of Cleves with the mighty fortress of Wesel on the lower Rhine, and Sweden on Prussian Pomerania.

The Holy Roman Empire also limbered into action. The *Reichstag* at Ratisbon, on pressure from Austria and France, declared war on Prussia and ordered a *Reichsarmee* be assembled. Even some of the Protestant princes dispatched contingents to join it.[130] Habsburg diplomats, however, failed in their attempts to have Frederick II placed under a *Reichsacht* (imperial ban). They had argued for such a move on the basis of judgements by the *Reichskammergericht* of 1495 and 1521, which they argued made the Prussian king a '*landfriedensbrüchigen Empörer*' (a disturber of the imperial peace). The envoys got nowhere with this argument. That they failed to win the support of the other German states illustrates the diminished inner cohesion of the Empire. It was no longer possible to wage an intra-German war under the emperor's direction.[131] War in the *Reich* was now just like any other European war, fought between independent states who were joined in alliances within the Empire and without.

If the anti-Prussian alliance had the bigger battalions, it nevertheless had weaknesses. A coalition of courts, its members shared few common interests but were divided by often barely suppressed suspicions. Its offensive purpose was obvious enough, but its effect on Prussian military power was attritional. The steady degrading of Frederick's warfighting capabilities was undeniable, yet his enemies never seized the initiative which was in their grasp in 1756.[132] In the absence of a unified command structure enemy commanders preferred manoeuvres to major engagements, a preference reinforced by the constant need to refer back to their governments for orders. Not all Austrian, French, or Russian generals were mediocre, or even inadequate. The Austrian commanders Count Leopold von Daun and Gideon Ernst von Laudon were more than averagely competent, but they could not match Frederick.[133] His overall strategy, although relying on swift offensives, was defensive. He stuck to simple principles but varied their application according to circumstances. This strategic simplicity and intellectual flexibility stood in marked contrast to the more cautious habits of thought and practice of the opposing generals. If the Prussian king broke conventions, it ought to be noted that he did not inaugurate a new type of warfare.[134] On the contrary, his bold manoeuvres, swift strikes, and surprise moves were rooted in contemporary warfighting doctrine, but he pushed it to its theoretical and practical limits.

Whatever its political ramifications, from a military perspective, Frederick's invasion went smoothly. On 29 August 1756, his 66,000-strong army advanced in three columns into Saxony. They met little organized resistance. Dresden, the capital, fell to them on 9 September. A few days later, one of the advancing columns under Field Marshal General Kurt Christoph von Schwerin crossed into Bohemia to lure the Austrians out of their reserve. Political gains, however, remained elusive. The Elector of Saxony, Frederick Augustus II, refused to surrender and align with Prussia, fleeing to Poland instead. Nor were the Austrians impressed by the Prussian surprise attack. The Hofburg dismissed the Prussian king's proposal of a mutual two-year peace guarantee.[135] The Saxon army, encircled at Pirna, bowed to the 'Ohnmöglichkeit' (impossibility) of holding out much longer and eventually surrendered on 16 October.[136] Still it had held out until Schwerin had beaten back an Austrian relief force under Field-Marshal Count Maximilian Ulysses Browne (Fig. 2.4), coming up from the Bohemian interior along the river Elbe, at Lobositz (Lovosice), not far from the Saxon border, on 1 October.[137]

Following their capitulation, the Saxon troops were forced into the Prussian army, and Saxony's wealth and resources were now in Frederick's hands. Saxon gold was welcome—some 48 million *Bankothalers* were squeezed out of the occupied country during the war—but the newly minted Prussian soldiers did not add much to the strength of Frederick's army. Most of them deserted as soon as they could, and only a few of the officers agreed to serve.[138] An end to the war was not in sight. Lobositz was a tactical setback for the Austrians, but the strategic situation had not changed. If anything, the campaign had lasted too long already, without producing any tangible results or enhancing Prussia's political or military position. Frederick could not determine the course of events, and the Austrians intensified their war preparations.[139] 'Perfectly sensible of the dangers to which he is exposed from the power and multiplicity of his enemies' he gave up his original plan to take up a strong position in Bohemia for the winter so as to draw on the Habsburg Monarchy's own resources in

Fig. 2.4 Maximilian Ulysses Browne. Alamy, 2F8NFAY.

preparation for renewed fighting in the spring, further evidence that his thinking did not transcend contemporary precepts.[140]

1757 did not start well for Frederick. In the spring, the anti-Prussian coalition had taken final shape, and the war began in earnest. With the Saxon ruler in Warsaw and Russia having joined the alliance against him, he had to abandon Eastern Prussia. A 24,000-strong force under General Hans von Lehwaldt was unable to protect this easternmost province of the kingdom with its commercial and administrative centre of Königsberg. A veteran of the first two Silesian wars and a capable field commander, Lehwaldt was unequal to the demands of independent command. The advancing Russians under Field Marshal Stepan Fyodorovich Apraksin, initially 100,000 strong, had shrunk by a fifth by May, logistic and supply failures and dysentery having taken their toll. Even so, numbers still mattered, and Lehwaldt lacked sufficient tactical nous to make up for his numerical disadvantage. He left the Russians reeling with an audacious attack at Grossjägersdorf (Motorno'e) on 30 August, but he could not overcome the enemy's artillery fire, and after desperate fighting at close quarters he had to break off the battle and withdraw. The Russians took possession of the province without firing a further shot. Until 1762, when a new tsar, Peter III, made peace with Frederick, East Prussia remained under Russian occupation.[141]

Prussia was on its own. Britain, the only ally who counted, was reluctant to enter the war on the continent.[142] Frederick had manoeuvred himself into a precarious situation. His position, even the survival of the Prussian state, was at risk. Its only remaining protection were the army and the military leadership of the king. But war was unpredictable, and its human and material cost immense.

The main theatres of the European war remained Saxony, Bohemia, and Silesia, and Frederick continued to seek salvation in offensives against the superior numbers of his enemies. His plans for the spring of 1757 revolved around the destruction of the 133,000-strong Austrian main army in its Bohemian winter quarters, which presented the most pressing immediate threat to his position. The occupation of Saxony in the previous autumn was the necessary preliminary for the planned attack. Capture of the great magazines in northern Bohemia would cripple the Habsburg war effort, effectively immobilizing the Austrian army, unable to attack Frederick in Silesia or Saxony. In April, four Prussian columns advanced towards Prague. On 6 May, underneath the city's walls, outnumbered by 24,000 to 60,000, they defeated the still unsuspecting Austrians under Prince Charles of Lorraine. Victory came at a heavy price, however. 6,350 Prussian soldiers lay dead, over a quarter of the forces engaged in the battled, amongst them Schwerin, Frederick's most experienced commander, who had earned his first military spurs under Marlborough at the battle of Blenheim (Browne was one of the 5,700 Austrian dead). Worse, the Prussians failed in their subsequent *coup de main* against the Bohemian capital, into which the retreating Austrians had escaped.[143]

Failure at Prague was followed by an even more severe setback. On 18 June, at Kolín in central Bohemia, Frederick was defeated by an Austrian relief army under Daun, whose orders had been to manoeuvre rather than fight so as to protect 'the interior of the hereditary territories of Bohemia and Moravia'.[144] Kolín taught Frederick the bitter lesson about the near-impossibility of a frontal attack. Finding Daun's forces in position on a range of hills parallel to his line of advance, he decided to press ahead, with the object of wheeling to his right so as to outflank the Austrians. All of this had to be done in plain view of the enemy, and Daun was not slow to divine Frederick's intentions. The field marshal changed his dispositions accordingly, strengthened his endangered flank, and then brought his artillery to bear on the Prussian marching columns. Such was the effect of Daun's batteries that the Prussian centre, against Frederick's orders, wheeled round prematurely and rushed the Austrian front. Three times the Austrians repulsed the advancing Prussian infantry, and then went to attack on the left. Frederick's plan was wrecked. Counterattacks by his cavalry were to no avail. The battle was lost. Only the difficulties inherent in linear warfare in pursuing a routed army saved the Prussian army from complete destruction.[145] Kolín was his first serious setback. The king, his adversary at Vienna purred with delight, was not 'unbeatable' after all.[146]

Defeat forced Frederick to lift the siege of Prague, before evacuating Bohemia altogether. No doubt, there had been an element of arrogance in his approach to the battle, and a corresponding tendency to dismiss Daun as a dithering nonentity. Even so, time was not on his side, and he had to act against the enemy where he found him, before the anti-Prussian coalition armies could unite. If defeat was painful,[147] it impressed upon Frederick the vital importance of surprise in a flanking attack, and the impossibility of achieving such surprise in full view of the enemy. He was to profit from that lesson at Leuthen.

For the moment, his situation was desperate. In Western Germany, the French main army, some 100,000 men strong, under Louis Charles César Le Tellier, Comte d'Estrées, opened operations by moving against Hanover. Prussia, facing Russia in the east and Austria in the southeast, could offer no material assistance. George II ordered his son, William Augustus, Duke of Cumberland, with his army of Hanoverians and allied German troops, to remain on the defensive. His 'Army of Observation', no more than 45,000 troops in all, kept the French in check for a good three months. But eventually Cumberland was outmanoeuvred by d'Estrées and then defeated at Hastenbeck, near Hameln on the river Weser, on 26 July.[148] Cleaving to his instructions, he retreated towards the Elbe estuary at Stade. Hemmed in, and facing a far superior enemy, he signed the Convention of Klosterzeven on 8 September. Its terms were disastrous for Hanover and Brunswick, and it left the French army free to press on '*sur les terres du Roi de Prusse*'.[149]

Frederick's enemies were closing in on him. His prospects were low, as the British envoy observed already in late summer:

> The King of Prussia has now against him the Russian army and fleet, 20m [i.e. thousand] Swedes, an army of the Empire supported by 30m French, and the great Austrian army of 100m, and, as if he had not

enemies enough, the convention [of Klosterzeven] to save Hanover from winter quarters will let loose 60 or 80m more French. What prospect can you have, my dear Lord, to exist till next year, far less to continue the war?[150]

To complete this catalogue of miseries, the Hungarian general Count András Hadik de Futak (Fig. 2.5) swept up from Thuringia with a force of 3,400 light troops in mid-October to seize Berlin. The corps was too small to hold the capital for any length of time, but it remained long enough to loot it and extract 269,474 *Thalers* from its citizens.[151]

Ultimately, Frederick's strategy and Prussia's survival did not depend on the fate of Berlin. Hadik's strike, however, disrupted his moves and provided an opening for allied commanders elsewhere in

Fig. 2.5 Weikert Count András Hadik de Futak. Alamy, MN084X.

central Germany—the essential purpose of irregular warfare, as Maria Theresa had repeatedly impressed upon her commanders.[152] Their forces continued to advance, but they did not exploit the opportunities given. On the contrary, the tide of military fortune receded. In October, Frederick turned against a Franco-German force of around 44,000 men, which had taken up a strong position in Thuringia and was *en route* to join Daun in Bohemia. If they succeeded, nothing could be done to prevent this vast force from invading Silesia. The forces in Thuringia consisted of the *Reichsarmee* under the Prince Joseph of Saxe-Hildburghausen and a French contingent under Charles de Rohan, Prince de Soubise.[153] On 5 November their combined troops were comprehensively defeated by Frederick at Rossbach near Weissenfels. The position of the allied army was so well chosen that Frederick could not risk attacking it. Soubise, relying on manoeuvres, then moved this army to another strong position, which had the added advantage of covering its communications, while threatening those of Frederick. At this point the divided command structure of the combined force became a weakness. Prince Joseph, the bulk of whose forces had been detached to cover the river Saale, decided to prolong the march of his army to reach the Prussian rear. Frederick, who was watching these movements, decided to attack, even though with his 22,000 men he was outnumbered by a ratio of two to one. He marched his army behind a ridge where it cut across the head of the approaching French columns. Poor liaison between Hildburghausen and Soubise caused confusion before the fight commenced. To compound matters, the French cavalry was some 2 km ahead of the infantry, while the columns of the latter impeded the imperial foot which dropped further behind. Disordered, the French had no time to regroup and were overwhelmed by Frederick's men. Rossbach was decided early on during the encounter by a daring cavalry attack. Following the first onslaught of the Prussian horse, the inherent weaknesses of *Reichsarmee* began to show. Most of its contingents had only recently been mustered.

They lacked the training and experience to resist the disciplined Prussians. Within two hours, some 5,000 Franco-German troops lay slain or wounded on the battlefield, while roughly the same number had been taken prisoner.[154]

Rossbach earned the *Reichsarmee* the soubriquet of *'Reissausarmee'* ('Run Away Army').[155] Prussian propaganda lost no time to exploit its unseemly flight. The rout at Rossbach gave shape to later perceptions of the old regime *Reich* as militarily inept; and since the force defeated by Frederick was predominantly French, this, too, was to acquire greater historical significance in the nineteenth and twentieth centuries. In the meantime, his victory was celebrated in a popular ditty: 'When our great Frederick comes, / And merely slaps his breeches, / Away run the whole imperial army, / Pandurs and Frenchmen, too' (*'Wenn unser grosser Friedrich kömmt, / Und klopft nur auf die Hosen, / So läuft die ganze Reichsarmee, / Panduren und Franzosen'*).[156]

Rossbach was a coup by a weakened commander who had his back to the wall and who had nothing to lose. It kept Prussia in the war; but it did not end the conflict. It nevertheless had an electrifying effect. In many parts of central and northern Germany, a pro-Prussian *'fritzische Gesinnung'* (pro-Frederician sentiments) gained ground, as the poet Goethe later noted when reflecting on his upbringing in the imperial free city of Frankfurt.[157]

More significant for Prussia's war effort was the effect on opinion in England where Frederick had steadily won admirers in polite society: 'Our constant toast here now is, success to the King of Prussia: he grows vastly popular amongst us.'[158] News of Rossbach increased Frederick's stock yet further. It also changed the strategic calculus of the government, which now revoked the Convention of Klosterzeven. Already on 16 November, Duke Ferdinand of Brunswick-Wolfenbüttel, Frederick's brother-in-law and one of his most able generals, was appointed commander of an allied army in the west.[159] Kaunitz, meanwhile, scrambled to keep the smaller German states aligned, exhorting them 'not to drop their courage, but to move against the King in Prussia with yet more steadfastness'.[160]

The battle of Leuthen was to complete what Rossbach had begun. Once more the Prussians faced an enemy force nearly double in size; once more Frederick seized the initiative; and once again he relied on the superior drill and firepower of his troops.

3

The Battle and Its Consequences

Rossbach transformed the Anglo-Prussian combination into a proper alliance, but it did not win Frederick any additional allies; nor did it significantly weaken the coalition ranged against him. Rossbach was a silver lining but no more. Prussia's continued existence as a great power was still at stake.

The Austrian main army remained an imminent danger. While Frederick manoeuvred in central Germany, Daun persisted with his concentric strategy against him and gradually tightened Austria's stranglehold on Silesia. In the course of a few weeks, he had captured the main Silesian fortresses, an unusual feat in winter. On 13 November, just a week after Rossbach, Schweidnitz surrendered, and a fortnight later Liegnitz fell. Control of both opened the prospect of secure winter quarters in Silesia.[1] Worse was to follow. On 22 November, the Austrians under Prince Charles of Lorraine (Fig. 3.1) defeated a 28,000-strong Prussian army under Frederick Francis, Duke of Brunswick-Bevern, a brother-in-law of Frederick's, who had been ordered to shield Lower Silesia and Breslau against the Austrian main army. In this he failed. A competent enough senior officer, he struggled with the demands of independent command. He dithered, hoping for a junction with the king's army before attacking the enemy. It was not to be. Outgeneralled and now outnumbered and outmanoeuvred by Charles' 54,000 troops (with a further 28,000 approaching), he was defeated outside Breslau.[2] The duke himself was taken prisoner, along with around 4,000 of his troops, and the scattered remnants of his army retreated down the Oder towards the fortress of Glogau. Bereft

Fig. 3.1 Portrait of Prince Charles Alexander of Lorraine (1712–80) by Martin van Mijtens. From a Private Collection. Alamy, 2GGNG0.

of all support, the Breslau garrison surrendered three days later.[3] Although offered free withdrawal, only some six hundred officers and men rejoined the king's army, the rest preferring to seek their fortunes elsewhere by melting into the civilian urban population or by scattering across the province.[4]

Austrian control of Silesia was now complete. In Vienna the empress ordered a *Te Deum* to be sung in at St. Stephen's cathedral. Frederick, meanwhile, pretended to be unimpressed: '[t]ous ces malheurs ne m'ont point abattu.'[5] If the recent misfortunes did not bring him down, there was nevertheless little doubt that the immediate aftermath of Rossbach offered a last chance to engage and defeat the enemy in battle. Letting it slip through his hands meant letting the Austrians winter in Silesia, ready to resume their attempts to combine with the Russian army in the spring of 1758. If that were to happen, their numbers would overwhelm the Prussians. Defeat, however, might force the Austrians to abandon Silesia and its resources, so delaying the resumption of their campaign until well into next year. Defeating them would also send a powerful signal to Prussia's Anglo-Hanoverian and other allies that Frederick remained alliance-worthy, because militarily capable. The wider political ramifications of victory for the remainder of the war could scarcely be exaggerated. A battle now, then, was both vital and hazardous. Victory meant survival and the prospect of preserving Prussia's recent gains. Defeat invited complete disaster. In such an event, Prussia's allies were likely to seek a way out of the war, and its survival and future status would be left to the mercy of the enemies. Against this backdrop Frederick's decision to risk another battle against a much larger enemy force was less reckless than might be thought. This was probably his last chance to stave off defeat: '*Je marche mon droit chemin vers ici, selon le plan que je m'était formé.*'[6]

The odds were nevertheless formidable. It was winter; the Austrians had the bigger battalions; and Frederick was still with his back to the wall. For two days after Rossbach he had mopped up the scattered remnants of the *Reichsarmee* in Thuringia. Having rested his troops he broke up his camp near Leipzig on 13 November and, accompanied by eight generals, he began the march southeastwards with eighteen infantry battalions and twenty-nine squadrons of cavalry. The recent presence of an Austrian army along the planned route of advance complicated supplying his army, but Frederick took the precaution of ordering the military governor of Dresden to despatch a supply train with flour and bread to Bautzen. In this manner, he made himself operationally more independent. He could also calculate with remarkable precision the date of his arrival in Silesia. He had informed Bevern on 10 November that he expected to reach Schweidnitz around the 28th. The duke's subsequent defeat and the fall of that fortress forced the king to move further north. Still, he arrived at Parchwitz (Prochowice), some 16 km (10 miles) from Liegnitz, the Austrian commander having neglected to cover the Glogau–Breslau road.[7] Along the route he gathered up the recovered wounded of Rossbach, who had been left at Torgau to recuperate.[8]

A skilful piece of deception aided Frederick's return to Silesia. Two Austrian forces hampered his progress, one under General Ernst Dietrich Count Marschall von Bieberstein with 12,000 infantry and 4,000 horse drawn up near Bautzen, the other a much smaller corps under Laudon at Freiberg on the Saxon-Bohemian frontier.[9] Frederick decided upon a diversionary move. On 16 November he ordered Field Marshal James Keith, a Jacobite Scot in Prussian service, to march into Bohemia with ten infantry battalions (c.6,300 men) and ten cavalry squadrons (c.900 men).[10] Alerted to movement to the south, Laudon and Marschall retreated towards Prague and the interior, ignoring orders to join the main army under Prince Charles. If Keith was meant to confuse the enemy, he was remarkably successful. On 26 November, he swooped down on Leitmeritz (Litoměřice), destroyed the magazine there and the bridge across the river Elbe, and 'unter Feuer und Schwerdt' confiscated some 250,000 Thalers, 'reciproque' with Hadik's robbery of Berlin.[11] He also spread the false rumour that the king himself was following with heavy artillery to besiege Prague. Marschall duly hastened back to prepare the city's defences, while Laudon and Hadik took up a shielding position at Mělník on the Elbe lest the Prussians, 'par revanche von Berlin', wreak havoc on the area. Keith had achieved his objective and returned to Chemnitz and Freiberg on 5 December to take up winter quarters there.[12] In similar fashion, General Ernest Heinrich August de la Motte Fouqué, the commandant of Glatz which covered the Breslau–Prague road, frequently sallied forth from that fortress to harass the Austrian forces in the mountain districts.[13]

In the meantime, by 2 December, having marched a distance of 272 km (169 miles), Frederick had reached, as anticipated, Parchwitz on the Katzbach (Kaczawa) River, a tributary of the Oder, with 20,000 men.[14] Here they were joined by the cavalry general Hans-Joachim von Zieten, who had fought at Breslau and who had afterwards gathered up the remnants of Bevern's demoralized and depleted force, some

18,000 men in all (thirty infantry battalions and one hundred cavalry squadrons). The veteran hussar leader was respected, indeed had acquired considerable popularity within the army and without it, and he kept Bevern's army in being. Scattered groups of Prussian soldiers, who had been taken prisoner at Schweidnitz but who had fled their captors on the march to Bohemia, also found their way into the king's camp. The joint force was not yet an army, ready to strike. Only one-third of it—eighteen infantry battalions and twenty-nine cavalry squadrons—had fought and won at Rossbach; the rest were the dregs of Bevern's force and the Breslau garrison. The former were no doubt motivated enough. But all of them were exhausted and underfed.[15]

Raising army morale was vital if the winter campaign was to succeed, as Frederick understood well enough. Bevern's earlier defeat left in tatters his original plan of using the duke's army to keep the Austrians in check before engaging them in battle. Victory would then be followed by Prussian advances into Bohemia. That was no longer feasible, which made it imperative now to force the Austrians out of Silesia before winter set in. In narrow military terms, he could not contemplate a new campaigning season with the enemy's main army so close to his state's centre of gravity. Silesia's material and manpower resources would fuel the Habsburg war effort, while Frederick would have to compensate this loss as best he could from Saxon and other sources. But he also understood that, politically, the fillip his cause had received by Rossbach would dissipate if the Austrians were allowed to remain entrenched in the contested province. Victory, then, necessitated another victory before the close of the year.

Under these circumstances Frederick could not break off the hazardous winter campaign. To carry on, however, he had to spur on his soldiers to fight and to win again. At Parchwitz, the troops were rested and, wherever possible, billeted in proper houses. Discipline was relaxed a little. As far as provisions allowed, there was plenty of food and drink, additional rations of warm meals and liquor being handed out. The king made a point of mingling with his soldiers. He presented himself to them as a fellow-soldier, weary as they were, his uniform even more tattered and snuff-stained than usual. He also appeared as their *Landesvater*, paternal but determined to secure victory in another battle, exchanging bluff banter with his grenadiers and musketeers, extoling the achievements at Rossbach to wipe out memories of Bevern's humiliation, and praising the virtues of the provinces from which his troops hailed. He sought out especially some of the units who had fought at Breslau, such as the 4th (Putkamer) Hussars, whose diminished ranks he greeted with the words: 'Good day, children! You have suffered much, but all shall be well', whereupon he exchanged pleasantries with the senior officers for half an hour.[16]

There may well have been an element of cynicism in Frederick's behaviour, but as an exercise in reverse military psychology it was an undoubted success. The troops responded in kind, calling their king by the familiar '*Du*' and the popular '*Fritz*'.[17] The diminutive, in fact, was an ingredient of the monarch's charismatic appeal and authority.[18] They were also felt by the officers whose response to Frederick's appearance was no less warm. Here, too, the king showed a sure touch. He took a dismal view of the bulk of his generals, as he confessed to his brother's *aide-de-camp* on arrival at Parchwitz: 'It is scarcely credible how major *fautes* have turned the heads of several of my generals, present here, and on account of which the affairs here are in such desperate conditions.'[19] Unusually, he called his senior officers—generals, regimental and battalion commanders—together at his headquarters. Several of them were promoted in rank, and the king promised further advancements and decorations in the aftermath of the battle he meant now to fight.[20] He appealed to their professional honour, and their loyalty to him and to Prussia. His 'adversities would grow immeasurably, were he not able to place the fullest confidence in their courage, steadfastness and patriotism'. They would have to demonstrate these once more. Silesia could not be left in enemy hands:

Understand, then: I shall attack, against all rules of the art [of war], the three times larger army of Prince Charles when I find it....I must risk this step, or else all will be lost; we must defeat the enemy, or be buried in front of his batteries. This is what I think, and I shall act accordingly ('*So denke ich—so werde ich handeln*').

Frederick then assured them of his unshakeable belief in their loyal service. Any officer unwilling to embark on the uncertain venture that lay before them 'may have his discharge at once, without the slightest displeasure on my part'. The assembled party had listened in silence, some, according to eyewitnesses, in tears. At this point Major Konstantin von Billerbeck, commander of the Infantry Regiment No. 17 ('Prinz Heinrich') and veteran of Prague and Kolín, cried out: 'Well, that would be a wretched scoundrel; it was time now.' Frederick might well have anticipated some such reaction, but there was also a warning of the harsh punishment that awaited men and regiments who failed in the hour of battle. 'Farewell, gentlemen', he concluded, 'soon we beat the enemy or we shall never see one another'.[21] If Frederick's eve-of-battle address was reminiscent of Henry V's at Agincourt, it was all the more effective for it. The king approached the coming encounter with a mixture of stoicism and a half-conscious striving for martyrdom. He took the precaution, at any rate, of drawing up a new will with detailed instructions as to the disposal of his body were he to be killed in battle.[22]

It is difficult to be precise about the numbers of troops under Frederick's command. Contemporary sources varied on that score, and later assessments came to equally varying conclusions. Frederick himself offered different estimates. On 1 December, prior to Zieten's arrival from Glogau, he anticipated to have 39,000 men at his disposal ('*Par ce que contiennent les listes, nous sommes 39,000 hommes*'). A week later, three days after the battle, he suggested that he had '*le jour de l'action*' a force of 35,000.[23] The latter figure seems more likely, consisting of forty-eight and a half infantry battalions, 133 cavalry squadrons, as well as ninety-four field guns and seventy-eight heavy artillery pieces, including seven mortars and ten 12-pounders which Zieten had transported over from Glogau. Estimates of the army that stood against him vary, too. But there were no fewer than 66,000 Austrian and allied imperial troops—eighty-five infantry battalions, 125 cavalry squadrons, and 5,000 light infantry with 170 field and sixty-five heavy guns. At least one Austrian platoon commander, however, was certain that 'we were around 80,000 men'.[24]

Frederick ventured all on a risky battlefield manoeuvre to compensate for his numerical disadvantage. And it was for this reason that the battle was remembered long afterwards as his apotheosis. No less important, however, were the dispositions made by the Austrian commanders prior to the battle and their behaviour during it. Nominal command over the main army in Silesia was in the hands of Charles of Lorraine, who owed his position entirely to dynastic considerations rather than intellect or capability—the Prussian envoy at Vienna described him as uncouth, 'of mediocre intelligence' and an officer out of 'a certain necessity' rather than conviction or ambition.[25] As Maria-Theresa's brother-in-law his appointment was to affirm the Habsburg-Lorraine character of the post-1740 Monarchy. Although experienced—he had served in the Turkish War (1737–9) and commanded the main army during the First Silesian War—Charles had a less than distinguished military record. He had come off worse against Frederick on no fewer than five previous occasions, at Chotusitz (1742), Hohenfriedberg, Soor, Kesselsdorf (all 1745), and Prague (1757); he had also been defeated by the French under Maurice de Saxe at Rocoux in the Flanders campaign of 1746.[26] Even by the standards of eighteenth-century warfare he was cautious and defensive, timid even.

Daun, the victor of Kolín, was placed by his side to add ballast to the prince's command (Fig. 3.2). And yet, although the field marshal denied that there was 'any *desunion*' amongst senior officers, he could not deny that opinion was frequently divided. Worse, Count Ferenc Nádasdy, one of the ablest generals, was sulking, having been passed over in favour of Daun, and now made a point, 'from exaggerated *accuratesse*', of seeking orders rather than taking decisions himself.[27]

Fig. 3.2 Leopold Count Daun. Wikimedia Commons.

On Daun's advice the army took up a secure position just outside the walls of Breslau on the near side of the Lohe (Ślęza), a small river flowing into the Oder north of the capital. From here the Austrians could scarcely be dislodged, and so could await further developments and strike out if circumstances appeared favourable. This was in line with Daun's methodical campaigning in Bohemia earlier. Daun's Fabian dispositions had stood him in good stead so far, and he had proved himself adept at the feints, manoeuvres, and countermarches that were the hallmarks of contemporary warfighting. But whatever his greater experience and however impressive his military record, the field marshal was not the emperor's brother's social equal, and he could not simply overrule him. Neither man, moreover, could act as he saw fit, but had to keep in close contact with the *Hofkriegsrat* and the Empress, whose deliberations took time.[28]

The latter never ceased to praise Daun's 'devotion, zeal, sense and war-experience', but there was never any doubt that she expected her views—usually expressed with considerable circumlocution—to be taken into consideration. If her brother-in-law and Daun disagreed with her suggestions, they had to notify her immediately and then await further orders.[29] Nor were matters in good order at Vienna itself, as one otherwise loyal courtier noted in late 1757: 'We have two lords, the Emperor and the Empress.' Francis directed, *'d'une certaine façon'*, the war and finance departments, and nothing could be done in these two *'Branches du gouvernement'* without his approval. But he was 'too indo-lent' for serious work. The Empress, by contrast, was 'rather too fiery, cannot wait and sticks in consequence to no order'. She was also apt to let herself be influenced by others and 'to turn over tomorrow again what had been decided today'. The *'capi'* (chiefs) of the various gov-ernment offices knew to manipulate this state of affairs 'and to delay or expedite matters according to their *convenance'*.[30]

Frederick's position was quite different. As *roi connétable* he was answerable to no one but himself.[31] As Daun reflected in 1758, he was at a disadvantage *'in denen maneuvrirungen'* against Frederick who was *'König-Souverein und commandirender General'*. The necessary conclu-sion for the Austrian army, reinforced by the previous year's defeats, then, was to involve him in protracted manoeuvres so that 'he weakens himself more than through a single battle in the various marches'.[32]

Whatever the internal constraints, there were sound reasons for caution at the end of 1757. Most of the Silesian fortresses were in the hands of the Austrians. Sitting tight might well be enough to force Frederick to withdraw from the province again. Scouting parties kept Charles and Daun informed about the king's advance and then his arrival at Parchwitz. Detailed and accurate though that intelligence was, it gave no indication of Frederick's ultimate objective. From his camp on the Katzbach he might move towards Liegnitz, cross the Oder, or push eastwards towards Neumarkt (Środa Śląska) on the main road to Breslau. On 3 December the duke decided to act. Although he considered his army 'rather weakened' by the absence of the two corps chasing Keith in Bohemia, it would move towards Neumarkt on the following morning. Frederick, he had concluded, meant to take nearby Liegnitz. It was therefore necessary 'to do everything to secure Ligniz [sic] and to expel the enemy from that region'.[33] The army would march in four columns along the Breslau-Liegnitz main road to camp the following day near the village of Leuthen.[34]

It is difficult to avoid the conclusion that the Austrian commanders projected their own concerns onto the enemy. Earlier in the autumn the *Hofkriegsrat* had instructed them to seize control of Silesia's fortress belt 'so that the whole region from Oder to Ligniz [sic] and thence to the Bohemian frontier fell under their command and they could count on a firm base in Silesia'.[35] They had acted accordingly. If Liegnitz fell to Frederick, he would dominate the northern parts of the province for the rest of the winter.

There were also reasons for giving battle. The events in Silesia that winter seemed to confirm the experience of the summer campaign in Bohemia. The Prussians were not invincible. Another defeat might well force Frederick to sue for peace. If he declined battle, and with the Austrians commanding most of the Silesian fortresses, he would have to evacuate the province and await the resumption of the war in the spring under yet more adverse circumstances. Given their numerical superiority, Charles and Daun could await either battle or fresh manoeuvres with equanimity. Perhaps also the recent '*herrlichen Eroberungen und Siege*' had made them overconfident.[36]

From one of Maria Theresa's letters it may be deduced that, contrary to historical consensus, the idea of meeting Frederick originated with Daun, presumably to prevent the Prussians from entrenching themselves at Parchwitz. The empress's deliberations elucidated the decision by her senior commanders. She welcomed Daun's offensive intentions. Securing Silesia for the winter was paramount: 'If this final objective can be attained without resorting to another *decisiven Schlacht*, the same should not be sought but, so far as possible, be avoided.' Then again, if the enemy took steps to deprive her army of its strong position, she considered it 'unavoidably necessary...to let it come to a *Haupt-Schlacht*.' Victory would provide a psychological boost, while 'an adverse outcome' would not likely have any serious consequences.[37] The letter, written on 5 December, arrived too late to influence its recipient, but it cast a light on the options before Charles and Daun.

The Austrians' greater strength in numbers was deceptive, however, and their tactical situation more precarious than Charles and Daun realized. Frederick's immediate object was Neumarkt, a small town some 37 km (23 miles) from Breslau, where the enemy had established a field bakery, crucial for any campaign. The place was protected by Major General Georg von Luszinsky with two regiments of hussars and two battalions of Croat light infantry, recently reinforced by 1,000 men infantry whose advance towards Liegnitz had been cut off by Frederick's appearance on the banks of the Katzbach. Neumarkt, it seems, was the intended next stop of the main army on its march westwards, it being on '*un terrain elevé et sec*'.[38] This circumstance left the field bakery and four-days' bread reserves stored there exposed to a Prussian move. It was to prove a costly tactical mistake.

Leuthen was a '*coup d'oeil*'.[39] Frederick's ability to 'read' the battlefield and to grasp the *genius loci* was exceptional, and by far exceeded that of the commanders on the other side of the hill. No less important was his careful battlefield reconnaissance, something the Austrian commanders rather neglected. The area between Breslau and Liegnitz was already well known to the king and his senior officers from the peacetime autumn manoeuvres in the interval between the second Silesian war and the present conflict. But Frederick left nothing to change. At daybreak, he led the strong vanguard of fourteen and a half battalions and sixty squadrons along the Breslau road, followed by the remainder of his army in four columns of infantry. After some skirmishing, the enemy outpost at Neumarkt was taken, five dismounted squadrons of hussars (H4) having broken down the town gate while the rest surrounded the place. Some five hundred Croat prisoners, 80,000 rations of bread and the bakery fell into Prussian hands.

Three Saxon *Cheveau-légers* regiments under Count Friedrich Moritz von Nostitz-Rieneck, light cavalry formations which had distinguished themselves at Kolín in the summer, had been readied to reinforce the Neumarkt garrison. But it was already too late. The Saxon horse had not left its camp between Kadlau (Kadłub) and Lampersdorf (Juszczyn), some 6.5 km (4 miles) from Neumarkt when the Prussians struck. All Nostitz could do was to halt the fleeing Austrian hussars and attach them to his own force which now took up position to the west of the village of Borne (Źródła), a further 3 km to the rear.[40] The failure to secure Neumarkt was the first of many questionable decisions the Austrian commanders took at Leuthen. Crucially, the skirmish confirmed to Frederick that the enemy's main army had left its encampment outside Breslau. 'The fox', he declared to Prince Francis of Brunswick, 'has crept out of his den; now I want punish his arrogance.'[41]

As night fell, the two armies were within a few miles of each other. The Prussian army bivouacked around Neumarkt, its van taking positions between the hamlets of Bischdorf (Święte) and Kammendorf (Komorniki), some 3 km to the east of the town. As before at Parchwitz, an attempt was made to house the troops in the surrounding farms and other proper buildings as opposed to letting them all spend the night in tents on open ground. Food was plentiful, at any rate, and soldiers received an additional ration of brandy to fuel their morale. Frederick finalized his order of battle, placing the units who had distinguished themselves at Rossbach in the first line. He added a sprinkling of formations beaten at Breslau, but for the most part these were kept in the second line. Thus prepared, the Prussians turned in for the night. There was calm in their camp.

The same could not be said of the Austrians. They, too, had left their camp in the early hours of the day, but the enemy's swift approach had caught them out. Frederick blocked the road of Liegnitz, and with the Neumarkt magazine lost, they had to face the prospect of a battle on the morrow. The rear, still somewhere on the Breslau road, was hastily brought up, and the whole army was ordered to bivouac 'under arms in battle order' just to the east of the village of Leuthen, along a north-south axis across the main Breslau—Liegnitz road on which the Prussian advance was expected.[42] Its centre lay just south of the road between Frobelwitz (Wróblowice) and Leuthen itself. The right wing—mostly infantry under the Charles Marie Raymond, 5th Duke of Arenberg—stretched north from there to the smaller village of Nippern (Mrozów), protected by massed cavalry under Lieutenant Field Marshal Count Joseph Lucchesi d'Averna at its back and, at its front, the Zettelbusch spinney which was secured by grenadier companies and light infantry. Further to its rear, the reserves took up their positions. The Austrian left wing extended to the farmsteads at Sagschütz (Zakrzyce) and the pineclad hills beyond it. At a retreating angle, facing Schriegwitz (Jarząbkowice), stood a separate cavalry corps under Nádasdy which had moved into position between 7 and 8 pm. Altogether the Austrian line covered a length of 8 km (5 miles).

Despite their considerable numerical superiority, the Austrian commanders had to contend with certain disadvantages. The soldiers had only taken 'the absolutely necessary', and the baggage train was some distance off still, on the other side of the river Weistritz (Bystrzyca Łomnicka) to the east of Lissa (Leśnica), the nearest town, about 12 km (7.5 miles) from Breslau. In consequence, not only did the troops have to spend the night in the open, they were also short of firewood, bedding straw, and food, conditions not conducive to raising morale. The mood amongst the officers was little better. The open, slightly undulating ground offered none of the advantages that had aided them at Kolín. Charles and Daun seemed content to rely on their superior numbers which would surely give them the edge in any battle, or else would force Frederick to move away. The Austrian infantry was also not as well rested as Frederick's foot soldiers; and, at 125 squadrons, the cavalry was slightly smaller in size than the Prussian horse with its 133 squadrons. Many were also below regular strength.[43] Further, although they had more field guns, Frederick had better and heavier artillery at his disposal, especially the so-called 'Brummer-Batterie' ('growler battery'), which had been assembled from the ten 12-pounder canon and four 50-pounder mortars Zieten had brought from Glogau. Both it and the cavalry were to play a significant role during different phases of the battle.

In addition, the fighting quality of the Prussians was greater than that of their opponents. The higher motivation after Rossbach and Breslau, albeit for sharply contrasting reasons, mattered. So did the setbacks in Bohemia in the summer. Subsequent desertions produced the rather curious effect of leaving the Prussian army smaller but also more homogenous, most non-native soldiers having absconded.[44] On the imperial side, by contrast, the Queen-Empress's Austrians and Hungarians fought alongside Bavarian and Saxon contingents as well as regiments furnished by smaller German princelings, such as the Prince-Bishop of Würzburg. There were also troops from Württemberg, whose Catholic duke, Charles Eugene, had joined the war against Frederick more out of fear of his near-neighbour Austria than out of real conviction. His largely Protestant subjects looked askance at the Habsburg alliance against Prussia; his younger brothers served in the Prussian army; and some of his soldiers had mutinied in June 1757, though drink may have been a more potent force than politics. Confidence in the Swabian '*Hülffstrouppe*' was low, and Charles later blamed Nádasdy for having placed these auxiliaries at an angle rather than, as instructed, in the second line.[45]

As day broke on 5 December, the Austrians and the allied *Reichstruppen* thus awaited Frederick's approach. There was nothing objectionable about the dispositions Prince Charles and Daun had made. They reflected conventional military wisdom. The line chosen covered the three possible approaches to Breslau. The duke moreover reasoned that Frederick's inferior numbers would make him baulk at the risk of a frontal attack. After the defeat at Kolín the Prussian king was not likely to attempt it at any rate. To do so was to invite the Austrians to bring the weight of their bigger numbers to bear. The safest option for Frederick, then, would be to decline battle in the hope that, through a series of skilful manoeuvres, he might eventually force the Austrians to retreat. If such assumptions were understandable, they were yet another instance of Charles and, to a lesser degree, Daun projecting their own preferences on their enemy.[46]

No doubt, a Prussian retreat would have suited the Austrians. Given the time of the year, deferring a decision now meant letting the two sides settle down until the spring. For that same reason, Frederick could not contemplate any such outcome. Now was his last chance to shift the military balance in his favour. He would have to attack. In the early hours of that day, his force was on the move. Reveille was sounded at 4 am. Within the hour the army, arranged in four columns with the cavalry on the wings, headed towards the Austrian lines which still lay a good 12 km (7.5 miles) ahead. The king himself led the van to reconnoitre the ground ahead,[47] a small force of light troops, three irregular *Freibatallione*, a few companies of dismounted *Jägers*, six regiments of hussars and the 12th ('Württemberg') Dragoons with nine battalions of infantry making up the rear. They were soon alerted by noise and the sight of watchfires on a height to the south of the main road between Neumarkt and Leuthen. If they indicated the Austrian lines, then the broken ground around Neumarkt would have hampered any attempt to engage the enemy in battle. It was not, however, the Austrian main army, but Nostitz's Saxon light horse and two regiments of hussars under Lieutenant Field Marshal Imre von Mórócz, which had been sent ahead to gather the scattered remnants of the Neumarkt contingent and to watch the high road to Breslau. Some Croat formations were also spotted by the Prussian *Jägers* in the woods around Borne. Frederick wasted no time and attacked with his hussars, deploying six grenadier battalions to the right to shield his advancing horse against the Croats, who soon retreated. Perhaps disorientated by the early morning mist, Nostitz and Mórócz were not only caught by surprise, they also failed to appreciate the attacker's bigger numbers. They clung to their position for too long, and before the Saxon horse had formed into two lines, they were thrown by the onrushing hussars. Eleven officers and *c.*600 men were taken prisoner and two Saxon standards captured. The rest retreated in great disorder, pursued by the hussars under Friedrich Wilhelm von Kleist beyond Gross Heidau (Błonie) within sight of the Austrian right wing. As the Saxons had played a major role at Kolín, 'Für Kolin' was the battle cry of the Prussian hussars as they harried Nostitz's retreating troopers.[48]

The appearance of the fleeing Saxons in front of their right wing heightened nervous anxiety amongst Austrian commanders. This was to play a significant role in their decision-making later that day. But as yet Frederick was in no position to give battle. The skirmish at Borne produced two crucial pieces of intelligence, however. Some of the captured horsemen disclosed that the Austrians had left most of their heavy artillery in Breslau. Further, surveying the terrain ahead of him from the Schönberg, an elevation near Borne, less than 3 km (2 miles) from the Austrian positions, Frederick now had a clear view of the prospective battlefield. The flickering lights of the campfires gleaming against the light dusting of snow that covered the ground marked out the enemy's line, and the gathering daylight revealed its full extent. Only the cavalry on the right remained hidden by the shrubby ground around the Zettelbusch, but the entire infantry and Nádasdy's left wing at Sagschütz were plainly visible.

Charles had chosen well enough. His line was too long perhaps, and this was a potential weakness. At the same time its sheer length made Frederick's task more complicated. More importantly, the ground to the west of Leuthen offered little protection to the Austrians. The countryside was open and gently rolling, like much of the Oder plain. It was broken only by a few hills and ridges, deceptively called 'Berge', though none rose to any great height. Only their right wing was shielded in front and flank by the dense copse of the Zettelbusch and by water meadows. This made it impossible for the Prussians to attack at any point between the Breslau road and Nippern (Mrozów). A move against the centre between Frobelwitz (Wróblowice) and Leuthen would bring down the enemy's right on them. Frederick's only option, then, was to attack the Austrian left wing, which was largely unprotected by any natural obstacles. It, in fact, ended well short of marshier ground that was crisscrossed by brooks and dotted with ponds, which might otherwise have anchored this wing.[49] Ironically, any move against it confirmed the essential correctness of the dispositions made by the Lorrainer and Daun. The Austrians' numerical advantage and the extent of their line meant that Frederick would have to spend much time on manoeuvring his army into position before he could attack the left wing; and with daylight fading between 4.30 and 5 pm, time was not on the Prussian king's side. It seemed as if the Austrians had achieved their object. A Prussian attack was all but impossible.

And yet on this point the Austrian commanders had miscalculated. From his vantage point on the Schönberg hill Frederick could see also that along nearly the whole length of the enemy's position ran a shallow ridge; and that to the south of Nádasdy's wing there were a number of low elevations around Sagschütz. The significance of these topographical features was not lost on the king, who reckoned that they might hide some of his approaching army and provide cover for a right wheel in front of the enemy's line to be followed by an attack against his vulnerable left. Frederick had noticed that the ground declined from there to Nippern, facilitating a push against the Austrian positions from the south. Declining the Prussian left would complete the deception.

This was not the first time Frederick sought to deploy this method. As an avid student of history, and reflecting contemporary *mores*, he was familiar with precedents from antiquity. Epaminondas, the Theban military leader, defeated the Spartans at the battle of Leuctra (371 BCE) by using an oblique order of battle, and this may well have inspired the Prussian king. At Chotusitz in May 1742 he had emulated the ancient Greek example with success, using the terrain to hide his principal strike force and then performing a half-wheel before attacking the exposed Austrian flank.[50] At Kolín he had failed because he had to move in plain sight of the enemy commanders. Now, the terrain allowed him to veil his real intentions from their prying telescopes. His plan did, indeed, run counter to contemporary tactical ideas. It was also an enormous gamble because it meant dividing his army, already inferior in numbers, with such a degree of precision that the diversionary force on his left wing was convincing enough to hold the attention of the Habsburg commanders while leaving his attacking forces on the right strong enough to break through the enemy lines. Deception was needed, and so was speed, for the longer the march to the south, the greater the danger of Frederick's real intention being discovered.

As seen, the terrain around Leuthen dictated the king's moves. The earlier cavalry skirmish at Borne also played into his hands. Nostitz's retreating vanguard had already alerted the enemy to his advance. Charles responded by advancing his troops by 1,000 paces so that the Austrian right wing came to rest against a wooded area southeast of Nippern and the main infantry line was positioned west of Frobelwitz and Leuthen, which latter place it thus enveloped. Heavy artillery was arranged in four batteries in front, while the reserves remained some distance behind the right. On the left, Nádasdy, now supported by Nostitz's Saxon cavalry, was ordered to move onto the hills at Sagschütz. The Magyar general deployed his heavy guns in two batteries and erected an abattis, a barricaded redoubt ('Verhau'), on the Kiefernberg hill.

By then, having cleared the village of Borne, some of the Prussian hussars, backed by a few infantry battalions, swung left, deployed in formation and advanced with deliberate slowness towards the Austrian right. It was the token force needed to keep the enemy's focus on the northern sector. The Austrians took the bait, but confusion reigned amongst the generals. From their vantage point on the Breslauer Berg Charles and Daun made out three advancing Prussian columns, 'making moves now on the left, then on the right, but the middle column remained immobile'.[51]

The Austrian right was under the command of Lieutenant Field Marshal Count Joseph Lucchesi d'Averna, a Neapolitan nobleman raised in Spain and a protégé of chancellor Kaunitz. From the moment Nostitz's Saxons had returned to his line, Lucchesi demanded the reserves be sent up as reinforcement. His wishes were granted. Charles ordered them to advance to Nippern at the far right of the Austrian line. It would prove to be another costly misjudgement. For these troops would be badly needed elsewhere later on that afternoon. It is important to note, however, that this was as much Charles' decision as Daun's.[52] The field marshal, usually so methodical, had accompanied the duke to inspect the situation on Lucchesi's wing, and he, too, expected the Prussian attack here. Both commanders, in fact, remained in what they took to be the threatened section of their line.

In the meantime, Frederick began his main manoeuvre. By 11 am the bulk of the army had passed through Borne, deployed in line, and then moved rightwards—to the south—in two snaking columns behind the ridge along the face of the enemy. It was an exceptionally complex manoeuvre. Its complexity, in fact, can scarcely be exaggerated. It involved various stops and starts and sideways shuffles. Above all, it required a high level of discipline to prevent individual units from becoming entangled and to ensure that they would deploy correctly in the next phase of the battle. Often passed over by historians, the wheel to the south was key to Frederick's success at Leuthen. Zieten's hussars formed the van, while the remaining twenty-five squadrons of hussars moved to the left (or east) to shield the infantry columns. Six of the nine infantry battalions of the advanced guard marched ahead of the bulk of the cavalry on the right, the other three under General Carl Heinrich von Wedel moving to the *tête* of the main force. Behind them were the heavy artillery pieces, arranged in five batteries. Frederick, accompanied by the commanding general of the main force, Prince Moritz of Dessau, son of the 'old Dessauer' of Mollwitz-fame, rode just below the brow of the ridge that gave cover to his marching troops.[53]

Perhaps only the Prussian army, well drilled in such moves, could have executed this manoeuvre. Moving such a force could not be hidden completely from the enemy. Charles and Daun, indeed, espied some of the movement, but only the initial turn to the right, whose suddenness and 'considerable speed' perplexed them.[54] Geography conspired against them, of course. The hills between Frederick's snaking columns and the Austrian line were of only modest height—the

Schleier-Berg, for instance, was 146 metres high, the Sophien-Berg 152 and the Heide-Berg 160. Yet the king had chosen well. The ground to the west of this ridge fell away enough to shield the Prussian troops from sight. After the war, the Prussian authorities conducted an experiment, sending a rider holding aloft a large white flag along the route taken by Frederick's troops. He was not visible to the observers on top of the Frobelwitz windmill who were scanning the landscape with their telescopes.[55]

However impeded their view, the Duke and the field marshal saw what previous experience told them to expect or what they wanted to see. They took it for a retreat in the face of overwhelming numbers. Frederick, it seemed, had been forced off the field; or else, he sought to coax the Austrian army out of its present strong position by threatening to cut off its communications with its Bohemian base, an idea in line with contemporary doctrine. 'Everyone', an unnamed Austrian officer later recalled, 'believed he was marching towards Schweidnitz'.[56] Whatever the Prussian king was planning, the immediate danger had seemingly passed. The 'Potsdam watch battalion' ('*Potsdamer Wachtbat-talion*') was withdrawing, Daun muttered, using the derogatory term for the Prussian army popular amongst Austrian officers on account of its much smaller size: 'They are marching off; let them go.'[57] Complacency played a role here. The failure of the Austrian commander to reconnoitre during this important phase of the engagement, at any rate, stood in marked contrast to the care with which the Prussian king had studied their position and movements. Had they been more attentive and less distracted by the Prussian feint on their right, they might well have discovered that Frederick's flank was left exposed while his troops continued their progress south.

Around noon the heads of the Prussian columns had reached the settlement of Schriegwitz, and Frederick ordered the troops to fall into line in readiness for the planned attack. It took another hour before they had completed their evolutions. They were now to southwest of Leuthen at a forty-five-degree angle to the Austrians. As the undulating ground sank into a plain here, the army wheeled left, its right wing now just south of the hamlet of Sagschütz. Further to their right, beyond Schriegwitz, was Zieten's cavalry, supported by six infantry battalions from the Prince of Bevern's brigade, which had formed the van during the march south and which now protected the flank of the army. The Prussian left extended along the Wachberg hill to the Heideberg hill to the southwest of Lobetinz (Łowęcice). To its left—at an angle, facing east, and screened by the Sophienberg heights—Frederick positioned the cavalry under Lieutenant General Georg Wilhelm von Driesen, an experienced commander of horse.[58] The twenty-five squadrons of hussars, which had previously protected the infantry columns on the march across the Austrian front, joined with the 12th Dragoons under Prince Frederick Eugene of Württemberg to form the reserve, positioned centrally behind the massed ranks of the infantry on the left and formed in two lines.

Key to the opening phase of the battle was the placing on the extreme right, in an advanced position, of the two battalions of Infantry Regiment 26 (Meyrinck) under Wedel, which were reinforced by the second battalion of IR 13 (Itzenplitz). The latter had moved steadily sideways during one of the evolutions as the army wheeled to the south to link up with the 26ers. Frederick had left nothing to chance. The 26th was an experienced regiment, battle-hardened and tough, a Brandenburg unit, whose recruitment *Kanton* lay to the east of Berlin along the Oder (Lebus, Cottbus, and Beeskow). It included members of the Wends, a Slavic-speaking ethnic minority, whose 'in-group' loyalties made it a formidable fighting force. The young Dessauer had recommended it to spearhead the attack: 'Your Majesty may entrust your crown and sceptre to the regiment—if they run away from the enemy, I would not remain behind myself.'[59] The 13th was another *Märkisch* regiment. Formed in 1685 from French *refugiés*, it now drew its recruits from the rural districts to the north and northwest of Berlin. Battle-hardened—it had fought at Lobositz, Prague, and Rossbach—it was nicknamed '*Donner und Blitzen*' ('Thunder and Lightening') in a pun on its regimental chief, August Friedrich von Itzenplitz.[60] Close behind Wedel's force were the II and III battalion of the Guard Regiment (IR 15) and IR 19 (Markgraf Carl), the former recruiting from the entire army, the so-called 'Unrangierten' and the 'Königskanton', six Silesian mountain districts, the latter from the core area of the Mark.[61]

Supported by the heavy guns of the 'Brummer-Batterie', which were drawn up on their left, Wedel's crack troops began the process of dislocating the whole Austrian line. Of the remaining four batteries, two were placed before the centre of the infantry line, the other two in front of each of the wings. The king himself chose the Wachberg, just a little to the left of the centre, as his command post. From there he had a clear view of the battlefield, and from there, at 1 pm, with no more than four hours of daylight left, he ordered his troops to attack. Dessau had already ridden over, fob watch in hand, urging Frederick to make haste. There could be no further delay. The battle now commenced.

To outflank the enemy's left, Frederick had to decline his own left wing and advance his troops at an angle. Fifty paces apart, they were to move forward towards the right 'en echelon', at a forty-five-degree angle and with the forces furthest to right in the most advanced position. It meant that the whole Prussian front could extend and contract again, accordion-style. It also meant that the centre and left were kept out of the firing during the opening stages of the fighting, preserving their strength until later in the battle. The main burden of the attack during that initial phase would be carried by Wedel's crack infantry battalions, supported by the heavy artillery.

Frederick had laid his plans carefully to avoid the mistakes of Prague and Kolín (Fig. 3.3). He had learned to appreciate that speed was vital, but it was not sufficient on its own. The earlier encounters at Prague and Kolín had impressed upon him that the Habsburg armies would stand their ground. The impact of the initial Prussian attack would have to be devastating, a hammer blow from which the enemy could not recover. Everything was concentrated on the three battalions that now advanced to administer that blow. The king took the trouble personally to indicate the 'Marschrichtungspunkt' (the point of attack) to

Fig. 3.3 Frederick the Great Surveying the Field of Battle by Hugo Ungewitter. Alamy, P4B3P5.

one of the junior officers of the 26th, *Fahnenjunker* (flag-bearing sub-lieutenant) Ernst von Barsewisch: '*Junker* of the life company, pay close attention. Towards that abattis (*Verhack*) yonder must you march. But do not advance too swiftly so that the army can follow.' He then turned to rank and file:

> Lads, do you see the whitecoats there? You must chase them out of their redoubt. All you have to do is to march forcefully and then drive them out with your bayonets. I will support you with five grenadier battalions and the whole army. It is a matter of winning or dying. You have the enemy before you, and behind you the entire army, so that you can move nowhere forward or back from the field of battle except as victors.

The heavy '*Brummer*' battery growled into action, and Wedel's grenadiers advanced. '*Mit klingendem Spiel*', to the sound of drums and fifes, the whole Prussian infantry was now moving in its staggered order to the right towards the Kiefernberg hill, south of Sagschütz, on the

Fig. 3.4 Advancing Prussian infantry by Carl Roechling. Wikimedia Commons.

Austrian left (Fig. 3.4). The troops kept excellent order, Barsewisch later recalled, 'as if at a review in Berlin'.[62]

Nádasdy, who was in command there, was not unaware of what was unfolding before him. He had watched the Prussian movement along his front for a while now, and he had repeatedly called for reinforcements to be sent to him. His warnings were in vain. His relations with Charles and Daun were fraught, and however experienced the Magyar general the two commanders were still convinced that the enemy was marching off. A Prussian attack this late in the day seemed impossible to them, and therefore implausible. Besides, the sheer length of the Austrian line now operated against them. Moving the reserves from the right to the left wing, over a distance of one German mile, or 7.5 km, would have taken too long to have an immediate effect.

Nádasdy's mounting concern may well have been caused by the uncertain fighting quality of the troops under his command. For in addition to Austro-German and Hungarian regulars of the Habsburg army, the bulk of the *Reich* auxiliaries had been allocated to him, Bavarians, Würzburgers, and Württembergers, widely considered unreliable and, more legitimately, less experienced.[63] In consequence, he had positioned them on the furthest left of his sector, ostensibly to protect his flank in the expectation that the serious fighting would occur elsewhere. Perhaps understandable, the decision would nevertheless cost him dearly because the weakest troops were thus deployed at precisely the point of impact of the Prussian attack.

Nádasdy was on the defensive throughout as, supported by heavy artillery, Wedel's three attack battalions steadily moved to their right towards the Kiefernberg hill at Sagschütz. The '*Brummers*' trained their fire on the Austrian positions with great effect, taking out two of their artillery pieces. As the Prussian infantry advanced, the battery was moved to the Glanzberg, another elevation between Schriegwitz and Sagschütz, to keep within range and to support the attack from there. Austrian light troops withdrew in the face of the advancing Prussians, pushing their way through three Württemberg battalions ensconced in the fir plantation around the Kiefernberg and throwing them into disorder. To compound the Swabians' difficulties, the Austrian field guns attached to them were short of ammunition and so had to reduce their rate of fire. Outgunned and outfired, they were no match for Frederick's heavy artillery. Charles later blamed the Württembergers for fleeing at the first salvo, thus throwing the Austrian line into disarray. It was a self-serving account, but sufficient to convince the Vienna court that responsibility for the defeat lay with the '*fatalen Alliirten*'.[64]

The Prussian battalions pushed forward to a drainage ditch fringed with willow trees within three hundred paces of the Kiefernberg, before they encountered any significant enemy fire. Once they had crossed the ditch, Wedel ordered them to fire a salvo and then to attack with felled bayonets. So rapid was their advance that they were in the midst of the Württembergers before they could aim a second salvo, 'beating them with their musket butts about the ears'.[65] The *Reichstruppen* wavered, broke, and then retreated, fearful also of being outflanked by Prussian cavalry. Three grenadier battalions that had been deployed in the nearby Kaulbusch spinney also retreated, without yet having come under fire. Seven regimental flags fell into the Wedel's hands. *Tout le corps Württembergeois est pris et dissipé*, Frederick noted after the battle.[66]

Nádasdy sought to counter-attack, if not to halt, at least to delay the Prussian advance. His best chance of success seemed to lie in an enveloping move against the Prussian front from the left. To that end he sent forty-three squadrons of cavalry, now under the command of Nostitz to attack the enemy. The charge failed. The rolling ground was dotted with pine trees and shrubs, which made it impossible for the cavalry to unfold properly. Caught on the hoof by the sudden Austrian charge, the Prussian cavalry on the right under Zieten had to contend with the same difficulty, of course. But Frederick's carefully planned battle order, especially the presence of the Prince of Bevern's brigade of infantry on Zieten's flank, now proved its worth. Nostitz's horse was halted and then driven back by the massed fire of Bevern's six battalions and the grapeshot of his field guns. Nostitz himself was killed at the *tête* of his *cheveaulégers*. Nádasdy now faced the prospect of being outflanked on his left himself. To avert this he decided to regroup his infantry, moving troops from the right of the second line of his sector to take up position in front of the Bavarian regiments just to the north of the Kiefernberg. In their haste, individual units became entangled, and confusion ensued. Three regiments, moreover, had to leave their artillery pieces behind. His predicament showed up the limits of conventional linear tactics. Reliant on the correct initial deployment, they were unable to adjust later on. To complicate matters further, the terrain was unsuitable for large-scale reordering.

All the while the Prussians continued to push forward, and they now hit Nádasdy's confused, disorganized and no longer fully equipped foot. Wedel's battalions were already well to the east of Sagschütz, steadily followed by the rest of the infantry in its '*en echelon*' advance. Firing salvo after salvo with the regularity of clockwork, this staggered line threatened to outflank the Austro-Bavarian regiments on the far left. At this point, the heavy guns of the *'Brummers'* and the two batteries in the centre of the Prussian front having by now been moved to the Judenberg, northwest of Sagschütz, resumed their fire. Austrian infantry, its now three lines tightly pushed against each other, took heavy casualties and began to back away. Already earlier, the two Austrian batteries there had withdrawn, unable to retaliate against the massed fire of the Prussian artillery. Now its own retreating infantry prevented it from replying at all. With heavy musket and grapeshot fire Wedel's battalions, supported by the battalion under Johann Bernhard von Kremzow—a unit formed of the grenadier companies of IR 17 (Manteuffel) and 22 (Prinz Moritz)—broke into the batteries and captured all its guns.[67]

At this point Prince Moritz ordered his troops, which were low on ammunition, to fall back into the second line, an order that, according to Barsewisch's recollections, was met with the cry: 'We should be scoundrels, if we now went into the second line. Cartridges! Cartridges!'[68] Such tales of heroism may elicit a degree of scepticism, and yet no fewer than fourteen of the officers of the 26th won the *Pour le Mérite*, the highest decoration for bravery, on that day and Frederick gave 1,500 *Thalers* to the ordinary soldiers of the regiment. Perhaps more significantly, the call for fresh ammunition highlighted a recent tactical innovation. Until Prague and Kolín, the Prussian infantry advanced without firing, sacrificing not only many of its men but also one of its chief advantages, its high rate of fire. Not so at Leuthen. By the time Wedel's crack battalions had reached the Austrian first line, they had used up their regulation sixty rounds. But Frederick had ordered that the munition carts be brought up behind the advancing infantry to ensure a steady supply of cartridges.[69]

The Prussian foot thus kept up a steady fire, and its push northwards continued apace, forcing the Austrian more and more to retreat. Nádasdy's force was heading for disaster now. He still managed to stabilize the line along the Gohlauer Graben, a drainage ditch southeast of Leuthen, but it allowed only for the briefest of respites.

Around 2 pm, Zieten's fifty-three cavalry squadrons moved from their original screening position, alert to the threat that Nádasdy's reassembled horse around the Gohlau hill posed to the right flank of the advancing Prussian infantry. Zieten's force could not easily deploy in formation, however, since the area between the Kaulbusch spinney and the ponds south of the hamlet of Gross Gohlau (Gałów) was dissected by dykes, drains, and gullies. Some dry, some waterlogged, many not easily visible, they afforded cover for the enemy's infantry. Under its fire the right of the Prussian cavalry under the Austrian-born Swiss nobleman General Robert Scipio von Lentulus faltered until reinforced by Zieten's hussars. Aided by the 2nd (Krockow) and 4th (Czettritz) Dragoons they rode down the Austrian infantry and then turned on Nádasdy's cavalry, just at the moment when he wanted to redeploy it to cover his beleaguered regiments of foot at the Gohlauer Graben.[70]

In the melée, Nádasdy could not rally his increasingly depleted mounted troops. The *Jung-Modena* and Savoy Dragoons were almost completely wiped out, both losing cannons and standards. Zieten's horsemen drove off what was left of the Austrian cavalry, the retreating riders then crashing into their own infantry. His own 2nd Hussars, until then kept at the rear, now overtook the Prussian first line and fell upon the enemy's infantry, completing the rout and taking 2,000 prisoners. At the same time, the six battalions of Bevern's brigade, coming up behind the cavalry, took the Kirchberg hill northeast of Sagschütz. The heavy 12-pounder battery drew up there and resumed its fire. At that point the Austrian line collapsed and retreated in complete disorder towards the village of Leuthen in the hope that its farmsteads and outbuildings would absorb the Prussian advance. The remains of the Austrian cavalry gathered north of Leuthen, at Rathen woods (Rathener Busch). Even so, Nádasdy's corps had ceased to exist as an effective fighting formation.

While the Prussian right continued its advance, keeping up a steady rate of fire, Zieten's mounted troops took up position on the south bank of the Fließ, a small stream that flowed into the river Weistritz at

Arnoldsmühle, some 4 km (2.5 miles) southeast of Leuthen.[71] By now, the Prussian heavy artillery had taken up its final position on Frederick's left on the tumulus-like Butterberg to the west of Leuthen, to support the assault on the village. Unusual by the standards of the day, this continual change of position underscored the increased importance of the artillery in battle, beyond the two field guns ('*Bataillonsgeschütze*') with which every infantry battalion was equipped.[72] Although the Prussian army was still to some extent dependent on importing gun barrels and assorted artillery equipment, it had made strides towards greater self-sufficiency. Eighteenth-century military writers appreciated the significance of the Prussian artillery in Frederick's wars, and so did the king himself: 'The results achieved by the artillery are the main element of the army's success.'[73]

It was at this late point, between 2.30 and 3 pm, that Charles and Daun grasped the extent of Frederick's deception. Until the moment that Nádasdy's wing dissolved, their main forces were still facing west. Now, with the imminent prospect of the entire army being rolled up from the left, Charles ordered the army to swing backwards at right angles—that is to the south—to face the swiftly oncoming Prussians on either side of Leuthen. Once more, the length of the Austrian line worked against it. Tens of thousands of troops had to stay in formation, three men deep, in two lines, and over several miles. The attempt ended in chaos. Muddled orders were compounded by disorganized units and confused and tired men, forced now to march three to four miles to confront an enemy already more or less in control of the battlefield. Troops surging back from what had been the left wing added to the sense of chaos and disorder. Yet the Austrian commanders accomplished the near-impossible. They established a new front, just under 3 km (2 miles) in length and in two lines, north of Leuthen to face the Prussians approaching from the south. Still, such was the turmoil that units became ensnared and in parts of the line they were one hundred men deep, an inviting target for the heavy '*Brummers*' on the Butterberg. As an Austrian officer recalled, '[t]he enemy's heavy artillery fire and the fast spreading fear amongst the common soldiers rendered all our all efforts fruitless.'[74]

The confusion also left the Austrian reserve, originally intended to protect the right wing at Nippern, unable to unfold into line formation. It merged as best it could with the main force, and some parts moved into the village of Leuthen itself to reinforce the soldiers who had barricaded themselves there. Also to the north, on the knoll of the Windmühlenberg (windmill hill), the Austrian artillery went into position, and behind it, to the right between the first and second lines, were Lucchesi and General Count Johann Baptist (also Giovanni Battista) Serbelloni, a veteran of Kolín and Breslau, with seventy squadrons of mostly heavy cavalry but with a few dragoon regiments attached, screened for now by the low ridge south of Gross Heidau (Błonie).[75] The Prussians, too, had regrouped before continuing their attack on Leuthen. Most of the battalions on their right wing had by now become involved in the fire fight, and the Prussian advance had gradually turned from a flanking movement into a frontal attack. They threw the scattered enemy infantry that had positioned itself outside Leuthen, and then paused to allow the troops under Dessau and Wedel to regroup on the hills northeast of Sagschütz to continue their flanking movement. As more troops entered the fight, Frederick, who had moved forward between the first and second line, took up a new position in the Radaxdorfer (Radakowice) Goy, a wooded area south of the Butterberg but affording a good view of Leuthen. Here he came under heavy fire from the Austrian batteries on the windmill hill.[76]

At around 3.30 pm the infantry began storming the *c*.1,800 paces long front at Leuthen. The village was a typical Silesian *Strassendorf*, the houses and farmyards threaded along the main thoroughfare, but walls, stables, and outbuildings formed natural obstacles to the advancing Prussians. House after house had to be taken. Resistance was fiercest around the Roman Catholic churchyard in the heart of the village, laid out in a square with the church at its centre and surrounded by a high wall of field stones and with corner roundels, an architectural folly of a local squire of the previous century (Fig. 3.5).

Fig. 3.5 Prussian fusiliers storming the churchyard at Leuthen by Menzel. Wikimedia Commons.

The Guards (IR 15) and the Retzow grenadiers (IR 6) were repulsed repeatedly as they sought to take the enclosure. They suffered heavy casualties, and the gaps in their ranks had to be filled with units from the second line. Eventually, the III battalion of the Guards under Captain Wichard Joachim von Moellendorff battered down the gate on the western side of the churchyard. Shortly afterwards, the battalion guns blew a breach into the south-facing wall.[77]

The guardsmen now filtered into the cemetery precinct where the fighting continued with great intensity.[78] The defenders, 'Roth-Würzburg', a regiment furnished by the Prince-Bishop of Würzburg as part of the Franconian *Kreis* contingent, were less experienced and less well equipped than the Austrian infantry. They held out until overwhelmed, at which point their remaining troops panicked and fled. The regiment suffered heavy losses. Three officers were killed, another five wounded and captured, a further fifteen junior officers were taken with the regimental colours and 350 men. As the day drew to a close, the regiment had shrunk to 217 men, of whom only four officers and thirty-three men with four flags managed to evade capture.[79] Altogether over 2,000 Würzburgers and Austrians were taken prisoners, as Prussian infantry cleared the village. Once the churchyard had been stormed, Austrian resistance faded. By 4 pm, after half-an-hour of bitter hand-to-hand fighting, Leuthen had been taken.[80]

With light fading the Prussians, exhausted from three hours of continuous fighting, formed a new line north of the village where they faced comparatively rested Austrian units from the enemy's original right wing. The final phase now began. It would be decided by the cavalry. As they made ready for a counterattack, the Austrians' position seemed well chosen, and the thinning line of bluecoats could scarcely be expected to overwhelm them. The presence of Dessau's nine battalions on their flank and the higher rate of Prussian infantry fire as well as the steady bombardment by the '*Brummers*' continued to tear holes into the Austrian lines. But the Prussian advance had come to a halt, some of the troops seeking shelter in the kilns (*Brechhause*)

dotted around the fields there to be used for drying flax.[81] The battle
hung in the balance; it had reached crisis point.

The Austrians nevertheless could not snatch victory at this late
hour. Once again, their earlier decisions, especially their reconnaissance failures, told against them. Prince Charles ordered Lucchesi and
Serbelloni to advance against the weakened enemy infantry. Seventy
fresh squadrons of heavy horse thus bore down on the Prussian left
wing between Gross Heidau and Frobelwitz. What neither the two
cavalry generals nor Prince Charles knew was that behind the Prussian
infantry stood Driesen's fifty squadrons in reserve between Borne, site
of the early-morning skirmish, and Radaxdorf. The force had followed
the army's advance earlier but had been ordered to remain behind and
at right angles to the infantry's flank. There it remained as the fighting
flared up elsewhere, shielded from sight by the rising ground around
Schleier- and Butterberg. Its position made up for Driesen's inferior
numbers, which comprised of fifteen squadrons cuirassiers and ten
squadrons of the Bayreuth Dragoons (D V) in the first line, followed by
fifteen more cuirassier squadrons and, in an extension to the left, by
ten squadrons of Putkamer's Hussars (H 4).

As the Austrian cavalry accelerated its advance across flat ground
towards the Prussian infantry, it rode across the front of Driesen's
units. The Prussians charged at full stretch. The first to hit Lucchesi's
regiments were the Bayreuth Dragoons, who had turned the battle of
Hohenfriedberg in 1745. They found the heavy Austrian cavalry a
more difficult proposition this time. But when the Prussian second
line came up, the cuirassiers, there was no stopping them. The 'White
Hussars' (H 4) joined in as well, and once again the shout '*Für Kolín*'
rang out as they tore into the Kolowrat Dragoons. The shock of
impact can scarcely be exaggerated. Lucchesi himself was killed in
the mêlée, and his cavalry pinned down. Worse, when thirty further
squadrons of the Prussian reserves under the Prince of Württemberg
joined in the fighting, the Austrian horse was driven eastwards
towards Leuthen. Over 150 squadrons, Prussians and Austrians, over
10,000 horses, were now at full tilt, stirrup-to-stirrup, ploughing into

the ranks of the right of the Austrian infantry which was still holding off the Prussians north of the village. In the ensuing panic the Austrian centre and left wavered, and then the whole of their front collapsed. There was no remedy for such disorder; linear tactics could not compensate for it. The battle was lost. Their poor field intelligence had contributed to the Austrians' defeat at the close of the fighting just as it had at its beginning.

As the imperial army was flung into confusion, the Prussian infantry launched a bayonet and musket butt charge and threw the enemy completely. A few whitecoats, the regiments Wallis and Baden-Durlach, stood their ground around the windmill hill. But they were mown down by the Prussian guard cuirassiers (*Leib-Carabiniers*) (K 11) and the Bayreuth Dragoons. Similarly, the Austrian gunners defended their batteries until they, too, were overwhelmed by the Schenckdendorff grenadiers (IR 35/36) at bayonet point, one of the elite battalions formed by Frederick by merging the grenadier companies of several regiments.[82]

Habsburg officers could no longer control their men, and the imperial army fled east across the river Weistritz towards Breslau in complete dissolution.[83] Daun, too, sustained an injury in the retreat. Ironically, it was to Nádasdy's foresight that the retreating Austrians owed their salvation. He had seen to it that bridges and other river crossings were kept open. Otherwise, the rout might have been complete. Frederick pursued some of the stragglers at the head of a small force gathered from his exhausted troops, mostly grenadiers and some cavalry, and with Zieten's hussars in the van. But in heavy snowfall and darkness he had to abort the chase. Behind him, the reformed infantry lines began to sing the chorale 'Nun danket alle Gott' ('Now thank we all our Lord'). As was custom in eighteenth-century armies, they had marched towards battle in the early hours of that day with another hymn, in the form of a morning prayer. But now, as the sound of their voices rolled over the scattered ranks of the survivors the 'Chorale of Leuthen' was born (Fig. 3.6).[84]

The losses were high on both sides. The Prussian casualties amounted to some 6,000, of whom 1,175 were dead, amongst them

Fig. 3.6 Prussian soldiers after the battle of Leuthen. Alamy, CPHX8D.

fifty-nine officers, and 5,043 wounded, or 3.35 per cent killed and 14.41 per cent wounded. The Austrians and the *Reichsarmee* contingents attached suffered even greater losses. They counted 3,000 dead, including Lucchesi and Nostitz as well as Generals Prince Gustav Adolf of Stolberg-Gedern and Franz Leopold, Baron Otterwolf von Niederstraeten, and 7,000 wounded, and over 12,000 of their troops were taken prisoner, though at least one statistic suggested 16,241 wounded and 25,249 missing amongst the infantry alone.[85] Some units suffered more than others. Of the troops in Prince Charles' regiment ninety-eight were killed and 320 wounded, and 454 were presumed missing or captured. No fewer than 789 men of Infantry Regiment Wallis were reported as missing, while a third of Infantry Regiment Harrach was recorded as wounded, though none was killed.[86] In addition, the Prussians, as Frederick reported to his sister, had captured 'une prodigieuse quantité de drapeaux et de canons', altogether some fifty-five regimental colours and 131 artillery pieces.[87]

In forcing the Austrians to engage in battle at Leuthen Frederick had a twin objective in view. In the short term, he wanted to force the enemy to vacate Silesia and to relinquish Breslau, which would then furnish him with winter quarters and an operational base for a spring campaign. Beyond that, it was imperative that the war, with its multiple fronts, be brought to an end as soon as possible. If the Austrians were able to recover during the winter, they would resume their efforts to join with the Russian or French armies. This had to be avoided. Once Austria had left the war, by contrast, the enemy coalition was likely to collapse. Frederick therefore sent Zieten in pursuit of the vanquished imperial troops. Wiping out the remaining Habsburg force in Silesia, he reasoned, would then enable him to march towards the Bohemian frontier, and so compel Vienna to enter into peace talks with the balance of advantage in his favour.[88] In this he failed. Retaking the Silesian capital took up all his resources for the moment. Even so, the king could be satisfied with the outcome of Leuthen. Breslau's 17,000-strong garrison surrendered on 20 December, and two days later, after several bloody skirmishes, Daun's depleted and demoralized army slunk back to Bohemia. Frederick had secure winter quarters, and the imperial army was in no position to resume active operations until later in 1758.[89]

At Leuthen Frederick pushed linear tactics to their utmost limits. His victory marked the zenith of eighteenth-century warfare and his own apogee as military leader in equal measure. For the first time, the concept of the oblique battle order had been applied fully and successfully; and this was possible because of a combination of Frederick's superior generalship, his better knowledge of the terrain and his ability to exploit it to his advantage, and the superior drill of the Prussian army. Frederick's regiments of foot combined movement and fire as precisely as prescribed in army manuals. The artillery, no mean feat for the period, moved forward with the advancing battalions, and the heavy 12-pounders were deployed to maximum effect. The cavalry meanwhile protected the flanks, and on two critical occasions, at the beginning and the end of the day, proved decisive, as indeed its significance had increased throughout the war.

No less important, though difficult to categorize, let alone quantify, was the cohesion of the Prussian army. The soldiers who fought at

Leuthen were no press-ganged civilians but hardened and motivated soldiers, 'Landeskinder', natives of the core Prussian areas, Brandenburgers, Mageburgers, Pomeranians, who felt a sense of loyalty towards Frederick and their native land, as their warm response to the king's eve-of-battle appeal underlined.[90]

Errors of commission and omission by the Austrian commanders undoubtedly contributed to Frederick's victory. Nádasdy's failure to keep scouting parties on his exposed flank is all the more extraordinary given his broad experience. No less remarkable were the blind spots of Charles and Daun. The Lorrainer's obsession with his right wing and his concomitant decision to deploy the weaker and less experienced auxiliaries on the left dealt the Prussian *roi connétable* a strong card, and so did Daun's disdain for the Potsdam 'Wachtparade'.

Whatever the individual failings, the general nature of eighteenth-century warfare also complicated matters for Daun and the prince. Having deployed the troops incorrectly, linear tactics did not allow them to reorder the units effectively. Conversely, they also hampered Frederick in his efforts to pursue the defeated remnants in the hours immediately after the fight and in the days following.

Victory at Leuthen nevertheless cemented Frederick's reputation as a military commander. Already on 6 December, the governor of Silesia hailed the king as 'the greatest general of our time'.[91] Frederick himself lost no time to broadcast news of his victory to the wider German and European public. A detailed *Rélation*, carefully composed by the monarch himself, was released three days later and then published in in German translation on 20 December. Although the document left little doubt as to the presiding genius behind the success, it praised the Prussian army, whose officers and soldiers and their 'fait des prodiges de valeur'.[92]

No less prodigious were the popular anecdotes into which Leuthen now congealed, such as the king's surprise visit to *Schloss* Lissa as night fell after the battle. In search of shelter for the night, the king and his small party chanced upon the chateau, which had served as Charles' headquarters, not realizing that senior Austrian officers were still present. With remarkable presence of mind, Frederick greeted the surprised officers courteously and asked to join them: '*Bonsoir Messieurs!* No doubt, you did not expect me here. May one also still find accommodation here?' It was a wonderful story, illustrating the monarch's *sangfroid* and *ésprit* and the Austrians' maladroit slow-wittedness in equal measure. It was also entirely fictitious.[93]

One fact, however, could not be denied. If Rossbach had bought Frederick time, Leuthen saved Prussia from imminent defeat. In the long term, Leuthen ensured more than the survival of the kingdom, it also affirmed its rise to the position of a European great power. In the event of defeat, with his army depleted yet further and his reserves nearly used up, Frederick would have had to end the war on terms dictated by the anti-Prussian coalition. No one would have rescued him. Prussia, save for a rump, would have been partitioned by its enemies. Leuthen, then, marked the second foundation of Prussia. Therein lies its historical significance.

At Vienna, the 'unfortunate outcome of the battle' was acknowledged as 'nothing if not painful', but fault lay with the German auxiliaries. The empress nevertheless feared the 'adverse impression' which the defeat could cause amongst her allies.[94] She was right to do so. The politico-strategic effect of the victory at Leuthen was immediate. Couriers carried the news of it abroad. Amongst the smaller princes allied to the Habsburgs, such as the Elector of Cologne, it created 'an indescribable consternation'.[95] Frederick also made sure to apprise the British government, a somewhat half-hearted ally so far. London revoked the convention of Klosterzeven, and Prince Ferdinand of Brunswick made moves to harry the French army in northwestern Germany.[96] The effect of Leuthen on public opinion in Britain was even more electrifying. Frederick, that old cynic and agnostic, emerged as the unlikely Protestant hero, and innkeepers and publicans rushed to rename their establishments in his honour: 'The sign-painters were everywhere employed in touching up Admiral Vernon into the King of Prussia.'[97]

In the spring, the second Convention of Westminster of 11 April 1758 reaffirmed the Anglo-Prussian alliance. Its material significance for Frederick's war effort cannot be exaggerated. The undertaking to keep an army of 50,000 in Germany aside, it guaranteed Prussia an annual subsidy of £670,000 (c.5.3 million *Thalers*). Altogether, no less than 27 million *Thalers* flowed into the king's coffers over the next few years.[98] He needed British guineas, for the war was far from over, and a political or military decision remained elusive. At the beginning of the new campaigning season, in spite of his grievous losses in the previous year, he was still able to put into the field the same number of troops as in 1757 (c.150,000). But over the next two years, Prussia was repeatedly on the brink of a catastrophe. Already in 1758, Frederick's reputation for military genius was tarnished by defeat. In vain he laid siege to Olmütz (Olumuce) between May and early July.

In late summer, on 25 August, at Zorndorf (Sarbinowo), a few miles to the east of the river Oder on the approaches to Berlin, Frederick managed to halt the advance of the Russian army under General Count Wilhelm (Villim Villimovich) von Fermor, thereby preventing it from joining with the Austrian main army. Fermor withdrew in stages into the interior of Poland. The Brandenburg heartlands were saved, but the cost was fearful. It was one of the bloodiest encounters of the war. Almost 13,000 Prussians and in excess of 18,000 Russians lay dead or wounded or were missing.[99]

Zorndorf was no victory, and worse was to come in the autumn. On 14 October, at Hochkirch, near Bautzen in Saxony, Daun, his doughty adversary, turned Frederick's tactics against him. He had learnt his previous lessons well. Frederick, frustrated by Daun's manoeuvring, accepted battle, but he had neglected to reconnoitre properly. Daun, who had been ordered to risk an encounter only if necessary, seized his chance by launching a surprise attack against the Prussian army. After bloody fighting, the Prussians had to retreat. Some 9,000 bluecoats were killed, including Keith; 200 cannons and the entire baggage train were lost. Only Daun's reluctance to pursue him allowed Frederick to slip back into Silesia, thereby forcing the Austrians to lift the siege of Neisse.[100]

The following year brought further setbacks. The strain of the war was beginning to show already. Frederick could put only around 100,000 men in the field, a third less than in the two previous years. He was no longer able to seize the initiative. On 12 August, at Kunersdorf (Kunowice), he suffered a near-catastrophic defeat. A new Russian army under a new commander, Count Pyotr Semyonovich Saltykov, had methodically and steadily pushed into Brandenburg and took Frankfurt on the Oder at the end of July. Reinforced by a small Austrian force, Saltykov routed Frederick's main army. More than 19,000 of his 50,000 men were killed or wounded. At the end of the battle his troops were deserting—he had no more than 3,000 men left. The king was plunged into utter despair. A decisive, combined thrust by the Russians and Austrians, of the kind that Frederick himself would have attempted in a similar situation, might very well have finished him off. Such a push never came. It was the moment of deliverance, of a miraculous turn of events, the 'Mirakel des Hauses Brandenburg', as Frederick himself put it a few weeks later. Suspicions riddled the anti-Frederician alliance. Daun feared for his extended supply lines from Bohemia, thereby rekindling Saltykov's suspicions of the Austrians, and anxious to preserve the fighting strength of his own army, he withdrew and headed east again.[101]

Over the next two years Frederick was frequently saved by the irresolution and disunity of his enemies. But he himself, often ill and worn out and above all lacking in numbers and resources, was no longer able to seek the offensive. He had also been taught to respect the Austrians. They were now in control of Saxony, and an attempt by an army under General Friedrich August von Finck to cut the communications between Dresden and Bohemia ended in Finck's surrender at Maxen on 21 November.[102]

The war reverted to the more traditional manoeuvre pattern. The king was still able to scrape together a 100,000-strong army in 1760.[103] In the northwest, his flank was protected by the Hanoverian

Observation Army, a force composed of British, Hanoverian, Prussian, and allied North German troops, some 94,000 in all. But against them, the anti-Prussian coalition could still muster around 369,000 troops, of whom 223,000 alone faced Frederick. The initiative lay with them. The Austrians invaded Silesia and, having defeated a Prussian army under Fouqué at Landeshut (Kamienna Góra) on 23 June, Laudon occupied the strategically important fortress of Glatz which commanded the routes into Bohemia across the middle part of the Sudeten range. Frederick held his own, defeating the combined Austro-Russian armies at Liegnitz on 15 August, another instance of the enemy coalition failing to coordinate its movements.[104]

Both sides suffered enormous casualties. Civilians were not excluded. In July 1760, for instance the Prussians bombarded Dresden to force a 14,000-strong enemy garrison out. The Saxon capital, with its famous baroque churches and palaces, often referred to as 'Elbflorenz' (Florence on the Elbe), was laid to waste during a two-week siege, its ruins, overshadowed by the skeletal tower of the city's *Kreuzkirche*, later captured in one of Bernardo Bellotti's (Canaletto's) evocative paintings. Even Prussian chroniclers were horrified by the wanton destruction: 'Many of the most noble streets were ablaze from one end to the other. Wherever one looked houses were collapsing.... Stately palaces that would have adorned any city in Europe fell victims to the flames. Often the poor inhabitants were buried under the rubble.'[105]

Prussia's capital did not escape unscathed either. Berlin fell into hands of a Russo-Saxon corps under the Russian general Count Gottlob Kurt Heinrich von Totleben (also Tottleben). Between 9 to 12 October 1760, the soldiers took revenge for Dresden, looting and plundering. They destroyed the army gunpowder mills and gun manufactures, and confiscated some 1.8 million *Thalers* from the local population.[106] Frederick had to hasten towards his capital but was unable to check Totleben's retiring force. Similarly, he was unable to dislodge the Austrians from Saxony. He defeated Daun at Torgau on 3 November—but the Austrians still held on to Dresden.[107] Frederick would take to the field one more time, during the War of the Bavarian

Succession (1778–9), but without recourse to fighting on any significant scale. This was a classic war of manoeuvre. In a sense, Torgau confirmed two things: Frederick was a master of tactics, and, strategically, the war had reached a stalemate. He still controlled Silesia, but Saxony eluded his grasp, and he had to withdraw from there altogether.

In July the following year, Allied forces defeated a French army in the west at Vellinghusen, near Hamm in Westphalia. It sufficed to keep the French in check for the rest of that year.[108] But relief in the west did not lead to any easing of the pressure in the east. On the contrary, the Russians seized the fortress of Kolberg (Kołobrzeg) on the Pomeranian coast and threatened to push once more towards Berlin. Frederick was ready to exploit what opportunities presented themselves, but he could no longer expect to vanquish his enemies. He could only hope to avoid defeat. The war had settled into a war of attrition.[109]

The decisions to end the war were made in the political and diplomatic sphere, not on the battlefield. In October 1760, George II died, and his successor, George III, changed course, hoping to free himself of his father's ministers and to present himself as a peacemaker. In February 1761, William Pitt, the architect of the Prussian alliance, resigned, and the new ministers were eager to extract Britain from the war. In the summer of 1762, the British government ended the subsidies to Prussia. It was a clear signal that London was ready to abandon the Prussian alliance, if that was the price of a separate Anglo-French peace.[110] The British could expect to gain little more from this war. North America was now in their hands, and in India the French had been pushed back, but a war with Spain now hove into view. French ministers, too, had tired of the war. On 3 November 1762, the two sides concluded a preliminary peace, condemned in vain by Pitt in a three-hour marathon speech in the House of Commons a month later, on 9 December, but it was to no avail. War weariness and a growing assumption that continental affairs were no longer of any concern won the day.[111]

Prussia's most significant ally had left the war. Already at the close of 1761 its position was precarious, as Frederick reflected: 'If fortune continues to treat me so mercilessly I shall undoubtedly succumb. Only she can deliver me from my present situation.'[112] Fortune unbent. Frederick had lost one ally but gained another, if only for a brief moment. On 5 January 1762, Elizabeth of Russia died. Her death removed from the political scene the driving force behind the anti-Prussian combination since 1759. She had opposed all suggestions of peace, determined to reduce Prussia territorially and her ruler to the rank of a mere elector. The contrast between the late tsarina and her successor could not have been starker. Peter III, a prince of Holstein-Gottorp, was an ardent admirer of the Prussian king. But if his admiration bordered on the obsessive, the new tsar was shrewd enough to realize that his empire's desolate finances did not allow Russia to stay in the war. He made peace on 5 May, restoring all Russian-occupied lands, including East Prussia and Pomerania, to Frederick. Sweden followed suit, fearful of its real enemy Russia, and made peace at Hamburg on 22 May. The tsar went further still, and concluded an alliance with Prussia in June 1762, which placed part of the Russian army at Frederick's disposal.[113] He was now able to turn on the isolated Austrians with renewed energy. Defeating Daun at Burkersdorf (Burkatów) on 21 July, their last encounter on the battle-field, he was in control of Lower Silesia again and took the nearby fortress of Schweidnitz after a brief siege on 9 October. Silesia was now secured to Prussia. In Saxony, the king's brother, Prince Henry, defeated the Austrians at Freiberg in Saxony on 29 October 1762, the only major engagement during this war in which a Prussian army was victorious when not commanded by Frederick. Defeat at Freiberg forced the Austrians to vacate Saxony and withdraw to Bohemia.[114]

The Russian alliance did not last for long. In fact, it probably cost Peter III his life—his wife, Catherine of Mecklenburg-Strelitz, plotted to have him murdered in July. As tsarina, she abrogated the Prussian alliance treaty, but did not re-enter the conflict, the war and the loss of British subsidies since 1756 having placed a heavy toll on Russia. France, moreover, had not abandoned its barrier policy in the East. On the contrary, Versailles' diplomats still worked towards containing

Russian influence in Eastern Central Europe. Russia had nothing to gain from this war. With Russia out of the war, the Prussian king rose like a Phoenix from the ashes of the previous six years. Drafting in the province of East Prussia, now free from Russian occupation, Frederick was able to put an army of 210,000 into the field in the summer of 1762. He pushed into Saxony, and so forced the Austrians back into Bohemia. Both sides found themselves in the same position as in 1756; both sides were also exhausted. It is important to note that it was not so much Russia's leaving the war—the myth created by Frederick—as the general exhaustion of all belligerents that made peace possible.

In a sense, Britain's abandoning of Prussia thus played into Frederick's hands. He had suggested earlier, in 1759 and again in 1761, that London should open talks with France for a separate peace. His rationale was sensible enough. Once the court of Versailles had made peace with its real enemy, thereby also leaving the coalition against Prussia, Louis XV and his ministers would find ways of coaxing or coercing Austria out of the war. Vienna's mounting financial difficulties made it biddable at any rate.[115] A separate Anglo-French treaty might thus serve as the basis for a general European peace. The obstacle in 1759 and 1761 was William Pitt, who wished to prosecute the war alongside Prussia until such time that Britain's maritime and commercial supremacy at France's expense had been secured. He would not preserve the Prussian alliance at all cost—just before his fall he had urged Frederick to make peace—but with his removal from office the alliance between London and Potsdam slowly waned.[116] British and Prussian interests had diverged beyond the point when the gaps between them could be papered over by a treaty or closed by guineas. Frederick's secret talks with Russia furnished the British government with a pretext to withhold any further subsidies. Much as he might still complain about it in the 1770s, eighteenth-century diplomacy was a matter of convenience rather than firm commitment, and Frederick was in no position to cavil at others' changing course or, indeed, sides. He had done so himself in 1742 and 1745, and he had encouraged the British to seek an understanding with France before Bute broke the alliance.[117]

In February 1763 a double peace settlement, the Anglo-French Peace of Paris and the Austro-Saxon-Prussian Peace of Hubertusburg (10 and 15 February), brought the Seven Years' War to an end.[118] The main beneficiary of the settlement was Britain. In addition to territorial gains in the Western hemisphere, London had secured trading advantages in the Atlantic and strengthened its position in India. Succeeding the Iberian powers and the Dutch Republic, Britain was now the dominant maritime and commercial power, though its dominance in North America was to be of limited duration. Britain's gains were well-nigh exclusively at France's expense, whose influence was significantly diminished.

The war in Germany ended where it had begun. The Treaty of Hubertusburg reaffirmed the status quo ante bellum, and Kaunitz's ambition to reduce Prussia to a second-rate power had to be abandoned, too.[119] The Austrians relinquished all claims to Silesia for good. Frederick formally recognized the Habsburg succession in the female line, and also undertook it to use his vote as Elector of Brandenburg to secure the election of Maria Theresa's eldest son, Joseph, as emperor, when he inherited the Habsburg possessions. The Prussian king could be satisfied with the settlement, but it was no triumph. His own cold, cynical habits of thought probably made it impossible for him to see it in such terms. He had done his duty, as he defined it, maintaining what he had once snatched in a daring coup from the Habsburgs. By guile and superior military ability, aided to no small degree by good fortune and the defective combination ranged against him, he saved Prussia from extinction as a great power. More, he had forced into existence a new great power system in the *Reich* and in Europe. What the elder Pitt had called the 'phenomenon of a second great power in Germany' had become a reality of international politics. Its relative strategic weakness notwithstanding, the Hohenzollern state had shown that it was capable of playing an independent political and military role amongst the other European powers, both, because of and despite the actions of its king. Yet the Prussia that emerged from the war was also isolated in Europe. Relations with Britain were strained, so were those with France, and Austria and Saxony remained hostile.[120] Some form of combination with Russia, then, was imperative, and Frederick made sure to act in conjunction with his powerful neighbour. In that sense, Russia, which had made no tangible or material gains from the Seven Years' War, benefitted from that European conflagration. Russia was now the 'arbiter of the North', and after the next Austro-Prussian war, the somewhat lacklustre affair of the War of the Bavarian Succession (1778–9), it was also the guarantor of Central European stability.[121] Its rise, and the uneasy state of Austro-Prussian relations, moreover, sealed the fate of the Polish republic, the principal victim of the war; Saxony, once a political rival of Branden-burg-Prussia was the other.[122]

The effect of the Seven Years' War on the German lands was nonetheless profound. As one of the chamberlains at the court of Queen Elizabeth Christine of Prussia, the gossipy but gifted Count Heinrich von Lehndorff observed at receiving the news of the Peace of Hubertusburg: 'All suffering has thus ended. But if one contemplates what incalculable sacrifices this war has demanded, how many families have been ruined, and all that to see the rulers confirmed in the *status quo ante*, one might scream at the madness of mankind.'[123]

Prussia and its king had held out for seven years against overwhelming numbers and often in seemingly hopeless situations. They did so with cunning, sheer bravery, superior generalship, and—perhaps most importantly—good fortune, above all the lack of internal cohesion of the anti-Prussian coalition. And they did so because of Frederick's ruthless determination to preserve, irrespective of, indeed often indifferent to, the enormous sacrifices the war entailed. Conservative estimates suggest, in total, around 500,000 casualties in the Seven Years' War. Of these, 180,000 were Prussians, and a further 60,000 ended up as Austrian prisoners. Prussia's population had decreased by 500,000 during the war, a ninth of her pre-war population of 4,500,000. The local nobility and the peasantry had suffered severe depravations; and it would take decades for Prussia to recover from the war. 'The state [Prussia] resembled a fighter weakened by blood loss, who nearly collapsed under his own weight.... Distress was widespread', Frederick later wrote.[124] In the Brandenburg heartlands of the Prussian monarchy, 25,000 horses had been lost, 17,000 bullocks, 20,900 cows, 121,000 sheep, and 35,000 pigs.[125] There was scarcely a noble family that had not lost members. In the three Silesian wars, 1,550 Prussian officers fell, sixty of them generals, all of them noblemen. The Kleists lost twenty-three of their family, the Münchows fourteen, and the Arnim, Bredow, Puttkamer, Seydlitz, and von der Schulenburg families lost seven or eight each. Of the (in 1756) 1,850 soldiers of the 26th Infantry Regiment, whose grenadiers had formed part of Wedel's crack troops at Leuthen, only some fifty lived to return home in 1763.[126] This blood sacrifice consecrated the union between the *Junker* landed elite and the Hohenzollern dynasty which was to last until 1918, and in some senses beyond. The names of the battles of that war were seared into Prussian collective memory and they were to shape the Borussian historical consciousness in the nineteenth century, with its *kleindeutsche* sense of mission that underpinned it.

The impact on German politics was no less profound. The old confessional differences that had plagued the Empire in the sixteenth and seventeenth centuries hardened into a political and cultural divide between northern Protestants, leaning towards Prussia, and a southern *kaiserlich* Germany that oriented itself towards the Habsburg monarchy. It limned the later antagonism of the nineteenth century. The question of mastery over Germany still remained to be settled.

4

The Leuthen Legacy in Military Thought before the First World War

One of the remarkable features of Leuthen's broader legacy was its slow maturation. Only gradually, and not until the middle of the nineteenth century, did it acquire its central status in historical memory. Its military legacy was also a matter of multiple and multi-layered misunderstandings. Frederick's 'greatness' had already been proclaimed by his contemporaries, but increasingly this complicated a proper appreciation of the king's military achievements and his historical significance.

This was less complicated for his erstwhile enemies. After 1763, the Prussian model inspired French military reforms and writers, particularly with regard to the problem of accurate deployment. Significantly, army instructions and, later in the 1770s, the works of Jacques-Antoine de Guibert placed great emphasis on columns as a means of obviating the cumbersome need to manoeuvre in order of battle. Especially for Guibert, brilliant but unstable and vain, such tactical changes were to increase an army's mobility, so compensating for any numerical superiority of the enemy. Here, Frederick's influence was undeniable, and the Frederician concept of battle *à la* Leuthen or Rossbach remained dominant. But to no small degree these innovations anticipated the *ordre mixte* which would form the backbone of Napoleonic tactics.[1]

By contrast, in post-Frederician Prussia generals, many of them apprenticed in war under Frederick, were less innovative. Instead, they sought to preserve the king's legacy. They did so by perfecting the careful choreography of linear tactics in all its possible permutations to such an extent that even in victory commanders were not to push their advantage.[2] Had Frederick lived, he might well have commented with his customary sarcasm on his successors' determination to cling to old practices as they marched towards catastrophic defeat in 1806. That task fell to the military reformers around Gerhard von Scharnhorst and August Neidhardt von Gneisenau when contemplating the scattered relicts of Prussia's army. They were in no doubt that intellectual inflexibility and a wilful ignoring of the profound changes the French Revolution had wrought in the military sphere were at the root of the catastrophe.[3] Carl von Clausewitz, who had taken part in the campaign, was scathing of the intellectually calcified generals. Since Leuthen, attacking *en echelon*, at an oblique angle, was 'the sublimated Prussian tactic'; and so, at Jena, General von Tauentzien advanced *en echelon* and was nearly wiped out: 'Now comes General Grawert, changes front, and advances likewise *en echelon* against the enemy and is beaten. Then General Rüchel arrives, advances *en echelon* and is beaten.'[4] Later, under the impression of Napoleon's 1812 campaign in which he had served as a Russian staff officer, Clausewitz came to a more nuanced judgement, and moved away from the 'primacy of the offensive', acknowledging that 'the defence is the stronger form in war'.[5]

Even so, to win one had to learn from Napoleon rather than the victor of Leuthen. Queen Louise, Prussia's 'Queen of Hearts', brought it to the point: 'We fell asleep on the laurels of Frederick the Great who, a master of his age, created a new era. We have not kept pace with the times and have now been outflanked by them.'[6] The collapse of the old Prussia and its subsequent, precarious existence at the mercy of Napoleon Bonaparte taught Prussian generals the humiliating lesson that Frederick's art of war did not, after all, mark a point of perfection. That assumption nevertheless re-emerged to shape Prusso-German military thought; and it also affected assessments of the significance of Leuthen.

Until the middle of the century, Leuthen lingered in the shadows of Rossbach. Frederick's earlier victory over the French army was capable of rousing patriotic sentiments, especially after the Napoleonic experience of defeat and occupation, that his rout of a dynastic enemy at Leuthen could not.[7] It was Rossbach, noted one early biographer, Friedrich Christoph Förster, 'through which Frederick won the hearts of the Germans and raised our nationality from deepest humiliation to a sense of self-worth again. For a hundred years the kings of France and their generals had maltreated the divided Germanies with haughty arrogance; and many princes of the Empire had ... betrayed and sold the honour of the fatherland and the lives of their subjects to France for base money. The nation, in its inner core still healthy, ... hailed Frederick as a hero-prince who restored honour to the name of Germany.'[8]

Contemporary concerns, political and cultural, were crucial to Leuthen's maturing legacy; and this needs to be borne in mind when assessing its impact on military thinking. The experience of French rule did not plant the seeds of German nationalism, but it provided the warmth necessary for their germination. In the years immediately after the defeat of France, the aspirations of the German national movement were focused on Austria. It seemed more likely to leading liberals in Germany that under Habsburg leadership a German nation state might eventually be established. It was in response to the failed 1848 revolution that they abandoned such *grossdeutsche* schemes and, instead, embraced, reluctantly at first and then with growing conviction, the idea of a *kleindeutsche* ('lesser German') solution, that is without Austrian participation.[9] Their hopes now rested on Prussia, whose 'German mission' was proclaimed by leading liberals. The German nation could secure its destiny—a unified nation state—only at the exclusion of Austria, and indeed with an explicit poise against her ruling dynasty.

By the 1850s, a 'Borussian'—that is Prussophile and *kleindeutsche*—school of thought was well established in Germany north of the river Main. An early exponent of this tendency was Johann Gustav

Droysen, in whose works rigorous scholarship and politics infused each other. In his *Geschichte der preussischen Politik*, the first volume of which appeared in 1855, he sought to trace the origins of Prussia's 'mission' to the advent of the Hohenzollern margraves in the early fifteenth century.[10] But it was the figure of Frederick that served as the pre-eminent representative of Prussia's historic claim to a leadership role in Germany. Ostensibly pursuing narrow Prussian state interests, in reality, so 'Borussian' historians argued, the king's political manoeuvres served larger ends. Droysen and others saw in him a pioneer of the idea of German unity. The rise of Frederick's sprawling and marginal kingdom to the position of a European great power in the course of three wars against Austria, then, was the necessary prelude to the next phase, the unification of the German lands under Prussian leadership and at the exclusion of the Habsburg dynasty and its dominions. There was a line of continuity from Frederick to Bismarck, and the Seven Years' War appeared as a forerunner of the wars of 1866 and 1870. In this reading, Prussia's 'mission' was accomplished with the proclamation of the new German Empire at Versailles in January 1871. It was taken as a political affirmation of the essential correctness of the 'Borussian' interpretation of Germany's past.[11] That Prussia's success—and hence the legitimacy of its 'mission'—came at the expense of the authority of the old Empire and its traditional rulers was an awkward complication, but not one that was insuperable to 'Borussian' historians. As Leopold von Ranke pointed out, Frederick's leaving the War of the Austrian Succession in October 1741, on having secured the possession of Silesia, allowed the Habsburg Monarchy to concentrate its resources against its real enemy, the Bourbon king.[12]

Such dialectic sophistry allowed the subsequent official histories of Frederick's wars largely to ignore their wider political contexts, to focus instead on strictly military aspects and the personality of the king. His stoicism in adversity, the seemingly well-ordered state he led, and above all the dogged determination shown by him and his soldiers in the struggles for Silesia served as models for the new

Kaiserreich. The 'strict military-monarchical discipline' of Frederician Prussia was regarded as having furnished the foundations of Prussia's great power status, its further rise and its historic mission, so enabling it 'to establish for itself, in the centre of the European continent, surrounded by powerful and often jealous neighbours, an independent existence and to secure respect in the world for Germany's name.'[13] It also lent historical legitimacy to the crypto-absolutist, pseudo-parliamentarian constitutional arrangements of Bismarckian Germany. To a considerable extent, then, Frederick served as the founding father of the new Prusso-German state, and his wars were the template for its wars.

The figure of Frederick also occupied a central position in the strategic thinking of the Prussian general staff. Its chief, Field Marshal Helmuth Count von Moltke, presented another fixed point in Prussia-Germany's seemingly linear rise to ever greater power. What the great king and Bismarck were in the political sphere, Frederick and Moltke were in the field of military leadership. Moltke's victorious operations in the wars of German unification, it seemed, marked the culmination of what Frederick had begun over a century earlier. Their strategy seemed to breathe the same spirit. The experiences of the three recent wars gave rise to the conviction amongst senior officers that the strategic offence was invariably superior to defensive dispositions. Moltke was a more nuanced military thinker, but amongst the next generation of military leaders this quest for the offensive hardened into the 'dogma of the battle of annihilation'.[14] Its most significant and influential— disastrously so—prophet was Moltke's successor but one as chief of the general staff, Alfred Count von Schlieffen.

This narrowing of the focus of strategic thought did not occur in a vacuum. The recent experiences of 1864, 1866, and 1870–1 aside, the evolution of this annihilationist doctrine was shaped to a significant degree by the work of the Prussian general staff's *Kriegsgeschichtliche Abteilung*, its military history section. Its research publications increasingly concentrated on Frederick's wars. In them the great monarch was held up as a role model of true strategic leadership.[15] Although they came heavily armed with the usual scholarly impedimenta of footnotes and appendices, the *Abteilung*'s publications did not conform to the standards of critical scholarship that especially German historians and theologians had developed in the nineteenth century. On the contrary, its researchers set their work apart from the quotidian concerns of 'civilian' academics, and treated military history and studies as '*Generalstabswissenschaft*', the exclusive preserve of high-ranking military specialists in the general staff who judged matters from a higher plane than '*Zivilstrategen*' in their ivory towers.[16] In practice, they tended to squeeze the wars of the previous century into the Procrustean formulae of their own strategic preconceptions. Hohenfriedberg, Rossbach, Torgau, and especially Leuthen were treated as little more than a giant quarry from which general staff officers could retrieve the building blocks for operational planning.

Military history ('*Kriegsgeschichte*') occupied a prominent place in the officer training programme at the Prussian *Kriegsakademie* at Berlin since its foundation in 1810. But unlike the also obligatory course in 'general history', it was treated as a '*kriegswissenschaftliche*' discipline, focused on practical aspects and designed to complement the budding officers' tactical studies. This tendency to treat the study of past wars as a source for practical lessons became more pronounced towards the end of the long nineteenth century.[17] The syllabus of 1912 specified the function of military history lectures thus:

> They must make discernible the immutable fundamental conditions of army leadership in relation to changing tactical forms, and throw light on the influence of outstanding personalities on the course of events and the weight of psychological factors. They must consider events with reference to their root causes and context, concern themselves with leadership questions, and give expression to the ideas of military leadership that were specific to their age. They will be the more valuable if the teacher succeeds in encouraging his audience's lively participation. Judgments, however, must never degenerate into purely negative criticism, but must take the form of well-founded proposals and decisions and measures.[18]

This was the so-called '*applikatorische Methode*' in its most pristine form. Usually attributed to the later Prussian war minister Julius Verdy du Vernois, who had taught at the academy from 1866 to 1872, it sought to apply insights and lessons derived from the past to the operational problems of contemporary warfighting. Erich Ludendorff, who was on secondment to the *Kriegsakademie* as an instructor in 1906–7, elaborated on the 'applied history' approach in his memoirs: 'When elucidating operations in war, I attempted...to think myself...ever more sensitively and thoroughly into the position of the commander whose campaign I was discussing, to get an impression of the many frictions and also the general conditions and the intelligence available, on the basis of which the leaders had to make their decisions.... I considered what I would have done in those conditions and further demonstrated how operations in earlier times would have unfolded under the influence of modern ideas and with modern weaponry.'[19]

Hindsight had to be avoided. The success or failure of the campaign under discussion was not to be the decisive criterion for judging the operational merits of the course of action pursued by past commanders. Clausewitz after all had argued that '[i]f the critical method is to apportion blame to a [past] commander, one first has to put oneself precisely into his position, that is to correlate everything that he knew and that motivated his actions, and conversely to ignore everything that he could not and did not know, above all, therefore, the outcome. Yet this is only the ideal, which to attain one may strive without ever doing so; for the state of affairs, from which an event arose, can never be the same in the eye of the critic as in the eye of the participant.... Much will always pass the critic by that was present to the participant's mind.'[20]

Ideal and attainment were far apart in the works of the *Abteilung*. In practice, its historians scoured Frederick's wars for evidence to prove the immutable verities of strategy—and they affirmed the spirit of the offence. The aim of their research was to provide the historical and intellectual underpinnings for the strategic and tactical ideas then dominant in German military circles. These revolved around wars of conquest, preventive wars, and battles of annihilation as the height of generalship. In addition, Leuthen and the oblique order of battle were taken to demonstrate the supreme importance of enveloping the enemy in flanking movements before delivering a devastating blow. In turn, this reinforced the preference for offensive operations as much as it seemed to reaffirm assumptions that they could compensate for numerical inferiority. Following from this, it was also taken as axiomatic that central to military success were outstanding commanders, men able to seize the initiative and exploit opportunities for offensive operations that more conventional minds failed to discern.

The emphasis on attack and conquest was no coincidence. Not the least, it offered a material justification for the annexation of Alsace and Lorraine after the Franco-German war. Perhaps inadvertently, Reinhold Koser, the (civilian) director of the Prussian state archives and one of the leading authorities on the Frederician period, revealed this latter-day connection between the conflicts over the two contested provinces. Both wars were defensive in motivation and nature, he averred: 'A defensive war loses nothing of its defensive origins and character if, in its course, it turns towards conquest; otherwise one might well come to the point of "discovering" the intentions of conquering Alsace-Lorraine as the origin ['*Ausgangspunkt*'] of the war of 1870'.[21] Koser's quasi-apologia reflected some of the dominant attitudes amongst senior officers. Defence and offence were no longer clearly separated, as a general staff memorandum of 1902 underlined: 'We do not wish to conquer but only to defend what we possess. We shall never be the attacking but always the attacked party. Only an offensive, however, can guarantee the necessary swift success.'[22]

Frederick's wars were a veritable cornucopia for contemporary strategic planning. His pre-emptive strike by invading Saxony in 1756 provided a moral justification for such an operation in the future, most likely against France. Frederick's wars in general thus established the paradigm for a just, because necessary, and exemplary offensive war, while his triggering of the Seven Years' War, in particular, was used to legitimize the idea of a preventive war against jealous neighbours, harbouring aggressive ambitions. History had been turned into the handmaiden of war planning; its chief purpose was to formulate an apologia for aggression. As Captain Walter von Bremen, who was attached to the *Abteilung* in the 1890s and again from 1899 until 1910, reflected in one of his studies of the monarch: 'This Frederician lesson to play the *Prävenire* has become a Prussian principle since his day and has remained so.'[23]

Instrumentalizing history for political purposes was pregnant with possibilities. Not least, the perceived analogy between Frederick's precarious position on the eve of the Seven Years' War and Germany's growing international isolation in the years after 1905/9 suggested a seemingly defensive strategy, the components of which were entirely offensive. The risks this entailed were great, of course. But the general staff consciously accepted them when finalizing the so-called Schlieffen Plan, with its implicit acceptance of the preventive war doctrine and its explicit breach of existing international treaties guaranteeing Belgium's neutrality. Just as Frederick in 1756, so Germany's leaders now were justified in resorting to extreme measures to pre-empt the country's complete encirclement by hostile powers. 'Humanitarian concerns', noted one author of one of the early volumes of the official history of the Seven Years' War, 'must not influence the commander when important military outcomes hang in the balance'.[24] It was but a small step from this notion to the idea of 'necessity knows no law', the argument used by Theobald von Bethmann Hollweg, the German chancellor, in August 1914 when seeking to justify the occupation of Luxemburg and the invasion of Belgium on 4 August 1914.[25]

Necessity had forced Frederick's hand in 1756, official historians averred. It dictated his decision to occupy ostensibly neutral Saxony, a move designed to prevent the formation of a powerful combination against Prussia.[26] Schlieffen, too, pointed to the continued hypothetical risk of an Austro-Saxon alliance in 1744–5, which had hampered Frederick's campaign in Bohemia: 'The experience of the Silesian Wars, especially of the second, had shown that Prussia could not achieve decisive successes ['*durchgreifenden Erfolge*'] against Austria if

Saxony, even if seemingly neutral and wholly passive, remained on its flank or, as in 1744, on its back.'[27]

This 'cult of the offensive' explains also the general staff's preoccupation with large-scale battles which were considered decisive for the outcome of wars. The victories at Königgrätz and Sedan, inevitably perhaps, had given rise to such ideas. The aim in future conflicts had to be to bring about similar encounters so as to annihilate the enemy's main forces, thereby compelling him to terminate the war immediately. This was the essence of real strategy. Wars had to be short and decisive, just as Prussia's eighteenth-century conflicts had been '*kurz und vifs*', as Walter von Bremen observed, citing Frederick. Battles decided the outcome of wars, hence the '*Drang nach vorwärts*' (the thrust forwards) which the great king had inculcated into his soldiers.[28] Only thus could Germany prevail over a numerically superior group of hostile powers. Battles of annihilation were the highest form of military leadership. And here, too, the lessons Frederick's wars held seemed to be incontrovertible. The road to ultimate victory over a mighty enemy coalition lay along a route via Mollwitz, Hohenfriedberg and Soor, Rossbach, and Leuthen. Ground down by repeated defeats—defeats, moreover, that conventional warfighting doctrines suggested should never have occurred—the enemies were forced to concede Prussia the great power status to which it was entitled, and for which historical necessity forced it to fight.

Theodor von Bernhardi, who had been Moltke's liaison officer at Vienna during the Franco-German war, and Lieutenant-General Adalbert von Taysen, head of the *Abteilung* from 1874 until 1881, were high-profile representatives of this line of argument. Neat as it was, it nevertheless contained a glaring inconsistency. Measured against Königgrätz and Sedan and judged by the general staff's standards, none of Frederick's victories was decisive. Not even at Rossbach and Leuthen was he able to annihilate the opposing armies. This much was incontrovertible. Against it, the *Abteilung's* historians held to the view that only the nature of warfare under the *ancien régime* prevented the intended outcome. Such constraints also extended to the cavalry and forced Frederick to refrain from pursuing the defeated enemy, observed an 1881 general staff study of modern mounted warfare.[29]

The king, in fact, had learnt more from his first encounter on the battlefield at Mollwitz than other commanders did from a hundred battles, asserted Max Jähns, a prominent instructor at the *Kriegsakademie* in the years between 1872 and 1885. Frederick had intuited 'the great maxim of the overwhelming force of initiative and attack' and of concentrating one's forces against one point on the enemy's flank. And with that 'came to him the revelation how to achieve this within the canon of linear tactics: he grasped the idea of the oblique battle order.' Thus Frederick 'inspired the formal language [of warfare] of his time with the breath of world historical significance', even though he could not wholly transcend the 'rigid forms of the old regime'.[30] Furthermore, the unreliable composition of eighteenth-century armies and their slow pace placed tight limits on what was achievable, noted Colonel Hugo von Freytag-Loringhoven, an instructor at the *Akademie* and later on Schlieffen's staff. Even so, for as long as Frederick 'had at his disposal a sizeable, splendidly drilled and in its attitude and mobility far superior army, he attempted to deal rapid, major blows.'[31]

That this had always been the king's ambition throughout was not to be doubted, Taysen argued. In all the battles which he had directed personally, Frederick aimed at the complete destruction of the enemy's forces. He had conceived of them as battles of annihilation. No other interpretation was admissible: 'Only he who has grasped this *Kardinalpunkt* completely, may be able fully to comprehend the King.'[32] Already a year previously, in two stout volumes on Frederick as commander, Bernhardi had made a similar argument. In sharp contrast to his contemporaries and marking a breach with *ancien régime* norms and practices, the king knew 'that the annihilation of the enemy forces was all-decisive, and that, therefore, for him who seeks the decision, the enemy army itself has to be, as we are now accustomed to say, the strategic object.' All his battles were 'conceived as battles of annihilation'. That none of the encounters ended in the wholesale destruction of the enemy armies was a measure of Frederick's political moderation: 'he knew of what Prussia was capable and of what not, [and] how easily the resources of his realm might be exhausted.'[33]

The assumed relevance of Frederician concepts for contemporary operational planning was made explicit by another staff officer in 1883. In a lecture to mark the king's birthday on 24 January, the so-called *Friedrichstag*, Major Rudolf von Caemmerer underlined the intellectual affinities between Prussian warfighting in the Seven Years' War, that of Napoleon and current practices: 'Fundamentally, both [Frederick and Napoelon] stand, with minor modifications, on the same ground, on which all great commanders of all times have stood; they see success guaranteed only by one means, by victory in battle.' Frederick's wars thus prepared the ground for the operations modern German armies might have to wage, and the monarch himself was 'a shining, effulgent example for the challenges which the future may hold for us.'[34]

A decade later, Bernhardi's son Friedrich (Fig. 4.1), who headed the general staff's first *Abteilung* in charge of recent military campaigns, emphasized the critical importance of Frederick's generalship for contemporary soldiering. Nothing was richer in 'deeply significant lessons than the campaigns of Frederick the Unique'. Bernhardi singled out his habit of taking to the offensive whenever necessary or possible. His object was always to bring about a battle in its 'absolute, most decisive form'. Ineluctably, it led the king to attempt flanking movements, so at Kolín, where he failed, and at Leuthen, where the operation succeeded. In its essence such a strategy remained relevant to modern warfare: 'The greater the masses of the defence, the greater the advantages of a flanking attack, still great enough to compensate for any numerical superiority [of the enemy]'. That, Bernhardi asserted, was 'the constant law of the art of war'.

In any future war, German war planners ought to emulate Frederick and opt for 'a resolute *va banque*' by concentrating their forces on whichever front the greatest threat lurked. Only thus could 'the still-valid law of war' be applied in the event of a two-front-war. The essence of Frederick's strategy remained valid still. Just as Prussia

Fig. 4.1 Friedrich von Bernhardi. Wikimedia Commons.

then, so Germany now had to seek its salvation in the offence, when forced to do so. These were the lessons which 'the battles of the King preach to us'. For Bernhardi had no doubt that the military balance in Europe had shifted to Germany's disadvantage. Nothing, he averred, was more certain than that 'we shall fight an equal or superior enemy'.[35] Bernhardi's monograph contained a blueprint of sorts for the Schlieffen Plan, work on which commenced in the same year. The object of the so-called 'Westaufmarsch'—the concentration of the bulk of the German armies against France, combined with a vast encircling operation swinging through the Low Countries to circumvent the French fortress belt on Meuse and Moselle—was the annihilation of the French army. The war would be decided on French soil.[36]

To some degree, Schlieffen's war plan of 1905 was a 'purely theor-etical operational study', just as its author, who had no experience of

Fig. 4.2 Alfred Graf von Schlieffen. Alamy, DRHHYX.

senior command in war, was more an austere theoretician than a practitioner (Fig. 4.2).[37] Throughout his tenure as Chief of the General Staff between 1891 and 1906, he continually developed and refined his ideas. None of the various plans he drafted in that period was in any sense 'final', no more than the elder Moltke's *Aufmärsche* were definitive.[38] Schlieffen's *Besprechungen*—summations and critiques—of the staff exercises and army manoeuvres in this period illustrate the gradual evolution of his planning models, but also the 'sudden and radical change' in them around 1900 in favour of prioritizing offensive operations in the west.[39]

Certain elements—a preference for attack and flanking movements—remained prominent features of his ideas. At the end of the staff exercise of 1893, designed around a sudden French attack with superior numbers through Lorraine and Luxemburg, he reprimanded those officers who adopted a defensive posture: 'the fundamental laws of warfare remain the same, and one of these laws says that without attack one cannot defeat the enemy,...one must attack the enemy when one has the means to do so and...one must attack in such a way that he will, if possible, be destroyed.'[40] The exercises at the end of that decade helped to crystallize Schlieffen's thinking about the need for swift strikes. In one of the scenarios for 1898, Russian forces threatened a German army corps in East Prussia on three sides. In the field marshal's analysis, the army had to turn on the nearest enemy force, defeat it and then turn against one of the other two. But the defeat had to be decisive. On no account must the German corps be pinned down by one of the Russian armies as this would give the other two time to prepare for an attack in the Germans' flank and rear before crushing them with their superior numbers.[41] The staff exercise in the following year envisaged a Russian invasion with forces double in size to the defending German *Ostarmee*. Here, too, Schlieffen urged the participants to contemplate enveloping ('*Umfassung*') the enemy: 'To secure success it is necessary to concentrate the available forces against one of the enemy's wings.' Dividing the defending forces entailed risks, but Schlieffen concluded that 'one had to run the risk of separation or give up the offensive and seek safety behind the Vistula'.[42]

By around 1900, all of Schlieffen's scenarios involved attacks on the enemy's flank. In the exercise of 1904, for instance, the participants had to meet a two-pronged Russian push into Lower Silesia while the bulk of the German forces was engaged in the west. The scenario was loosely based on Frederick's victory at Liegnitz in 1760. Technical advances made it impossible to replicate the moves in every detail, but the underlying concept of attack against one army while holding off another remained relevant to modern warfare, Schlieffen contended. In all their decisions commanders were never to lose sight of the:

notion of annihilation, which shines forth from all the battles of Frederick the Great, which pervaded all the operations of Napoleon and on the basis of which Field Marshal Moltke achieved his unrivalled successes.... In the many staff exercise submissions, I have only twice seen the intention expressed: I will annihilate the enemy!... All great commanders have fundamentally done the same thing. When Frederick the Great, on a foggy December morning, marched round the flank of the Austrians... [it was] based on the same idea: the enemy was to be forced against a different front, be defeated and pushed back in a disadvantageous direction.[43]

In his final *Schlussbesprechung* at the end of the 1903 staff ride in the East—a wargaming exercise involving some twenty-five to thirty-five staff officers of all ranks—Schlieffen reiterated that a two-front war, now considered inevitable, 'is not to be brought to an end by repelling one or the other enemy but by the annihilation, first, of the one and then, if possible, of the other'. History furnished enough examples of successful strategies of annihilation: 'Frederick the Great repeatedly aimed at it; Napoleon applied it in 1800, 1805, 1806, 1807, and would have applied in 1809, had not Berthier and his own arrogance ruined it for him. The Allies used the same means in October 1813 to break Napoleonic rule. The late Field Marshal Count Moltke based his successes in August and September 1870 on that same means.' Ultimately, he concluded, the idea of using massed armies to attack the enemy's flank and rear had to be at the core of any future German war plan: 'That is the only way in which we, following the examples of past times, not only can resist our enemies but can also destroy them.'[44]

Whatever its intellectual antecedents and whatever the precise status of Schlieffen's war plan, following his retirement in 1906 he developed in more detail the concept of a large-scale envelopment, followed by the complete destruction of the enemy's forces. Ostensibly inspired by the example of Hannibal's victory over a Roman army twice the size of his Carthaginian force at Cannae in 216 BCE, his reflections appeared in the general staff's in-house strategic studies journal between 1909 and 1913. Cannae furnished the label for Schlieffen's model, but in its essence it was a replica of Leuthen. Revealingly, Schlieffen referred to such a Cannae-style operation as the '*Leuthener Programm*', a far more accurate description than the Carthaginian label.[45] Leuthen had underpinned his modelling exercises since 1901. Now he sought to demonstrate that a campaign of encirclement and annihilation, as the acme of all leadership, was practicable with inferior numbers and—note the echo of Parchwitz—'in spite of all theories.'[46] According to the basic principle ('*Grundform*') of a Cannae-style encounter, 'a broader battle line moves against a narrower but usually deeper battle line. The overhanging wings swing against the flanks and the advancing cavalry against the rear.'[47]

Schlieffen is known to have read the account of Cannae by the Berlin historian Hans Delbrück sometime around 1900 (Fig. 4.3). He was impressed enough to order the *Abteilung* to prepare a series

Fig. 4.3 Hans Delbrück. Wikimedia Commons.

of studies to demonstrate that Hannibal's Apulian victory was a prototype of major modern battles.[48] Varro's rout by a numerically inferior army, led by a gifted general, held obvious attractions for Schlieffen. Frederick, moreover, was placed in a similarly precarious strategic situation in a struggle for Prussia's survival. In this reading Cannae became infused with memories of Leuthen, while the latter was recast as an eighteenth-century version of the former and a template for Germany's next war. Extrapolating from Leuthen, Schlieffen demanded the concentration of all available forces against one point: 'The enemy's front is not the object of the main attack. It is not against it that the masses are to be assembled and the reserves deployed; the essential point is to crush the flanks.'

Frederick, Schlieffen argued, had rediscovered and refined the strategic principle of strategic flanking operations. At Leuthen, his *'inegale force'* of 35,000 was insufficient for any frontal attack. Had he attempted it, his army would have been enveloped itself. In consequence, he 'directed his main attack against the flank'. Contemporary communication was too fragile and the Prussian force 'too *inegale*', and the encounter could only end in a 'truncated Cannae'. And yet, had it not been for the return of a Russian army to Central Europe, Schlieffen speculated, 'Leuthen might well have brought the war to an end soon'. In its conception, a complete Cannae was an integral part of Frederician warfare: 'All these battles, whether Frederick succeeded or failed, are marked by a desire, from the beginning, to attack one flank or perhaps the rear of the enemy, to push him, if possible, against an impassable obstacle and then to destroy him by means of enveloping one or two wings.'[49] Frederick moreover had learnt from experience, and at Leuthen he ignored the enemy's front altogether to concentrate his troops for a flanking manoeuvre. Overwhelmed by the swift Prussian advance and their disciplined fire, Charles of Lorraine's belated formation of a new front left the Austrians as a 'narrow, deep mass'. They could thus be enveloped on the left and right alike: 'They were beaten and because of the imposed change of front were forced into a retreat along the flank with significant losses.'[50]

If this interpretation of Leuthen was somewhat schematic and lacking in complexity, the tendency to invest the person of the monarch with almost super-human qualities was even more problematic. From the pages of the studies produced under the auspices of the general staff Frederick emerged as a commander, whose genius and whose conception of warfare were, in essence, modern. He seemed to anticipate Napoleon Bonaparte and Moltke. There was, in fact, an irrational element to this interpretation. It marked the beginning of his mythologization as a *Feldherr*, a real military leader, a rank to which, according to Schlieffen, one could 'not be appointed, but had to be born and predestined'. General and monarch were indivisibly one, and the combination of Frederick's charismatic personality and superior generalship was the recurring and decisive theme in the *Abteilung*'s historical studies. For Schlieffen, indeed, the grenadiers who stormed the churchyard at Leuthen were not so much Prussian as Frederick's.[51] A 'perfect Cannae' was rarely found in the history of war. It required a commander who had something of 'a Frederick the Great, who brings all cannon and rifles into action, of a Frederick the Great or a Napoleon, who directs the main attack against the flank or rear, or of a Frederick the Great or a Moltke, who replaces the absent Hasdrubal with a natural obstacle or the frontier of a neutral state'.[52]

This one-sided interpretation of Frederick and of Leuthen, with its strong emphasis on the operational aspects of warfighting at the exclusion of other elements of grand strategy, was to sink under the weight of its own wishful propositions in the mud of Flanders. Previous large-scale battles, Schlieffen had propounded in his last essay on the subject, had been 'approximate battles of annihilation'. Yet there was to be no new Leuthen, no complete Cannae.

Already before then Schlieffen's and the general staff's reading of Frederick's strategy was challenged by contemporary writers. Turning Frederick into a near-infallible hero was not only questionable in scholarly terms, it was also deeply problematic with a view to the general staff's core activities. For the officially approved version of Frederick as the heroic leader was so tightly enmeshed with the strategic axioms and operational plans of the military leadership of the *Kaiserreich* that any form of revisionism threatened their coherence, and by implication the exalted position of the general staff itself.[53]

Revisionism, of course, reared its head, and it did so at the prompting of an unlikely source. In 1878 Taysen produced the first ever edition of Frederick's military testament of 1768, replete with extensive commentary and scholarly annotations. In his observations Taysen touched on an obvious discrepancy between the views expressed in this document and the ideas propounded, a decade earlier, in Frederick's reflections on military tactics and the concept of the battle of annihilation with which senior staff officers had invested Frederick's operations. In 1758, the king had stressed that the 'fate of a state may often depend on a single decisive battle; if one detects an advantage in it, one should engage in it'.[54] This was in line with the official reading of Frederician warfare. But a complication arose in the king's advocacy, in his later testament, of a defensive, positional type of warfare, focused on taking up strong positions and avoiding field battles whenever possible, the kind which he was to practise in the War of the Bavarian Succession ten years later.

This discrepancy between Frederick the ideal-type annihilationist and the reality of the battle-hardened tactician whom experience had taught caution was awkward. Taysen was enough of a scholar, however, not to suppress or redact the document: 'In the place of bold initiative and the instigation of major tactical decisions we witness here almost exclusively the so-called "methodical warfare"...—in short, one sometimes cannot believe these to be Frederick's words but of one of those generals who let him win his bold and risky game by their ponderosity and caution.' Taysen sought to explain the disparity away by suggesting that it was more apparent than real. The king, he asserted, was discussing here the specific, if hypothetical, case of another conflict with Austria. The further weakening of the Habsburg Empire was politically inopportune since it might induce Vienna to enter another anti-Prussian coalition. For that reason Frederick had to avoid battles if war itself could not be averted.[55]

It was a neat explanation; it was also a sleight of hand. For Frederick's reflections on the greater merits of defensive dispositions were part of the chapter on the fundamental principles of war. With this sleight of hand, Taysen sought to salvage Frederick the strategist of annihilation, founding father of modern warfare and forerunner of Moltke. What made it more ironic still was the fact that Taysen's emphasis on context—standard for any professional historian—flew in the face of the general staff's assertion of immutable principles of warfare.

Chief among the revisionist critics was the historian and political commentator Hans Delbrück. It was one of the ironies of the ensuing 'Strategiestreit' between him and general staff historians that it was his analysis of Cannae that had inspired Schlieffen. In some respects, Delbrück was an impeccable insider. His was a typical Bildungsbürger, middle-class family which had furnished Prussia with numerous civil servants and professors—he himself had tutored the youngest son of the future emperor Frederick III and was later a Freikonservativ deputy in the Prussian diet (1882–5) and the Reichstag (1884–90).[56] And yet his dedication to rigorous scholarship, irrespective of political convenience, made him something of an outsider in academia and public life, and a professorial chair at Berlin University long eluded him.[57] By chance he became the biographer of Gneisenau, and the immersion in the general's papers whetted his interest in military history as much as it sharpened his appreciation of the chasm between Napoleonic warfare and the wars of the Old Regime, something that Clausewitz had grasped but that the historians of the Abteilung tended to ignore.[58]

Delbrück's early work sowed a life-long concern with military history and strategy, conceived of as embedded in broader historical developments, and culminating in his four-volume History of the Art of War.[59] The history of war, he observed in a later essay on ancient Rome's legendary sixth king, was to no small degree constitutional history. More, it needed to be placed in its precise geographical and political as well as economic and social contexts:

'The historian who wishes to narrate wars or more still the history of the art of war also has to study the material conditions and the technical possibilities of past events until he controls them with complete mastery.'[60]

This broader understanding ran counter to the intellectual habits of the official military historians, who could conceive of their subject only in narrow 'technical' terms and who assumed that, in their innermost essence, the underlying principles of strategy remained unchanged across the centuries. Delbrück, by contrast, was a happy iconoclast and no respecter of taboos, if the logic of his research demanded it. Already in 1879 he had taken aim at Taysen's commentary on Frederick's military testament. The monarch's express 'disinclination to fight battles' was nothing but a 'continuation of an already existing idea', he argued.[61] He returned to the charge over the next few years, most notably in his 1887 comparative study of Frederician and Napoleonic strategy, in which he demonstrated that the king had insufficient means for a strategy of annihilation. Meticulously he threaded quote after quote on a long string of evidence that presented Frederick as an accomplished practitioner of 'methodical' warfare. None of this, Delbrück asserted, perhaps to deflect charges of unpatriotic sentiments, could detract from Frederick's historic greatness. Leuthen, Rossbach, Zorndorf, and Torgau, and even the defeats at Kolín and Kunersdorf, stood out against the 'drab grey background of manoeuvres evolving year on year': 'Only once one has placed oneself with him [Frederick] in his century can one discern how the figure of the great king towers not above a bunch of pygmies but even an assembly of heroes.'[62]

Frustrated at the limited echo his arguments found, Delbrück then resorted to the means of parody, in the guise of an examination of the strategy of Pericles, whose seemingly dilatory and defensive operations were frequently criticized by classical scholars. Delbrück dismissed such criticism by arguing that his strategy was conditioned by the nature of the Athenian *polis* and its society. Neither permitted the kind of extensive military service needed to pursue the sustained offensives Pericles' latter-day critics seemed to envisage. With these constraining factors and faced by a large hostile coalition, the Athenian leader pursued a strategy of attrition ('*Ermattungsstrategie*') and of limited war, as opposed to one of subjection and annihilation ('*Niederwerfungsstrategie*').[63] At the root of modern criticism of Periclean strategy, he argued, lay a misunderstanding of Clausewitz's apparent preoccupation with the idea of annihilation, even though the general himself had sought to develop a concept of attrition.[64] To drive home this point, Delbrück compared Pericles to Frederick, who faced similar challenges and whose strategic genius was no less than Napoleon's. But ancien régime warfare did not allow for the complete *Niederwerfung* of the enemy. No doubt deliberately, Delbrück's argument was provocative. He accused his opponents of 'party politicking by the so powerful royalism in this state'. Above all, it was a direct attack on the '*Friedrich-Theologen*' and other dogmatists of annihilation who rhapsodized on the quasi-apostolic line of succession from Frederick through Napoleon and on to Moltke.[65]

Delbrück's nomenclature was also bound to jar. '*Ermattung*' implied a state of exhaustion, and the corresponding adjective, '*matt*', indicated feebleness or lethargy, neither attributes usually associated with the great king. This terminological choice alone was designed to rile official historians, and it explains some of the bile in their response.[66] To compound his act of sacrilege, Delbrück prefixed his study of Pericles with what he called a 'methodical parody', in which he examined Frederick's campaign in the Seven Years' War. Its purpose was to show the king as acting within the parameters of eighteenth-century war and society. Frederick had drawn up four war plans, but all of them defensive. The initiative always lay with his enemies. Could, he asked facetiously, a commander who understood the importance of seizing the initiative make his own decisions dependent on the actions of others? Far from aiming at the destruction of Habsburg military power, a goal unattainable with his resources, Frederick sought to weaken Austria so that only part the Prussian forces was needed to keep it pinned back in Bohemia, while the remainder of his army could take on the French or Russians. Rossbach and Leuthen were the high points the war, deeds of courage and determination. But, ultimately, the one was a victory over the miserable *Reichsarmee* rabble, the other an easy whipping of Württembergers, fellow-Protestants reluctant to fight a Protestant prince. From 1758 on, Frederick's campaigns conformed more and more to the precepts of manoeuvre warfare, and he fought no more battles after 1762. In the end little was left of Frederick the statesman or strategist. His reputation lay in tatters. And yet his operations 'exuded a certain magic. There are, it seems, names in whom humanity believes and once that belief has become entrenched, it cannot be disputed away by criticism. Odd, very odd!'[67]

Delbrück's reflection was prescient, but the entrenched resistance to his efforts to historicize Frederick's wars was not so odd after all. They posed a dual threat to the intellectual and institutional hegemony of Germany's military leadership. If Frederick's aim was not the annihilation of the enemy, then this removed the principal intellectual prop from underneath current war planning. Staff officers in the *Abteilung* were wont to brush the professor off as a mere '*Zivilstratege*' or a '*Kathederstratege*', a 'strategist of the lectern', who presumed 'to understand Clausewitz better than the army had ever done'.[68] His meticulous source analysis and incisive logic could not be gainsaid so easily, however. Delbrück's oeuvre, indeed, threatened the general staff's defence-intellectual monopoly on war studies and military history. Jealously shielded against the forays of civilian interlopers, it was yet another aspect of the military's privileged political and social position in the *Kaiserreich*.[69]

The general staff qua institution refrained from becoming embroiled with the disputatious Delbrück. Individual officers, especially the two Bernhardis, and other historians affiliated with it, however, were encouraged to attack his criticism of the heroic Frederick orthodoxy. For three decades the so-called *Strategiestreit* ('strategy dispute') rumbled on with varying degrees of intensity.[70]

Often his adversaries descended to low ad hominem jibes. Yet the more aggressive their line of attack, the more deeply Delbrück dug into the original sources to refute the arguments of his opponents. The controversy thus stimulated the production of a whole series of document collections around the turn of the century, not just relating to Frederick's wars but to Brandenburg-Prussian history in the round.[71] And the more original sources were brought to light, the more untenable became the officially approved version of Frederick as the apostle of annihilation.

The original sources also laid bare Frederick's real strategic dilemma. Prussia's limited material and manpower resources militated against a protracted conflict. In this context, battle, especially a decisive one, was an attractive proposition. Victory might bring about a swift end to the war. On the other hand, Frederick's army, composed of native recruits as much as non-native mercenaries, was no more trustworthy than other armies of the period. And the king was very much a man of his times, who would not risk such a potentially unreliable instrument unnecessarily. The tension between the two objects of destroying the enemy and preserving his own forces therefore always lay at the heart of his operations.

Gradually, Delbrück's superior scholarship prevailed in the *Strategiestreit*. Even Frederick's political calculations, assumed to be defensive, were no longer sacrosanct. In 1894, the Göttingen historian Max Lehmann argued on the basis of the king's hitherto unpublished political testament of 1752 that he hoped to acquire parts of Saxony, West Prussia, and Swedish Pomerania. Thus, '[t]here was a confluence of two offensives in 1756; that of Maria Theresa, aimed at the reconquest of Silesia, that by Frederick, aimed at conquering West Prussia and Saxony'.[72] The process of professionalization of military history was now under way, and Delbrück had provided the initial spark.

The collapse of the *Kaiserreich* relieved the general staff from the painful need to reassess the Frederician military tradition in line with proper scholarly methods. Yet Frederick's name continued to exude its 'odd' magic. His popular reputation as a German national battle hero survived the Kaiser's flight into exile to serve as a counterfoil to the perceived chaos of the Weimar years and then as a means of mobilizing the masses in support of the Nazi regime.

5

Myth and Memory

Leuthen's Political and Cultural Legacy

The wider cultural and political legacy of the battle of Leuthen mirrored its reception in Prusso-German military thought. Leuthen emerged as a shorthand for a specific Prusso-Protestant sense of national mission, a certain habit of mind, a general attitude that reflected and, in turn, influenced the cultural and political life of nineteenth- and twentieth-century Germany.

It was not until the second half of the nineteenth century that Leuthen took on a specific cultural meaning. Even the imagery associated with battle-weary and exhausted soldiers intoning the 'Chorale of Leuthen', so potent later on, did not take shape until then. For contemporaries, manifestations of religious sentiments were anything but remarkable. Prayers before battle, thanks-giving services afterwards, hymns and other religious practices, after all, were a firm part of early modern battle rituals, just as marches—the punctuated rhythm and 4/4 tact of an infantry march and the 6/8 of a cavalry one—accompanied soldiers into and during battle. Princes commissioned their court composer to write a *Te Deum* or a mass to celebrate victory; soldiers expressed their emotions, not least their gratitude for having survived the ordeal of battle, in religious song.[1] Religion, as a political factor might well have declined since the seventeenth century, but war was still infused with religious sentiments. At Rossbach, for instance, Frederick's victorious troops were reported to have sung church hymns: 'All around, probably from every regiment, arose the solemn sounds of their chorales into the night sky.'[2]

The notion of *the* 'Chorale of Leuthen' was clearly a later construct. That *'Nun danket alle Gott'*, the chorale later synonymous with Leuthen, was sung after the battle, is beyond doubt. Very likely, it was one of many that were intoned, probably spontaneously by different units. It was only in the final war against Napoleon Bonaparte that the 'Leuthen chorale' was designated the Prussian army's thanks-giving anthem, first after the battle of Möckern (5 April 1813) and then after Waterloo (15 June 1815).[3]

Until the collapse of the Prussian state at Jena and Auerstedt, memories of Rossbach outshone the victory at Leuthen. In popular imagery, Frederick, the austere and unostentatious monarch, who had withstood the onslaught of overmighty enemies and their knavish machinations, predominated. His stoicism in the face of adversity, his military genius, the courage of his troops and the unbreakable bond between monarch and soldiers were the *leitmotif* in popular culture. It already influenced the odes of Johann Wilhelm Ludwig Gleim, especially his *Preussische Kriegslieder*, inspired in their conception and their metre by old English ballads, such as *Chevy Chase*. Gleim's verses idealized and idolized the king, who was not only heroic and wise but also an instrument of Divine intervention: 'When Frederick, or God through him, / Has accomplished the great work, / Tamed proud Vienna, / And set Germany free' (*Wenn Friedrich, oder Gott durch ihn, / Das grosse Werk Vollbracht, / Gebändigt hat das stolze Wien, / Und Deutschland frey gemacht*).[4]

Pictorial art likewise represented the king, his officers and soldiers as a unit. Especially the etchings by Daniel Nikolaus Chodowiecki gave shape to the popular figure of *'der alte Fritz'*, as the epitome of the ideal monarch, doughty in war, neglectful of his own appearance, covered in snuff and dust, but ever-solicitous to the needs of his subjects.[5] This was also very much the king as depicted by the Swiss artist Anton Graff in 1781 (Fig. 5.1). Eschewing all ornaments, it sharply deviated

Fig. 5.1 Frederick II by Anton Graff. Wikimedia Commons.

from the usual style of in royal portraiture, and to some extent anticipated nineteenth-century bourgeois aesthetics. Graff focused on the king's face, his large eyes, watchful yet benevolent, and his Roman nose. His forehead is bathed in light, and there is the hint of a smile about his lips. This was a benign ruler and solicitous *Landesvater*.[6] In this fashion, the person of the Prussian king became the focus of proto-patriotic ideas.

The first detailed account of the Seven Years' War, published in 1789 and revised in 1793, captured some of that atmosphere. Johann Wilhelm von Archenholtz, a Prussian army captain who, as a young cadet, had fought in the conflict and who later earned a reputation as a political and military writer, concluded his *Geschichte des Siebenjährigen Krieges* by reflecting on the wider significant of this war. With the war, he suggested, began the cultural rise of the German nation:

It was at this period in the midst of the most fearful war that the
refinement and progress of arts took their rise among the Germans; and
it would appear that such has been the case among the most celebrated
people.... So it was in the time of Frederic with the Germans.... During
the time that all Europe was astonished at their deeds in the field they were
gaining laurels in the regions of learning and taking up a position as
an educated people that few nations had attained for the last thousand
years.... The muses, who had been scared by the tumult of war so soon
after their first appearance in Germania now returned to their peaceful
homes...; and the most brilliant period in Germany was, as in Rome,
when... the temple of Janus was closed.[7]

As with the earlier cases of artistic and cultural flourishing, so German
culture turned away from the Prussian monarch. Popular memory,
often drawing on anecdotes and taking inspiration from images, stood
at variance to late eighteenth-century high culture. Even some of the
leading Prussian reformers, such as Baron von Stein, while apprecia-
tive of the king's achievements, were critical of his autocratic habits:
'all elements expected the necessary impulse from above; nowhere
was there autonomy or a sense of self-worth.'[8] To the representatives
of early German romanticism the seemingly desiccated enlightenment
roi philosophe Frederick held little attraction. Such diverse writers as
Ernst Moritz Arndt, the poet Novalis (Friedrich von Hardenberg), and
Adam Müller laid stress on the cold-hearted functionality of Frederician Prussia, which they contrasted with their own idealized conception of popular, above all Christian monarchy. Politics to them were in
essence a matter of aesthetics, and to them Frederick's state was a
soulless machine which lacked the nobility of higher ideals.[9]

Prussian ultra-conservatives during the restoration period found
Frederick equally unappealing. They could not deny that his *Macht-
politik* had laid the foundations of Prussia's rise. Yet, the monarch
proved rather problematic for their purposes on several counts. Intellectually, his sardonic secularism ran counter to the principal tenets of
the Holy Alliance and the idea of the divine right of kings that
underpinned this neo-mediaeval ideological and diplomatic pact. In

his materialism they saw the yeast of potential revolutionary ferment, which could only endanger the organic order they hoped to preserve. Here, too, aesthetics was interlaced with ideology and practical politics. Celebrations to mark the centenary of Frederick's succession in 1840 struck Ernst Ludwig von Gerlach, one of the most sophisticated of ultra-conservatives, as 'taste- and thoughtless flatteries' and he refused to join the toast to the spirit of Frederick in the presence of the then king.[10] Considerations of current politics also made celebrations of this sort appear inopportune. At a time when the small craft of Prussian diplomacy drifted in the wake of the major conservative powers Austria and Russia, any manifestation of Prussian patriotism that was rooted in the great king's wars with his Habsburg rival was politically awkward. Conservatives of the period, moreover, shared with their liberal opponents an abiding suspicion of Frederick's charismatic personality and his autocratic tendencies, which, they contended, had stifled the live elements and creative forces of his people.[11]

Whatever the aversions of poets and intellectuals, Frederick the ideal monarch never entirely disappeared from public discourse. Already during the French occupation, Friedrich Daniel Ernst Schleiermacher, the leading Protestant theologian of that time, sought to establish him as an exemplar of wise of kingship, frugal in his habits but inspired by a sense of duty towards his people. In one of his 'Patriotic Sermons', delivered on 24 January 1808, the anniversary of Frederick's birth, he stressed the progressive aspects of the king's reign:

> For ... just as certainly as the construction of the state that he erected, the spirit in which he ruled it, bore the imprint of greatness, so equally was goodness in it, which we must not lose.... Nor must we forget how always during the reign of that great king the principle of equality of all before the law predominated. Let us remind ourselves how public opinion followed his example even more strongly, how the sharp dividing lines between the different Estates ... began to disappear ... and how, by contrast, the more unforced, more harmonious association between persons of different rank became possible.[12]

Schleiermacher's progressive interpretation of Frederick anticipated the monarch's re-evaluation by mid-century German liberals. It reflected the 'cult of the genius' that shaped so much of Germany's cultural output in the first half of the century.[13] And it resonated with the popular image of the Frederician era and its monarch, as disseminated in the biography—really a string of anecdotes—by Franz Kugler, an art historian and sometime official in the Prussian Ministry of Education,[14] and illustrated by Adolph (von) Menzel, then a largely unknown artist but soon to be the most significant representative of historical portraiture in Germany.[15] Menzel's illustrations were to shape the popular image of Frederick for generations of Germans until well into the twentieth century. Kugler accorded Leuthen a more prominent place than had been customary. Significantly, he fused the king's scepticism in all matters religious with the religiosity of the common soldier. In so doing, he reasserted an older theme. On a regimental commander enquiring whether he should forbid his troops from singing the usual eve-of-battle chorale, he records Frederick as having replied: 'No, let them be: with men like these God will surely grant me victory.'

It was not this, however, not the victory against the odds nor its musical coda, that stood in the foreground, but Frederick's address to his generals at Parchwitz. The main focus, then, was not on the king as monarch or as heroic leader but on a collective, the ruler and his loyal and brave generals and soldiers, who jointly vanquished a far superior enemy. Frederick's genius inspired them to fight 'against all the rules [of war]'. His address, Kugler wrote, 'coursed through the veins of the gentlemen present, fanned a new fire to distinguish themselves through exceptional gallantry and to sacrifice blood and life for their great monarch.... This was followed by a solemn silence on the part of his audience, and a certain enthusiasm...signalled to him the complete devotion of his army.' The enthusiasm 'flooded over all officers and soldiers of the army.... Since then a certain inner feeling of resolve and confidence was noticeable in everyone, commonly a happy omen of future victory.'[16] In this manner the Kugler—Menzel biography framed one of the principal themes of the nineteenth- and twentieth-century Leuthen myth.

A visual representation of the union of monarch and army was furnished by Christian Daniel Rauch's equestrian statue of Frederick on *Unter den Linden* in the heart of Berlin, a 43-foot-high (13.34 m) monument of the king resting on a three-tiered pedestal, the central section of which is surrounded by smaller statues of Frederick's generals as well as a smaller number of artists, composers, ministers, and other intellectual figures (Fig. 5.2). A monument of some kind had been discussed variously in the 1790s and 1820s only for the idea to be dropped, until Gustav Adolf von Rochow, then an official in the Ministry of the Interior, brought revived it again. It was not commissioned until 1839, however, and not completed for another dozen years after that. When unveiling the statue in May 1851, Frederick William IV laid particular stress on the alliance of monarchy and army. In its design Rauch's monument was closely modelled on examples from antiquity, such as the equestrian statue of Marcus Aurelius on the Capitoline Hill in Rome. His head is tilted slightly, accentuating his sharp profile with the famous Roman nose, and with a cloak draped, toga-like, around his shoulders. Yet the monument deviated from classical models in certain respects, not least in that instead of a sabre Frederick is holding his well-known cane. Here was the ideal type of a '*Volkskönig*', for which Rauch drew heavily on the popular idea of the '*alte Fritz*', as popularized by Kugler and Menzel.[17] Ironically, although it was meant to symbolize the old, pre-1848 Prussia, the statue also appealed to Liberals who appropriated it for their own purposes. Soon after its formal unveiling an anonymous ditty was glued to its pedestal: '*Alter Fritz* descend to us below, / And rule the Prussians once again. / Let in these terrible times, Frederick William ride away.'[18]

Inadvertently, Rauch's Frederick had become a counterfoil to Prussia's current ruler. The melancholy monarch, whose accession to the throne coincided with the centenary of that of his great-great uncle, held conflicting views in which ancestral veneration and moral

Fig. 5.2 Frederick II (1712–86). Bronze equestrian statue on Unter den Linden in Berlin, completed in 1851 by Christian Daniel Rauch. Photographed *c.*1900. Alamy, FFANAA.

disapprobation mingled in equal measure. He was the first ruler since Frederick to live at Sanssouci on a regular basis, and during his reign Frederick's collected works were published. At the same time, he felt revulsion at the great king's notorious irreligiosity. No less significant,

162

while Frederick's fame rested on his victories on the battlefield, he saw his own role as that of a guarantor of European peace. Such was his commitment to this idea, it has been suggested, that Potsdam's *Friedenskirche* (Church of Peace) in the park of Sanssouci, begun in 1845, exactly one hundred years after Frederick's palace, was intended as an architectural statement, a deliberate 'ideological counterpoint' to the enlightened scepticism epitomized by the king's retreat.[19]

His pacific sentiments notwithstanding, Frederick William IV's affirmation of the union of army and state three years after the revolutionary events of 1848 was significant. It was the army, after all, which had saved the near-absolute monarchy. The events of that year and then the re-emergence of the Austro-Prussian dualism set in motion a profound reassessment of Frederick and of Leuthen. In Liberal circles the so-called Punctation of Olmütz (Olomouc) of November 1850 was resented as a humiliating political defeat at the hands of Habsburg diplomacy, which strove to preserve in aspic the old structures of 1815 and keep Prussia in a junior position. Most Liberals turned into *kleindeutsche* disciples of *realpolitik*, abjuring the 'castles in the air' that had characterized the rostrums of *Vormärz*-Liberals. However reluctantly, they now embraced the notion of a *Machtstaat*, a state forged by and based on military might.[20] Those years also marked the beginning of Frederick's transformation into a national hero for a new century.[21]

There was another aspect to his posthumous transfiguration. At a time when the Austro-Prussian dualism resurfaced, Frederick's military successes were invested with a decidedly anti-Austrian, *kleindeutsche*, and Protestant meaning. For Liberals as much as for moderate conservatives, such as the prime minister Otto von Manteuffel, he now appeared as an early advocate of German unification under Prussian leadership.[22] To fulfil its 'German mission', Prussia needed a powerful army and a latter-day *roi connétable*. In the final decade of Frederick William IV's reign both were noticeable only by their absence. The monarch himself slowly descended into a debilitating depression, buffeted by the demands of competing factions, as reforming ministers jostled for position with a reactionary *camarilla* at court, before a series of apoplectic strokes completely incapacitated him; and the army was in a desolate condition.[23]

The stasis in Prussian politics also affected the manner in which Leuthen was memorialized. By 1858/9 Frederick William IV's prostration was complete. In a curious reversal, liberal opinion now pinned its hopes on the Regent, Prince William. Liberals of the previous decade had condemned him as the '*Kartätschenprinz*' ('shrapnel prince') in view of his strong advocacy, at least for a while, of suppressing revolutionary activities in 1848. Now they increasingly saw in him and the Hohenzollern dynasty a suitable vehicle for overdue reforms and for achieving some form of German unification. If startling, the reversal was real enough. It also affected the painter Menzel, whose illustrations had done so much to popularize the image of Frederick as '*Volkskönig*'. As a pictorial homage to the *Neue Ära* inaugurated by William's regency, he conceived of a painting of Frederick's Parchwitz address (Fig. 5.3). Menzel planned on a large scale, and with it he returned to a subject with which he had dealt on numerous occasions before, not least in his illustrations for Kugler's biography. In the summer of 1859, he wrote: 'I am once more engaged in something big...: namely, Fritz's address to his men before the *va banque* at Leuthen. It means painting a moral effect.'[24] In its composition, the painting revealed Menzel's programme. It placed the king off centre, speaking to his generals, who form a semi-circle around him. Their posture, leaning forward and their heads mostly bowed, signalled attentiveness to their monarch's quietly spoken words and devotion to his person. Yet there could be no doubt that he was one of them. He could not be confident of victory. It was his officers, their loyalty to him, their courage, and their military skill that would decide the outcome of the battle against a far superior enemy. The spectator's eye, moreover, is drawn towards a few cavalrymen and beyond, indistinct in the mist-shrouded distance, dispersed foot soldiers. On view was the symbolic union of monarch, army, and people.

Fig. 5.3 Parchwitz address, Adolph von Menzel's unfinished painting. Wikimedia Commons.

Menzel's high hopes for William's regency remained unfulfilled and their artistic expression unfinished. Indeed, the areas of blank canvas, the scratched faces and obvious traces of later attempts at repainting suggest a tragedy.[25] The constitutional crisis over control of the army budget did not bode well for Menzel's artistic concept of a symbolic union between monarch and people. Worse, the Liberals' defeat in the *Verfassungskonflikt*, engineered by the new prime minister, Otto von Bismarck, now serving King William I, made the army independent of parliament, an instrument of the monarch and his chief minister. The subsequent collapse of Prussian Liberalism rendered obsolete the notion of a union of ruler, army, and people. The experience of a common, 'national' endeavour during the Wars of Liberation in 1813–15 had popularized this idea. It had survived the failure of the 1848 revolution; it ended with barely a whimper when the Liberal majority in the *Landtag* broke in the face of Bismarck's immovability. Disappointed, Menzel abandoned his monumental painting.[26]

What was now wanted was a clearer identification of the monarch with the army and greater emphasis on the military genius of Frederick. The Silesian-born novelist and playwright Gustav Freytag's *Bilder aus der deutschen Vergangenheit* gave literary expression to this new image of the monarch. A work on popular, middle-brow lines, illustrating the history and customs of the German people from the late Roman period to the middle of the nineteenth century, it drew on previous anecdotal Frederician literature. During the Seven Years' War, Freytag wrote, Frederick's:

> conduct of war astounded all armies of Europe. How he positioned his lines against the enemy, always the faster and more nimble one, how he so often in oblique order outflanked, drove back and threw over the weaker wing of the enemy, how his cavalry...threw itself furiously onto the enemy, tore apart his ranks, all that was recognized everywhere as the latest progress in the art of war, [and] praised as an invention of the greatest genius. For almost half a century the tactics and strategy of the Prussian army became the model and pattern for all forces of Europe. There was unanimity that Frederick was the greatest commander of his time, that before him...there had been few army leaders who could be compared to him.[27]

The successes of 1864, 1866, and 1870/1 were taken to vindicate the quasi-autonomous position of the army. Dybbøl, Königgrätz, and Sedan affirmed the essential correctness of the *kleindeutsche* programme, as whose pioneer Frederick was now invariably presented. Inevitably, perhaps, '*Nun danket alle Gott*' was sung at the proclamation of William I as German emperor in Versailles' *salle des glaces*.[28]

The Frederician and the Leuthen myths underwent yet another subtle change in the years after 1870. Prussia's 'German mission' now took on a decidedly more Protestant hue. Frederick stood in the tradition of Martin Luther and Gustavus II Adolphus, the Swedish king whose intervention in the Thirty Years' War had made him a Protestant hero in Germany. A political genealogy that reached from the Vasa king to the victor of Leuthen and on to William I was a prominent theme in the historiography and political journalism of the time.[29] Heinrich von Treitschke, the influential historian and apostle of Prusso-German nationalism, drew an explicit line from the *Reformator* and the Nordic ruler to Frederick: 'Just as Luther and Gustavus Adolphus, the only real heroes before him, . . . so Frederick was feared in the lands under the crozier [i.e. the ecclesiastical principalities of the *ancien régime*] on Rhine and Main as the great enemy.'[30] In this reading the Prussian monarch emerged as a fighter for Protestant liberties against ultramontane obscurantism, a useful ally in the *Kulturkampf* struggle of the 1870s between the Berlin government and the Catholic clergy in Germany.[31]

The impact of the elective Gustavus Adolphus—Frederick affinity was by no means confined to the years around the *Reichsgründung*. The mythogenesis of Frederick as a Protestant hero continuing the work of the Swedish warrior-king illustrates the unique blend of Protestantism and racialism that proved highly effective until well into the twentieth century. The Reformation scholar Max Lenz, one of the leading historians of the Wilhelmine period, repeatedly drew a parallel between the two soldier-kings' Protestant and German missions, both of which he invested with confessional significance.[32] Lenz and others could draw on their inherent sense of destiny in the summer of 1914. In a pamphlet with the revealing title *Der deutsche Gott* he invoked the 'wonderous beatifying power of war' when establishing beyond doubt that God had always stood on the side of the righteous. Germany would emerge victorious from this war because she had to and because God would not abandon them. Just as Gustavus Adolphus musketeers at Lützen, Lenz reminded his readers during the Reformation jubilee in 1917, so Prussian soldiers fought under the motto of '*Gott mit uns*'.[33]

The Gustavus–Frederick genealogy was not a matter of confessional aspects alone. It was also marked by a racialist undertone. A strongly developed, essentially Germanic sense of national duty, Lenz and others asserted, reinforced the two rulers' sense of Protestant mission. Combined, they fuelled the rise of the until then small and insignificant Swedish and Prussian states. In a lecture to mark the 200th anniversary of the creation of the kingdom of Prussia in 1901, Erich Marcks, one of the rising stars of German historical scholarship, articulated this argument with admirable, if perhaps dubious, clarity. He reflected on the union between Prussia and 'Protestant-Germanic England' in the Seven Years' War, which had secured 'the Germanic race and its creed their existence in the wide world'.[34] Assumptions of affinities between kindred 'races' were common in educated discourse in the long nineteenth century, with its highly developed sense of international and other hierarchies. Nor were they confined to Germany.[35] Even so, the emphasis on a Germanic racial identity created a new dimension to the Frederician myth which was to be revived to devastating effect in the years after 1918.

In the 1870s, following the creation of the German Empire, Prussia appeared to have fulfilled its 'German mission'; it had redeemed the *Reich* out of the spirit of Northern Protestantism.[36] Against this backdrop Leuthen and its 'Chorale' were now invested with a quasi-sacral significance. The court chaplain Adolf Stoecker, whose theology combined Protestant orthodoxy with Prusso-German exceptionalism and a hefty dose of antisemitism, played a significant role in this process. In one of his sermons, he asserted that 'the trace of God' was clearly discernible in the development of the German lands from 1517 onwards, culminating in the proclamation, in 1871, of the 'Holy Protestant Empire of the German Nation'.[37] Frederick's chorale-singing grenadiers had thus been recruited as early fighters for a new empire.

As seen in the previous chapter, in the 'Borussian' reading Frederick's three Silesian wars created the necessary political conditions for the Bismarck's creation in 1871. Yet the de facto division of Germany following the extrusion of Austria from German affairs in 1866 lessened the immediate political utility of the Leuthen myth, the anti-Austrian poise of the myth having been made largely redundant. Its anti-Catholic element, moreover, was less than opportune given the continued strains between political Catholicism and the Berlin government in the wake of the *Kulturkampf*.[38] Leuthen, then, was reimagined once again, this time as symbolizing a specific type of

Fig. 5.4 Parchwitz address by Karl Roeber. Image from the author's own collection.

Prusso-German warfare, centred principally on the figure of the king as heroic warrior and leader.

The 1888/9 painting of Frederick at Parchwitz by Fritz Roeber, an artist associated with the Düsseldorf school of painting, known for its use of subdued colours, captured the post-1871 version of the Leuthen myth (Fig. 5.4). In contrast to Menzel's more ambiguous treatment of the subject, the king is the focal point of the compositional arrangement here. With his arm raised for declamatory effect, and nonchalantly leaning on his cane, his is a commanding presence that exudes confidence. His generals surround the king in two semi-circles, their attitude a mixture of attention, devotion, and determination. Roeber's painting sought to glorify Frederick's military genius, and by implication his offensive type of warfare. But equally, it sought to give visual expression to the now dominant military orthodoxy that considered itself rooted in Frederick's strategy in the Seven Years' War. Tellingly,

Roeber's painting was commissioned by the Prussian war ministry to adorn the walls of Berlin's *Zeughaus* (Royal Armoury).[39] Frederick's historic achievements were thus linked to an assumed specifically Prussian ethos. Its Protestant roots inculcated a strong sense of duty and loyalty towards the state and the ruling dynasty; its Germanic roots, meanwhile, lent it warrior-like qualities.[40]

Such qualities were also foregrounded in popular literature. A brief survey of Prussian history to mark the bicentenary of the monarchy for younger readers by Friedrich Polack, a pedagogue and writer of patriotic and local history books, made this point emphatically. His readers learnt that Frederick defeated an enemy three times stronger. The Parchwitz address was mentioned, and so was the 'Chorale': 'and finally the whole army sang the uplifting "Chorale of Leuthen".' Frederick's 'wonderful victory', Polack observed, 'cleansed Silesia of the enemies. Soldiers and young country lads sang: "Long live by the Grace of the Highest the King, who shall protect us / And so he will beat with his *Wachtparade* yet another eighty thousand men."'[41] The figure of Frederick was frequently presented as the epitome of ideal kingship in popular works. It was '"the" King *per se* that materialized in the person of the Frederick the Great', asserted Gustav Mendelssohn Bartholdy in introducing his character sketch *Der König*, a work covering the full gamut of the Leuthen myth, from Parchwitz to the chorale—Mendelssohn referred to it as 'the German Te Deum'—and the apocryphal aftermath of the battle at the chateau at Lissa.[42]

Artistic representations nevertheless played a prominent role in entrenching the Leuthen myth in its latest *Kaiserreich* incarnation. As seen, under the auspices of the General Staff, historical research into Frederick's campaigns was a form of applied history. The great king's operations were sacrosanct, and the purpose of research was to distil the essential core of strategy so as to supply the necessary historical and intellectual underpinnings for current military planning. The three Silesian wars, and individual campaigns in the Seven Years' War in particular, furnished a form of historical legitimation of future offensive wars and a sort of intellectual guarantee of successes of such operations against a coalition of enemy powers.

Art helped to perpetuate and popularize such ideas, often through the medium of lavishly produced illustrated books, such as *Bildersaal deutscher Geschichte* by Adolf Bär and Paul Quensel, and cheaper postcard reproductions. To an extent it was a form of vulgarization that stripped out the moral ambiguities and complex relations in Menzel's portraiture and replaced them with them with simpler messages. In the historical paintings by the appropriately named Arthur Kampf fighting scenes and the depiction of heroic deaths on the battlefield predominated. For one of them, reproduced in the Bär and Quensel compendium, he chose the aftermath of Leuthen as his subject. Titled 'Nun *danket alle Gott*', it was but the latest variation on the 'Chorale' theme. In the foreground a motley crew of Prussian soldiers from different units are seen kneeling on the rutted and snow-covered ground against a slate-grey sky, their hands folded in prayer, their faces etched with exhaustion and yet illuminated by the elation of victory. In the distance looms a group of officers, their heads bared and bowed, but already looking towards whatever lay beyond the horizon.[43] More striking still, *Fridericus immortalis* (*c.*1890) by Georg Schöbel showed the king ascending from the vault of the Potsdam garrison church, a sword in his right and in the left the standard of the elite *Garde du Corps* cuirassiers (Fig. 5.5). With a halo-like light effect around his head, the picture is strongly reminiscent of contemporary images of the resurrection of Christ, and, to an extent, it anticipated the reimaging of the king during the crisis years of the 1920s and early 1930s.[44]

Another, even more popular, painter of the Wilhelmine period was Carl Roechling, who specialized in military subjects and whose illustrations for a popular children's book *Der Alte Fritz* made him a household name.[45] His paintings of the onslaught on the walled churchyard of Leuthen, and especially the grenadiers of the 15th (Guards) Regiment storming the breach in the wall, quickly established themselves as part of the popular Frederician canon. They were

Fig. 5.5 Fredericus Immortalis von Georg Schöbel. Wikimedia Commons.

a core element of the historical-educational experience of successive generations.[46] This applied with even greater force to *Der Alte Fritz*, a co-production by Röchling and Richard Knötel, the pioneer of historical and military costume studies known for his attention to minute details. Anecdotal in its conception and aimed at a mass and especially a younger audience, it was inspired by a suggestion of William II and sponsored by the former Prussian war minister General Heinrich von Gossler.[47] Its text was suitably loyal in tone, and there was—a typically Wilhelmine product—more than a whiff of the theatrical about it. Although the major political and military episodes were not ignored, the two artists focused on more intimate scenes designed to reveal Frederick's charisma and character. Significantly, Leuthen featured in three of the fifty *tableaux* that provide the artistic spine of the book. Parchwitz set the scene, and Knoetel, too, shifted the monarch into the foreground of his composition. Dressed in his customary blue army coat, his left rests on his cane, while his right is lifted for emphasis and his big eyes are turned on his generals who face him solemnly and attentively. Above their heads the key passage from the king's speech is reproduced in a rococo-style cartouche. Frederick's fictitious encounter at Lissa, also drawn by Knoetel, provides a comic coda to the events of the day—'a funny prank after so serious a day'. But above all, it was meant to demonstrate the king's quickness of mind and his *sangfroid*. The latter was underscored by the middle picture of the Leuthen-triptych in *Der alte Fritz*, Roechling's depiction of the Potsdam *Wachtparade* advancing in line against Nádasdy's left wing, muskets shouldered, bayonets fixed and ready (see Fig. 3.4). The accompanying text offered a condensed account of the battle, culminating in the now canonical final scene: 'Towards Heaven rises a mighty chorale. Trumpets, fifes, drums and kettle-drums join in. In mighty chords, sung by thousands and thousands of voices, rises into the starry night: "*Nun danket alle Gott!*" That was the Day of Leuthen.'[48] The image of the *Wachtparade*, disciplined, resolute and irresistible, was now firmly established in the popular Frederician canon. A memorial plaque in the wall around the Leuthen churchyard, mounted in 1907 to mark the sesquicentennial of the battle, repeated the rhyming couplets, already known from Polack's popular history, extolling the prowess of the Potsdam guard.[49]

Wilhelmine Germany was not short of occasions for military remembrance. Commemorations of the victory at Sedan, the '*Sedantag*', a semi-official public holiday since 1873, enjoyed great popularity. Rooted in recent events they had, perhaps, greater contemporary resonance.[50] Even so, the memory of Leuthen was firmly established as a crucial landmark in the development of Prussia and Germany. It was, in fact, a constitutive element of nineteenth-century Prussian and later Wilhelmine Prusso-German historical consciousness. Public monuments and other memorials in the vicinity of Leuthen underlined this fact. The battlefield became a memorial landscape.[51] Usually, the monuments combined the patriotic with the religious. Both elements were important, but their relative weight shifted over time.

In the aftermath of the Napoleonic wars Frederick William III (1770–1840) revived his great uncle's tradition of holding the main annual manoeuvre, the *Königsmanöver*, in Lower Silesia and the area around Leuthen more especially. During the manoeuvres of 1824 he enquired after any surviving veterans of that campaign. One was duly produced, an 85-year-old local man, who identified the spot on which he and his comrades had intoned the famous chorale. The monarch was satisfied, and ordered the planting of a grove of lime and maple trees, not so much to commemorate Frederick II but to express his gratitude for the divine protection bestowed upon Prussia since the days of the great king. To underline the sacral nature of the spot, Frederick William also ordered the erection of a field altar for the holding of religious services there. Locally, indeed, the place was known for a long time as the 'Altar of Leuthen'.[52]

Thirty years later, in 1854, at a time of domestic and external crisis, officers of VI army corps erected a 39-feet-high (12 m) column, fashioned from Silesian granite, on the Schöneberg, between Gross-Heidau and Radaxdorf, to the west of Leuthen, where Frederick reputedly finalized his battle plans. It was a simple memorial, unadorned except for a tablet dedicated to the king's victory and a replica of Rauch's Victoria with a laurel wreath on its top (Fig. 5.6).[53]

Changes in the memorialization of the battle in the Leuthen locale reflected the shifting perceptions of Frederick and his military campaigns in the nineteenth century. Frederick William III's sacralized

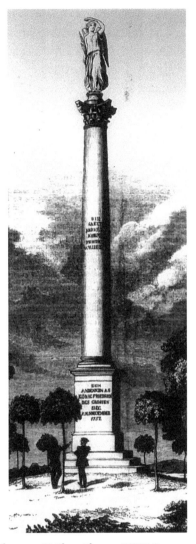

Fig. 5.6 Victory column at Heidau. Alamy, 2BEFN3B.

grove gave expression to his belief that victory at Leuthen had been a matter of divine intervention on behalf of Prussia and her army. The plain column of 1854, stripped of all overt religious symbols, was intended as a simple manifestation of Prussian patriotism. But in its dedication to Frederick's memory lay an implicit anti-Austrian poise. The intra-German and international contexts—post-Olmütz tensions with Austria and Vienna's dithering as Europe teetered on the brink of the Crimean War—lent it its specific meaning.

Similarly, the sandstone obelisk, erected to mark the 150th anniversary of Leuthen in 1907, reflected Wilhelmine historical and aesthetic sensibilities. It stood in the place which, in 1824, had been identified as the spot where Frederick's battle-weary soldiers broke into the 'Chorale of Leuthen'. At nearly 79 feet (24 m), it was double the height of the Crimean-era column. On its front was fixed a bronze relief of Frederick, above which an inscription read '*Nun danket alle Gott*'. Its rear bore the Kaiser's dedication 'To the Victors of Leuthen'. The reassertion of religious elements, the affirmation of divine assistance, were obvious. On William II's orders, a cross was also erected opposite the column of 1854,[54] the juxtaposition symbolizing the alliance of throne and altar. The inscription '*Nun danket alle Gott*' signalled the beginning of a line of historical development that led to the '*Gott mit uns*' of 1870. What had begun at Leuthen ended at Sedan. This was the secularized, historicized teleology of Prussia's rise set in sandstone and granite (Fig. 5.7);[55] and it was meant to bestow legitimacy to the Prussian roots and character of the *Kaiserreich* and its rise since 1871. Finally, the emperor's dedication to the victors of Leuthen emphasized the collective and its martial virtues. Here, the explicit invocation of the 'Chorale of Leuthen' affirmed the official, nationalist-Protestant character of post-1871 Germany. It provided the *leitmotif* against all those branded as *Reichsfeinde*, Catholics, Socialists, and others, who challenged either the new state's dominant Protestantism, its quasi-modern, quasi-constitutional order, or Prussia's alleged 'German mission'. Leuthen exemplified the strength of spirit of Frederician Prussia: 'Prussia has since been recognized as the pre-eminent military power of the world. The name Prussia acquired a lustre, and the various provinces began to feel part of a bigger whole.'[56]

Even those less susceptible to the official bombast of the Kaiser's regime had imbibed some of the Leuthen and Frederick myths. This

Fig. 5.7 Monuments on the battlefield. Wikimedia Commons.

was of particular importance during the First World War. It helped to entrench the idea that Prussia's development as a modern state represented not only a viable but in fact a superior alternative to Western parliamentary regimes—a belief brilliantly articulated by Thomas Mann in a 1915 essay, in which he drew an explicit parallel between the international constellations of 1756 and 1914. By invading Saxony Frederick might be said to have done a wrong, but necessity knew no law. He had to strike first or else be crushed by his enemies. In a similar manner the German leadership had to pre-empt the designs of the encircling enemies or else submit to them later.[57] 'Germany today', Mann wrote, 'is Frederick the Great. It is his struggle that we now bring to an end. And it was the king's soul that has re-awakened in us, this invincible mixture of activity and moral radicalism which made him appear to others so revolting and terrifying as an unknown and evil animal.' Germany's ultimate victory, 'will be a paradox, yes, a miracle, a prevailing of the soul over the multitude—entirely without equal'.[58]

On the eve of the First World War, Frederick and Leuthen had become hardwired into the official politics of the *Kaiserreich*.

A Prussian-Protestant core was fused with a secularized teleological view of Prusso-German history, and all of this was wrapped up in the exaltation of the military. Leuthen had become a shorthand for what were considered to be specifically Prussian virtues: unquestioning loyalty, a disposition towards the offence, a readiness to sacrifice one's life in the service of the Prussian state. The latter was sacralized in the iconography of the 'Chorale of Leuthen' and the *lieux de memoire* associated with 5 December 1757.

Neither memories of the great king nor the invocation of a *deutscher Gott* were sufficient to secure victory in the First World War. In the aftermath of defeat and revolution in 1918/19 the Leuthen myth underwent another transformation. If anything, it became yet more potent. The malleability of the sacral symbols associated with it allowed for the figure of Frederick once again to be expropriated for political purposes. But whereas previously it had conveyed multiple meanings, in the 1920s and 1930s it lost its utility as a shorthand for traditional conservatism. Instead, the monarch and Leuthen were used to project a new ideology. Already in the early 1920s, Erich Ludendorff, the brainier half of Germany's de facto war-emergency military dictatorship after 1916, blamed the defeat on an un-Prussian, un-Frederician pacifism and internationalism that, he alleged, had been rife in pre-war German society and had weakened the nation's moral fibre.[59] Soon he was to add Jews, Jesuits and freemasons, and assorted other occult elements to his list of culprits. His almost pathological obsession with dark forces made him something of a fringe figure in post-war Germany. Some of his arguments, however, and the assumptions that underpinned them, especially the notion of a psychological unity as the basis of future warfare gained ground amongst the military elite and in right-wing circles.[60] Leuthen was now a shorthand for the total militarization of society.

At a time when the Prussian state government was the perhaps 'unlikely rock of democracy' in Weimar Germany,[61] the utility of the 'Fredericus' myth for the anti-republican parties of the right was all too obvious. In particular, the German-National People's Party

(*Deutschnationale Volkspartei* (DNVP)), a mass party under whose banner the notables of the pre-war monarchy and a newer breed of far-right populists rallied, frequently used images of eighteenth-century grenadier drummers or of the great monarch himself. A 1932 election poster featured Frederick, raising his famous cane, under the slogan 'Rettet mir mein Preussen!' ('Save my Prussia!').[62]

The early leaders of the nascent National Socialist movement were also not slow to realize the potential of the Leuthen myth as a vehicle for spreading their ideas under the guise of traditional values. Leuthen not only stood for resilience in the face of adversity; it also demonstrated the importance of strong leadership. Defeat in 1918 reinforced this argument. The late emperor had been anything but a charismatic, determined, and purposeful warrior-leader, and in its current state of national humiliation and economic prostration Germany needed a charismatic leader to rise again. Although marginal until the early 1930s, the leaders of the Hitler movement laid claim to Frederick's legacy. In 1932, for instance, Count Wolf-Heinrich von Helldorff, a bankrupt aristocrat who led the Berlin *Brownshirts*, proclaimed him 'the first National Socialist'.[63]

Nazi propaganda then and later could draw on the nineteenth-century imagery of Knoetel, Menzel, and Roechling. Above all, it could harness the even more effective visual power of film. Already towards the end of the First World War, the German high command had cast about for ways to use Frederick-themed films for 'the carefully planned manipulation of the domestic masses'.[64] The war was over before any of these plans could take practical shape, and the first feature-length, silent 'Fridericus-Film' was not shown in German cinemas until 1923. It and the subsequent films of this genre were all box-office hits. They were not universally popular, however. One, Gustav Uccicky's *Das Flötenkonzert von Sanssouci* (1930), triggered street brawls in working-class districts of Berlin. Starting with the '*Fridericus Rex*' tetralogy, directed by Arzén von Cserépys, the films reflected the declining fortunes of the Weimar Republic and the gathering public mood of pessimism. They invited their audiences to see in the story of

Prussia's staring into the abyss a parable of the nation's current predicament. By implication, if the viewer accepted the parallel between Leuthen then and Weimar now, there was hope for a better future.[65] All of this fitted into an interpretative pattern, well established since the previous century, of popular resilience and charismatic leadership forming a symbiotic union. Accordingly, a leader of Frederick's type, stern yet charismatic, neglectful of his needs but always focused on the interests of the nation, a military leader of genius and selfless servant of his people, could demand any sacrifices from them. If the films conveyed a political message, albeit disguised in rococo costumes, they also serviced a broad popular psychological disposition towards such notions.[66]

The films, fourteen of them starring Otto Gebühr in the title role, drew on the anecdotal material and visual imagery in Kugler–Menzel and Roechling–Knoetel, and they were inspired by the austere aesthetics of Arthur Moeller van den Bruck[67] or the fictional treatment of the Fridericus-theme by the middle-brow novelist Walter von Molo, both of them associated with the so-called 'Conservative Revolution'.[68] The directors deliberately replicated the scenes that were so familiar from Menzel's illustrations or the paintings by Kampf, Roechling, and other nineteenth-century historical painters, and further popularized on collectors' cigarette cards.[69] It made the film scenes instantly recognizable to most viewers. This and the lavish scale on which they were produced insinuated a heightened degree of authenticity. The scriptwriters, in fact, claimed a considerable degree of artistic licence, playing fast-and-loose with the chronology of Frederick's life, reign and wars, and offering little more than a patchwork of clichés. But because the visual images they recreated were so well known, they were highly effective. Even their star, Otto Gebühr, bore an uncanny resemblance to the Prussian king (Fig. 5.8). To many Germans, indeed, he was the king.[70]

The eighth and last of the Weimar 'Fridericus' films was Carl August Froehlich's 'Der Choral von Leuthen', which was financed by Alfred Hugenberg, media-mogul and linkman between old-style nationalists

Fig. 5.8 Actor Otto Gebühr. Image from the author's own collection.

and the Hitler movement.[71] It was one of the great successes of late Weimar cinema, filmed during 1932, a time when Heinrich Brüning's chancellorship of emergency decrees and draconian austerity measures neared its end and the Social Democrat-led Prussian government was suspended by the conservative camarilla that succeeded Brüning.[72] It was passed by the film censor on 29 January of the following year, the day prior to Adolf Hitler's appointment as chancellor. 'Der Chorale' marked Frederick's cinematic apotheosis. From its opening shot, showing a memorial stone adorned with sword and laurel and dedicated to 'Seinem Gedächtnis' ('To His Memory'), to the final scene in which the torches carried by cheering soldiers create a halo around the king, it was a paean to Prussia's great monarch. Gebühr's Frederick was in turn charismatic and autocratic, possessed of the popular touch, noble and full of courtly courteoisie. Only in one scene loses

Fig. 5.9 The Day of Potsdam—Hitler and Crown Prince William. Alamy, 2J6FHD1.

the king self-control, when meeting his brother Henry, an advocate of peace talks. Frederick raises his voice in dismissing his brother's arguments: 'For whom do I wage this war? For the *Heimat*.' It was as anachronistic as it was suggestive, and it chimed in with the ideological precepts of the Nazi movement.[73]

The film was released in the cinemas several weeks later, neatly coinciding with the '*Tag von Potsdam*' on 21 March (Fig. 5.9). Ostensibly the opening of the new *Reichstag*—parliament itself was unavailable following the infamous fire in February—the event was carefully staged to mark the quasi-sacral 'marriage of the symbols of previous greatness and the young force'.[74] Old Prussia was represented by the aged President, Paul von Hindenburg, the victor of Tannenberg, in the full-dress uniform of an imperial field marshal, and the new Germany by the *Führer*, dressed in bourgeois morning suit, and his movement with its paramilitary formations. Little was left to chance in the staging of the '*Potsdamer Rührkomödie*' ('sentimental comedy').[75] The service was held in the nearby St. Nikolaus church, while the opening of the

Reichstag took place in the garrison church. The *Generalsuperintendent* (presiding bishop) of the Protestant church in the Kurmark, Otto Dibelius, invoked memories of August 1914: '*Ein Reich, ein Volk, ein Gott.*'[76] The ceremony in the garrison church supplied the relics needed for the symbolic union of old and new, the remains of Frederick and the other Prussian kings buried in the crypt. Hindenburg took his place underneath the pulpit in close proximity of the royal vault, his presence implying a revived alliance of throne and altar, a return to Prussia's mission in Germany, just as the date of the event marked the anniversary of the opening of the first *Reichstag* of the Second Reich in 1871.[77]

The garrison church and its royal relics were stage props, and they gave Hitler a rhetorical and symbolic point of reference. He delivered what was his formal opening address to the *Reichstag* from the pulpit of the church. He called upon the assembled dignitaries and deputies—only the Social Democrats boycotted the event—to imbibe the spirit of old Prussia: 'May providence lend us that courage and that resilience, that we feel in this for every German sacred space, as men who are fighting for the freedom and greatness of our people at the feet of the casket of its greatest king.'[78] At the close of proceedings, Hindenburg rose to salute the royal pew, deserted since November 1918, with his marshal's baton. The organ fell in with '*Nun danket alle Gott*'. Events seemed to have come full circle. It was Hitler's nod to the monarchist right who still yearned for a Hohenzollern restoration. Those attending the service, the thousands who thronged the streets of Potsdam and the millions across the *Reich* who listened to it on their wireless sets should feel reassured of the continuity between an old, seemingly better, past and the now more promising future.[79] They included some of the Kaiser's field marshals, such as August von Mackensen, who enthused about Hitler as '*so wunderbar*' and now became his ardent supporter.[80] They also included a young officer in the 9th Infantry Regiment, the successor to the old Prussian guard regiments, whose battalions took part in the Potsdam parade, and who, as a senior general staff officer, was to become one of the organizers of the plot against Hitler.[81]

The 'Tag von Potsdam' was meant to consecrate the Austrian-born *Führer*, a typical product of the Habsburg Empire and the antithesis of everything Prussian, as the lineal descendant of the great Hohenzollern monarch. It turned Frederick into an instrument chosen by providence to fulfil Germany's destiny and the Potsdam garrison church into a place of national pilgrimage. In the Leuthen chorale the new regime found its *canto fermo* that linked Prussia's past glory with the ideological tenets of Nazism. It provided the soundtrack to the historical imagery, consciously and skilfully conjured up by Hitler's propaganda chief, Joseph Goebbels, to insinuate continuity and an uplifting promise of greater things to come. If Frederick's victory at Leuthen marked the second foundation of the Kingdom of Prussia, the gathering around his burial vault on 21 March 1933 was the third *Reichsgründung*. Suggesting continuity was also a form of political 'reinsurance', visual and musical symbols and the ostentatious embrace of the outward signs of the older Prussian tradition establishing a vital link with conservative circles and above all the senior army commanders. It was an important element of added stability for a regime that, particularly in its early years, still felt fragile.[82]

Leuthen in its 'Tag von Potsdam' incarnation remained a recurring theme in official propaganda throughout the years of the Third Reich. It was an effective vehicle for projecting well-established memories of past Prussian greatness onto the present, an effectiveness heightened by the infusion of religious motifs. This also applied to the *Wehrmacht*. Until the outbreak of the Second World War the young recruits of Infantry Regiment No. 9 ('*Graf Neun*') swore their oath of allegiance to the *Führer* in the vault of the garrison church while the organ played the 'Chorale of Leuthen', followed by the *Hohenfriedberger Marsch*.[83] Leuthen, then, continued to provide the accompanying chords to Nazi propaganda. It could do so because a specific image of Frederick, his wars, epitomized by Leuthen, and his stoicism were deeply entrenched in popular consciousness. Especially memories of a king 'confronting one of the greatest coalitions' and prevailing over it was a potent propaganda tool in wartime. Frederick's victory in three wars, Hitler asserted on 1 September 1939, was a matter of 'that believing stout heart' which he had possessed 'and that we, too, require in these times'.[84] The Silesian wars remained a favourite point of reference for the *Führer*. On the eve of the attack on Poland he confided to his army adjutant that all he desired was 'the First Silesian War', but if others were foolish enough to escalate the war, they would have to be destroyed.[85]

The Leuthen myth remained malleable and could be bent to the changing demands of the hour, as was demonstrated by the final 'Fridericus' film, *'Der Grosse König'* of early 1942. Although it was set in the final three years of the Seven Years' War, in the aftermath of Kunersdorf, it was infused with the essence of the Leuthen myth. As the earlier films of this genre had done, it combined Wilhelmine iconography with a quasi-sacral atmosphere, inspired by the notion of a Prussian-Protestant mission, to great cinematic effect. The two storylines—the king's travails during this period and the love story of a miller's daughter—introduced a subtle variation. Frederick was no longer the sole focus of the war effort. Goebbels, who controlled film production, had insisted on it.[86] In the closing scene, sowing and ploughing peasants, swaying wheat fields and the rising Prussian eagle are projected on to Frederick's eye, while a choir intoned a hymn to the king: 'Black Eagle of Frederick the Great, / Cover you, like the sun, / Those abandoned and expelled / With your golden wings.' The film was an appeal to unite in a common endeavour, to show the same resilience, and to bring any sacrifice for the greater national good, firm in the conviction that Germany's cause would ultimately prevail. On the eve of Stalingrad the union of Prussia and National Socialism was complete. In a speech at the Berlin *Philharmonie* on 19 April 1942, Goebbels praised the film for its 'depiction of the human and individual essence of a unique political and military genius'. Frederick's greatness merely prefigured Hitler's genius, for 'style and expression' of true genius were always the same. The idea of genius in the guise of Frederick was thus instrumentalized to affirm the *Führerprinzip*.[87]

Frederick and Leuthen were more than merely tactical instruments in the service of regime propaganda. For Hitler and Goebbels they were a vital prop of their own sense of destiny; it was a case of autosuggestion. Not only did they consider the monarch 'a heroic genius'; they also saw in him, along with Luther and Bismarck, a 'forerunner' of Nazism.[88] Both often referred to Frederick as a role model. The *Führer's* decisions, Goebbels rhapsodized at the beginning of the war, were of a magnitude comparable only to those of the great king: 'He stands above all figures from Prusso-German history.... Faced with his greatness we should all humbly sink into the dust. Not the dimensions, in which the historical genius works, are decisive for his greatness, but the courage and the boldness with which he confronts dangers.'[89]

Although Hitler subscribed to the view 'that numerical superiority is decisive in war', he also believed that the strong-willed would ultimately prevail *à la Frédéric*. During the last years of the war, 'with his wrecked body and his nerves increasingly out of control', noted a historian in the General Staff, he was 'sustained by the infernal, intransigent will'.[90] Above his desk in one of his two rooms inside the fuggy *Führerbunker* in the grounds of the chancellery, hung Graff's oval portrait of Frederick, and Hitler often sat in broody contemplation in front of it 'as if he was in silent conversation with the king'.[91]

Whatever went on in Hitler's mind, popular memories of Frederick's wars now furnished the raw material for appeals to sacrifice (Fig. 5.10). The 'steadfastness of one man [Frederick]', he impressed on his commanders in late 1944, 'made it possible to carry on the struggle' until 'a miraculous turn of events occurred'.[92] In his 'total war' speech at Berlin's *Sportpalast* in February 1943, Goebbels exhorted the German people to emulate the example of the great king, '*like him* to remain unshakeable under all blows which fate deals, like him to force victory..., and never to doubt the great cause for which we fight'.[93] In his final public appearances at Lauban on 8 March 1945, and

Fig. 5.10 Propaganda poster by the Nazi party, 24 Aug. 1941. Hennepin County Library, MPW00643.

later that evening in Görlitz, both now within the range of Soviet artillery, he played on the sacral aspects of the Leuthen myth. He invoked the memory of Frederick 'whose resilience and unbroken heart' had saved Prussia. In like manner the *Führer* would now lead Germany to victory if the people stood by him 'as with the great Prussian king…faithful and loyal'. Troops, he claimed, had been rallied around Berlin, ready for a counter-offensive against the Red Army, and would go into battle 'as into a church service'.[94]

The Frederician and Leuthen themes remained a potent force. When news broke of President Roosevelt's death on 13 April 1945, a Friday, Hitler was ecstatic. He declared it a repeat of the '*Mirakel des Hauses Brandenburg*', though he postdated it by three years, of course. As in 1762 following the death of tsarina, so now the enemy coalition would break apart, he was sure.[95] No less revealingly, Goebbels, in one of his last acts as Plenipotentiary for the Total War Effort, Goebbels gave plans for a final offensive around Berlin the code name 'Leuthen'.[96]

In the years after 1945 Leuthen largely disappeared from public memory in the two Germanies. The legacy for which it stood was defiled and discredited by its manipulation by a criminal regime, whose twelve years were best forgotten. The Prussian state had been abolished by an Allied decree in 1947. Even the battlefield itself was no longer on German soil. The chorale lingered on in the collective consciousness, but its meaning was now simply one of redemption. When, in June 1947, the villagers of Palmnicken (Yantarni'i) in Eastern Prussia were allowed to leave for now Soviet-occupied Eastern Germany, as their train crossed the river Oder at Frankfurt, the Protestant pastor sang '"Now thank we all God", the words taken up by others, echoing through the wagons and out over the river as the East Prussians reached their new home.'[97]

It was but a faint echo. Both post-war German states were, to some extent, anti-Prussian creations. The Rhenish, Catholic-dominated West Germany of the *Wirtschaftswunder* years had little in common with Frederick's Spartan Prussia. Nor did the new republic's leaders seek inspiration from the *roi connétable* in their attempts to reintegrate their country into the comity of nations. East Germany, meanwhile, was ruled by Moscow-trained apparatchiks whose thick Saxon accents suggested that the victims of 1756 had had their secret revenge at last.

In both states there was nevertheless a 'Prussia renaissance' of sorts in the late 1970s and early 1980s. The division of Germany appeared now to be a durable, if not indeed a permanent, feature of the post-war world; and on both sides of the Berlin Wall political and intellectual leaders were re-evaluating older historical traditions for their present-day relevance or utility. In the Federal Republic a major exhibition in West Berlin's Gropius-Bau in 1981 sought to offer a retrospect on the new defunct state.[98] This was followed by a flurry of Frederick biographies to mark the bicentenary of his death in 1986.[99] At the same time, in East Berlin, the leadership of the GDR went to some lengths, accompanied by a good deal of dialectical gymnastics, to utilize certain aspects of Prussia's political traditions, without, however, reviving any *gesamtdeutsche* tendencies in their half of the divided nation.[100] As part of a drive to rediscover Prussia's 'second' or 'progressive' face, the figure of Frederick was reassessed with a view to its, at least, partial, appropriation for the regime's efforts to cultivate a separate East German cultural heritage.[101]

In neither Germany was there much appetite for reviving memories of Frederick the military leader. That was a problematic legacy for either republic. Nor did the fall of the Berlin Wall alter that assessment. The trauma of the Third Reich had severed the ties of tradition. And yet a faint echo of the 'Chorale of Leuthen' could be heard again in reunited Germany. In August 1991, at the initiative of the Hohenzollerns, Frederick's remains were transferred to Potsdam to be reinterred on the terraces of his beloved Sanssouci palace, as he had stipulated in his will on the eve of the battle of Leuthen (Fig. 5.11). The night-time ceremony took place in private, but in the presence of a *Bundeswehr* watch battalion and the federal chancellor, Helmut Kohl. In an uneasy nod to the age of television, a recording of the ceremony was then broadcast the following day.[102] Apparently at the chancellor's request, the ceremony was closed with '*Nun danket alle Gott*'. The religious

Fig. 5.11 Frederick II's tomb at Sanssouci, Potsdam. Image from the author's own collection.

element had reasserted itself, albeit without any pretence to any sort of mission by the now defunct Prussian state. It signalled some form of reconciliation between the modern Federal Republic and its traumatic past, though the name of Prussia still proves something of an historical itch[103]—confirmation of sorts of the philosopher Helmuth Plessner's observation that 'Prussia can be wiped off the map but never from memory, for we live off it'.[104]

Conclusion

The Seven Years' War was particularly rich in battlefield encounters, perhaps uniquely so for the early modern period. The sites are scattered across a series of theatres of war in Western and Central Europe, and indeed the globe, if one includes the Anglo-French transoceanic, imperial conflict. Leuthen was not the largest of these battles. Other encounters can lay claim to that distinction, if distinction it is. Some 125,000 and 157,000 combatants fought at Prague (1757) and Kunersdorf (1759), respectively; and at Vellinghausen (1761), a 70,000-strong allied Anglo-Hanoverian-Prussian army under Prince Ferdinand of Brunswick took on 140,000 French troops. Leuthen perhaps lacked the drama of the cavalry charges at Rossbach (1757). Nor was it as bloody as Zorndorf (1758) or Torgau (1760), at the end of which 38,000 and 33,000 wounded and dead, respectively, littered the field. Leuthen was also not a decisive battle in the way in which Blenheim (1704) or Poltava (1709) or later Waterloo (1815) are usually judged to have been. The notion of 'decisiveness', as especially Chapter 4 of this study has shown, is a questionable criterion that betrays elements of a later nineteenth-century fixation with the Napoleonic period and its legacy.[1]

Leuthen was nevertheless the most consequential of the battles in the European theatres of the Seven Years' War. It saved Prussia as a military power capable of fighting the war. Defeat would not only very likely have ended the conflict. It would also have brought with it the end of Prussia as a kingdom. Victory kept it in the war and preserved the Prussian state. It is no exaggeration to suggest that Leuthen

191

marked the Second Foundation of Prussia. Further, it confirmed and entrenched the dualistic structure of German politics. Potsdam and Vienna were now the two opposing programmatic poles around which the lesser German states were to orbit with varying degrees of proximity for the next century. Frederick's victory on that foggy December day in 1757 pointed towards the territorial and property arrangements the exhausted belligerents were to agree six years hence. They were to shape the affairs of the German-speaking (and, indeed, the non-German-speaking) lands of Central and Eastern Central Europe until 1866, and arguably beyond, until 1938 or 1945.

For all these profound, longer-term consequences, it is important to reiterate, as was seen in Chapter 3, that the battle of Leuthen was nevertheless not decisive enough to end the war in Prussia's favour immediately. Numbers and material resources were stacked too much against it to allow for such an outcome. For the next six years, Frederick would have to grind out a favourable outcome by means of attrition, inflicting sufficiently painful setbacks on his adversaries until he fought them to a standstill. Leuthen, then, did not mark a transition to a more modern form of warfare. Frederick had pushed linear warfighting to its practical and doctrinal limits, but he could not transcend contemporary constraints.

The fact that later nineteenth- and twentieth-century military thinkers and writers saw in the Prussian king's operations at the close of 1757 an expression of the immutable essence of true leadership in war underlines the broader significance of Leuthen. None was more profound than its impact on operational planning by the Prusso-German general staff. The German armies marched to war in the summer of 1914 to the drum beat of Schlieffen's 'Leuthener Programm'.

Leuthen also illustrates key aspects of European remembrance culture. The past is malleable, capable of, indeed liable to, being manipulated to serve current political and other needs. Even so, memories of Leuthen were not a case of infinite plasticity. *Pace* postmodern theories, it could not be told in an infinite variety of ways. As Chapter 5 has underlined, the historical figure of Frederick was just too enlightened and too anti-religious, if not altogether atheist, for early Prussian ultra-conservatives during the restoration period. Mid-century liberals were attracted by some aspects of the Frederician legacy, but circumstances tended to conspire against them and their ambitions. The *roi connétable* and Leuthen proved more fertile grounds for their successors. Later nineteenth-century historians discerned in the king and his wars an underlying Protestant sense of duty and a proto-nationalist sense of mission, the so-called 'Borussian' view of Prusso-German history that was to shape public historical conscious-ness from the 1860s and the formation of the *Kaiserreich* until the collapse of the Third Reich.

In the aftermath of the First World War, during the disturbances of the late Weimar years, Leuthen, in its cinematic and literary drama-tization, offered the counterfoil of a better past and future to new mass audiences. As a manifestation of Prussian resilience in adversity, prof-fering the enticing prospect of ultimate victory against a world of enemies, it also proved an effective vehicle for mass propaganda during the war years after 1939. With 'Operation Leuthen' Goebbels sought to initiate the great counter-offensive that would turn around Nazi Germany's fortunes in the last weeks of the Second World War.

For the two Germanies that emerged out of the dying embers of the Third *Reich* Leuthen and Frederick had little political utility. For East German communists, as for nineteenth-century Prussian ultra-conservatives and liberals, the king was an awkward subject. They hailed the 'cunning of history' that had turned the monarch into a tool of forces that would ultimately destroy the feudal order and pave the way for the industrialization of Central Europe; they even acknow-ledged through gritted teeth his 'second', rogressive, face. But he was too much the product of East Elbian Junkerdom and its perceived militarist-imperialist spirit to be usable for their own regime's pur-poses. Nor did Leuthen find any echo in the West Germany, Rhenish, Catholic and more inspired by Charlemagne than Frederick the Great.

Leuthen's role in fostering a Silesian regional identity must not be ignored. There was no museum at Leuthen or in its vicinity. But the battle was commemorated locally throughout the nineteenth and twentieth centuries. The monuments erected on the battlefield and the groves planted there testified to its status as a *lieu de mémoire*, a collective landscape of memory. Frederick's three wars for Silesia formed a key element of its Prussian regional identity; and Frederick occupied a special place in the province's sense of self, especially so in the many popular anecdotes surrounding Leuthen and its immediate aftermath.[2] With the transfer of Silesia to Polish rule and the expulsion of its ethnic German population that tradition came to an end. The subsequent decay and demolition of the memorials in and around Leuthen testified to that fact. It also underscores the limits to which battles can be used to generalize, or indeed universalize, the human experience of war. Their remembrance rests on specific circumstances and the distinct narratives that succeeding generations create of them.

NOTES

Preface

1. Edward Creasy established the genre of 'decisive' battle literature, id., *The Fifteen Decisive Battles of the World: From Marathon to Waterloo* (London, 1851). In a similar vein, J. C. F. Fuller, *Decisive Battles of the Western World and Their Influence upon History* (3 vols, London, repr. 2003 [1st 1955]). Ibid., ii, 207–15, deals with Leuthen. For a recent discussion see M. Füssel, 'Die Krise der Schlacht: Das Problem der militärischen Entscheidung im 17. und 18. Jahrhundert', R. Schlögl, P. R. Hoffmann-Rehnitz, and E. Wiebels (eds), *Die Krise der frühen Neuzeit* (Göttingen, 2016), 311–32.
2. C. von Clausewitz, *Vom Kriege*, ed. W. Hahlweg (Bonn, 19th ed. 1991 [1832]), 469 (original emphasis). Here and elsewhere I am using my own translation; the standard English translation by P. Paret and M. Howard, *On War* (Princeton, NJ, 1989 (pb) [1st 1976]), here 259, is occasionally too loose.

Chapter 1

1. Frederick II report, 9 Dec. 1757 (published 20 Dec.), H. Jessen (ed.), *Friedrich der Gross und Maria Theresia in Augenzeugenberichten* (Munich, 1972), 305–8.
2. P. W. Schroeder, *The Transformation of European Politics, 1763–1847* (Oxford, 1994), 3–11.
3. The literature has become vast since Michael Roberts' inaugural essay on the subject, id., *The Military Revolution, 1560–1660* (Belfast, 1956); see also for a mildly revisionist assessment, G. Parker, *The Military Revolution: Military Innovation and the Rise of the West, 1500–1800. The Lees Knowles Lectures 1984* (Cambridge, 1988); D. Parrott, *The Business of War: Military Enterprise and Military Revolution in Early Modern Europe* (Cambridge, 2012); J. Luh, 'Early Modern Military Revolution: The German Perspective', J. Black (ed.), *Global Military Transformation: Change and Continuity, 1450–1800* (Rome, 2023), 205–24. For pertinent critiques, P. A. Lorge, *The Asian Military Revolution: From Gunpowder to the Bomb* (Cambridge, 2008), and J. Black, 'Eighteenth-Century Warfare in a Global Perspective', A. S. Burns (ed.), *The Changing Face of Old Regime Warfare: Essays in Honour of Christopher Duffy* (Warwick, 2022), 21–35.

4. O. Hintze, 'Wesen und Wandlung des modernen Staats' [1931], id., *Staat und Verfassung: Gesammelte Abhandlungen zur Allgemeinen Verfassungsgeschichte*, ed. G. Oestreich (Göttingen, 2nd ed. 1962), 480. This was also the real motive behind the so-called 'soldier trade', see P. Wilson, 'The German "Soldier Trade" of the Seventeenth and Eighteenth-Centuries: A Reassessment', *IHR* xviii, 4 (1996), 757–92.

5. S. de Monzambano (pseud. S. von Pufendorf), *Über die Verfassung des Deutschen Reiches*, ed. H. Bresslau (Berlin, 1922).

6. For the constitution of the Holy Roman Empire and the different agreements and conventions on which it rested, see E. Bussi, *Il diritto publico del Sacro Impero alla fine del XVIII secolo* (2 vols, Milan, 1957–9); also A. Schindling, 'Der Westfälische Frieden und der Reichstag', H. Weber (ed.), *Politische Ordnungen und Soziale Kräfte im Alten Reich* (Wiesbaden, 1980), 113–54.

7. See Art. VIII, § 2 of the Peace of Osnabrück: '*ita tamen ne eiusmodi foedera sint contra imperatorem et imperium pacemque eius publicam vel hanc imprimis transactionem fiantque salvo per omnia iuramento quo quisque imperatori et imperio obstrictus est*', K. Müller (ed.), *Instrumentum Pacis Westphalicae: Die Westfälischen Friedensverträge 1648* (Berne, 1966), 48.

8. Elector Frederick William I, Political Testament, 1667, R. Dietrich (ed.), *Politische Testamente der Hohenzollern* (Munich, 1981 (pb)), 62. This right was never clearly defined, however. The French translation of the Treaty of Westphalia spoke of the *souveraineté* of the individual states, but the French version had no legal validity in imperial law. The Latin version referred to *superioritas territorialis*, which fell well short of modern ideas of sovereignty, see H. H. Hofmann, 'Einleitung', id. (ed.), *Quellen zum Verfassungsorganismus des Heiligen Römischen Reiches Deutscher Nation, 1495–1815* (Darmstadt, 1976), XXXV.

9. 'Reichs-Kammergerichts-Ordnung' [1521], Hofmann (ed.), *Quellen*, doc. 1b; K. O. von Aretin, *Kaiser Joseph II. und die Reichskammergerichtsvisitation, 1767–1776* (Wetzlar, 1991), and R.-P. Fuchs, 'The Supreme Court of the Holy Roman Empire: The State of Research and the Outlook', *SCJ* xxxiv, 1 (2003), 9–27.

10. P. H. Wilson, *German Armies, War and German Politics, 1648–1806* (London, 1998), 17–22; for southern Germany see H. Neuhaus, 'Reichskreise und Reichskriege in der Frühen Neuzeit', H. Wüst (ed.), *Reichskreis und Territorium: Die Herrschaft über der Herrschaft: Supraterritoriale Tendenzen in Politik, Kultur, Wirtschaft und Gesellschaft* (Stuttgart, 2000), 71–86.

11. 'Reichsgutachten in puncto securitatis', 13/23 May 1681, Hofmann (ed.), *Quellen*, doc. 40; also R. A. Wines, 'The Imperial Circles: Princely Diplomacy and Imperial Reform, 1681–1714', *Journal of Modern History* xxxix, 1 (1967), 1–29.

12. C. Dipper, *Deutsche Geschichte, 1648–1789* (Frankfurt, 1991), 293. For a nuanced revision of older interpretations see P. H. Wilson, *The Holy Roman Empire: A Thousand Years of European History* (London, 2016).

13. J. Kunisch, 'La guerre c'est moi?: Zum Problem der Staatenkonflikte im Zeitalter des Absolutismus', *ZHF* xiv (1987), 407–38.

14. Religious motivations never disappeared entirely, and the wars of Frederick II bore, at least outwardly, confessional aspects. For a more emphatic assertion of the continued importance of religion see J. Black, *Kings, Nobles and Commoners: States and Societies in Early Modern Europe* (London, 2004), 2–5 et passim.

15. G. Zeller, *Histoire des relations internationales*, iii, *De Louis XIV à 1789* (Paris, 1955), 17–50; J. A. Lynch II, 'The Grand Strategy and the *Grand Siècle*: Learning from the Wars of Louis XIV', W. Murray, R. H. Sinnreich, and J. Lacey (eds), *The Shaping of Grand Strategy: Politics, Diplomacy and War* (Cambridge, 2011), 34–62.

16. Frederick to Jordan, 24 Feb. 1741, O. Bardong (ed.), *Friedrich der Grosse* (Darmstadt, 1982), no. 73; J. Luh, *Der Grosse: Friedrich II. von Preussen* (Berlin, 2011), 49–60; for Brandenburg claims on Silesian territories, see M. Weber, *Das Verhältnis Schlesiens zum alten Reich in der Frühen Neuzeit* (Cologne, 1992), 122–6 et passim; W. Bein, *Schlesien in der habsburgischen Politik: Ein Beitrag zur Entstehung des Dualismus im Alten Reich* (Sigmaringen, 1994), 85–132.

17. For some illustrations, see G. de Werd, *Schenkenschanz, "de sleutel van den hollandschen tuin"* (Cleves, 1996), 96–103. Visualizing dynastic success had a long tradition, see C. M. Klinkert, *Nassau in het nieuws: Nieuwsprenten van Maurits van Nassaus militaire ondernemingen uit de periode 1590–1600* (Zutphen, 2005), 35–56.

18. G. Jordan and N. Rogers, 'Admirals as Heroes: Patriotism and Liberty in Hanoverian England', *Journal of British Studies* xxviii, 3 (1989), 201–22.

19. The Saxon army camp at Zelthain in June 1730 was a case in point, see R. Müller, *Die Armee August des Starken: Das sächsische Heer von 1730 bis 1733* (East Berlin, 1984), 14–18.

20. Frederick II of Prussia, 'Geschichte meiner Zeit' [1775], G. B. Volz (ed.), *Die Werke Friedrich des Grossen* (Berlin, 1913), ii, 59.

21. E. Fehrenbach, 'Die Ideologisierung des Krieges und die Radikalisierung der Französischen Revolution', D. Langenwiesche (ed.), *Revolution und Krieg: Zur Dynamic historischen Wandels seit dem 18. Jahrhundert* (Paderborn, 1989), 57–66; K. and S. Möbius, *Prussian Army Soldiers and the Seven Years' War: The Psychology of Honour* (London, 2019).

22. M. S. Anderson, *The Rise of Modern Diplomacy, 1494–1919* (London, 1994), 69–95, 163–80, and 219–35; J. T. Johnson, *Ideology, Reason and the Limitation of War: Religious and Secular Concepts, 1200–1740* (Princeton, NJ, 1975); K. Müller, *Das Kaiserliche Gesandtschaftswesen im Jahrhundert nach dem Westfälischen Frieden* (Bonn, 1976), 144–61 and 338–52.

23. W. Robertson, 'The History of the Reign of the Emperor Charles V, from the Subversion of the Roman Empire to the Beginning of the Sixteenth Century' [1782], *The Works of William Robertson, DD* (London, one vol. ed. 1852), 364.

24. E. Kaeber, *Die Idee des europäischen Gleichgewichts in der publizistischen Literatur vom 16. bis zum 18. Jahrhundert* (Hildesheim, repr. 1971 [1st 1907]), 77–87.

25. D. Gerhard, *England und der Aufstieg Russlands* (Berlin, 1933); W. Mediger, *Moskaus Weg nach Europa: Der Aufstieg Russlands zum europäischen Machtstaat im Zeitalter Friedrich des Grossen* (Braunschweig, 1952), 1–107; J. P. LeDonne, *The Russian Empire and the World, 1700–1917: The Geopolitics of Expansion and Containment* (Oxford, 1997), 23–42; C. B. Stevens, *Russia's Wars of Emergence, 1460–1730* (Harlow, 2007), 243–73.

26. See H. M. Scott, *The Rise of the Eastern Powers, 1756–1775* (Cambridge, 2001); B. Simms, *The Struggle for Mastery in Germany, 1779–1850* (London, 1998).

27. H. Duchhardt, *Gleichgewicht der Kräfte, Convénance, europäisches Konzert: Friedenskongresse und Friedensschlüsse vom Zeitalter Ludwigs XIV. bis zum Wiener Kongress* (Darmstadt, 1976).

28. For some thoughts on the *Reichskriegsverfassung* see G. Papke, 'Von der Miliz zum stehenden Heer: Wehrwesen im Absolutismus', Militärgeschichtliches Forschungsamt (ed.), *Deutsche Militärgeschichte, 1648–1939* (6 vols, Munich, 1983), i/1, 236–43.

29. L. and M. Frey, 'A Question of Empire: Leopold I and the War of Spanish Succession, 1701–1705', *Austrian History Yearbook* xiv (1978), 56–72.

30. V. Press, 'Österreichische Grossmachtbildung und Reichsverfassung: Zur Kaiserlichen Stellung nach 1648', *Mitteilungen des Institutes für Österreichische Geschichte* xcviii, 1–2 (1990), 131–54.

31. L. Just, 'Grenzsicherungspläne im Westen des Reiches zur Zeit des Prinzen Eugen', id., *Um die Westgrenze des alten Reiches: Vorträge und Aufsätze* (Cologne, 1941), 75–92; M. Braubach, 'Kurfürst Joseph Clemens von Köln als Vermittler zwischen Versailles und Wien', *AHVN* cxlviii (1948), 228–38.

32. J. C. Allmayer-Beck, 'Bedrohung und Befreiung Wiens 1683: Eine weltgeschichtliche Einführung', id., *Militär, Geschichte und Politische Bildung*, ed. P. Broucek and E. A. Schmidl (Vienna, 2003), 261–74.

33. K. A. Roider, *Austria's Eastern Question, 1700–1790* (Princeton, NJ, 1982) remains the most authoritative work on the subject.

34. A. Schindling, *Die Anfänge des immerwährenden Reichstages zu Regensburg* (Mainz, 1991).

35. R. Gerba, *Feldzüge des Prinzen Eugen von Savoyen*, xix, *Polnischer Thronfolgekrieg: Feldzug 1733 und 1734* (Vienna, 1891), 119–22 and, for the campaign, 163–91.

36. Maximilian Franz to Karg von Bebenburg, 14 Sept. 1792, LANRW, Kurköln VII/242.

37. U. Dann, *Hanover and Great Britain, 1740–1760: Diplomacy and Survival* (Leicester, 1991), 3; Müller, *Armee Augusts des Starken*, 8; C. Becker, 'Über die finanziellen Aufwendungen Kurkölns im Siebenjährigen Kriege für den Reichskrieg gegen Friedrich den Grossen', *AHVN* xcii (1912), 72–3.

38. Wilson, 'German "Soldier Trade"', 757–92; and also C. W. Ingrao, *The Hessian Mercenary State: Ideas, Institutions and Reform under Frederick II* (Cambridge, 1987).

The poet and writer Johann Gottlieb Seume (1763–1810) who, as a student, was pressed into Hessian service and sent to America, described his fellow-recruits as a student from Jena, a bankrupt Viennese merchant, a lace-maker ('*Posamentierer*') from Hanover, a sacked postal clerk from Gotha, a Würzburg monk, a senior administrator of Meiningen, a sergeant in the Prussian hussars, and a cashiered Hessian major, id., 'Mein Leben', id., *Seumes Werke*, ed. A. and K.-H. Klingenberg (2 vols, East Berlin and Weimar, 1983), i, 86 [83–121].

39. See O. Hintze, 'Der österreichische und der preussische Beamtenstaat im 17. und 18. Jahrhundert' [1910], id., *Staat und Verfassung*, 321–58.

40. e.g. J.-M. Constant, *La vie quotidienne de la noblesse Français aux XVIe et XVIIe siècles* (Paris, 1985), 11–35.

41. J. H. Elliot, 'A Europe of Composite Monarchies', *P&P* no. 137 (1992), 48–71; J. C. Allmayer-Beck, 'Das Heerwesen in Österreich und Preussen', R. A. Kann and F. E. Prinz (eds), *Deutschland und Österreich: Ein bilaterales Geschichtsbuch* (Vienna and Munich, 1980), 490–521.

42. H.-G. Riqueti de Mirabeau, 'Letter Memorial Presented to Frederick William II', id., *Secret Memoirs of the Court of Berlin* (2 vols, London, s.a. [1908]), ii, 275; C. Clark, *Iron Kingdom: The Rise and Downfall of Prussia, 1600–1947* (Cambridge, MA, 2006), 178–9.

43. Convention of Wehlau, 19 Sep. 1657, F. W. Ghillany, *Europäische Chronik von 1492 bis Ende April 1865, mit besonderer Berücksichtigung der Friedensverträge* (3 vols, Leipzig, 1865), i, 170–1; C. Hinrichs, *Friedrich Wilhelm I., König in Preussen: Eine Biographie* (Darmstadt, enlarged ed. 1974), 134–46.

44. L. Hüttl, *Friedrich Wilhelm von Brandenburg, der Grosse Kurfürst: Eine politische Biographie* (Munich, 1981), 189–90 and 295–8; Clark, *Iron Kingdom*, 38–66. The rulers at Berlin continued to look with suspicion at their Western provinces. Frederick William I thought the Cleves nobles '*dumme Oxen aber Malicieus wie der deuffel*' and fixated on their '*Privilegia*', while the County of Moers was '*sehr guht Hollendisch*', Frederick William I, Political Testament, 22 Jan.–17 Feb. 1722, G. Küntzel and M. Hass (eds), *Die Politischen Testamente der Hohenzollern, nebst ergänzenden Aktenstücken* (2 vols, Leipzig, 1911), i, 80–1.

45. G. Oestreich, 'Zur Heeresverfassung der deutschen Territorien', id., *Geist und Gestalt des frühmodernen Staates* (Berlin, 1969), 290–310.

46. A. Schindling, 'Kurbrandenburg im System des Reiches während der zweiten Hälfte des 17. Jahrhunderts', O. Hauser (ed.), *Preussen, Europa und das Reich* (Cologne and Vienna, 1987), 33; figures in W. Neugebauer, 'Brandenburg im absolutistischen Staat: Das 17. und 18. Jahrhundert', I. Materna and W. Ribbe (eds), *Brandenburgische Geschichte* (Berlin, 1995), 322.

47. O. Büsch, 'Die Militarisierung von Staat und Gesellschaft im alten Preussen', M. Schlenke (ed.), *Preussen: Beiträge zu einer politischen Kultur* (Reinbek, 1981), 45–60. Büsch's concept of 'social militarization' is problematic, see P. H. Wilson, 'Social Militarization in Eighteenth-Century Germany', *German History* xviii, 1 (2000), 1–39.

48. H.-G. Riqueti de Mirabeau, *De la monarchie prusse sous Frédéric le Grand* (8 vols, London, 1788), i, 70.

49. H. Rosenberg, *Bureaucracy, Aristocracy and Autonomy: The Prussian Experience, 1660–1815* (Cambridge, MA, 1958); also C. Hinrichs, 'Die preussische Zentralverwaltung in den Anfängen Friedrich Wilhelms I.', id., *Preussen als historisches Problem: Gesammelte Aufsätze*, ed. G. Oestreich (Berlin, 1964), 138–60.

50. R. Koser, 'Der preussische Staatsschatz von 1740–1756', *FBPG* iv, (1891), 529–51; for its adverse effects on economic activity, see F.-W. Henning, 'Die preussische Thesaurierungspolitik im 18. Jahrhundert', I. Bog, G. Franz, K.-H. Kaufhold, H. Kellenbenz, and W. Zorn (eds), *Wirtschaftliche und Soziale Strukturen im saekularen Wandel: Festschrift für Wilhelm Abel zum 70. Geburtstag* (2 vols, Hanover, 1974), ii, 399–416.

51. C. Jany, *Geschichte der königlich-preussischen Armee bis zum Jahre 1807* (3 vols, Berlin, 1928–9), i, 691–4.

52. O. Büsch, *Militärsystem und Sozialleben im Alten Preussen, 1713–1807: Die Anfänge der sozialen Militarisierung der preussisch-deutschen Gesellschaft* (Berlin, 2nd ed. 1981), 11–20 et passim; for 'foreign' elements see M. Winter, *Untertanengeist durch Militärpflicht: Das preussische Kantonsystem in brandenburgischen Städten im 18. Jahrhundert* (Bielefeld, 2005), 167–70.

53. A. Corvisier, *Armies and Societies in Europe, 1494–1789* (Bloomington, IN, 1979), 113; see also O. Büsch, 'Militärwesen und Militarisierung', W. Treue (ed.), *Preussens grosser König: Lebenswerk Friedrichs des Grossen* (Freiburg, 1986), 96.

54. Büsch, *Militärsystem*, 75–143; E. Melton, 'The Prussian Junkers, 1600–1786', H. M. Scott (ed.), *The European Nobilities in the Seventeenth and Eighteenth Centuries* (2 vols, London, 1995), ii, 99–100.

55. Wilson, 'Social Militarization', 29–33; H. Bleckwenn, 'Bauernfreiheit durch Wehrpflicht—ein neues Bild der altpreussischen Armee', Militärgeschichtliches Forschungsamt (ed.), *Friedrich der Grosse und das Militärwesen seiner Zeit* (Bonn, 1987), 55–72.

56. O. Hintze, 'Das Politische Testament Friedrich des Grossen von 1752' [1904], id., *Regierung und Verwaltung: Gesammelte Abhandlungen zur Staats-, Rechts-, und Sozialgeschichte Preussens*, ed. G. Oestreich (Göttingen, 2nd ed. 1967), 432.

57. The Hohenzollern dynasty converted from Lutheranism to Calvinism in 1613. For the Dutch influences, W. Stratmann, 'Die Militärreform der Oranier—Wurzeln, Umsetzung und Rezeption', H. J. Vogt, H.-J. Giersberg, and A. W. Vliegenhart (eds), *Onder den Oranje Boom: Niederländische Kunst und Kultur im 17. und 18. Jahrhundert an den deutschen Fürstenhöfen* (Munich, 1999), 77–105.

58. Papke, 'Miliz zum stehenden Heer', 218–22.

59. P. Mansel, 'Monarchy, Uniform and the Rise of the *Frac*, 1760–1813', *P&P* no. 116 (1982), 103–22; P.-M. Hahn, 'Aristokratisierung und Professionalisierung: Der Aufstieg der Obristen zu einer militärischen und höfischen Elite in Brandenburg-Preussen, 1650–1725', *FBPG* n.s. i (1991), 161–208.

60. Fiedler, *Grundriss* i, 104.

61. M. Hochedlinger, *Austria's Wars of Emergence: War, State and Society in the Habsburg Monarchy, 1683–1797* (London, 2003), 26–7; id., 'The Habsburg Monarchy: From "Military-Fiscal State" to "Militarization" ', C. Storrs (ed.), *The Fiscal-Military State in Eighteenth-Century Europe: Essays in Honour of P. G. M. Dickson* (Farnham, 2009), 55–95; see also the detailed examination by P. G. M. Dickson, *Finance and Government under Maria Theresa, 1740–1780* (2 vols, Oxford, 1987).

62. W. Schulze, 'Das Ständewesen in den Erblanden der Habsburger Monarchie bis 1740: Vom dualistische Ständestaat zum organisch-föderativen Absolutismus', P. Baumgart and J. Schmädeke (eds), *Ständetum und Staatsbildung in Brandenburg-Preussen* (Berlin, 1983), 263–79.

63. Even in 1756, the loss of Silesia was of little intrinsic significance to the Magyar nobles, see anon. memo., 'Animadvertiones qu[a]e de utilium Hungaricae Insurrectionis huis aliquid offerunt', n.d. [1756], KA, AFA, Cabinets-Acten 1756, K. 598, XIII-2; P. Maťa, 'Die Habsburgermonarchie', id., M. Hochedlinger and T. Winkelbauer (eds), *Verwaltungsgeschichte der Habsburgermonarchie in der frühen Neuzeit* (2 vols, Vienna, 2019), i, esp. 40–3 [29–62].

64. Military professionals could nevertheless rise far in Austria, M. Hochedlinger, 'Mars Ennobled: The Ascent of the Military and the Creation of a Military Nobility in Mid-Eighteenth-Century Austria', *GH* xvii, 2 (1999), 141–76.

65. O. Regele, *Der Hofkriegsrat, 1556–1848* (Vienna, 1949) offers a succinct account; for Joseph's reforms M. Hochedlinger, *Thron und Gewehr: Das Problem der Heeresergänzung und der Militarisierung der Habsburger Monarchie im Zeitalter des aufgeklärten Absolutismus, 1740–1790* (Graz, 2021), 645–81.

66. Unsigned to Maria Theresa, 4 Sept. 1756, KA, AFA, Cabinets-Acten 1756, K. 598, IX-3.

67. In exile, Napoleon rued his decision to let Prussia survive, G. Gourgaud, *Sainte-Hélène: Journal inédit de 1815 à 1819* (2 vols, Paris, 1899), ii, 402: 'J'aurais dû la changer, je le pouvais' ('I should have changed it, I could have'); also W. D. Godsey, *The Sinews of Habsburg Power: Lower Austria in a Fiscal-Military State, 1650–1820* (Oxford, 2018), 359–92.

68. A partial exception were the forces maintained by the free cities, see e.g. T. Schwark, *Lübecks Stadtmilitär im 17. und 18. Jahrhundert: Untersuchungen zur Sozialgeschichte einer reichsstädtischen Berufsgruppe* (Lübeck, 1990), 45–54; for the the contested nature of the term 'absolutism' see H. Duchhardt, 'Die Absolutismusdebatte: Eine Antikritik', *HZ* cclxxv, 3 (2002), 323–31.

69. M. Braubach, *Die Bedeutung der Subsidien für die Politik im Spanischen Erbfolgekriege* (Bonn, 1923); C. Becker, 'Von Kurkölns Beziehungen zu Frankreich und seiner wirtschaftlichen Lage im Siebenjährigen Kriege', *AHVN* c (1917), esp. 43–9; H. Weber, 'Frankreich, Münster und Kurtrier, 1692–1693', K. Repgen and S. Skalweit (eds), *Spiegel der Geschichte: Festgabe für Max Braubach zum 10. April 1964* (Münster, 1964), 501 49.

70. Hinrichs, *Friedrich Wilhelm I.*, 763–4.

71. As quoted in Hardwicke to Newcastle, 14 Sept. 1760, P. C. Yorke, *The Life and Correspondence of Philip Yorke, Earl of Hardwicke, Lord High Chancellor of Great Britain* (3 vols, Cambridge, 1913), iii, 247.

72. See e.g. the promise by Lieutenant-Field Marshal Claudius Baron de Sincère to keep 'a watchful eye' on the battalion von Haller as it arrived at Olmütz, Sincère to Hofkriegsrat, 13 Sept. 1756, KA, AFA, Hofkriegsrath 1756, K. 596, IX-38K.

73. Ulrich Bräker, a Swiss pressed into Prussian service, used the confusion after the battle of Lobositz (Lovosice) of 1 October 1756 to desert, id., *Lebensgeschichte und Natürliche Ebentheuer des Armen Mannes im Tockenburg*, ed. S. Voellmy (Basel, 1978 [1st 1788]), 183–8.

74. G. A. Craig, *The Politics of the Prussian Army, 1640–1945* (Oxford, 1955), 8.

75. J. Black, *War in the Eighteenth Century* (London, repr. 2002), 164–95.

76. For a discussion of contemporary ideas see A. Gat, *A History of Military Thought: From the Enlightenment to the Cold War* (Oxford, 2001), 27–96.

77. C. Duffy, *Siege Warfare: The Fortress in the Early Modern World, 1494–1660* (London, repr. 1996) and *Fire and Stone: The Science of Fortress Warfare, 1660–1860* (Newton Abbot, 1975).

78. R. Waddington, *La guerre de sept ans* (5 vols, Paris, 1899–1914), i, 444–95.

79. G. Ritter, *Staatskunst und Kriegshandwerk: Das Problem des Militarismus in Deutschland* (4 vols, Munich, 1954–68), i, 50–9.

80. In the case of the Polish succession, matters were complicated because the question also furnished Versailles with a pretext for meddling in the affairs of Lorraine and an opportunity for reactivating the dormant Franco-Spanish alliance, A. M. Wilson, *French Foreign Policy during the Administration of Cardinal Fleury* (Cambridge, MA, 1938), 232–48; also R. Taverneaux, 'La Lorraine, les Habsbourg et l'Europe', id., J.-P. Bled and E. Faucher (eds), *Les Habsbourg et la Lorraine* (Nancy, 1988), 11–28.

81. T. Schieder, *Friedrich der Grosse: Königtum der Widersprüche* (Frankfurt, 1983), 153–4.

82. See W. Bleyl, *Silberberg: Die Passfestung Schlesiens. Darstellung einer friderizianischen Festungsanlage auf Grund örtlicher und aktenmässiger Bauforschungen* (Cologne, repr. 1977 [1st 1938]), 13–14.

83. Frederick II, 'Generalprincipien des Krieges in Anwendung auf die Taktik und auf die Disciplin der preussischen Truppen' [1753], H. Merkens (ed.), *Ausgewählte Kriegswissenschaftliche Schriften Friedrichs des Grossen* (Jena, 1876), 5.

84. But see the important revisionist take by I. Berkovich, *Motivation in War: The Experience of the Common Soldier in Old Regime Europe* (Cambridge, 2017), 17–54.

85. Mitchell to Holderness (private), 4 Nov. 1756, Mitchell MSS., BL, Add. MSS. 6831.

86. Yorke to Hardwicke, 31 July 1758, Yorke, *Life of Hardwicke* iii, 218–29; see also the cultural study by K. and S. Möbius, *Prussian Army Soldiers and the Seven Years' War: The Psychology of Honour* (London, 2019).

87. As quoted in P. Gaxotte, *Frédéric II* (Paris, repr. 1982), 217.

88. A. Jones, *The Art of War in the Western World* (Oxford, 1989 (pb)), 289–94.

89. S. Fiedler, 'Die taktische Entwicklung der Armee unter Friedrich dem Grossen', Wehrgeschichliches Museum Schloss Rastatt (ed.), *Die Bewaffnung und Ausrüstung der Armee Friedrich des Grossen: Eine Dokumentation* (Rastatt, 1986), 15–31. For a technical study see A. Wirtgen, *Die preussischen Handfeuerwaffen: Modelle und Manufaktur, 1700–1806* (2 vols, Osnabrück, 1976).

90. Grosser Generalstab, *Die Kriege Friedrich des Grossen*, 3rd ser., *Der Siebenjährige Krieg* (13 vols, Berlin, 1901–12), x, 245–78.

91. This is not to suggest that the regions traversed by belligerent armies escaped altogether unscathed, see M. Braubach, 'Politik und Kriegsführung am Niederrhein während des Siebenjährigen Krieges', *DJ* xlviii (1956), 65–103, and for 1689 K. von Raumer, *Die Zerstörung der Pfalz von 1689 im Zusammenhang der französischen Rheinpolitik* (Munich, 1930).

Chapter 2

1. A useful survey of Russia's growth is G. Nekrasov, *Rol' Rossii v evropeiskoi mezhdunarodnoi politike 1725–1739 gg.* (Moscow, 1976).

2. J. L. Sutton, *The King's Honor and the King's Cardinal: The War of the Polish Succession* (Lexington, KT, 1980); K. O. von Aretin, *Das Alte Reich, 1648–1806*, ii, *Kaisertradition und österreichische Grossmachtpolitik, 1648–1745* (Stuttgart, 1997), 288–96.

3. K. A. Roider, *Austria's Eastern Question, 1700–1790* (Princeton, NJ, 1982), 71–90; id., 'Perils of Eighteenth-Century Peacemaking: Austria and the Treaty of Belgrade', *CEH* v, 2 (1972), 195–207; J. Whaley, *Germany and the Holy Roman Empire* (2 vols, Oxford, 2013 (pb)), ii, 163–8.

4. A. M. Wilson, *French Foreign Policy during the Administration of Cardinal Fleury* (Cambridge, MA, 1938), 321–3.

5. See Frederick's instruction to the envoy to France, Paul Heinrich von Camas and A. Berney, *Friedrich der Grosse: Entwicklungsgeschichte eines Staatsmannes* (Tübingen, 1934), 113–14.

6. R. Browning, *The War of the Austrian Succession* (London, 1994) offers a discussion of the background.

7. O. Redlich, *Das Werden einer Grossmacht: Österreich von 1700 bis 1740* (Brno and Vienna, 3rd ed. 1942), 320–49, offers much detail; see also M. S. Anderson, *The War of the Austrian Succession, 1740–1748* (London, 2nd ed. 1999), 7–11. C. W. Ingrao, 'The Pragmatic Sanction and the Theresian Succession', W. J. McGill (ed.), *The Habsburg Dominions under Maria Theresa* (Washington, PA, 1980), 3–18, offers the best modern analysis.

8. H. von Zwiedeneck-Südenhorst, 'Die Anerkennung der pragmatischen Sanktion durch das Deutsche Reich', *MIÖG* xvi (1894), 276–341.

9. L. Hüttl, 'Die bayerischen Erbansprüche auf Böhmen, Ungarn und Österreich in der frühen Neuzeit', F. Seibt (ed.), *Die böhmischen Länder zwischen Ost und West: Festschrift für Karl Bosl* (Munich, 1983), 7–88; F. Wagner, *Kaiser Karl VII und die grossen Mächte, 1740–1745* (Stuttgart, 1938); L. Schilling, 'Der Wiener Hof und Sachsen-Polen, 1697–1764', Verein für sächsische Landesgeschichte (ed.), *Sachsen-Polen zwischen 1697 und 1765* (Dresden, 1998), 124–8.

10. A. Schmid, 'Franz I. und Maria Theresia, 1745–1765', A. Schindling and W. Ziegler (eds), *Die Kaiser der Neuzeit, 1519–1918: Heiliges Römisches Reich, Österreich und Deutschland* (Munich, 1990), 232–48; H. Collin, 'François-Etienne, dernier duc de Lorraine (1729–1737) et premier Empereur de la maison de Lorraine-Habsbourg (1745–1765)', J.-P. Bled and E. Faucher (eds), *Les Habsbourg et la Lorraine* (Nancy, 1988), 151–9.

11. Wilson, *Fleury*, 262–3; for the text see F. W. Ghillany, *Europäische Chronik von 1492 bis Ende April 1865, mit besonderer Berücksichtigung der Friedensverträge* (3 vols, Leipzig, 1865), i, 251–4.

12. Public debt amounted to 101 million florins, G. Otruba, *Die Wirtschaftspolitik Maria Theresias* (Vienna, 1963), 21–2.

13. I. Kállay, 'Die Staatsrechtliche Stellung Ungarns un des Landtags unter Maria Theresia', G. Mraz and G. Schlag (eds), *Maria Theresia als Königin von Ungarn* (Eisenstadt, 1980), 22–9.

14. Erizzo relazione, 7 Oct. 1738, A. von Arneth (ed.), *Die Relationen der Botschafter Venedigs über Österreich im achtzehnten Jahrhundert* (Vienna, 1863), 150–1.

15. Charles Albert had sought to raise his army from 6,200 in 1733 to 60,000, a target never reached. His 42,000-strong force swallowed 68.4 per cent of government expenditure. By the end of the decade, he had to reduce the army to 10,000 men, A. Schmid, 'Karl VII., 1742–1745', Schindling and Ziegler (eds), *Kaiser*, 218–20; Wagner, *Kaiser Karl VII.*, 22–9.

16. P. C. Hartmann, *Karl Albrecht—Karl VII.: Glücklicher Kurfürst, unglücklicher Kaiser* (Regensburg, 1985), 126–31.

17. P. Geyl, *Willem IV en Engeland tot 1748 (Vrede van Aken)* (The Hague, 1924), 76–82. Essential reading for the background is J. Black, *Natural and Necessary Enemies: Anglo-French Relations in the Eighteenth Century* (London, 1986).

18. For an earlier attempt see R. Schnur, *Der Rheinbund von 1658 in der deutschen Verfassungsgeschichte* (Bonn, 1955), 40–9.

19. Frederick to Voltaire, 26 Oct. 1740, as quoted in R. Peyrefitte, *Voltaire et Fréderic II* (2 vols, Paris, 1991), i, 174; P. H. Wilson, 'Prussia's Relations with the Holy Roman Empire, 1740–1786', *HJ* li, 2 (2008), 347.

20. The extent of Brandenburg aspirations was outlined in Frederick William, 'Entwurf', 1670, R. Dietrich (ed), *Politische Testamente der Hohenzollern* (Munich, 1981 (pb)), 80–7; R. Koser, *Geschichte Friedrichs des Grossen* (4 vols, Stuttgart and Berlin, 5th ed. 1912), i, 225–47.

21. W. Maurenbrecher, 'Die Politik Friedrich des Grossen (I)', *Preussische Jahrbücher* xxvii, 5 (1871), 549–51.

22. C. Grünhagen, *Schlesien unter Friedrich dem Grossen* (2 vols, Wolfenbüttel, repr. 2014 [1st 1889]), i, 31–9; H.-W. Büchsel, 'Oberschlesien im Brennpunkt der Grossen Politik', *Forschungen zur Brandenburgisch-Preussischen Geschichte* xli, 1 (1939), 83–102; also P. Baumgart, 'Schlesien', J. Ziechmann (ed.), *Panorama der Fridericianischen Zeit: Friedrich der Grosse und seine Epoche—ein Handbuch* (Bremen, 1985), 705–15.

23. Minutes of Rheinsberg conference, 29 Oct. 1740, *PC* i, no. 119. An excellent analysis is offered by T. Schieder, 'Macht und Recht: Der Ursprung der Eroberung Schlesiens durch König Friedrich II. von Preussen', *HJWG* xxiv (1979), 235–91; this should be read in conjunction with J. Kunisch, *Friedrich der Grosse: Der König in seiner Zeit* (Munich, 2004), 159–63.

24. Frederick to Podewils, 16 Dec. 1740, *PC* i, no. 208; T. Schieder, *Friedrich der Grosse: Königtum der Widersprüche* (Frankfurt, 1983), 145–6; G. Ritter, *Friedrich der Grosse: Ein historisches Profil* (Königstein im Taunus, repr. 1978), 96–8.

25. Koser, *Geschichte* i, 271–87.

26. C. W. Ingrao, 'Habsburg Strategy and Geopolitics during the Eighteenth Century', G. Rothenberg (ed.), *East Central European Society and War in the Pre-Revolutionary Eighteenth Century* (Boulder, CO, 1982), 49–66.

27. Robinson to Harrington, 22 Feb. 1741, TNA, SP 80/144.

28. J. Black, 'The Hanoverian Nexus: Walpole and the Electorate', and H. M. Scott, 'Hanover in Mid-Eighteenth-Century Franco-British Geopolitics', B. Simms and T. Riotte (eds), *The Hanoverian Dimension in British History, 1714–1837* (Cambridge, 2007), 18–19, and 275–300; for tensions within the Hanoverian ministry, U. Dann, *Hanover and Great Britain: Diplomacy and Survival, 1740–1760* (Leicester, 1991), 22–40.

29. W. Mediger, *Moskaus Weg nach Europa: Der Aufstieg Russlands zum europäischen Machtstaat im Zeitalter Friedrich des Grossen* (Braunschweig, 1952), 510–16; J. Kunisch, 'Der Aufstieg neuer Grossmächte im 18. Jahrhundert und die Aufteilung der Machtsphären in Ostmitteleuropa', G. Klingenstein and F. A. J. Szabo (eds), *Staatskanzler Wenzel Anton von Kaunitz-Rietberg, 1711–1794: Neue Perspektiven zur Politik und Kultur der europäischen Aufklärung* (Graz, 1996), 70–90.

30. E. Guglia, *Maria Theresia: Ihr Leben und ihre Regierung* (2 vols, Munich and Berlin, 1917), i, 138–9; P. H. Wilson, *The Holy Roman Empire: A Thousand Years of European History* (London, 2017), 476.

31. P. G. M. Dickson, 'English Negotiations with Austria, 1737–1752', A. Whiteman (ed.), *Essays in Eighteenth-Century History, Presented to Dame Lucy Sutherland* (Oxford, 1973), 81–112; and Anderson, *Austrian Succession*, 80–9.

32. Wagner, *Karl VII*, 117–33; M. Sautai, *Les préliminaires de la guerre de la Succession d'Autriche* (Paris, 1907), 133–52 and 157–60.

33. Koser, *Geschichte* i, 304–20; M. Rohrschneider, 'Leopold I. von Anhalt-Dessau. Die oranische Heeresreform und die Reorganisation der preussischen Armee unter Friedrich Wilhelm I.', P. Baumgart, B. R. Kroener, and H. Stübig (eds), *Die Preussische Armee: Zwischen Ancien Régime und Reichsgründung* (Paderborn, 2008), 45–72.

34. D. E. Showalter, *The Wars of Frederick the Great* (London, 1996), 45–51. Poor generalship on the Austrian side helped the Prussian secure victory, O. Regele, 'Die Schuld des Grafen Reinhard Wilhelm von Neipperg am Belgrader Frieden, 1739, und an der Niederlage bei Mollwitz, 1741', MÖSA vii (1954), 373–98; for Frederick's reforms of the cavalry, C. Duffy, *The Army of Frederick the Great* (London, 1974), 106–7.

35. The text is Ghillany, *Europäische Chronik* i, 259–60; Hartmann, *Karl VII.*, 180–99.

36. Frederick was still something of a diplomatic 'beginner' Berney, *Friedrich der Grosse*, 144–5.

37. J. Black, 'Mid-Eighteenth-Century Conflicts with Particular Reference to the Wars of the Polish and Austrian Succession', id. (ed.), *The Origins of War in Early Modern Europe* (Edinburgh, 1988), 228.

38. Kunisch, *Friedrich der Grosse*, 193–7.

39. Still useful A. Unzer, *Die Konvention von Klein-Schnellendorf (9. Oktober 1741)* (Frankfurt, 1889); R. Lodge, *Great Britain and Prussia in the Eighteenth Century* (Oxford, 1923), 36–8 and 67–8.

40. See Koser's apposite comments, id., *Geschichte* i, 367; for Vienna's hesitations see T. Lau, *Die Kaiserin: Maria Theresia* (Vienna, 2016), 84–5.

41. Grünhagen, *Schlesien* i, 179–93; R. Butler, *Choiseul, i, Father and Son, 1719–1785* (Oxford, 1980), 296–301.

42. J. Black, *A System of Ambition?: British Foreign Policy, 1660–1793* (London, 1991), 168–9.

43. Wagner, *Karl VII.*, 187–212. Fewer than half the Bohemian nobles recognized Charles Albert as king, Hartmann, *Karl VII.*, 202–4.

44. B. Stollberg-Rollinger, *Maria Theresia: Die Kaiserin in ihrer Zeit* (Munich, 2017), 80–95.

45. The plan was attractive enough, but the Republic was now but a shadow of its former self and its internal situation paralyzed Dutch politics, see Bentinck to Countess of Portland, 13 Mar. 1742, C. Gerretson and P. Geyl (eds), *Briefwisseling en Aantekeningen van Willem Bentinck, Heer van Rhoon (tot an de dood van Willem IV)* (3 vols, The Hague, 1976), i, no. XLV.

46. Showalter, *Wars of Frederick the Great*, 59–61; O. Herrmann, 'Von Mollwitz bis Chotusitz: Ein Beitrag zur Taktik Friedrich des Grossen', FBPG vii, 2 (1894), 13–61, offers a nineteenth-century perspective.

47. Carteret to Hyndford, 30 Mar. 1742, Carteret MSS., BL, Add. MSS. 22,531.

48. Lodge, *Britain and Prussia*, 40; the text is in Ghillany, *Europäische Chronik* i, 263–4.

49. R. Lodge, *Studies in Eighteenth-Century Diplomacy, 1740–1748* (London, 1930), 31–79; B. Williams, 'Carteret and the So-Called Treaty of Hanau', *English Historical Review* xliv, 4 (1934), 684–7.

50. Kunisch, *Friedrich der Grosse*, 173–4 and 209–10.

51. Grünhagen, *Schlesien* i, 219–32; Showalter, *Wars of Frederick the Great*, 75–9.

52. Wagner, *Karl VII.*, 604–33; Hartmann, *Karl VII.*, 296–304.

53. J. Muth, *Flucht aus dem militärischen Alltag: Ursachen und individuelle Ausprägung der Desertion in der Armee Friedrichs des Grossen* (Freiburg, 2003).

54. On this point see also H. Hantsch, *Die Entwicklung Österreich-Ungarns zur Grossmacht* (Freiburg, 1933), 104; for the Treaty of Füssen see Browning, *War of the Austrian Succession*, 203; the text is in Ghillany, *Europäische Chronik* i, 270–1.

55. Frederick to Podewils, 8 May 1745, *PC* iv, no. 1828; Koser, *Geschichte* i, 484.

56. C. Duffy, *Frederick the Great: A Military Life* (London, 1985), 59–62; see also the reminiscences of J. A. F. Logan-Logejus, *Meine Erlebnisse als Reiteroffizier unter dem Grossen König in den Jahren 1742–1759* (Breslau, 3rd ed. 1934), 90–108.

57. H. Stabenau, *Die Schlacht bei Soor* (Frankfurt, 1901) offers a detailed account; see also C. Jany, *Geschichte der Königlich Preussischen Armee* (4 vols, Berlin, 1928–33), ii, 146–9.

58. Showalter, *Wars of Frederick the Great*, 87.

59. Ghillany, *Europäische Chronik* i, 273–4. For the Prussians the arrangement was defensive, for the Austrians it was an offensive means in the struggle for Silesia, H.-W. Bergerhausen, 'Nur ein Stück Papier?: Die Garantieerklärung für die österreichisch-preussischen Friedensverträge von 1742 und 1745', H. Neuhaus and B. Stollberg-Rillinger (eds), *Menschen und Strukturen in der Geschichte Alteuropas: Festschrift für Johannes Kunisch zur Vollendung seines 65. Lebensjahres* (Berlin, 2002), 267–78.

60. Lodge, *Studies*, 311–411, offers a detailed account of the negotiations; see also W. Bein, *Schlesien in der habsburgischen Politik: Ein Beitrag zur Entstehung des Dualismus im Alten Reich* (Sigmaringen, 1994), 291–4.

61. For a critical judgement, albeit from an orthodox Marxist perspective, see I. Mittenzwei, *Friedrich II. von Preussen: Biographie* (Cologne, 3rd ed. 1983), 80–3.

62. For a discussion of the armaments programmes of the powers between the late 1740s and 1756 see the important study by B. R. Kroener, 'Herrschaftsverdichtung als Kriegsursache: Wirtschaft und Rüstung der europäischen Grossmächte im Siebenjährigen Krieg', B. Wegener (ed.), *Wie Kriege entstehen: Zum historischen Hintergrund von Staatenkonflikten* (Paderborn, 2000), 145–74.

63. See J. Kunisch, 'Der Historikerstreit über den Ausbruch des Siebenjährigen Krieges', id., *Friedrich der Grosse in seiner Zeit: Essays* (Munich, 2008), 48–105.

64. F. A. J. Szabo, *Kaunitz and Enlightened Absolutism, 1753–1780* (Cambridge, 1980), 20–51, provides a thorough overview; more impressionistic, but still useful, A. Novotny, *Staatskanzler Kaunitz als geistige Persönlichkeit: Ein österreichisches Kulturbild aus der Zeit der Aufklärung und des Josephinismus* (Vienna, 1947).

65. 'Additional Instructions' for Count Podewils, 12 May 1746, C. Hinrichs (ed.), *Friedrich der Grosse und Maria Theresia: Diplomatische Berichte von Otto Christoph Graf von Podewils, Königlich Preussischer Gesandter am Österreichischen Hofe in Wien* (Berlin, 1937), 29–32.

66. Schieder, *Friedrich der Grosse*, 168–9; for a sceptical note see F. A. J. Szabo, *The Seven Years' War in Europe, 1756–1763* (Abingdon, repr. 2013), 105–16.

67. L. von Ranke, 'Die Grossen Mächte', id., *Sämtliche Werke* (Leipzig, 1874), xxiv, 23.

68. *Staats-Betrachtungen über gegenwärtigen Preussischen Krieg in Teutschland, in wie fern solcher das allgemeine Europäische vornehmlich aber das Teutsche Interesse betrifft, mit untermischten völkerrechtlichen Bemerkungen* (Vienna, 1761), repr. in J. Kunisch, *Das Mirakel des Hauses Brandenburg: Studien zum Verhältnis von Kabinettspolitik und Kriegsführung im Zeitalter des Siebenjährigen Krieges* (Munich, 1978), app. II, 136.

69. Memo. 'Memoire sur les dangers dont l'Autriche et toute Allemagne sont menaces de le part de Prusse', n.d. [1749/50], HHStA, Staatskanzlei, Preussen, Collecteana, K. 201.

70. See Kunisch, *Mirakel*, 30–1; F. Walter, *Die Paladine der Kaiserin: Ein Maria-Theresia-Buch* (Vienna, 1959), 40–2.

71. Memo. Kaunitz, 'Opinion du Prince Kaunitz-Rietberg sur l'état des circon-stances militaires et politiques', 7 Sept. 1778, repr. in K. O. von Aretin, *Heiliges Römisches Reich, 1776 bis 1806: Reichsverfassung und Staatssouveranität* (2 vols, Wiesbaden, 1967), ii, doc. no. 1; also L. Schilling, *Kaunitz und das Renversement des alliances: Studien zur aussenpolitischen Konzeption Wenzel Antons von Kaunitz* (Berlin, 1994), 19–52.

72. See inter alia M. Füssel, *Der Siebenjährige Krieg: Ein Weltkrieg des 18. Jahrhunderts* (Munich, 2010); D. Baugh, *The Global Seven Years' War, 1754–1763* (London, 2013); and E. Dziembowski, *La guerre de sept ans (1756–1763)* (Paris, 2015).

73. Parliament was wary at any rate of paying Austria more subsidies, Pelham to Carteret, 15 July 1743, Carteret MSS., BL, Add. MSS. 22,536.

74. D. B. Horn, 'The Cabinet Controversy on Subsidy Treaties in Time of Peace, 1749–1750', *EHR* xliii, 3 (1930), 463–6; R. Browning, 'The Duke of Newcastle and the Imperial Election Plan, 1749–1754', *JBS* i, 1 (1967), 28–67; T. R. Clayton, 'The Duke of Newcastle, the Earl of Halifax, and the American Origins of the Seven Years' War', *HJ* xxiii, 4 (1981), 571–603.

75. P. Baumgart, 'Schlesien als eigenständige Provinz im altpreussischen Staat (1740–1806)', N. Conrads (ed.), *Deutsche Geschichte im Osten*, iii, *Schlesien* (Berlin, 1994), 384–94.

76. Instructive, J. Burkhardt, 'Geschichte als Argument in der Habsburgisch-Französischen Diplomatie: Der Wandel des frühneuzeitlichen Geschichtsbewusstseins in seiner Bedeutung für die Diplomatische Revolution von 1756', R. Babel (ed.), *Frankreich im Europäischen Staatssystem der Frühen Neuzeit* (Sigmaringen, 1995), 196–9.

77. G. Zeller, *Histoire des relations internationales*, iii, *De Louis XIV à 1789* (Paris, 1955), 227–35; J. Black, *From Louis XIV to Napoleon: The Fate of a Great Power* (London, 1999), 100–6.

78. Tensions had been building in North America for some time, see L. H. Gipson, *Zones of International Friction: North America, south of the Great Lakes Region, 1748–1754* (New York, 1937); P. Higgonet, 'The Origins of the Seven Years' War', *JMH* xl, 1 (1968), 57–90; also J. Black, 'Anglo-French Relations in the Mid-Eighteenth Century, 1740–1756', *Francia* xlii, 2 (1990), 70–3.

79. W. J. McGill, 'The Roots of Policy: Kaunitz in Italy and the Netherlands, 1742–1746', *CEH* i, 2 (1968), 131–49. Maria Theresa had already decided in the autumn of 1750 to make Kaunitz chancellor but had to await a suitable opportunity, G. Klingenstein, 'Kaunitz contra Bartenstein: Zur Geschichte der Staatskanzlei in den Jahren 1749–1753', H. Fichtenau and E. Zöllner (eds), *Beiträge zur neueren Geschichte Österreichs* (Vienna, 1974), 243–63; Stollberg-Rillinger, *Maria Theresia*, 230–7.

80. W. J. McGill, 'Wenzel Anton von Kaunitz-Rietberg and the Conference of Aix-la-Chappelle, 1748', *DR* xiv, 2 (1969), 154–69.

81. Memo. Kaunitz, 'Meynungen des Graffen Kaunitz über das auswärtige System', 24 Mar. 1749, repr. R. Pommerin and L. Schilling, 'Denkschrift des Grafen Kaunitz zur mächtepolitischen Konstellation nach dem Aachener Frieden von 1748', J. Kunisch (ed.), *Expansion und Gleichgewicht: Studien zur europäischen Mächtepolitik des ancien régime* (Berlin, 1986), here 207–9.

82. Maria Theresa to Daun, 24 July 1759, repr. in J. Kunisch, 'Der Ausgang des Siebenjährigen Kriegs: Ein Beitrag zum Verhältnis von Kabinettspolitik und Kriegsführung im Zeitalter des Absolutismus', *ZHF* ii, 2 (1975), 220.

83. For the Protestant dimension of the dualism see P.-M. Hahn, *Friedrich II. von Preussen* (Stuttgart, 2013), 69.

84. Kaunitz's secret reports from Paris are to be found in H. Schlitter (ed.), *Correspondance secrète entre le comte Anton Wenzel Kaunitz-Rietberg, Ambassadeur impérial à Paris, et le Baron Ignaz de Koch, Secrétair de l'Imperatrice Marie-Thérèse, 1750–1752* (Paris, 1895); see also W. J. McGill, 'The Roots of Policy: Kaunitz in Vienna and Versailles', *JMH* xlii, 2 (1971), 228–44; R. Browning, 'The British Orientation of Austrian Foreign Policy, 1749–1754', *CEH* i, 3 (1968), 299–323.

85. Memo. Kaunitz, July 1756, F. Dickmann (ed.), *Geschichte in Quellen*, iii, *Renaissance, Glaubenskämpfe, Absolutismus* (Munich, 1966), 686–7.

86. In 1750 senior Dutch diplomats still thought that any British ministry '*dans toute affaire du continent ne peut aller que de pair avec la République, s'il ne veut se perdre*', as quoted in Geyl, *Willem IV*, 291, n. 2.

87. See 'Nouveau projet de convention', Feb. 1755, A. F. Pribram (ed.), *Österreichische Staatsverträge: England* (2 vols, Vienna, 1913), i, no. 62.

88. *Weisung* Kaunitz to Colloredo, 27 Aug. 1755, HHStA, Staatenabteilung, England, K. 107.

89. Memo. Kaunitz, 28 Aug. 1755, ibid., Staatskanzlei, Vorträge, K. 76; also in G. B. Volz and G. Küntzel (eds), *Preussische und Österreichische Acten zur Vorgeschichte des Siebenjährigen Krieges* (Osnabrück, repr. 1965), no. II/1.

90. French views of the Prussian king veered between notions of an '*allié naturel*' and an '*indigné allié*', see S. Skalweit, *Frankreich und Friedrich der Grosse: Der Aufstieg Preussens in der öffentlichen Meinung des "ancien régime"* (Bonn, 1952), 9–39 et passim.

91. The classic accounts are R. Waddington, *Louis XV et le renversement des alliances: Préliminaires de la guerre de sept ans* (Paris, 1896), and M. Braubach, *Versailles und Wien von Ludwig XIV. bis Kaunitz: Die Vorstadien der diplomatischen Revolution im 18. Jahrhundert* (Bonn, 1952); also W. G. Rödel, 'Eine geheime französische Initiative als Auslöser für das Renversement des Alliances?', Kunisch (ed.), *Expansion und Gleichgewicht*, 98–112.

92. E. M. Satow, *Frederick the Great and the Silesian Loan* (London, 1907) offers a dry but detailed account of this thorny dispute; otherwise Lodge, *Britain and Prussia*, 76–81.

93. Frederick II, 'Political Testament', 27 Aug. 1752, R. Dietrich (ed.), *Die Politischen Testamente der Hohenzollern* (Munich, 1981 (pb)), 176, 179, 186 and 180–2; E. Bosbach, *Die "Rêveries Politiques" in Friedrichs des Grossen Politischem Testament von 1752: Historisch-Politische Erläuterungen* (Cologne and Graz, 1960), 41–59.

94. In 1756, the French navy had nearly seventy ships of the line ready for action, enough perhaps to reverse the outcome of the previous wars at sea, provided France did not have to fight a war in Europe at the same time.

95. Newcastle to Hardwicke, 6 Sept. 1751, W. Coxe, *Memoirs of the Administration of the Rt. Hon. Henry Pelham* (2 vols, London, 1829), ii, 406; also Mitchell to Holderness (secret), 14 May 1756, Mitchell MSS., BL, Add. MSS. 6871.

96. R. Pommerin, 'Bündnispolitik und Mächtesystem: Österreich und der Aufstieg Russlands im 18. Jahrhundert', Kunisch (ed.), *Expansion und Gleichgewicht*, esp. 118–34.

97. H. H. Kaplan, *Russia and the Outbreak of the Seven Years' War* (Berkeley, CA, 1968), 44–7; M. J. Müller, 'Russland und der Siebenjährige Krieg: Beitrag zu einer Kontroverse', *JbfGO* xxviii (1980), 198–219.

98. G. Küntzel, 'Die Westminster Konvention', *Forschungen zur Brandenburgisch-Preussischen Geschichte* ix, 4 (1897), 541–69, provides a detailed account, which should be read in conjunction with K. W. Schweitzer, *Frederick the Great, William Pitt, and Lord Bute: The Anglo-Prussian Alliance, 1756–1763* (New York, 1991).

99. As quoted in Koser, *Geschichte* ii, 346.

100. Mitchell to Newcastle (private), 4 Nov. 1756, Mitchell MSS., BL, Add. MSS. 6831; D. B. Horn, 'The Duke of Newcastle and the Origins of the Diplomatic Revolution', J. H. Elliott and H. G. Koenigsberger (eds),

The Diversity of History: Essays in Honour of Sir Herbert Butterfield (London, 1970), 245–68.

101. Frederick to Knyphausen, 16 Feb. 1756, *PC* xii, no. 7275.
102. Maria Theresa to Starhemberg, 27 Mar. 1756, Volz and Küntzel (eds), *Acten*, no. II/59a.
103. Braubach, *Versailles und Wien*, 423–56; Bein, *Schlesien*, 336–7.
104. Starhemberg to Kaunitz, 2 May 1756, Volz and Küntzel (eds), *Acten*, no. II/82; see also J. C. Batzel, *Austria and the First Three Treaties of Versailles, 1755–1758* (Ann Arbor, MI, 1975); J. Black, 'Strategic Culture and the Seven Years' War', W. Murray, R. H. Sinnreich, and J. Lacey (eds), *The Shaping of Grand Strategy: Politics, Diplomacy and War* (Cambridge, 2011), 68–9.
105. *Weisung* Kaunitz to Esterházy, 22 May 1756, HHStA, Staatenabteilung, Russland II, K. 163.
106. Starhemberg to Kaunitz, 17 Apr. 1756, Volz and Küntzel (eds), *Acten*, no. II/68; Szabo, *Seven Years' War*, 14–16.
107. A. C. Carter, *The Dutch Republic in Europe in the Seven Years' War* (London, 1971), 56–68.
108. Mediger, *Moskaus Weg*, 247–329; H. Bagger, 'The Role of the Baltic in Russian Foreign Policy, 1721–1773', H. Ragsdale (ed.), *Imperial Russian Foreign Policy* (Cambridge, 1993), 36–74.
109. Yorke to Holdernesse, 23 Mar. 1756, Mitchell MSS., BL, Add. MSS. 6871. The source was a Dutch agent.
110. See already H. Butterfield, *The Reconstruction of an Historical Episode: The History of the Enquiry into the Origins of the Seven Years' War* (Glasgow, 1951) (= Eighteenth David Murray Lecture), 30–8.
111. G. Lind, 'The Making of the Neutrality Convention of 1756: France and the Scandinavian Alliance', *SJH* viii, 2 (1983), 171–92.
112. The Prussians had recruited their first spy around March 1747, Frederick to Fredersdorf, 10 Mar. 1747, J. Richter (ed.), *Die Briefe Friedrich des Grossen an seinen vormaligen Kammerdiener Fredersdorf* (Moers, repr. 1979 [1st 1926]), 101; also R. Hanke, *Brühl und das Renversement des Alliances: Die antipreussische Politik des Dresdener Hofes, 1744–1756* (Berlin, 2006).
113. Frederick to Fouqué [commandant of Glatz], 25 June 1756, KA, AFA, Cabinets-Acten 1756, K. 598, VI-7. The Austrians regularly intercepted the king's communications.
114. Frederick to Mitchell, 24 July 1756, *PC* xiii, no. 7746; J. Kunisch, *Friedrich der Grosse: Der König in seiner Zeit* (Munich, 2004), 350–8.
115. See already, though apologetic in tone and substance, Ritter, *Friedrich der Grosse*, 130–1.
116. Brusso to Francis I Stephen, 12 July 1756, KA, AFA, Cabinets-Acten 1756, K. 598, VII-1; also Browne to Neipperg, 24 June 1756, ibid., Hofkriegsrath 1756, K. 596, VII-1; A. Naudé, *Beiträge zur Entstehungsgeschichte des Siebenjährigen Krieges* (Berlin, 1895), 52–94, for Prussian preparations.

117. Frederick to Klinggräffen, 26 Aug. 1756, *PC* xiii, no. 7914; also memo. Klinggräffen, 'Mémoire', 28 Aug. 1756, KA, AFA, Cabinets-Acten 1756, K. 598, VIII-1; R. Waddington, *La guerre de sept ans* (5 vols, Paris, 1899–1914), i, 8–9.

118. The *Hofkriegsrat* still considered Frederick's dispositions as *'eine bloße deffensive'*, Neipperg to Browne, 1 Sept. 1756, KA, AFA, Hofkriegsrath 1756, K. 596, IX-2.

119. Szabo, *Seven Years' War*, 36, even speaks of a 'failed gamble', which seems harsh; also Schieder, *Friedrich der Grosse*, 170–82; W. Baumgart, 'Der Ausbruch des Siebenjährigen Kriegs: Zum gegenwärtigen Forschungsstand', *MGM* xi (1972), 157–65.

120. For a discussion of some of this see R. Middleton, *The Bells of Victory: The Pitt-Newcastle Ministry and the Conduct of the Seven Years' War, 1757–1762* (Cambridge, 1985), 7–13; P. F. Doran, *Andrew Mitchell and Prussia's Diplomatic Relations during the Seven Years' War* (New York, 1986), 50 et passim.

121. For the frantic attempts to preserve the electorate's neutrality see R. Meyer, *Die Neutralitätsverhandlungen des Kurfürstentums Hannover beim Ausbruch des Siebenjährigen Krieges* (Kiel, 1912); A. C. Thompson, *George II: King and Elector* (New Haven, CT, 2011), 253–7.

122. Frederick II, 'Politisches Testament', 27 Aug. 1752, Dietrich (ed.), *Politische Testamente*, 187.

123. Fredrick II, *Considerations sur l'état présent du corps politique de l'Europe* (1739), as quoted in P. Gaxotte, *Frédéric II* (Paris, 1982 (pb)), 179.

124. As reported by the British envoy, Mitchell to Holdernesse (private), 4 Dec. 1756, Mitchell MSS., BL, Add. MSS. 6381.

125. Kunisch, *Mirakel des Hauses Brandenburg*, 77–91.

126. Winterfeldt, one of Frederick's generals, had travelled through Saxony prior to the war, see W. Petter, 'Hans-Karl von Winterfeldt als General der friderizianischen Armee', J. Kunisch (ed.), *Persönlichkeiten im Umfeld Friedrichs des Grossen* (Cologne and Vienna, 1988), 82–4. For the geographical conditions instructive, F. Ratzel, *Politische Geographie* (Munich, 3rd ed. 1925), 564 and 582–3.

127. Podewils to Eichel, 22 July 1756 (summarizing his conversation with Frederick), *PC* xiii, no. 7735; see also H. M. Scott, 'Frederick the Great and the Administration of Prussian Diplomacy', R. Oresko, G. C. Gibbs, and H. M. Scott (eds), *Royal and Republican Sovereignty in Early Modern Europe: Essays in Memory of Ragnhild Hatton* (Cambridge, 1997), 501–26.

128. Stollberg-Rillinger, *Maria Theresia*, 415–17.

129. Note by Austrian government, 'Réponse au Mémoire par Monsr de Klinggraeff, le 2 Sept^{re}', 6 Sept. 1756, KA, AFA, Cabinets-Acten 1756, K. 598, IX-ad 1; also Waddington, *Renversement des Alliances* (Paris, 1896), 475–6, on the unreliability of Bernis' protestations to the contrary.

130. No small achievement for Habsburg diplomacy which was aware of suspicions at the smaller courts that the Austro-French combination

aimed at the suppression of Protestantism, Maria Theresa circular to envoys abroad, 24 July 1756, KA, AFA, Hofkriegsrath 1756, K. 596; see further M. Plassmann, 'Bikonfessionelle Streitkräfte', M. Kaiser and S. Kroll (eds), *Militär und Religiosität in der Frühen Neuzeit* (Münster, 2004), 33–48.

131. Schieder, *Friedrich der Grosse*, 267–8; J. Waley, *Germany and the Holy Roman Empire* (2 vols, Oxford, 2013 (pb)), ii, 359.

132. E. von Kessel, 'Zum Problem des Wandels des Krieges', *Wehr und Wissen* xx, 4 (1939), 103; J. Kunisch, 'Die grosse Allianz der Gegner Preussens sim Siebenjährigen Krieg', B. R. Kroener (ed.), *Europa im Zeitalter Friedrichs des Grossen* (Munich, 1989), 79–97.

133. F. Walter, 'Feldmarschall Leopold Joseph Graf Daun und Feldmarschall Gideon Ernst von Laudon', H. Hantsch (ed.), *Gestalten der Geschichte Österreichs* (Innsbruck, 1962), 263–78; F.-L. von Thadden, *Feldmarschall Daun: Maria Theresias grösster Feldherr* (Vienna, 1967); T. M. Barker, 'Military Nobility: The Daun Family and the Evolution of the Austrian Officer Corps', id., *Army, Aristocracy and Monarchy: Essays on War, Society and Government in Austria, 1618–1780* (Boulder, CO, 1980), 128–46; J. Kunisch, 'Feldmarschall Laudon oder das Soldatenglück', id., *Fürst—Gesellschaft—Krieg: Studien zur bellizistischen Disposition des absoluten Fürstenstaaten* (Cologne and Vienna, 1992), 107–29.

134. e.g. R. Koser, 'Die preussische Kriegsführung im Siebenjährigen Krieg', *HZ* xcii, 2 (1904), esp. 259–62; vide infra Chapter 4.

135. Frederick to Frederick Augustus II, 29 Aug. and 5 Sept. and vice versa, 3 Sept. 1756, *PC* xiii, nos. 7955 and 7981; an agreeable for the Austrians, Kaunitz to Browne, 5 Sept. 1756, KA, AFA, Cabinets-Acten 1756, K. 598, IX-4.

136. Brühl to Browne, 14 Oct. 1756, ibid., X-11a; *Précis de la Retraite de l'Armée Saxonne de son Camp de Pirna* (Frankfurt, 1756), 4 (copy in ibid., XIII-7).

137. See Browne's account, to Kaunitz, 4 Oct. 1756, ibid., X-3. The emperor had impressed on him the '*avantages des Terrains bey Lobositz*', Francis I Stephen to Browne, 17 Sept. 1756, KA, AFA, Hofkriegsrath 1756, K. 596, IX-45; see also C. Duffy, *Feldmarschall Browne: Irischer Emigrant, Kaiserlicher Heerführer, Gegenspieler Friedrich II. von Preussen* (Vienna, 1966), 283–99.

138. O. Groehler, *Die Kriege Friedrichs II.* (Berlin, 6th ed. 1990), 79–81; see also the detailed study by M. von Salisch, *Treue Deserteure: Das Kursächsische Militär und der Siebenjährige Krieg* (Munich, 2008).

139. Mins. Hofkriegsrat, 9 Oct. 1756, KA, Hofkriegsrath Protocolli in Publicis, 1756, vol. 908.

140. Mitchell to Holderness (most secret), 4 Nov. 1756, *PC* xiii, no. 8261; R. Koser, 'Zur Geschichte des preussischen Feldzugplanes vom Frührjahr 1757', *HZ* xcii, 1 (1904), 71–4.

141. A. Kossert, *Ostpreussen: Geschichte und Mythos* (Munich, 2007 (pb)), 92–4; J. H. L. Keep, 'Die russische Armee im Siebenjährigen Krieg', Kroener (ed.),

Europa, 147–52; for the structural flaws in Russian military supplies see D. E. Bangert, *Die russisch-österreichische militärische Zusammenarbeit im Siebenjährigen Krieg in den Jahren 1758–1759* (Boppard am Rhein, 1971), 319–20.

142. The Austrians were nevertheless concerned about the presence of a Royal Navy squadron in the Adriatic and feared an attack on Triest, see Liechtenstein to Maria Theresa, 29 July 1757, KA, AFA, Hofkriegsrath 1757, K. 632.

143. Showalter, *Wars of Frederick the Great*, 152–7, who however cites higher casualty figures.

144. Maria Theresa to Daun, 10 May 1757, KA, AFA, Cabinets-Acten 1757, K. 634, V-2.

145. See Daun's account, id. to Maria Theresa, 19 June 1757, ibid., VI-28; see also Thadden, *Daun*, 263–86. D. Goslich, *Die Schlacht bei Kolin am 18. Juni 1757* (Berlin, 1911) offers a detailed Prussian view of the battle; a useful, modern corrective is P. Broucek, *Der Geburtstag der Monarchie: Die Schlacht von Kolin 1757* (Vienna, 1982), esp. 93–126.

146. Maria Theresa to Daun, 21 June 1756, KA, AFA, Cabinets-Acten 1757, K. 634, VI-31. She also ordered a *Te Deum* to be sung at St. Stephen's cathedral.

147. For Frederick's reaction see Koser, *Geschichte* ii, 501–4; J. Luh, *Der Grosse: Friedrich II. von Preussen* (Berlin, 2011), 63–5.

148. W. von Wersebe, *Geschichte der Hannoverschen Armee* (Hanover, 1928), 150–5; D. Albers, 'Nordwestdeutschland als Kriegsschauplatz im Siebenjährigen Krieg', *NJbfLG* xv (1938), 142–81.

149. Dombasle to Hofkriegsrat, 20 Aug. 1757, KA, AFA, Hofkriegsrath 1757, K. 632; Dann, *Hanover*, 83–105; W. Mediger, 'Hastenbeck und Zeven: Der Eintritt Hannovers in den Siebenjährigen Krieg', *NJbfLG* lvi (1984), 143–5.

150. Mitchell to Holdernesse, 28 Aug. 1757, Yorke MSS., Add. MSS. 6831.

151. Hadik, 'Unterthänigste Relation über die Expedition in die Marck Brandenburg und die Einnahme der Königl: Preuß: Haubt- und Residentz-Stadt Berlin', 22 Oct. 1757, KA, AFA, Hofkriegsrath 1757, K. 632, X-42a; for the contributions see memo. Hadik, 'Specification, waß an auß der Marckt [sic] Brandenburg eingebrachtenen Contributions Königl: Feld-Kriegs-Cassa eingelieferet worden', n.d., ibid., XI-8d; see further F. Escher, 'Die brandenburgisch-preussische Residenz und Hauptstadt im 17. und 18. Jahrhundert', W. Ribbe (ed.), *Geschichte Berlins* (2 vols, Munich, 1987), 398; J. R. McIntyre, 'The Raid on Berlin, 1757', *Journal of the Seven Years' War Association* xxii, 3 (2019), 20–42.

152. Maria Theresa to Daun, 28 May 1757, KA, AFA, Cabinets-Acten 1757, K. 634, V-8, insisting that the 'kleine Krieg' was to be initiated.

153. H. F. Potempa, '"Und kommt der grosse Friedrich...": Die Reichsarmee im Siebenjährigen Krieg', Birk et al. (eds), *Wie Friederich "der Grosse" wurde*, 64–9.

154. Showalter, *Wars of Frederick the Great*, 186–91; Wilson, *German Armies*, 272–4; Kunisch, *Friedrich der Grosse*, 374–8.

155. H. Neuhaus, 'Das Problem der militärischen Exekutive in der Spätphase des alten Reiches', J. Kunisch (ed.), *Staatsverfassung und Heeresverfassung in der europäischen Geschichte in der frühen Neuzeit* (Berlin, 1986), 299; further T. Nicklas, 'Die Schlacht bei Rossbach (1757) zwischen Wahrnehmung und Deutung', *FBPG*, n.s. xii (2002), 35–51.

156. W. J. Kaiser (ed.), *Friedrich der Grosse: Sein Bild im Wandel der Zeiten* (Frankfurt, 1986), 97; K. and S. Möbius, '"They imbibed their hatred of the French with their mother's milk…": The Battle of Rossbach and Mid-18th Century Gallophobia', *JSYWA* xxiii, 2 (2019/20), 4–26.

157. J. W. von Goethe, *Aus Dichtung und Wahrheit*, ch. IV, para 1, 300–1; K.-J. Bremm, *Preussen bewegt die Welt: Der Siebenjährigen Krieg* (Düsseldorf, 2017), 164–5.

158. Holderness to Mitchell, 8 Sept. 1756, A. Bisset, *Memoirs and Papers of Sir Andrew Mitchell, Envoy Extraordinary and Minister Plenipotentiary from the Court of Great Britain to the Court of Prussia, from 1756 to 1771* (2 vols, London, 1850), i, 204.

159. Schweitzer, *Anglo-Prussian Alliance*, 60–1; R. Savory, *His Britannic Majesty's Army in Germany during the Seven Years' War* (Oxford, 1966), 42–60.

160. Kaunitz to Brossart [imperial envoy at Cologne], 18 Nov. 1757, HHStA, Reichskanzlei, Diplomatische Akten Köln, Weisungen 4; C. Becker, 'Die Erlebnisse der kurkölnischen Truppen im Verbande der Reichsarmee während des Siebenjährigen Krieges', *AHVN* xci (1914), 81–2.

Chapter 3

1. Note Hofkriegsrat, 17 Nov. 1757, KA, AFA, Hofkriegsrath 1757, K. 632, XI-7; and Luszinsky to Charles of Lorraine, 1 Dece. 1757, ibid., Haputarmee 1757, K. 614, XII-158; J. W. von Archenholtz, *Geschichte des Siebenjährigen Kriegs* (Halle, s.a. (c.1913/14) [1st 1791]), 90. The Silesian fortresses were basic constructions, intended to be used as *points d'appui* rather than as strongholds, their defences often resting on a ring of detached forts and lunettes which were not connected by continuous entrenchment, see C. Duffy, *Fire and Stone: The Science of Fortress Warfare, 1660–1860* (Newton Abbott, repr. 1976), 68–9.

2. Grosser Generalstab, *Die Kriege Friedrichs des Grossen*, 3rd ser., *Der Siebenjährige Krieg*, vi, *Leuthen* (Berlin, 1904), 7 and 136–7 n.; C. Duffy, *Prussia's Glory: Rossbach and Leuthen 1757* (Chicago, 2003), 114–23.

3. Austrian officials struggled to count the prisoners, but came to 3,982 '*Köpfe*' (heads), Plöckherrn to Daun, 6 Dec. 1757, KA, AFA 1757, Hauptarmee 1757, K. 614, XII-8; F.-L. von Thadden, *Feldmarschall Daun: Maria Theresias grösster Feldherr* (Vienna, 1967), 312–13.

4. Instrument of surrender, 24 Nov. 1757, KA, AFA, Hofkriegsrath 1757, K. 632, XII-3a; see also J. A. F. Logan-Logejus, *Meine Erlebnisse unter dem Grossen König in den Jahren 1741–1759* (Breslau, 3rd ed. 1934), 199–200.

5. Frederick to Prince Henry, 27 Nov. 1757, *PC* xvi, no. 9549. For the *Te Deum* at St. Stephen's see Khevenhüller diary, 15 Nov. 1757, R. Khevenhüller-Metsch and H. Schlitter (eds), *Aus der Zeit Maria Theresias: Tagebücher des Fürsten Johann Joseph Khevenhüller-Metsch, Kaiserlicher Oberhofmeister, 1742–1776* (7 vols, Vienna, 1907–25), iv, 180–1.

6. Frederick to Prince Henry, 27 Nov. 1757, *PC* xvi, no. 9549.

7. Anon., *Bericht von dem Marsch des Preußischen Corps aus Sachsen nach der Bataille bey Weissenfels [i.e. Rossbach] bis in Schlesien nach der Bataille bey Lissa [i.e. Leuthen]* (s.loc., s.a. [1757]), 1–2; further C. F. R. [*recte* E. F. R.] von Barsewisch, *Meine Kriegs-Erlebnisse während des Siebenjährigen Krieges, 1757–1763* (Berlin, 2nd ed. 1863), 24.

8. For details see Grosser Generalstab, *Siebenjähriger Krieg* vi, 2–5.

9. Ibid., 134, for a breakdown of the troops.

10. Memo., 'Die dermahlige Position des Keithischen Corps in Sachsen', n.d., KA, AFA 1757, K. 614, XII-132; S. Coull, *Nothing but my Sword: The Life of Field Marshal James Francis Edward Keith* (Edinburgh, 2000).

11. Arnstett to Frederick, 26 Nov. 1757 (copy), KA, AFA, Hauptarmee 1757, K. 614, XII-147b. The news of Marschall's retreat caused dismay at Vienna, min. Hofkriegsrat, 29 Nov. 1757, KA, Hofkriegsrath Protocolli 1757, vol. 908.

12. Netolitzky to Charles, 2 Dec. 1757, and Laudon to Charles, 4 Dec. 1757, KA, AFA, Hauptarmee 1757, K. 614, XII-182 and 216.

13. Los Rios to Daun, 1 Dec. 1757, ibid.; see also E. Köhl, *Die Geschichte der Festung Glatz* (Würzburg, 1972), 73.

14. The Austrians kept a careful watch on Frederick's army, Palasty to Daun, 1 Dec. 1757, KA, AFA, Hauptarmee 1757, K. 614, XII-162.

15. For the high rate of desertion, Kyau to Frederick, 27 Nov. 1757, Königlich Preussischer Generalstab (ed.), *Friedrich der Grosse von Kolin bis Rossbach und Leuthen nach den Cabinetts-Ordres im Königlichen Staats-Archiv* (Berlin, 1858), 112. For Zieten's role, I. Rockel, *"Aller gnädigster König und Herr! Ich bin Euer Knecht Zieten": Die Familien Hans Joachims von Zieten* (Berlin, 2012), 142–5.

16. Logan-Logejus, *Meine Erlebnisse*, 206; Duffy, *Prussia's Glory*, 130.

17. R. Koser, 'Vor und nach der Schlacht von Leuthen: Die Parchwitzer Rede und der Abend im Schloss Lissa', *FBPG* i (1888), 288–94. For the charge of cynicism, see C. Nolan, *The Allure of Battle: A History of How Wars Have Been Won and Lost* (Oxford, 2017), 179.

18. Applying Max Weber's ideal type of 'charismatic rule' to Frederick has obvious attractions, T. Schieder, *Friederich der Grosse: Königtum der Widersprüche* (Frankfurt, 1983), 220; J. Kunisch, *Friederich der Grosse: Der König und seine Zeit* (Munich, 2004), 379–80; and also T. Blanning, *Frederick the Great: King of Prussia* (London, 2015), 276–7.

19. Frederick to Finck, 3 Dec. 1757, Generalstab (ed.), *Friedrich der Grosse*, 117.

20. One of the officers receiving promotion to the rank of general was Carl Heinrich von Wedel (1712–82), whose battalions led the attack at Leuthen, Barsewisch, *Kriegs-Erlebnisse*, 25; D. E. Showalter, *The Wars of Frederick the Great* (London, 1996), 194.

21. Anon. [W. F. von Retzow], *Charakterbild der wichtigsten Ereignisse des siebenjährigen Krieges, in Rücksicht auf Ursachen und Wirkungen von einem Zeitgenossen* (2 vols, Berlin, rev. ed. 1802), i, 240–2. For the aspect of punishment, see Berkovich, *Motivation*, 169–70. There is no doubt that Frederick addressed his officers at Parchwitz, but none of the extant versions can be considered strictly authentic, many of them sporting later (nineteenth-century) embroideries, see Koser, 'Vor und nach der Schlacht von Leuthen', 288–94. Retzow (1700–58), who was present and whose version seems the most reliable, obviously recorded later what he thought he remembered. He earned the king's displeasure on account of his failure to execute his orders during the battle of Hochkirch in October 1758, resigned and died shortly afterwards.

22. 'Testament du roi avant la bataille', 28 Nov. 1757, *PC* xvi, no. 9559.

23. Frederick to Prince Henry, 1 Dec., and Princess Wilhelmine of Bayreuth [his sister], 8 Dec. 1757, *PC* xvi, nos. 9557 and 9570.

24. 'Extract-Schreiben Oesterreichischen Officirs', 15–19 Dec. 1757, KA, AFA, Hauptarmee 1757, K. 614, XII-223 1/2; also 'Ordre de Bataille', Dec. 1757, ibid., XII-1. The calculations of the official Prussian historians seem accurate enough, Grosser Generalstab, *Siebenjähriger Krieg* vi, 136–8.

25. Podewils to Frederick, 22 Mar. 1747, C. Hinrichs (ed.), *Friedrich der Grosse und Maria Theresia: Diplomatische Berichte von Otto Christoph Graf von Podewils* (Berlin, 1937), 72–3.

26. B. Stollberg-Rillinger, *Maria Theresia: Die Kaiserin in ihrer Zeit* (Munich, 2017), 116–17. Charles had also married the empress's sister, the Archduchess Maria Anna (1718–44).

27. Memo. Daun, n.d. [before mid-November 1757], KA, AFA, Cabinets-Acten 1757, K. 634, XIII-13.

28. See Maria Theresa's earlier half-apology, id. to Daun, 6 June 1757, KA, AFA, Cabinets-Acten 1757, K. 634, VI-9.

29. Maria Theresa to Daun, 10 May 1757, and to Charles, 16 Dec. 1757, ibid., V-5 and XII-7.

30. Khevenhüller diary, 31 Dec. 1757, R. von Khevenhüller-Metsch (ed.), *Aus der Zeit Maria Theresias: Tagebuch des Fürsten Johann Josef Khevenhüller-Metsch, 1742–1776*, iv, *1756–1757* (Vienna, 1914), 141.

31. J. C. Allmayer-Beck, 'Wandlungen im Heerwesen zur Zeit Maria Theresias', Heeresgeschichtliches Museum (ed.), *Maria Theresia: Beiträge zur Geschichte des Heerwesens ihrer Zeit* (Graz, 1967), 7–24; J. Kunisch, *Das Mirakel des Hauses Brandenburg: Studien zum Verhältnis von Kabinettspolitik und Kriegsführung im Zeitalter des Siebenjährigen Kriegs* (Munich, 1978), 77–83.

32. Daun to Maria Theresa, 5 Aug. 1758, KA, AFA, Hauptarmee 1758, K. 670, VIII-2.

33. Charles to Laudon, 3 Dec. 1757, ibid., Hauptarmee 1757, K. 614, XII-202; for reconnaissance reports and speculations as to Frederick's aims, see e.g. Morocz to Charles, 2 Dec. 1757, and Beck 'rapport', 2 Dec. 1757, ibid., XII-170 and 175.

34. Charles to Kálnoky, Nostitz and Beck, 3 Dec. 1757, and 'Marche Zetterl', 3 Dec. 1757, ibid., XII-109a and 117.

35. Hofkriegsrat to Charles, 30 Sept. 1757, KA, Hofkriegsrath 1757, K. 632, IX-30.

36. Hadik to Charles, 4 Dec. 1757, KA, AFA, Hauptarmee 1757, K. 614, XII-212.

37. Maria Theresa to Charles, 5 Dec. 1757, KA, AFA, Cabinets-Acten 1757, K. 634, XII-ad 1. The Empress acknowledged the 'unpleasantness' of such late campaigning, id. to Charles, 5 Dec. 1757, ibid., XII-1.

38. According to a report by Guasco de Clavières, 3 Dec. 1757, ibid., XII-201; for Luszinski's position see id. to Charles, 3 Dec. 1757, ibid., XII-200.

39. R. Waddington, La Guerre de Sept ans: Historie Diplomatique et Militaire (5 vols, Paris, 1899–1914), i, 705.

40. Nostitz to Charles, 3 Dec. 1757, and Sprecher to Draskovich, 4 Dec. 1757, KA, AFA, Hauptarmee 1757, K. 614, XII-195 and 215.

41. Grosser Generalstab, Siebenjähriger Krieg vi, 18. For an eyewitness account of the Neumarkt raid, see Logan-Logejus, Meine Erlebnisse, 207–11.

42. Report Charles, 'Bericht über die am 5. Dezember nächst dem Dorfe Leuthen vorgefallene Schlacht', n.d. [Dec. 1757], KA, AFA, Hauptarmee 1757, K. 614, XII-218, from which the subsequent quote is also taken.

43. For a calculation of the numbers see Grosser Generalstab, Siebenjähriger Krieg vi, 140–3.

44. The Austrians kept a tally of the deserters as best they could, see e.g. 'Extract derer seit 22ten Octobris 1757 angelangten Königl: Preuss: Prisonirs und Deserteurs', n.d., KA, AFA, Hauptarmee 1757, K. 614, XII-73.

45. Neipperg to Charles, 8 Oct. 1757, ibid., X-218. The Württemberg court also had a habit of asking for more money, see note Rentz, 'Pro-Memoria', 18 May 1757, ibid., Cabinets-Acten 1757, K. 634, V-5b; further P. H. Wilson, 'Violence and Rejection of Authority on Eighteenth-Century Germany: The Case of the Swabian Mutiny in 1757', GH xii, 1 (1994), 1–26.

46. P. Gerber, Die Schlacht bei Leuthen (Berlin, 1901), 53–4. Gerber was a doctoral student of Hans Delbrück, vide infra Chapter 4.

47. Frederick's careful, usually personal, reconnoitring of the terrain was a contributory factor to his eventual success, see [E.] von Deutelmoser, 'Die Gefechtsaufklärung Friedrichs des Grossen im Siebenjährigen Kriege', VfTH viii, 2 (1911), 198–9.

48. Logan-Legejus, Meine Erlebnisse, 211–12, who also confirms the murky weather conditions; for an account of the skirmish at Borne see Grosser Generalstab, Siebenjähriger Krieg vi, 20–2.

49. The area was drained in the nineteenth century, and subsequent intensive tilling and gravel extractions in the twentieth have altered the landscape somewhat.

50. Xenophon, *Hellenica* 7.5.19. The parallel had already been spotted in Frederick's time, Archenholtz, *Siebenjähriger Krieg*, 95–6. For Frederick's dispositions at Chotusitz see R. Keibel, 'Die schräge Schlachtordnung in den beiden ersten Kriegen Friedrichs des Grossen', *FBPG* xiv, 1 (1901), esp. 127–30.

51. Charles, 'Bericht', n.d., KA, AFA, Hauptarmee 1757, K. 614, XII-218.

52. For the traditional view suggesting Daun's reservations, see Grosser Generalstab, *Siebenjähriger Krieg* vi, 24; C. Duffy, *The Army of Maria Theresa: The Armed Forces of Imperial Austria, 1740–1780* (London, 1977), 185–6.

53. Grosser Generalstab, *Siebenjähriger Krieg* vi, 25; Duffy, *Glory*, 145–6.

54. Charles, 'Bericht', n.d., KA, AFA, Hauptarmee 1757, K. 614, XII 218.

55. Grosser Generalstab, *Siebenjähriger Krieg* vi, 146, n. 14. Although an overcast day, there was no mist as on the day of the battle. In a rare lapse, Showalter, *Wars of Frederick the Great*, 196, is mistaken in suggesting that the day was 'clear'.

56. 'Extract-Schreiben Oesterreichischen Officirs', 15–19 Dec. 1757, KA, AFA, Hauptarmee 1757, K. 614, XII-223 1/2a.

57. Archenholtz, *Siebenjähriger Krieg*, 96; S. Fiedler, *Grundriss der Militär- und Kriegsgeschichte*, i, *Die stehenden Heere im Zeitalter des Absolutismus, 1640–1789* (Munich, 2nd ed. 1981), 262.

58. For a biographical vignette see H. Count Praschma, *Das Kürassier-Regiment von Driesen (Westfalen) Nr. 4, 1717–1900* (Münster, 1901), 37–8.

59. As quoted in Bleckwenn, *Uniformen* i, 168; for the point about 'in-group' loyalties, see Showalter, *Wars of Frederick the Great*, 199.

60. Bleckwenn, *Uniformen* i, 104; E. Lange, *Die Soldaten Friedrich des Grossen* (Leipzig, 1853), 56–7.

61. Bleckwenn, ibid., 117 and 137.

62. Barsewisch, *Kriegs-Erlebnisse*, 32–3. Barsewisch put the begin of the attack at 12.30 pm; R. Koser, *Geschichte Friedrich des Grossen* (4 vols, Stuttgart and Berlin, 5th ed. 1912), ii, 555–6.

63. Waddington, *Guerre de Sept Ans* i, 707–8.

64. Hofkriegsrat to Kriegs-Präsident, 10 Dec. 1757, KA, AFA, Hauptarmee 1757, K. 614, XII-220.

65. Report Schlabrendorff, 6 Dec. 1757 (copy), ibid., XII-217 1/3. Schlabrendorff was the Prussian governor of Silesia, 1756–91.

66. Frederick to Wilhelmine of Bayreuth, 8 Dec. 1757, PC xvi, no. 9570; for the Württembergers' experiences see P. H. Wilson, 'The Württemberg Army in the Seven Years' War', A. S. Burns (ed.), *The Changing Face of Old Regime Warfare. Essays in Honour of Christopher Duffy* (Warwick, 2022), 78–80.

67. G. Naumann, *Sammlung ungedruckter Nachrichten, so die Geschichte der Feldzüge der Preußen von 1740 bis 1779 erläutern* (2 vols, Dresden, 1782), i, 464. Neither regiment took part in the battle as such.

68. Barsewisch, *Kriegs-Erlebnisse*, 37.

69. Grosser Generalstab, *Siebenjähriger Krieg* vi, 146, n. 13.

70. The Silesian manoeuvres of 1754 took place around Gross Gohlau. Zieten had evidently gained a good understanding of the local terrain, see Grosser Generalstab, *Siebenjähriger Krieg* vi, 30 n.

71. Gerber, *Leuthen*, 62–3; Duffy, *Prussia's Glory*, 154–5.

72. R. Wirtgen, 'Das Feldgeschützmaterial der preussischen Artillerie zwischen 1740 und 1786', E. H. Schmidt and A. Wirtgen (eds), *Die Bewaffnung und Ausrüstung der Armee Friedrichs des Grossen* (Rastatt, 1986), 56.

73. As quoted in V. Schmidtchen, 'Der Einfluss der Technik auf die Kriegsführung zur Zeit Friedrich des Grossen', Militärgeschichtliches Forschungsamt (ed.), *Friedrich der Grosse und das Militärwesen seiner Zeit* (Herford, 1987), 139; also H. Strachan, *European Armies and the Conduct of War* (London, 1983 (pb)), 33.

74. 'Extract-Schreiben Oestereichischen Officirs', 15–19 Dec. 1757, KA, AFA, Hauptarmee 1757, XII 228 1/2a.

75. Charles, 'Bericht', n.d., ibid., XII-218.

76. Eichel to Podewils, 7 Dec. 1757, PC xvi, no. 9569.

77. K. von Priesdorf, *Soldatisches Führertum* (10 vols, Hamburg, 1935–42), i, 516–20.

78. Waddington, *Guerre de Sept Ans*, i, 713; Duffy, *Prussia's Glory*, 161.

79. L. Freiherr von Thüna, *Die Würzburger Hilfstruppen im Dienste Österreichs 1756—1763. Ein Beitrag zur Geschichte des Siebenjährigen Krieges. Nach archivalischen Quellen* (Würzburg, 1893), 135–8. The regiment consisted of two battalions and two grenadier companies, altogether fourteen companies with a nominal strength of 1,860 men.

80. Gerber, *Leuthen*, 67–71.

81. See the account by Retzow, *Charakteristik* i, 250–1.

82. Logan-Logejus, *Meine Erlebnisse*, 215; P.-M. Hahn, *Friedrich II. von Preussen: Feldherr, Autokrat, Selbstdarsteller* (Stuttgart, 2013), 134–5.

83. Charles claimed that he retreated 'in decent order', but this ought to be taken *cum grano salis*, Charles, 'Bericht', n.d., KA, AFA, Hauptarmee 1757, K. 614, XII-218.

84. Retzow, *Charakteristik* i, 251; for the singing of the morning prayer, see Koser, *Geschichte* ii, 553; C. von Krockow, *Friedrich der Grosse: Ein Lebensbild* (Munich, 1993 (pb)), 79–80. The tune may be familiar from two of J. S. Bach's cantatas, BWV 24 and 45.

85. See memo. Benaglio, 'Extract, des Löbl. Hertzog Carl Lothring: Infant. Regiment über der bey dato 5ten Decembris 1757 vorgefallenen Action Todte, blessirte und unwissend Verlohren gegangenen Mannschaft betreffend', n.d.; anon, 'Extract derer Commandirt, Absent, Blessirt und Krancken auch der Standt und Dienst Tabella pro Decembri 1757, nachstehend Kayl:

Königl: Infanterie Regimenter betreffend', n.d., and 'Aufsatz, über bey der den 5ten Decembris nägst Lissa in Schlesien gewesenen Action von der K.K. Armée ergebenen Todt, Blessirt und Verlohren gegangenen Staabs, Ober-Officirs und Gemeinen', n.d., KA, AFA, Hauptarmee 1757, K. 614, XII-222/ VIII, XII-142 and XII-222.

86. Anon., 'Loco-Standt des Löbl. General-Feldzeugmeister Graf Harrach'schen Infanterie-Regiments', 7 Dec. 1757, ibid., XII-80.

87. Frederick to Wilhelmine of Bayreuth, 5 Dec. 1757, J. D. E. Preuss (ed.), *Oeuvres de Frédéric le Grand* (30 vols, Berlin, 1846–56), xxvii, no. 334.

88. Frederick to Zieten, 10 Dec. 1757, *PC* xvi, no. 9574; Serbelloni to Charles, 9 Dec. 1757, KA, AFA, Hauptarmee 1757, K. 614, XII-219.

89. Frederick to d'O [commandant Glatz], 29 and 30 Dec. 1757, KA, AFA, Cabinets-Acten 1757, K. 634, XII-12 and 13; further Grosser Generalstab, *Siebenjähriger Krieg* vi, 43–53.

90. Kunisch, *Friedrich der Grosse*, 383.

91. Report Schlabrendorff, 6 Dec. 1757, KA, AFA, Hauptarmee 1757, K. 614, XII-217 1/3; G. Ritter, *Friedrich der Grosse: Ein historisches Profil* (Königstein im Taunus, repr. 1978), 141, encapsulates the traditional Prussian view.

92. 'Rélation de la marche du Corps prussien de la Saxe, après la bataille de Weissenfels [i.e. Rossbach], jus'quen Silesie après la bataille de Lisse [i.e. Leuthen], n.d. [9 Dec. 1757], *PC* xvi, no. 9572.

93. Koser, 'Vor und nach der Schlacht', 288–94; also W. J. Kaiser (ed.), *Friedrich der Grosse: Sein Bild im Wandel der Zeiten* (Frankfurt, 1986), 99, 144, and 147.

94. Maria Theresa to Charles and Daun, 9 Dec. 1757, KA, AFA, Cabinets-Acten 1757, K. 634, XII-3.

95. Bossart to Kaunitz (no. LXI), 18 Dec. 1757, HHStA, Staatskanzlei, Diplomatische Korrespondenz, Köln 11.

96. Frederick to Podewils, 6 Dec., and to Mitchell, 13 Dec. 1757, *PC* xvi, nos. 9568 and 87; also R. Savory, *His Britannic Majesty's Army in Germany during the Seven Years' War* (Oxford, 1966), 42–60.

97. Bisset, *Memoirs of Andrew Mitchell*, 287 n.; M. Schlenke, *England und das friderizianische Preussen, 1740–1763: Ein Beitrag zum Verhältnis von Politik und Öffentlicher Meinung im England des 18. Jahrhunderts* (Freiburg, 1963), 241–9; for the politics see R. Middleton, *The Bells of Victory: the Pitt-Newcastle Ministry and the Conduct of the Seven Years' War, 1757–1762* (Cambridge, 1985), 57–63.

98. C. Parry (ed.), *Consolidated Treaty Series* (New York, 1969), xli, 184–6; and further I. Mittenzwei, *Friedrich II. von Preussen: Biographie* (Cologne, 3rd ed. 1983), 125.

99. Fermor's 'Relation' is in KA, AFA, Cabinets-Acten 1758, K. 670, VIII-15; O. Herrmann, 'Zur Schlacht von Zorndorf', *FBPG* xxiv (1911), 547–66; C. Duffy, *Frederick the Great: A Military Life* (London, 1985), 163–8. For the complexities of Austro-Russian cooperation see D. Bangert, *Die russisch-österreichische Zusammenarbeit im Siebenjährigen Krieg, 1758–1759* (Boppard am Rhein, 1971), here 52–6.

100. Maria Theresa to Daun, 19 Oct. 1758, KA, AFA, Cabinets-Akten 1758, K. 670, X-13; for her order see id. to Daun, 15 May 1758, ibid., K. 669, V-10; Waddington, *Guerre de Sept Ans* ii, 301–16.

101. Frederick to Prince Henry, 1 Sept. 1759, *PC* xviii, no. 11451; for the battle see Duffy, *Frederick*, 183–90; Waddington, *La Guerre de Sept Ans* iii, 154–81; for a discussion of the lack of allied cooperation see Kunisch, *Mirakel*, 91–4.

102. Kunisch, *Friedrich der Grosse*, 404–7; C. Duffy, *The Army of Maria Theresa: The Armed Forces of Imperial Austria, 1740–1780* (London, 1977), 195–7.

103. For the reorganization of 1759/60 see C. Duffy, *The Army of Frederick the Great* (London, 1974), 189–91.

104. Waddington, *Guerre de Sept Ans* iv, 55–74. Glatz was second only to Magdeburg as a fortress, Archenholtz, *Siebenjähriger Krieg*, 230.

105. Archenholtz, *Siebenjähriger Krieg*, 233–4. Archenholtz also noted that plundering Austrians added to the plight of the Saxon capital.

106. F. Escher, 'Die brandenburgisch-preussische Residenz und Hauptstadt Berlin im 17. und 18. Jahrhundert', W. Ribbe (ed.), *Geschichte Berlins* (2 vols, Munich, 1987), i, 398.

107. Frederick's losses at Torgau were significant, around 17,000 or nearly 40 per cent of his army; for detailed studies see E. Kessel, *Quellen und Untersuchungen zur Schlacht bei Torgau* (Berlin, 1937), and H. Schnitter, 'Die Schlacht bei Torgau 1760', *Militärgeschichtliche Mitteilungen* xviii (1979), 216–24; further T. Lindau, *Die Peripetie des Siebenjährigen Krieges: Der Herbstfeldzug in Sachsen und der Winterfelzug in Hessen, 1760/61* (Berlin, 1993).

108. See L. Kennett, *The French Armies in the Seven Years' War: A Study in Military Organization and Administration* (Durham, NC, 1967), and J. C. Riley, *The Seven Years' War and the Old Regime in France: The Economic and Financial Toll* (Princeton, NJ, 1986).

109. Szabo, *Seven Years' War*, 361–73, who however emphasizes Prussia's likely defeat at that point in the war, which seems an unduly pro-Habsburg assessment.

110. For the Hanoverian side Dann, *Hanover*, 117–21; for public opinion, Schlenke, *England*, 249–65; for the high politics, Middleton, *Bells of Victory*, 170–211, and K. W. Schweizer, *England, Prussia and the Seven Years' War* (Lewiston, NY, 1989), 240–60.

111. Waddington, *La Guerre de Sept Ans* iv, 494–601; F. Spenser, 'The Anglo-Prussian Breach of 1762', *English Historical Review* xli, 1 (1956), 100–12; see also M. Roberts, *Splendid Isolation, 1763–1780* (Reading, 1970).

112. Frederick to d'Argens, Dec. 1761, as quoted in E. Daniels, 'The Seven Years' War', A. W. Ward, G. W. Prothero, S. Leathes (eds), *The Cambridge Modern History*, vi, *The Eighteenth Century* (Cambridge, 1909), 297–8.

113. G. Küntzel, 'Friedrich der Grosse am Ausgang des Siebenjährigen Krieges und sein Bündnis mit Russland', *FBPG* xiii (1901), 75–122; H. Fleischhacker, 'Porträt Peters III.', *JbfGO*, n.s. v (1957), 127–89.

114. For the Silesian campaign see the detailed study by A. Kloppert, *Der Schlesische Feldzug von 1762* (Bonn, 1988). Henry was an accomplished, if perhaps conventional, commander, see W. Gembruch, 'Prinz Heinrich von Preussen, Bruder Friedrich des Grossen', J. Kunisch (ed.), *Persönlichkeiten im Umfeld Friedrich des Grossen* (Cologne and Vienna, 1988), 99–103; also E. Ziebura, *Prinz Heinrich von Preussen. Biographie* (Berlin, 1999), 147–58.

115. G. Otruba, *Die Wirtschaftspolitik Maria Theresias* (Vienna, 1966), 25–7; still important, A. Beer, 'Die Staatsschulden und die Ordnung des Staatshaushalts unter Maria Theresia', AÖG lxxxii (1894), 1–135.

116. K. W. Schweizer, 'William Pitt, Lord Bute and the Peace Negotiations with France, May–September 1761', *Albion* xiii, 2 (1981), 262–75.

117. J. H. Rose, 'Frederick the Great and England (II)', *EHR* xxix, 114 (1914), 269–70; and also R. Pares, 'American versus Continental Warfare', ibid., li, 203 (1936), 462–3.

118. F. W. Ghillany, *Europäische Chronik von 1492 bis Ende April 1865, mit besonderer Berücksichtigung der Friedensverträge* (3 vols, Leipzig, 1865), i, 301–8.

119. M. Hochedlinger, *Austria's Wars of Emergence: State and Society in the Habsburg Monarchy, 1683–1797* (London, 2003), 348–9.

120. W. Stribny, *Die Russlandpolitik Friedrich des Grossen, 1764–1786* (Würzburg, 1966), 12–35 et passim; F. Althoff, *Untersuchungen zum Gleichgewicht der Mächte in der Aussenpolitik Friedrich des Grossen nach dem Siebenjährigen Krieg (1763–1786)* (Berlin, 1995), 33–40; H. M. Scott, *The Emergence of the Eastern Powers, 1756–1775* (Cambridge, 2001), 103–34.

121. Already in 1762, Frederick remained studiously neutral in the Gottorf succession question, E. Hübner, *Staatspolitik und Familieninteressen in der russischen Aussenpolitik, 1741–1773* (Neumünster, 1984), 75–8.

122. U. Schulze, *Die Beziehungen zwischen Kursachsen und Friedrich dem Grossen nach dem Siebenjährigen Krieg bis zum Bayerischen Erbfolgekrieg* (Jena, 1930), 4–8 et passim; K. Zernack, *Polen und Russland: Zwei Wege in der europäischen Geschichte* (Berlin, 1994), 256–95.

123. Lehndorf diary, 16 Feb. 1763, H. von Kuehnheim (ed.), *Aus dem Tagebuch des Grafen Lehndorff* (Berlin, 1982), 146.

124. Frederick, 'Denkwürdigkeiten vom Hubertusburger Frieden bis zum Ende der polnischen Teilung', A. Ritter (ed.), *Die Werke Friedrichs des Grossen* (2 vols, Berlin, 1915), i, 505; see also E. Frie, *Friedrich II.* (Reinbek, 2012), 74–6.

125. For the statistics see W. Hubatsch, *Frederick the Great: Absolutism and Administration* (London, repr. 1975), 148–9; further L. Beutin, 'Die Wirkungen des Siebenjährigen Kriegs auf die Volkswirtschaft Preussens', *VSWG* xxvi, 2 (1933), 209–43; and W. O. Henderson, *Studies in the Economic Policy of Frederick the Great* (London, 1968), 38–58. Useful data can also be gleaned from I. Mittenzwei, *Preussen nach dem Siebenjährigen Krieg: Auseinandersetzung zwischen Bürgertum und Staat in der Wirtschaftspolitik* (East Berlin, 1979).

126. Duffy, *Frederick the Great*, 242–3; Schieder, *Friedrich der Grosse*, 65, 122–3, 184.

Chapter 4

1. R. S. Quimby, *The Background of Napoleonic Warfare: The Theory of Military Tactics in Eighteenth-Century France* (New York, 1957), 101–5 et passim. For Guibert's emphasis on columns see id., 'Essai générale de tactique [1772]', *Œuvres militaires du comte de Guibert* (5 vols, Paris, 1803), i, esp. 208–20.

2. Especially in the writings of Adam Heinrich Dietrich von Bülow, A. Kuhle, *Die preussische Kriegstheorie um 1800 und ihre Suche nach dynamischen Gleichgewichten* (Berlin, 2018), 85–249; further D. E. Showalter, 'Hubertusburg to Auerstädt: The Prussian Army in Decline', *German History* xii, 3 (1994), 308–33.

3. Inter alia P. Paret, *York and the Era of Prussian Reforms, 1807–1815* (Princeton, NJ, 1966), 117–90; R. Höhn, *Scharnhorsts Vermächtnis* (Bonn, 1952), 176–298; W. Görlitz, *Der deutsche Generalstab: Geschichte und Gestalt, 1657–1945* (Frankfurt, s.a. [1953]), 45–66.

4. C. von Clausewitz, *Nachrichten über Preussen in seiner grossen Katastrophe* (Berlin, 1888), 505 and 512; for the wider context, P. Paret, 'Jena and Auerstedt', id., *Understanding War: Essays on Clausewitz and the History of Military Power* (Princeton, NJ, 1992), 85–92 and *The Cognitive Challenge of War: Prussia 1806* (Princeton, NJ, 2009), 72–103.

5. C. von Clausewitz, 'Der Russische Feldzug von 1812', id., *Sämtliche Hinterlassene Werke über Krieg und Kriegführung* (3 vols, s.loc. [Stuttgart], 1999), iii, 84. More emphatic in book eight of *Vom Kriege*, ed. W. Hahlweg (Berlin, 19th ed. 1991 [1st 1832]), 999–1008; see further H. Strachan, 'The Case for Clausewitz: Reading *On War* Today', id., *The Direction of War: Contemporary Strategy in Historical Perspective* (Cambridge, 2013), 52–4.

6. As quoted in O. Hintze, *Die Hohenzollern und ihr Werk: Fünfhundert Jahre vaterländische Geschichte* (Berlin, 1915), 461–2; D. E. Showalter, 'The Retaming of Bellona: Prussia and the Institutionalization of the Napoleonic Legacy, 1815–1876', *MA* xliv, 2 (1976), 57–63.

7. S. Skalweit, *Frankreich und Friedrich der Grosse: Der Aufstieg Preussens in der öffentlichen Meinung des "Ancien Régime"* (Bonn, 1952), 100.

8. F. C. Förster, *Leben und Thaten Friedrichs des Grossen, König von Preussen, geschildert als Mensch, Regent und Feldherr* (Meissen, 1840), 173. The work proved very popular and went through four editions by 1860.

9. G. Wollstein, *Das "Grossdeutschland" der Paulskirche: Nationale Ziele in der bürgerlichen Revolution 1848/49* (Düsseldorf, 1977), 291–306.

10. See J. G. Droysen, *Geschichte der preussischen Politik* (14 vols, Leipzig, 1855–86); also J. Rüsen, 'Johann Gustav Droysen', H.-U. Wehler (ed.), *Deutsche Historiker II* (Göttingen, 1971), 7–23.

11. F. Gilbert, *Johann Gustav Droysen und die preussisch-deutsche Frage* (Munich, 1931); W. Hardtwig, 'Von Preussens Aufgabe in Deutschland zu Deutschlands Aufgabe in der Welt: Liberalismus und borussianisches Geschichtsbild

zwischen Revolution und Imperialismus', id., *Geschichtskultur und Wissenschaft* (Munich, 1990), 103–60.

12. L. von Ranke, *Der Ursprung des Siebenjährigen Krieges* (Leipzig, 1871), 4; vide infra Chapter 5.

13. Hintze, *Hohenzollern*, vi; G. Breit, *Das Staats- und Gesellschaftsbild deutscher Generale beider Weltkriege im Spiegel ihrer Memoiren* (Boppard am Rhein, 1973), 45.

14. J. L. Wallach, *Das Dogma der Vernichtungsschlacht: Die Lehren von Clausewitz und Schlieffen und ihre Wirkungen in zwei Weltkriegen* (Frankfurt, 1967) is the standard account.

15. Grosser Generalstab, Kriegsgeschichtliche Abteilung, *Die Kriege Friedrichs des Grossen*, ser. 1, *Der Erste Schlesische Krieg, 1740–1742* (3 vols, Berlin, 1890–3), ser. 2, *Der Zweite Schlesische Krieg, 1744–1745* (3 vols, Berlin, 1895), ser. 3, *Der Siebenjährige Krieg, 1756–1763* (13 vols, Berlin, 1901–14). For a discussion of the *Abteilung's* organization see R. Brühl, *Militärgeschichte und Kriegspolitik: Zur Militärgeschichtsschreibung des preussisch-deutschen Generalstabs, 1816–1945* (East Berlin, 1975), 162–5, and M. Raschke, *Der politisierende Generalstab: Die friderizianischen Kriege in der amtlichen Militärgeschichtsschreibung, 1890–1914* (Freiburg, 1993), 63–92, the latter of which is essential reading.

16. For the dismissive epithet see e.g. C. von der Goltz, 'Antikritik zu Delbrücks Rezension von Adalbert von Taysens "Das Militärische Testament Friedrich des Grossen"', *ZfPGL* xvi, 2 (1879), 292.

17. D. Bald, *Der deutsche Generalstab, 1859–1939: Reform und Restauration in Ausbildung und Bildung* (Munich, 1977), 67–9; M. Kutz, *Realitätsflucht und Aggression im deutschen Militär* (Baden Baden, 1990), 28–38.

18. *Lehrordnung* 1912, as quoted in B. Schwertfeger, *Die grossen Erzieher des deutschen Heeres: Aus der Geschichte der Kriegsakademie* (Potsdam, 1936), 59–60; also D. Bald, G. Bald-Gerlich, and E. Ambros, *Tradition und Reform im militärischen Bildungswesen: Von der preussischen Allgemeinen Kriegsschule zur Führungsakademie der Bundeswehr* (Baden-Baden, 1985), 32–5; K. Demeter, *Das deutsche Offizierskorps in Gesellschaft und Staat, 1650–1945* (Frankfurt, 1963), 69–94.

19. As quoted in Schwertfeger, *Erzieher*, 85; for Verdy, see Raschke, *Generalstab*, 36–9.

20. Clausewitz, *Vom Kriege*, 326; anon., *Die Lehren der Kriegsgeschichte für die Kriegführung* (Berlin, 1881) (= *Beiheft zum Militär-Wochenblatt* 9).

21. R. Koser, 'Zum Ursprung des Siebenjährigen Krieges', *Historische Zeitschrift* lxxiv, 1 (1895), 77. Koser was an adjunct lecturer at the Kriegsakademie, [H.] von Freytag-Loringhoven, *Menschen und Dinge wie ich sie in meinem Leben sah* (Berlin, 1923), 55.

22. As quoted in G. Ritter, *Staatskunst und Kriegshandwerk: Das Problem des "Militarismus" in Deutschland*, ii, *Die Hauptmächte Europas und das Wilhelminische Reich* (Munich, 1960), 147.

23. W. von Bremen, *Friedrich der Grosse* (Leipzig, 2nd ed. 1905), 36; Raschke, *Generalstab*, 77–8.

24. Generalstab, *Die Kriege Friedrichs des Grossen*, 3rd ser. iii, *Kolin* (Berlin, 1901), 201; for a breakdown of the authors of the individual volumes see Raschke, *Generalstab*, App. A, 187–9.

25. *Verhandlungen des Reichstages, Stenographische Berichte: Legislaturperiode XIII, Session 2 (1914–16)* cccvi (Berlin, 1914), 5–7.

26. Generalstab, *Die Kriege Friedrichs des Grossen*, 3rd ser. i, *Pirna und Lobositz* (Berlin, 1901), 45 and 170–1. For the growing popularity of the idea of a preventive war in army circles see M. Kitchen, *The German Officer Corps, 1890–1914* (Oxford, 1968), 96–114.

27. A. von Schlieffen, *Friedrich der Grosse* (Berlin, 1912), 39.

28. W. von Bremen, *Friedrich der Grosse: Der Siebenjährige Krieg* (Berlin, 1912), 16.

29. [H. O. R.] Brix, *Gedanken über die Organisation, Ausbildung und Verwendung der Cavallerie bei der modernen Kriegsführung* (Berlin, 1881), 10–11.

30. M. Jähns, 'Die Kriegskunst als Kunst' [1874], id., *Geschichtliche Aufsätze*, ed. K. Koetschau (Berlin, 1903), 123–4. Jähns achieved prominence with his *Geschichte der Kriegswissenschaften, vornehmlich in Deutschland* (3 vols, Munich and Leipzig, 1883–1901); for his career at the *Kriegsakademie*, see Schwertfeger, *Erzieher*, 141.

31. H. von Freytag-Loringhoven, 'Theorie und Praxis bei König Friedrich, Napoleon und Moltke', *VfTH* vi, 1 (1909), 34–5; id., 'König Friedrich als Kriegsherr und Heerführer', *BMW* no. 2/3 (1912), 32–3.

32. A. von Taysen, *Zur Beurteilung des Siebenjährigen Krieges* (Berlin, 1882), 3; L. von Scharfenort, *Die Königlich-Preussische Kriegsakademie* (Berlin, 1910), 249–50. Taysen initiated the official histories of Frederick's wars at the suggestion of the elder Moltke, see A. Bucholz, *Hans Delbrück and the German Military Establishment: War Images in Conflict* (Iowa City, 1985), 57; Brühl, *Militärgeschichte*, 121.

33. T. von Bernhardi, *Friedrich der Grosse als Feldherr* (2 vols, Berlin, 1881), i, 2–3 and 17–18.

34. R. von Caemmerer, *Friedrichs des Grossen Feldzugsplan für das Jahr 1757* (Berlin, 1883), 1 and 30. Caemmerer later supervised the official histories of the campaigns of 1813–15, Brühl, *Militärgeschichte*, 197.

35. F. von Bernhardi, *Das Studium der friderizianischen Kriege in seiner Bedeutung für die moderne Kriegskunst* (Berlin, 1892), 165, 178, 184, and 22–3; id., 'Die Elemente des modernen Krieges', *BMW* no. 9 (1898), 430–53, and 'Über angriffsweise Kriegführung', ibid., no. 4 (1905), 125–52. For a sketch of Bernhardi's career see Kitchen, *Officer Corps*, 97–100, and for his time at the head of the *Abteilung* see his *Denkwürdigkeiten aus meinem Leben* (Berlin, 1927), 211–31.

36. This is not the place to rehearse the arguments surrounding the controversy surrounding Terence Zuber's arguments about the status, indeed the reality,

of the Schlieffen Plan, id., *Inventing the Schlieffen Plan: German War Planning, 1871–1914* (Oxford, 2006). Suffice it to say that I am leaning towards the critique offered by G. P. Gross, 'There Was a Schlieffen Plan: Neue Quellen', id., H. Ehlert and M. Epkenhans (eds), *Der Schlieffen Plan: Analysen und Dokumente* (Paderborn, 2006), 117–60.

37. G. Ritter, *The Schlieffen Plan: Critique of a Myth* (London, 1958), 46; for Schlieffen's career see E. Kessel, 'Graf Alfred von Schlieffen: Der Mensch und die Persönlichkeit in seinen Briefen', id. (ed.), *Generalfeldmarschall Graf Alfred von Schlieffen: Briefe* (Göttingen, 1958), 9–55.

38. F. von Schmerfeld (ed.), *Die deutschen Aufmarschpläne, 1871–1890* (Berlin, 1929).

39. Ritter rightly identified this as 'the central problem in the historical understanding of the Schlieffen Plan', id., *Schlieffen Plan*, 43. A. Bucholz, *Moltke, Schlieffen and Prussian War Planning* (New York, 1991) remains the most thorough analysis.

40. Generalstab des Heeres, Kriegswissenschaftliche Abteilung (ed.), *Generalfeldmarschall Graf von Schlieffen: Dienstschriften des Chefs des Generalstabs der Armee* (2 vols, Berlin, 1937), i, 22. For an impression of such an exercise, see E. Birchner and W. Bode, *Schlieffen: Mann und Idee* (Zurich, 1937), 123–36.

41. Schlieffen, *Dienstschriften* i, 51; S. Förster, 'Der deutsche Generalstab und die Illusion des kurzen Krieges, 1871–1914: Metakritik eines Mythos', MGM liv, 1 (1995), esp. 76–82.

42. *Dienstschriften* i, 61 and 63.

43. Ibid., 138–9.

44. Ibid., ii, 301–2 and 309.

45. A. von Schlieffen, 'Cannae (I)', *VfTH* vi, 4 (1909), 535.

46. Ibid., 530. The study appeared in instalments at irregular intervals, 'Cannae (II)', ibid., vii, 1 (1910), 11–30, (III), ibid., vii, 2 (1910), 196–232, (IV), ibid., vii, 4 (1910), 485–521, (V), ibid., viii, 3 (1911), 355–64, (VI), ibid., viii, 4 (1911), 523–45, (VII), ibid., ix, 2 (1912), 185–214, and (VIII), ibid., x, 1 (1913), 1–41.

47. Schlieffen, 'Cannae (VIII)', 35; for the *Vierteljahreshefte* see Brühl, *Militärgeschichte*, 188–91.

48. See Bucholz, *Delbrück*, 63–4, and H. Delbrück, *Geschichte der Kriegskunst* (4 vols, Hamburg new ed. 2000 [1st 1900–20]), i, 364–92.

49. Schlieffen, 'Cannae (I)', 529, 530–1, 535.

50. Id., 'Cannae (VIII)', 34; [B.] Schwertfeger, 'Die Strategie Friedrichs des Grossen im Siebenjährigen Kriege', BMW no. 2 (1913), 56–7.

51. A. von Schlieffen, 'Der Feldherr' [1909], id., *Cannae*, ed. H. von Freytag-Loringhoven (Berlin, 1925), 264 and 265; W. von Blume, *Feldherrntum* (Berlin, 1914) (= Beiheft zum Militär-Wochenblatt no. 4), 134–5; see also F. von Bernhardi, *How Germany Makes War* (London, 1914), 147–8.

52. Schlieffen, 'Cannae (VIII)', 40.

53. See inter alia D. J. Hughes, *The King's Finest: A Social and Bureaucratic Profile of Prussia's General Officers, 1871–1914* (Westport, CT, 1987), 142–44.

54. Frederick II, 'Betrachtungen über die Taktik und einzelne Theile des Krieges, oder Betrachtungen über einige Veränderungen in der Art, Krieg zu führen', 27 Dec. 1758, H. Merkens (ed.), *Ausgewählte Kriegswissenschaftliche Werke Friedrichs des Grossen* (Jena, 1876), 135.

55. A. von Taysen, 'Das militärische Testament Friedrich des Grossen', in Königlich-Preussische Archiv-Verwaltung (ed.), *Miscellaneen zur Geschichte König Friedrich des Grossen* (Berlin, 1878), 184–5. Already in 1758 Frederick placed greater emphasis on the situational context, see id., 'Betrachtungen über die Taktik', 134–6.

56. H. Delbrück, 'Persönliche Erinnerungen an den Kaiser Friedrich III und sein Haus [1888]', id., *Erinnerungen, Aufsätze und Reden* (Berlin, 1902), 64–86.

57. See H. Schleier, 'Hans Delbrück: Ein politischer Historiker zwischen Preussen-Legende, amtlicher Militärgeschichtsschreibung und historischer Realität', G. Seeber (ed.), *Gestalten der Bismarckzeit* (East Berlin, 1978), 383–6.

58. H. Delbrück, *Das Leben des Feldmarschalls Grafen Neidhardt von Gneisenau* (2 vols, Berlin, 3rd ed. 1908), 45–54. Delbrück also published posthumously one of Clausewitz's essays on the subject, id., 'Carl von Clausewitz: Über das Fortschreiten und den Stillstand der kriegerischen Begebenheiten', *ZfPGL* iv, 3 (1878), 233–41, and also 'Clausewitz', ibid., xv, 2 (1878), 217–31.

59. Bucholz's monograph aside, succinct assessments of Delbrück's scholarship are offered by G. A. Craig, 'Delbrück: The Military Historian', id., *War, Politics, Diplomacy* (London, 1966), 59–87; A. Hillgruber, 'Hans Delbrück', H.-U. Wehler (ed.), *Deutsche Historiker IV* (Göttingen, 1972), 40–52; W. Deist, 'Hans Delbrück: Militärhistoriker und Publizist', *Militärgeschichtliche Zeitschrift* lvii, 2 (1998), 371–84; and U. Raulff, 'Politik als Passion: Hans Delbrück und der Krieg in der Geschichte', Delbrück, *Kriegskunst* i, ix–xlvi. For Delbrück as a public intellectual, see A. Thimme, *Hans Delbrück als Kritiker der wilhelminischen Epoche* (Düsseldorf, 1953).

60. H. Delbrück, *Kriegskunst* i, lii; id., 'Die Verfassung des Königs Servius Tullius' [1908], id., *Vor und nach dem Weltkrieg: Politische und historische Aufsätze, 1902–1925* (Berlin, 1926), 470 (quote from former).

61. H. Delbrück, review of 'Das militärische Testament Friedrich des Grossen', *ZfPGL* xvi, 1 (1879), 31; Lange, *Delbrück*, 85–6.

62. H. Delbrück, 'Über die Verschiedenheit der Strategien Friedrichs und Napoleons' [1887], id., *Historische und politische Aufsätze* (Berlin, 2nd ed. 1907), 300–1.

63. H. Delbrück, *Die Strategie des Perikles, erläutert durch die Strategie Friedrichs des Grossen. Mit einem Anhang über Thukydides und Kleon* (Berlin, 1890), 77–107 et passim.

64. Ibid., 7–12.

65. Ibid., 37 and 45. Delbrück used the theological jibe twice, ibid., 37 and 42. He was a gifted and ready polemicist, see K. Molinski, 'Der Historiker

Delbrück', id., F. J. Schmidt and S. Mette, *Hans Delbrück: Der Historiker and Politiker* (Berlin, 1928), 46–8.

66. See Freytag-Loringhoven, *Menschen und Dinge*, 94–5.

67. Delbrück, *Perikles*, 42, 47, and 48 (quote from latter). Delbrück was by no means immune to the 'magic', see 'Der Ursprung des Siebenjährigen Krieges', id., *Erinnerungen*, 268–9.

68. Bernhardi, *Denkwürdigkeiten*, 133 and 143. The 'Zivilstratege' epithet was deployed by the *Norddeutsche Allgemeine Zeitung*, 4 Aug. 1892, as quoted in Bucholz, *Delbrück*, 38; for the relations between officer corps and the middle classes see also Breit, *Staats- und Gesellschaftsbild*, 29–37.

69. Bucholz, *Delbrück*, 52–85, and Lange, *Delbrück*, 83–124; the latter also gives a schematic chronological survey, ibid., App. D, 150–5.

70. See the reflections by Delbrück's disciple Martin Hobohm, 'Delbrück, Clausewitz und die Kritik des Weltkrieges', *PJ* clxxxi, 2 (1920), 202–32, and O. Hintze, 'Delbrück, Clausewitz und die Strategie Friedrichs des Grossen: Eine Erwiderung', *FBPG* xxxiii, 1 (1921), 131–77; for Hobohm see H. Schleier, *Die bürgerliche Geschichtsschreibung der Weimarer Republik* (East Berlin, 1975), 531–74.

71. Most notably in the works of Koser and Hintze and in the document collection of the *Acta Borussica: Denkmäler der Preußischen Staatsverwaltung im 18. Jahrhundert*, instigated by Gustav Schmoller, which began to appear from 1892.

72. M. Lehmann, *Friedrich der Grosse und der Ursprung des siebenjährigen Krieges* (Leipzig, 1894), 85. Lehmann explicitly condemned the treatment of Delbrück as 'akin to a literary autodafé', ibid., v.

Chapter 5

1. U. Liedtke, *Ich bin Komponist: Friedrich II. als Musiker* (Berlin 2012), 139–43. Frederick understood such emotions. After Zorndorf he quipped that 'my *Lumpenkerle* are afraid, . . . for they sing psalms by Clément Marot. We shall get to listen to quite different music soon', Catt diary, 25 Aug. 1758, W. Schüssler (ed.), *Friedrich der Grosse: Gespräche mit Henri de Catt* (Munich, 1983 (pb)), 231. Clément Marot (1495–1544), French court poet and protégé of Margaret of Navarre.

2. R. Koser, *Geschichte Friedrichs des Grossen* (4 vols, Stuttgart and Berlin, 5th ed. 1913), ii, 543. Following his victory at Prague in May 1757, Frederick ordered his court musician Carl Heinrich Graun (1703/4–59) to write *Te Deum*, an unusually mellow composition, without timpani and brass instruments that tended to feature in such works, L. Näf, 'Carl Heinrich Graun: *Te Deum*', CD booklet (CPO 777 158–2), 5–7.

3. G. Graf, *Gottesbild und Politik: Eine Studie zur Frömmigkeit in Preussen während der Befreiungskriege, 1813–1915* (Göttingen, 1993), 95.

4. J. W. L. Gleim, 'Siegerlied nach der Schlacht von Rossbach', in R. F. Lacher, *"Friedrich unser Held"*: *Gleim und sein König* (Göttingen, 2017), 53.

5. E. Wormsbächer, *Daniel Nikolaus Chodowiecki (1726–1804): Erklärungen und Erläuterungen zu seinen Radierungen* (Hanover, 1988). Frederick, notoriously reluctant to sit for painters, understood the use of portraits as diplomatic and other gifts, F. Mankarz, 'Die Marke Friedrich: Der preussische König im zeitgenössischen Bild', Stiftung Preussische Schlösser und Gärten (ed.), *Friederisico: Friedrich der Grosse* (Munich, 2012), 206 and 211.

6. See Ekhart Berckenhagen's *catalogue raisonée Anton Graff: Leben und Werk* (Berlin, 1967), no. 328; also V. Veltzke, 'Das brandenburgisch-preussische Herrscherbild: Kontinuität und Wandel', id. (ed.), *Macht und Dienst: Zur Darstellung des brandenburgisch-preussischen Herrscherhauses in Gemälde und Graphik, 1650–1900* (Minden, 1993), 8.

7. F. [recte J.] W. von Archenholtz, *The History of the Seven Years War in Germany*, transl. F. A. Catty (Frankfurt, 1843), 541–2; J. W. von Archenholtz, *Geschichte des Siebenjährigen Krieges* (repr. Halle, s.a. [1st 1791]), 394–5.

8. K. von Stein, 'Geschichte des Zeitraumes von 1789 bis 1799', G. Wilmenus (ed.), *Friedrich der Grosse im Urteil der Mit- und Nachwelt* (Stuttgart, s.a. [1957]), 13–14.

9. A. Müller, *Die Elemente der Staatskunst: Sechsunddreissig Vorlesungen* (Berlin, 1936 [1st 1808–9]), 195; see also J. Willms, 'Posthume Zeitgenossenschaft: Anmerkungen zur Rezeption Friedrichs II von Preussen', *Aus Politik und Zeitgeschichte* nos. 20–1 (1986), 29.

10. H.-J. Schoeps, *Das andere Preussen* (Stuttgart, 1952), 36.

11. Id., 'Die preussischen Konservativen', G. K. Kaltenbrunner (ed.), *Rekonstruktion des Konservatismus* (Bern, 3rd ed. 1978), 180–8.

12. Sermon, 24 Jan. 1808, in F. Schleiermacher, *Patriotische Predigten*, ed. W. Schotte (Berlin, 1935), 57 and 60. It was perhaps no coincidence that Schleiermacher was a native of Breslau; for his political theology see T. Vial, 'Schleiermacher and the State', J. Mariña (ed.), *The Cambridge Companion to Friedrich Schleiermacher* (Cambridge, 2005), 277–9.

13. J. Schmidt, *Die Geschichte des Genie-Gedankens in der deutschen Literatur, Philosophie und Politik, 1750–1945* (2 vols, Darmstadt, 1985), i, 467–76.

14. R. Lüdicke, *Die Preussischen Kultusminister, ihre Beamten im ersten Jahrhundert des Ministeriums, 1817–1917* (Stuttgart and Berlin, 1918), 58–9.

15. Menzel studied Sanssouci and period costumes in considerable detail, G. Eckhardt, 'Der junge Menzel in Sanssouci', K. Thiele (ed.), *Staatliche Museen zu Berlin: Forschungen und Berichte 26* (East Berlin, 1987), 251–8.

16. F. Kugler and A. Menzel, *Geschichte Friedrichs des Grossen* (Cologne, repr. s.a.), 358 and 356–7; for the genesis of the work, anon., 'Nachwort', ibid., 624–31; further G. Lammel, *Zwischen Legende und Wahrheit: Bilderfolgen zur brandenburgisch-preussischen Geschichte* (Münster, 1997), 50–1.

17. B. Schmitz, 'Nachwort', anon., *Denkmal König Friedrichs des Grossen, enthüllt am 31. Mai 1851* (Leipzig, repr. 1987 [1st 1851]), [15] (original unpaginated);

H. Mackowski, *Das Friedrich-Denkmal nach den Entwürfen Schinkels und Rauchs* (Berlin, 1894), 16–45. Rochow was later Minister of the Interior (1834–42).

18. K. Merckle, *Das Denkmal Friedrichs des Grossen in Berlin: Aktenmässige Geschichte und Beschreibung des Monuments* (Berlin, 1894), 137.

19. D. E. Barclay, *Frederick William IV and the Prussian Monarchy, 1840–1861* (Oxford, 1995), 73; J. Angelow, 'Friedenskirche und Grabmal Friedrich Wilhelms IV.: Monarchie und Armee in der Revolution von 1848', B. R. Kroener and H. Ostertag (eds), *Potsdam: Staat, Armee, Residenz in der preussisch-deutschen Militärgeschichte* (Berlin, 1993), 377–92. Frederick William was later criticized for favouring a style alien to German traditions, A. Kitschke, *The Peace Church in Potsdam-Sanssouci* (Passau, 2011), 12–13.

20. A. L. Rochau, *Grundsätze der Realpolitik*, ed. H.-U. Wehler (Berlin, 1972 [1st 1853]), 26–7; see also D. Langewische, *Liberalismus in Deutschland* (Frankfurt, 1988), 65–72.

21. As with so many other nationalisms, German national identity defined itself 'against' others, especially France, M. Hughes, *Nationalism and Society: Germany, 1800–1945* (London, 1988).

22. No romantic reactionary, Manteuffel hoped that the Frederician enlightened absolutism could be revived in a modernized form, Barclay, *Frederick William IV*, 258–65.

23. G. A. Craig, *The Politics of the Prussian Army, 1640–1945* (Oxford, 1955), 120–35.

24. Menzel to Schöll, 1 July 1859, as quoted in C. Keisch, 'Adolph Menzels "Ansprache Friedrich des Grossen vor der Schlacht bei Leuthen"', Thiele (ed.), *Forschungen und Berichte*, 259.

25. See the catalogue entry in C. Keisch and M. U. Riemann-Reyher (eds), *Adolph Menzel, 1815–1905: Between Romanticism and Impressionism* (New Haven, CT, 1996), 291–4.

26. Menzel may even have tried to destroy the picture, Keisch, 'Menzels "Ansprache"', 278–9; O. Pflanze, *Bismarck and the Development of Germany*, i, *The Period of Unification, 1815–1871* (Princeton, NJ, 2nd ed. 1973), 192–230.

27. G. Freytag, *Bilder aus der deutschen Vergangenheit* (3 vols, Leipzig, s.a. [1st 1857]), iii, 458. For the racial undertones in Freytag's work, H. O. Horch, 'Judenbilder in der realistischen Erzählliteratur: Jüdische Gestalten bei Gustav Freytag, Fritz Reuter, Berthold Auerbach und Wilhelm Raabe', H. A. Strauss and C. Hoffmann (eds), *Juden und Judentum in der Literatur* (Munich, 1985), esp. 143–50.

28. M. Epkenhans, *Die deutsche Reichsgründung 1870/71* (Munich, 2020), 9; for contemporary sentiment, G. Friedrich, *Fontanes preussische Welt: Armee-Dynastie-Staat* (Herford, 1988), 268–87.

29. S. Oredsson, *Gustav Adolf, Sverige och Trettioåriga kriget: Historieskrivning och kult* (Lund, 1992), esp. 67–86; also P. H. Wilson, *Lützen* (Oxford, 2018), 142–52.

30. H. von Treitschke, *Deutsche Geschichte im 19. Jahrhundert* (5 vols, Berlin, 1879–94), i, 269–98; id., 'Gustav Adolf und Deutschlands Freiheit', id.,

Historische und Politische Aufsätze (Leipzig, 4th ed. 1920), 23–37; W. Bussmann, *Treitschke: Sein Welt- und Geschichtsbild* (Göttingen, 1952), 294–9.

31. M. L. Anderson, 'The Kulturkampf and the Course of German History', *CEH* xix, 1 (1986), 86–115; K. Cramer, 'The Cult of Gustavus Adolphus: Protestant Identity and German Nationalism', H. Walser Smith (ed.), *Protestants, Catholics and Jews in Germany, 1800–1914* (Oxford, 2001), 97–120.

32. M. Lenz, 'Gustav Adolf', id., *Kleine historische Schriften*, ii, *Von Luther bis Marx* (Munich, 1922); see also B. Faulenbach, *Ideologie des deutschen Weges: Die deutsche Geschichte in der Historiographie zwischen Kaiserreich und Nationalsozialismus* (Munich, 1980), 125–31. Emphasizing the Protestant aspect of the king's policy was not the preserve of German historians alone, see inter alia the work of the Oxford historian C. R. L. Fletcher, *Gustavus Adolphus and the Struggle of Protestantism for Existence* (London, 1890).

33. As quoted in Oredsson, *Gustav Adolf*, 75–6; for an appreciation of Lenz's work, K.-H. Krill, *Die Rankerenaissance: Max Lenz und Erich Marcks: Ein Beitrag zum historisch-politischen Denken in Deutschland* (Berlin, 1962).

34. E. Marcks, 'Das Königtum des grossen Friedrich [1901]', O. Büsch (ed.), *Moderne preussische Geschichte* (3 vols, Berlin, 1981), i, 132; Faulenbach, *Ideologie*, 44–7.

35. W. Mock, 'The Function of "Race" in Imperialist Ideologies: The Example of Joseph Chamberlain', P. M. Kennedy and A. J. Nicholls (eds), *Nationalist and Racialist Movements in Britain and Germany before the First World War* (London, 1981), 190–203; for the fissiparous nature of radical nationalism, G. Eley, *Reshaping the German Right: Radical Nationalism and Political Change after Bismarck* (New Haven, CT, 1980), 160–238.

36. Thus Dietrich Schäfer, Treitschke's successor at Berlin, *Weltgeschichte der Neuzeit* (2 vols, Berlin, 1912), i, 570–1.

37. As quoted in H.-U. Wehler, *Deutsche Gesellschaftsgeschichte*, iii, *Von der "Deutschen Doppelrevolution" bis zum Beginn des Ersten Weltkrieges, 1849–1914* (Frankfurt, 1995), 383; H. M. Green, 'Adolf Stoecker: Portrait of an Antisemite', *Politics & Policy* xxxi, 1 (2003), 106–29.

38. M. L. Anderson, *Practising Democracy: Elections and Political Culture in Imperial Germany* (Princeton, NJ, 2000), 106–16.

39. Keisch, 'Menzel's "Ansprache"', 273.

40. M. Messerschmidt, 'Nachwirkung Friedrichs II. in Preussen-Deutschland', B. R. Kroener (ed.), *Europa im Zeitalter Friedrichs des Grossen: Wirtschaft, Gesellschaft, Kriege* (Munich, 1989), 274.

41. F. Polack, *Zweihundert Jahre preussisches Königtum: Volks- und Jugendschrift zur zweihundertjährigen Jubelfeier des preussischen Königtums* (Berlin, s.a. [1901]), 91. Pollack was an educational official in Thuringia, before becoming a freelance writer, G. Kley, *Friedrich Polack (1835–1915): Der Pestalozzi der Eichsfelder* (Bad Langensalza, 2021).

42. G. Mendelssohn Bartholdy, *Der König: Friedrich der Grosse in seinen Briefen und Erlassen, sowie in zeitgenössischen Berichten und Anekdoten* (Ebenhausen bei München, 1912), 4 and 320–6. The author was the great-great-great grandson of Moses Mendelssohn.

43. A. Bär and P. Quensel (ed.), *Bildersaal deutscher Geschichte: Zweitausend Jahre deutschen Lebens in Wort und Bild* (Stuttgart, 1890), 286–7.

44. Reproduced in V. Veltzke, 'Herrscher und Haus in Beispielen der Ölmalerei', id., *Macht und Dienst*, 33.

45. R. Knoetel and W. Friedrich, *Der Alte Fritz in fünfzig Bildern für Jung und Alt* (Dortmund, repr. 3rd ed. 1986 [1st 1905]).

46. B. R. Kroener, '"Nun danket alles Gott": Der Choral von Leuthen und Friedrich der Grosse als protestantischer Held. Die Produktion politischer Mythen im 19. und 20. Jahrhundert', G. Krumeich and H. Lehmann (eds), *"Gott mit uns": Nation, Religion und Gewalt im 19. und frühen 20. Jahrhundert* (Göttingen, 2000), 119.

47. H. Müller-Bohn, 'Einleitung', in Knoetel and Friedrich, *Der Alte Fritz*, 16; also C. Pilske, 'Vermittlung der Geschichte in den Medien zur Zeit Anton von Werners', D. Bartmann (ed.), *Anton von Werner: Geschichte in Bildern* (Munich, 1993), 171.

48. Knoetel and Friedrich, *Der alte Fritz*, 66–71.

49. A. Schiller, *Die Schlacht bei Leuthen: Zur 150-jährigen Erinnerung an die Schlacht bei Leuthen und an die Einweihung des Denksteines auf dem Schlachtfelde am 5. Dezember 1907 durch seine Majestät Kaiser Wilhelm II* (Schweidnitz, 1907), 24.

50. C. Lepp, 'Protestanten feiern ihre Nation: Die kulturprotestantischen Ursprünge des Sedanstages', *Historisches Jahrbuch* cxviii (1998), 201–22; F. Schellack, 'Sedan- und Kaisergeburtsfeste', D. Düding, P. Friedemann, and P. Münch (eds), *Öffentliche Festkultur: Politisches Fest in Deutschland von der Aufklärung bis zum ersten Weltkrieg* (Reinbek, 1988), 278–97; J. Koch, *Von Helden und Opfern: Kulturgeschichte des deutschen Kriegsgedenkens* (Darmstadt, 2013), 51–64.

51. In general P. Nora, *Les Lieux de Mémoire* (3 vols, Paris, 1984) ; and for Germany, T. Nipperdey, 'Nationalidee und Nationaldenkmal in Deutschland im 19. Jahrhundert', id., *Kann Geschichte ojektiv sein?: Historische Essays*, ed. P. Nolte (Munich, 2013), 105–60.

52. R. Conrad, 'Auf dem Schlachtfelde von Leuthen: Zur Erinnerung an die Schlacht am 5. Dezember 1757', *Schlesische Heimatblätter: Zeitschrift für Schlesische Kultur* (1907–8), 87–91. According to another popular anecdote Zieten attributed victory to the 'great ally', pointing his index finger skywards.

53. Schiller, *Schlacht bei Leuthen*, 3. The photograph in T. Rehtwisch, *Leuthen: Blätter der Erinnerung an den grossen König und das Jahr 1757* (Leipzig, 1907), 252, gives an impression of the monument. It was destroyed in 1945, and only the foundations remain, H. Trierenberg, *Reisewege zu historischen Stätten in Niederschlesien* (Dülmen, 1996), 147.

54. H. Weczerka, *Handbuch der Historischen Stätten: Schlesien* (Stuttgart, 1977), 280.

55. For the prevalence of such teleological views, T. Nipperdey, *Deutsche Geschichte, 1800–1866: Bürgerwelt und starker Staat* (Munich, 1987), 300.

56. O. Hintze, *Die Hohenzollern und ihr Werk: Fünfhundert Jahre vaterländsicher Geschichte* (Berlin, 1915), 368 and 380.

57. T. Mann, *Friedrich und die grosse Koalition* (Frankfurt, repr. 1916), 83–93 109–10; further K. Sontheimer, *Thomas Mann und die Deutschen* (Frankfurt, 1965 (pb)), 18–25, and S. D. Stirk, *The Prussian Spirit: A Survey of German Literature and Politics* (London, s.a. [1941]), 109–11.

58. Mann, *Friedrich*, 15–16; for the context, W. J. Mommsen, 'Der Geist von 1914: Das Programm eines politischen "Sonderwegs" der Deutschen', id., *Der autoritäre Nationalstaat: Verfassung, Gesellschaft und Kultur des deutschen Kaiserreichs* (Munich, 1990), 407–21.

59. E. Ludendorff, *Kriegsführung und Politik* (Berlin, 2nd ed. 1922), 320–42; also M. Kitchen, *The Silent Dictatorship: The Politics of the German High Command under Hindenburg and Ludendorff, 1916–1918* (New York, 1976).

60. E. Ludendorff, *Der totale Krieg* (Munich, 1933), 11–28 et passim; R. Chickering, *Imperial Germany and the Great War* (Cambridge, 1998), 189–91; K.-J. Müller, 'Deutsche Militär-Elite in der Vorgeschichte des Zweiten Weltkrieges', M. Brozsat (ed.), *Die deutschen Elite und der Weg in den Zweiten Weltkrieg* (Munich, 1989), 226–90.

61. D. Orlow, *Weimar Prussia, 1918–1925: The Unlikely Rock of Democracy* (Pittsburgh, PA, 1986); also K. D. Bracher, 'Preussen und die deutsche Demokratie', M. Schlenke (ed.), *Preussen: Beiträge zu einer politischen Kultur* (Reinbek, 1981), 295–311.

62. For examples, G. Korff (ed.), *Preussen: Versuch einer Bilanz* (Reinbek, 1981), 598.

63. As quoted in H. Wilderotter, 'Das widerspenstige Erbe', *Preussen JahrBuch: Ein Almanach* (Berlin, 2001), 141 [140–3]. Helldorff became chief of the Berlin police in 1933, D. Siemens, *Stormtroopers: A New History of Hitler's Brownshirts* (Newhaven, CT, 2017), 130–1; I. Harrison, 'Alter Kämpfer im Widerstand: Graf Helldorff, die NS-Bewegung und Opposition gegen Hitler', *VjfZG* xlv, 3 (1997), 385–424.

64. Ludendorff to War Ministry, 4 July 1917, repr. in U. W. Wolf, *Preussen Glanz und Gloria im Film: Die berühmten deutschen Tonfilme über Preussens glorreiche Vergangenheit* (Munich, 1981), 158–61. Preparations were already in train since late 1916, minutes of meeting, *Kriegspresseamt*, 20 Nov. 1916, W. Deist (ed.), *Militär und Innenpolitik, 1914–1918* (2 vols, Düsseldorf, 1970), i, no. 136.

65. H. Regel, 'Die Fridericus-Filme der Weimarer Republik', A. Marquardt (ed.), *Preussen im Film* (Reinbek, 1981), 124–34, and H. Feld, 'Potsdam gegen Weimar oder Wie Otto Gebühr den Siebenjährigen Krieg gewann', ibid., 68–73.

66. S. Kracauer, *From Caligari to Hitler: A Psychological History of German Film* (Princeton, NJ, 1947), 266–7. Unsurprisingly, alongside Bismarck, Frederick was a counter-projection to the confused conditions of the present,

K. Sontheimer, *Antidemokratisches Denken in der Weimarer Republik: Die politischen Ideen des deutschen Nationalismus zwischen 1918 und 1933* (Munich, 3rd ed. 1992), 150.

67. A. Moeller van den Bruck, *Preussischer Stil* (Berlin, 1916); D. Bartetzko, 'Unter dem Berufe des Kriegerischen—Ein Missverständnis: Arthur Moeller van den Brucks preussischer Stil', P. Bahners and G. Roellecke (eds), *Preussische Stile: Ein Staat als Kunststück* (Stuttgart, 2001), 380–90.

68. *Der Grosse Fritz im Krieg* (Stuttgart, 1917); *Fridericus* (Munich, 1918); *Das Fridericus-Rex-Buch* (Berlin, 1923); *Vom alten Fritz: Vier Erzählungen aus dem leben des grossen Königs* (Nuremberg, 1924). Molo, best known for his exchanges in 1945 with Thomas Mann about so-called 'internal exile', fell out of favour with the Nazi cultural authorities and some of his works were suppressed by the censor, A. Werner, 'Die Verbotsschlaufe: Der Schriftsteller Walter von Molo, der "Fridericus"-Film von 1936 und die Zensur', A. Dorgerloh and M. Becker (eds), *Preussen aus Celluloid: Friederich II. im Film* (Berlin, 2011), 111–22.

69. e.g. Cigaretten-Bilderdienst (ed.), *Bilder deutscher Geschichte* (Hamburg, repr. 1936), nos. 74–6. The pictures show the Parchwitz address, Frederick on the Borne hill and the 'meeting' at Lissa.

70. The leading theatre critic Alfred Kerr quipped that German audiences had now made Frederick's acquaintance *'über Gebühr'* (beyond measure), see A. Kilb, 'Der Mann aus Marmor: Friedrich der Grosse als Heldenfigur in den Filmen der Weimarer Republik und des Nationalsozialismus', Dorgerloh and Becker (eds), *Preussen aus Celluloid*, 18.

71. A. Thimme, *Flucht in den Mythos: Die Deutschnationale Volkspartei und die Niederlage von 1918* (Göttingen, 1969), 50–60; E. Dovifat, 'Die Publizistik der Weimarer Zeit: Presse, Rundfunk, Film', L. Reinisch (ed.), *Die Zeit ohne Eigenschaften: Eine Bilanz der Zwanziger Jahre* (Stuttgart, 1961), 130–1.

72. H.-P. Ehni, *Bollwerk Preussen?: Preussen-Regierung, Reich-Länder-Problem und Sozialdemokratie, 1928–1932* (Bonn, 1975), 263–76; H. Schulze, *Otto Braun oder Preussens demokratische Sendung* (Frankfurt, 1977), 725–44.

73. Kilb, 'Marmor', 25.

74. 'Der Tag von Potsdam' commemorative issue of *Die Woche*, no. 7 (Mar. 1933), 8; Thimme, *Flucht*, 61–5.

75. Friedrich Meinecke's scathing comment after 1945, id., *Die deutsche Katastrophe* (Wiesbaden, 1946), 25.

76. The sermon also contained a veiled warning against 'thirst for revenge and arrogance', M. Grünzig, *Für Deutschtum und Vaterland: Die Potsdamer Garnisonskirche im 20. Jahrhundert* (Berlin, 2017), 165–6. Dibelius, a self-proclaimed antisemite and anti-republican, later became an opponent of Nazism. At least initially, there was a good deal of support for the Nazi movement amongst lay members of the Protestant church, R. von Thadden, 'Kirche im Schatten des Staates?: Zur Problematik der evangelischen Kirche in der preussischen Geschichte', H.-J. Puhle and H.-U. Wehler (eds), *Preussen im Rückblick* (Göttingen, 1980), 174.

77. K. D. Bracher, W. Sauer, and G. Schulz, *Die nationalsozialistische Machtergreifung: Studien zur Errichtung des totalären Herrschaftssystems 1933/34* (Cologne and Opladen, 1962), 149–52; also A. von der Goltz, *Hindenburg: Power, Myth, and the Rise of the Nazis* (Oxford, 2009), 174–8.

78. Hitler speech at the opening of the *Reichstag*, 21 Mar. 1933, E. Klöss (ed.), *Reden des Führers: Politik und Propaganda Adolf Hitlers, 1922–1945* (Munich, 1967), no. 4, 92–5.

79. K. Scheel, *Der Tag von Potsdam* (Berlin, 1996), 101–2.

80. As quoted in T. Schwarzmüller, *Zwischen Kaiser und Führer: Generalfeldmarschall August von Mackensen. Eine politische Biographie* (Paderborn, 1995), 237.

81. B. Scheurig, *Henning von Tresckow: Eine Biographie* (Oldenburg, 2nd ed. 1973), 44–5; K.-J. Müller, 'Der Tag von Potsdam und das Verhältnis der preussisch-deutschen Militär-Elite zum Nationalsozialismus', B. R. Kroener and H. Ostertag (eds), *Potsdam: Staat, Armee, Residenz in der preussische-deutschen Militärgeschichte* (Berlin, 1993), 435–50.

82. V. Ulrich, *Hitler, i, Ascent, 1889–1939* (London, 2013), 434–76.

83. F. L. Carsten, 'Potsdam in historischer Sicht', Kroener and Ostertag (eds), *Potsdam*, 26. It was also used by world war veterans, Grünzig, *Deutschtum*, 225–7.

84. Hitler *Reichstag* speech, 1 Sept. 1939, Klöss (ed.), *Reden*, no. 12, 215.

85. As quoted in M. Messerschmidt, 'Aussenpolitik und Kriegsvorbereitung', Militärgeschichtliches Forschungsamt (ed.), *Das Deutsche Reich und der zweite Weltkrieg* (10 vols, Stuttgart, 1979–2008), i, 699.

86. Goebbels diary, 26 Apr. 1940, R. G. Reuth (ed.), *Joseph Goebbels: Tagebücher* (5 vols, Munich, 1992), iv, 1412; also W. van Kampen, 'Das "preussische Beispiel" als Propaganda und politisches Lebensbedürfnis: Anmerkungen zur Authentizität und Instrumentalisierung von Geschichte im Preussenfilm', Marquardt (ed.), *Preussen im Film*, 176–7.

87. Goebbels speech, 19 Apr. 1942, H. Heiber (ed.), *Goebbels-Reden, 1932–1945* (2 vols, Düsseldorf, 1971–2), ii, 115–17; K. Barthel, *Friedrich der Grosse in Hitlers Geschichtsbild* (Wiesbaden, 1977), 22.

88. A. Hitler, *Mein Kampf*, translated by R. Manheim (Boston, MA, 1943), 238; for the notion of *Vorläufer*, see H. H. Hofmann, *Der Hitlerputsch: Krisenjahre deutscher Geschichte, 1920–1924* (Munich, 1961), 263–4.

89. Goebbels diary, 16 Jan. 1940, Reuth (ed.), *Goebbels Tagebücher* iv, 1370; further Schmidt, *Geschichte des Genie-Gedankens* ii, 207–12.

90. P. E. Schramm, *Hitler: The Man and the Military Leader* (London, 1972), 119.

91. J. Fest, *Der Untergang: Hitler und das Ende des Dritten Reiches: Eine historische Skizze* (Reinbek, 2002), 32.

92. Hitler address to divisional commanders, 12 Dec. 1944, H. Heiber (ed.), *Hitlers Lagebesprechungen: Die Protokollfragmente seiner Konferenzen, 1942–1945* (Stuttgart, 1962), 721.

93. Goebbels speech, 18 Feb. 1943, H. Heiber (ed.), *Goebbels-Reden* ii, 172–6.

94. *Völkischer* Beobachter, 8 Mar. 1945, as quoted in Reuth (ed.), *Goebbels Tagebücher* v, 2145, n. 19, and 2147, n. 21.

95. H. Trevor-Roper, *The Last Days of Hitler* (London, rev. ed. 1965 (pb)), 142–3.

96. US Army Center of Military History, *Military Improvisation during the Russian Campaign* (Washington, DC, repr. 1986), 90–1.

97. As quoted in M. Egremont, *Forgotten Land; Journeys among the Ghosts of East Prussia* (London, 2011), 297.

98. G. Korff (ed.), *Preussen: Versuch einer Bilanz. Katalog* (5 vols, Reinbek, 1981).

99. The most notable works of this period were T. Schieder, *Friedrich der Grosse: Ein Königtum der Widersprüche* (Frankfurt, 1983) and K. O. von Aretin, *Friedrich der Grosse: Grösse und Grenzen des Preussenkönigs* (Freiburg, 1985).

100. I. Mittenzwei, 'Das unerwünschte Erbe: Preussen und die DDR', *Preussen Jahr-Buch: Ein Almanach* (Berlin, 2001), 136–9.

101. Id., 'Die zwei Gesichter Preussens', *Deutschland-Archiv* xvi, 2 (1983), 214–18 [first published in East Germany in 1978], and *Friedrich II. von Preussen. Biographie* (East Berlin, 1979). The latter is more remarkable as testifying to the changes in regime attitudes than on grounds of scholarship. E. Kehrt, 'Das ganze Erbe soll es sein: Die Erweiterung des Erbe- und Traditionsverständnisses im Geschichtsbild der SED'; id. and H. von Löwis, *Griff nach der deutschen Geschichte: Erbaneignung und Traditionspflege in der DDR* (Paderborn, 1988), 128–43; and A. Dorpalen, *German History in Marxist Perspective: The East German Approach* (London, 1967), 138–67. The more orthodox position of East German scholars was exemplified in G. Vogler and K. Vetter, *Preussen: Von den Anfängen bis zur Reichsgründung* (East Berlin, 1970), 81–126.

102. H. Caspar, 'Friedrich der Grosse: Letzte Ruhe auf dem Weinberg', *Tagesspiegel*, 16 Aug. 1991; see also Hajo Funke's sardonic reflections 'Potsdamer Notizen', *Die Neue Gesellschaft/Frankfurter Hefte* xxxviii, 10 (1991), 874–6.

103. At the time of writing, federal authorities were contemplating renaming the *Stiftung Preussischer Kulturbesitz*, the largest heritage organization in Germany, D. Kurbjuweit and C. Schult, 'Kulturkampf um Preussen', *Der Spiegel*, no. 52, 31 Dec. 2022, and J. Kaube, 'Das ungeliebte Preussen', *Frankfurter Allgemeine Zeitung*, 31 Dec. 2022.

104. Id., *Die verspätete Nation* (Stuttgart, 1959), 21.

Conclusion

1. See also the case-study by J. Ostwald, 'The "Decisive" Battle of Ramillies, 1706: Prerequisites for Decisiveness in Early Modern Warfare', *Journal of Military History* lxiv, 4 (2000), 649–78.

2. Colmar Grünhagen's *Schlesien unter Friedrich dem Grossen* (2 vols, Wolfenbüttel, repr. 2014 [1st 1889]) gives ample testimony to this fact.

BIBLIOGRAPHY

I. Archival Sources

Official Papers

AUSTRIA

Haus-, Hof- und Staatsarchiv, Vienna

Reichskanzlei
    Diplomatische Akten Köln, Weisungen
Staatenabteilung
    England
    Russland
    Preussen, Collecteana
Staatskanzlei
    Vorträge

Kriegsarchiv, Vienna

Alte Feldakten
    Cabinets-Acten 1756
    Cabinets-Acten 1757
    Cabinets-Acten 1758
    Hauptarmee 1756
    Hauptarmee 1757
    Hauptarmee 1758
    Hofkriegsrath 1756
    Hofkriegsrath 1757
Hofkriegsrat
    Protocolli in Publicis 1756

BRITAIN

The National Archives (Public Record Office), Kew

SP 80 The Empire

GERMANY

Landesarchiv Nordrhein-Westfalen, Abteilung Rheinland, Duisburg
Kurköln VII Kriegsakten.

Private Papers

British Library, London

Carteret MSS
Mitchell MSS
Yorke MSS

Printed Sources and Contemporary Works

Anon., *Bericht von dem Marsch des Preußischen Corps aus Sachsen nach der Bataille bey Weissenfels [i.e. Rossbach] bis in Schlesien nach der Bataille bey Lissa [i.e. Leuthen]* (s.loc., s.a. [1757]).

Anon., *Denkmal König Friedrichs des Grossen, enthüllt am 31. Mai 1851* (Leipzig, repr. 1987 [1st 1851]).

Anon. [W. F. von Retzow], *Charakteristik der wichtigsten Ereignisse des siebenjährigen Krieges, in Rücksicht auf Ursachen und Wirkungen von einem Zeitgenossen* (2 vols, Berlin, rev. ed. 1802).

J. W. von Archenholtz, *Geschichte des Siebenjährigen Krieges* (repr. Halle, s.a. [1st 1791]) (Engl. Translation: F. [*sic*] W. von Archenholtz, *The History of the Seven Years War in Germany*, transl. F. A. Catty (Frankfurt, 1843)).

A. von Arneth (ed.), *Die Relationen der Botschafter Venedigs über Österreich im achtzehnten Jahrhundert* (Vienna, 1863).

O. Bardong (ed.), *Friedrich der Grosse* (Darmstadt, 1982).

H. Caspar, 'Friedrich der Grosse: Letzte Ruhe auf dem Weinberg', *Tagesspiegel*, 16 Aug. 1991.

C. von Clausewitz, *Vom Kriege*, ed. W. Hahlweg (Bonn, 19th ed. 1991 [1st 1832]).

Id., *Nachrichten über Preussen in seiner grossen Katastrophe* (Berlin, 1888).

Id., *Sämtliche Hinterlassene Werke über Krieg und Kriegführung* (3 vols, s.loc. [Stuttgart], 1999).

H. Delbrück (ed.), 'Carl von Clausewitz: Über das Fortschreiten und den Stillstand der kriegerischen Begebenheiten', *Zeitschrift für Preussische Geschichte und Landeskunde* iv, 3 (1878), 233–41.

F. Dickmann (ed.), *Geschichte in Quellen*, iii, *Renaissance, Glaubenskämpfe, Absolutismus* (Munich, 1966).

R. Dietrich (ed.), *Politische Testamente der Hohenzollern* (Munich, 1981 (pb)).

J. G. Droysen, M. Duncker and H. Sybel (eds), *Politische Correspondenz Friedrich des Grossen* (46 vols, Berlin, 1879–1939).

C. Gerretson and P. Geyl (eds), *Briefwisseling en Aantekeningen van Willem Bentinck, Heer van Rhoon (tot an de dood van Willem IV)* (3 vols, The Hague, 1976).

F. W. Ghillany, *Europäische Chronik von 1492 bis Ende April 1865, mit besonderer Berücksichtigung der Friedensverträge* (3 vols, Leipzig, 1865).

Generalstab des Heeres, Kriegswissenschaftliche Abteilung (ed.), *Generalfeldmarschall Graf von Schlieffen: Dienstschriften des Chefs des Generalstabs der Armee* (2 vols, Berlin, 1937).

G. Gourgaud, *Sainte-Hélène: Journal inédit de 1815 à 1819* (2 vols, Paris, 1899).

J. A. de Guibert, *Œuvres militaires du comte de Guibert* (5 vols, Paris, 1803).

H. Heiber (ed.), *Hitlers Lagebesprechungen: Die Protokollfragmente seiner Konferenzen, 1942–1945* (Stuttgart, 1962).

Id. (ed.), *Goebbels-Reden, 1932–1945* (2 vols, Düsseldorf, 1971–2).

C. Hinrichs (ed.), *Friedrich der Grosse und Maria Theresia: Diplomatische Berichte von Otto Christoph Graf von Podewils, Königlich Preussischer Gesandter am Österreichischen Hofe in Wien* (Berlin, 1937).

A. Hitler, *Mein Kampf*, translated by R. Manheim (Boston, MA, 1943).

H. H. Hofmann (ed.), *Quellen zum Verfassungsorganismus des Heiligen Römischen Reiches Deutscher Nation, 1495–1815* (Darmstadt, 1976).

E. Kessel (ed.), *Generalfeldmarschall Graf Alfred von Schlieffen: Briefe* (Göttingen, 1958).

R. Khevenhüller-Metsch and H. Schlitter (eds), *Aus der Zeit Maria Theresias: Tagebücher des Fürsten Johann Joseph Khevenhüller-Metsch, Kaiserlicher Oberhofmeister, 1742–1776* (7 vols, Vienna, 1907–25).

E. Klöss (ed.), *Reden des Führers: Politik und Propaganda Adolf Hitlers, 1922–1945* (Munich, 1967).

Königlich Preussischer Generalstab (ed.), *Friedrich der Grosse von Kolin bis Rossbach und Leuthen nach den Cabinetts-Ordres im Königlichen Staats-Archiv* (Berlin, 1858).

H. von Kuehnheim (ed.), *Aus dem Tagebuch des Grafen Lehndorff* (Berlin, 1982).

G. Küntzel and M. Hass (eds), *Die Politischen Testamente der Hohenzollern, nebst ergänzenden Aktenstücken* (2 vols, Leipzig, 1911).

H. Merkens (ed.), *Ausgewählte Kriegswissenschaftliche Schriften Friedrichs des Grossen* (Jena, 1876).

H.-G. Riqueti de Mirabeau, *De la monarchie prusse sous Frédéric le Grand* (8 vols, London, 1788).

S. de Monzambano (pseud. S. von Pufendorf), *Über die Verfassung des Deutschen Reiches*, ed. H. Bresslau (Berlin, 1922).

K. Müller (ed.), *Instrumentum Pacis Westphalicae: Die Westfälischen Friedensverträge 1648* (Berne, 1966).

G. Naumann, *Sammlung ungedruckter Nachrichten, so die Geschichte der Feldzüge der Preußen von 1740 bis 1779 erläutern* (2 vols, Dresden, 1782).

C. Parry (ed.), *Consolidated Treaty Series* xli (New York, 1969).

J. D. E. Preuss (ed.), *Oeuvres de Frédéric le Grand* (30 vols, Berlin, 1846–1856).

A. F. Pribram (ed.), *Österreichische Staatsverträge: England* (2 vols, Vienna, 1913).

R. G. Reuth (ed.), *Joseph Goebbels: Tagebücher* (5 vols, Munich, 1992).

J. Richter (ed.), *Die Briefe Friedrich des Grossen an seinen vormaligen Kammerdiener Fredersdorf* (Moers, repr. 1979 [1st 1926]).

A. Ritter (ed.), *Die Werke Friedrichs des Grossen* (2 vols, Berlin, s.a. [1915]).

W. Robertson, *The Works of William Robertson, DD* (London, one vol. ed. 1852).

F. Schleiermacher, *Patriotische Predigten*, ed. W. Schotte (Berlin, 1935).

H. Schlitter (ed.), *Correspondance secrète entre le comte Anton Wenzel Kaunitz-Rietberg, Ambassadeur impérial à Paris, et le Baron Ignaz de Koch, Secrétair de l'Imperatrice Marie-Thérèse, 1750–1752* (Paris, 1895).

F. von Schmerfeld (ed.), *Die deutschen Aufmarschpläne, 1871–1890* (Berlin, 1929).

W. Schüssler (ed.), *Friedrich der Grosse: Gespräche mit Henri de Catt* (Munich, 1983 (pb)).

Verhandlungen des Reichstages, Stenographische Berichte: Legislaturperiode XIII, Session 2 (1914–16) cccvi (Berlin, 1914).

G. B. Volz (ed.), *Die Werke Friedrich des Grossen* (10 vols, Berlin, 1913).

Id. and G. Küntzel (eds), *Preussische und Österreichische Acten zur Vorgeschichte des Siebenjährigen Krieges* (Osnabrück, repr. 1965).

G. Wilmenus (ed.), *Friedrich der Grosse im Urteil der Mit- und Nachwelt* (Stuttgart, s.a. [1957]).

'Der Tag von Potsdam' commemorative issue of *Die Woche*, no. 7 (Mar. 1933).

Xenophon, *Hellenica*, ed. C. L. Brownson (2 vols, Cambridge, MA, 1921).

Memoirs and Autobiographical Materials

C. F. R. [*recte* E. F. R.] von Barsewisch, *Meine Kriegs-Erlebnisse während des Siebenjährigen Krieges, 1757–1763* (Berlin, 2nd ed. 1863).

F. von Bernhardi, *Denkwürdigkeiten aus meinem Leben* (Berlin, 1927).

U. Bräker, *Lebensgeschichte und Natürliche Ebentheuer des Armen Mannes im Tockenburg*, ed. S. Voellmy (Basel, 1978 [1st 1788]).

J. W. von Goethe, *Aus Dichtung und Wahrheit*.

J. A. F. Logan-Logejus, *Meine Erlebnisse als Reiteroffizier unter dem Grossen König in den Jahren 1742–1759* (Breslau, 3rd ed. 1934).

H.-G. Riqueti de Mirabeau, *Secret Memoirs of the Court of Berlin* (2 vols, London, s.a. [1908]).

J. G. Seume, *Seumes Werke*, ed. A. and K.-H. Klingenberg (2 vols, East Berlin and Weimar, 1983).

Biographical Studies

K. O. von Aretin, *Friedrich der Grosse: Grösse und Grenzen des Preussenkönigs* (Freiburg, 1985).

A. Berney, *Friedrich der Grosse: Entwicklungsgeschichte eines Staatsmannes* (Tübingen, 1934).

E. Birchner and W. Bode, *Schlieffen: Mann und Idee* (Zurich, 1937).

A. Bisset, *Memoirs and Papers of Sir Andrew Mitchell, Envoy Extraordinary and Minister Plenipotentiary from the Court of Great Britain to the Court of Prussia, from 1756 to 1771* (2 vols, London, 1850).

T. Blanning, *Frederick the Great: King of Prussia* (London, 2015).

R. Butler, *Choiseul, i, Father and Son, 1719–1785* (Oxford, 1980).

H. Collin, 'François-Etienne, dernier duc de Lorraine (1729–1737) et premier Empereur de la maison de Lorraine-Habsbourg (1745–1765)', J.-P. Bled and E. Faucher (eds), *Les Habsbourg et la Lorraine* (Nancy, 1988), 151–9.

W. Coxe, *Memoirs of the Administration of the Rt. Hon. Henry Pelham* (2 vols, London, 1829).

C. Duffy, *Feldmarschall Browne: Irischer Emigrant, Kaiserlicher Heerführer, Gegenspieler Friedrich II. von Preussen* (Vienna, 1966).

Id., *Frederick the Great: A Military Life* (London, 1985).

H. Delbrück, *Das Leben des Feldmarschalls Grafen Neidhardt von Gneisenau* (2 vols, Berlin, 1880).

F. C. Förster, *Leben und Thaten Friedrichs des Grossen, König von Preussen, geschildert als Mensch, Regent und Feldherr* (Meissen, 1840).

[H.] von Freytag-Loringhoven, *Menschen und Dinge wie ich sie in meinem Leben sah* (Berlin, 1923).

E. Frie, *Friedrich II.* (Reinbek, 2012).

P. Gaxotte, *Frédéric II* (Paris, repr. 1982).

E. Guglia, *Maria Theresia: Ihr Leben und ihre Regierung* (2 vols, Munich and Berlin, 1917).

P.-M. Hahn, *Friedrich II. von Preussen* (Stuttgart, 2013).

C. Hinrichs, *Friedrich Wilhelm I., König in Preussen: Eine Biographie* (Darmstadt, enlarged ed. 1974 [1st 1943]).

L. Hüttl, *Friedrich Wilhelm von Brandenburg, der Grosse Kurfürst: Eine politische Biographie* (Munich, 1981).

W. J. Kaiser (ed.), *Friedrich der Grosse: Sein Bild im Wandel der Zeiten* (Frankfurt, 1986).

R. Knoetel and W. Friedrich, *Der Alte Fritz in fünfzig Bildern für Jung und Alt* (Dortmund, repr. 3rd ed. 1986 [1st 1905]).

R. Koser, *Geschichte Friedrichs des Grossen* (4 vols, Stuttgart and Berlin, 5th ed. 1912).

C. von Krockow, *Friedrich der Grosse: Ein Lebensbild* (Munich, 1993 (pb)).

F. Kugler and A. Menzel, *Geschichte Friedrichs des Grossen* (Cologne, repr. s.a.).

J. Kunisch, *Friedrich der Grosse: Der König in seiner Zeit* (Munich, 2004).

T. Lau, *Die Kaiserin: Maria Theresia* (Vienna, 2016).

J. Luh, *Der Grosse: Friedrich II. von Preussen* (Berlin, 2011).

I. Mittenzwei, *Friedrich II. von Preussen: Biographie* (Cologne, 3rd ed. 1983).

A. Novotny, *Staatskanzler Kaunitz als geistige Persönlichkeit: Ein österreichisches Kulturbild aus der Zeit der Aufklärung und des Josephinismus* (Vienna, 1947).

S. K. Padover, *The Revolutionary Emperor: Joseph the Second, 1740–1790* (London, 1939).

W. Petter, 'Hans-Karl von Winterfeldt als General der friderizianischen Armee', J. Kunisch (ed.), *Persönlichkeiten im Umfeld Friedrichs des Grossen* (Cologne and Vienna, 1988), 59–87.

R. Peyrefitte, *Voltaire et Fréderic II* (2 vols, Paris, 1991).

O. Pflanze, *Bismarck and the Development of Germany*, i, *The Period of Unification, 1815–1871* (Princeton, NJ, 2nd ed. 1973).

K. von Priesdorf, *Soldatisches Führertum* (10 vols, Hamburg, 1935–42).

G. Ritter, *Friedrich der Grosse: Ein historisches Profil* (Königstein im Taunus, repr. 1978).

I. Rockel, *"Aller gnädigster König und Herr! Ich bin Euer Knecht Zieten": Die Familien Hans Joachims von Zieten* (Berlin, 2012).

B. Scheurig, *Henning von Tresckow: Eine Biographie* (Oldenburg, 2nd ed. 1973).

T. Schieder, *Friedrich der Grosse: Königtum der Widersprüche* (Frankfurt, 1983).

P. E. Schramm, *Hitler: The Man and the Military Leader* (London, 1972).

A. Schmid, 'Karl VII., 1742–1745', A. Schindling and W. Ziegler (eds), *Die Kaiser der Neuzeit, 1519–1918: Heiliges Römisches Reich, Österreich und Deutschland* (Munich, 1990), 215–31.

Id., 'Franz I. und Maria Theresia, 1745–1765', ibid., 232–48.

T. Schwarzmüller, *Zwischen Kaiser und Führer: Generalfeldmarschall August von Mackensen. Eine politische Biographie* (Paderborn, 1995).

B. Stollberg-Rillinger, *Maria Theresia: Die Kaiserin in ihrer Zeit* (Munich, 2017).

F. A. J. Szabo, *Kaunitz and Enlightened Absolutism, 1753–1780* (Cambridge, 1980).

F.-L. von Thadden, *Feldmarschall Daun: Maria Theresias grösster Feldherr* (Vienna, 1967).

A. C. Thompson, *George II: King and Elector* (New Haven, CT, 2011).

V. Ulrich, *Hitler*, i, *Ascent, 1889–1939* (London, 2013).

F. Walter, *Die Paladine der Kaiserin: Ein Maria-Theresia-Buch* (Vienna, 1959).

Id., 'Feldmarschall Leopold Joseph Graf Daun und Feldmarschall Gideon Ernst von Laudon', H. Hantsch (ed.), *Gestalten der Geschichte Österreichs* (Innsbruck, 1962), 263–78.

P. C. Yorke, *The Life and Correspondence of Philip Yorke, Earl of Hardwicke, Lord High Chancellor of Great Britain* (3 vols, Cambridge, 1913).

E. Ziebura, *Prinz Heinrich von Preussen. Biographie* (Berlin, 1999), 147–58.

Monographs

Anon., *Die Lehren der Kriegsgeschichte für die Kriegführung* (Berlin, 1881) (= *Beiheft zum Militär-Wochenblatt* 9).

J. C. Allmayer-Beck, *Militär, Geschichte und Politische Bildung*, ed. P. Broucek and E. A. Schmidl (Vienna, 2003).

F. Althoff, *Untersuchungen zum Gleichgewicht der Mächte in der Aussenpolitik Friedrich des Grossen nach dem Siebenjährigen Krieg (1763–1786)* (Berlin, 1995).

M. L. Anderson, *Practising Democracy: Elections and Political Culture in Imperial Germany* (Princeton, NJ, 2000).

M. S. Anderson, *The War of the Austrian Succession, 1740–1748* (London, 2nd ed. 1999).

J. Angelow, 'Friedenskirche und Grabmal Friedrich Wilhelms IV.: Monarchie und Armee in der Revolution von 1848', B. R. Kroener and H. Ostertag (eds), *Potsdam: Staat, Armee, Residenz in der preussisch-deutschen Militärgeschichte* (Berlin, 1993), 377–92.

K. O. von Aretin, *Heiliges Römisches Reich, 1776 bis 1806: Reichsverfassung und Staatssouveranität* (2 vols, Wiesbaden, 1967).

Id., *Kaiser Joseph II. und die Reichskammergerichtsvisitation, 1767–1776* (Wetzlar, 1991).

Id., *Das Alte Reich, 1648–1806* (2 vols, Stuttgart, 1997).

A. Bär and P. Quensel (ed.), *Bildersaal deutscher Geschichte: Zweitausend Jahre deutschen Lebens in Wort und Bild* (Stuttgart, 1890).

D. Bald, *Der deutsche Generalstab, 1859–1939: Reform und Restauration in Ausbildung und Bildung* (Munich, 1977).

Id., G. Bald-Gerlich and E. Ambros, *Tradition und Reform im militärischen Bildungswesen: Von der preussischen Allgemeinen Kriegsschule zur Führungsakademie der Bundeswehr* (Baden-Baden, 1985).

D. E. Bangert, *Die russisch-österreichische militärische Zusammenarbeit im Siebenjährigen Krieg in den Jahren 1758–1759* (Boppard am Rhein, 1971).

D. E. Barclay, *Frederick William IV and the Prussian Monarchy, 1840–1861* (Oxford, 1995).

K. Barthel, *Friedrich der Grosse in Hitlers Geschichtsbild* (Wiesbaden, 1977).

J. C. Batzel, *Austria and the First Three Treaties of Versailles, 1755–1758* (Ann Arbor, MI, 1975).

W. Bein, *Schlesien in der habsburgischen Politik: Ein Beitrag zur Entstehung des Dualismus im Alten Reich* (Sigmaringen, 1994).

E. Berckenhagen, *Anton Graff: Leben und Werk* (Berlin, 1967).

F. von Bernhardi, *Das Studium der friderizianischen Kriege in seiner Bedeutung für die moderne Kriegskunst* (Berlin, 1892).

Id. Bernhardi, *How Germany Makes War* (London, 1914).

T. von Bernhardi, *Friedrich der Grosse als Feldherr* (2 vols, Berlin, 1881).

J. Black, *Natural and Necessary Enemies: Anglo-French Relations in the Eighteenth Century* (London, 1986).

Id., *A System of Ambition?: British Foreign Policy, 1660–1793* (London, 1991).

Id., *War in the Eighteenth Century* (London, repr. 2002).

Id., *Kings, Nobles and Commoners: States and Societies in Early Modern Europe* (London, 2004).

H. Bleckwenn, *Die friderizianischen Uniformen, 1753–1786* (4 vols, Osnabrück, 1984).

W. Bleyl, *Silberberg: Die Passfestung Schlesiens. Darstellung einer friderizianischen Festungsanlage auf Grund örtlicher und aktenmässiger Bauforschungen* (Cologne, repr. 1977 [1st 1938]).

W. von Blume, *Feldherrntum* (Berlin, 1914) (= *Beiheft zum Militär-Wochenblatt* no. 4).

E. Bosbach, *Die "Rêveries Politiques" in Friedrichs des Grossen Politischem Testament von 1752: Historisch-Politische Erläuterungen* (Cologne and Graz, 1960).

K. D. Bracher, W. Sauer, and G. Schulz, *Die nationalsozialistische Machtergreifung: Studien zur Errichtung des totalären Herrschaftssystems 1933/34* (Cologne and Opladen, 1962).

M. Braubach, *Die Bedeutung der Subsidien für die Politik im Spanischen Erbfolgekriege* (Bonn, 1923).

Id., *Versailles und Wien von Ludwig XIV. bis Kaunitz: Die Vorstadien der diplomatischen Revolution im 18. Jahrhundert* (Bonn, 1952).

G. Breit, *Das Staats- und Gesellschaftsbild deutscher Generale beider Weltkriege im Spiegel ihrer Memoiren* (Boppard am Rhein, 1973).

W. von Bremen, *Friedrich der Grosse* (Leipzig, 2nd ed. 1905).

Id., *Friedrich der Grosse: Der Siebenjährige Krieg* (Berlin, 1912).

K.-J. Bremm, *Preussen bewegt die Welt: Der Siebenjährigen Krieg* (Düsseldorf, 2017).

[H. O. R.] Brix, *Gedanken über die Organisation, Ausbildung und Verwendung der Cavallerie bei der modernen Kriegsführung* (Berlin, 1881).

P. Broucek, *Der Geburtstag der Monarchie: Die Schlacht von Kolin 1757* (Vienna, 1982).

R. Browning, *The War of the Austrian Succession* (London, 1994).

R. Brühl, *Militärgeschichte und Kriegspolitik: Zur Militärgeschichtsschreibung des preussisch-deutschen Generalstabs, 1816–1945* (East Berlin, 1975).

A. Bucholz, *Hans Delbrück and the German Military Establishment: War Images in Conflict* (Iowa City, 1985).

Id., *Moltke, Schlieffen and Prussian War Planning* (New York, 1991).

O. Büsch, *Militärsystem und Sozialleben im Alten Preussen, 1713–1807: Die Anfänge der sozialen Militarisierung der preussisch-deutschen Gesellschaft* (Berlin, 2nd ed. 1981).

E. Bussi, *Il diritto publico del Sacro Impero alla fine del XVIII secolo* (2 vols, Milan, 1957–9).

W. Bussmann, *Treitschke: Sein Welt- und Geschichtsbild* (Göttingen, 1952).

H. Butterfield, *The Reconstruction of an Historical Episode: The History of the Enquiry into the Origins of the Seven Years' War* (Glasgow, 1951) (= Eighteenth David Murray Lecture).

R. von Caemmerer, *Friedrichs des Grossen Feldzugsplan für das Jahr 1757* (Berlin, 1883).

A. C. Carter, *The Dutch Republic in Europe in the Seven Years' War* (London, 1971).

R. Chickering, *Imperial Germany and the Great War* (Cambridge, 1998).

Cigaretten-Bilderdienst (ed.), *Bilder deutscher Geschichte* (Hamburg, repr. 1936).

C. Clark, *Iron Kingdom: The Rise and Downfall of Prussia, 1600–1947* (Cambridge, MA, 2006).

J.-M. Constant, *La vie quotidienne de la noblesse Français aux XVIᵉ et XVIIᵉ siècles* (Paris, 1985).

A. Corvisier, *Armies and Societies in Europe, 1494–1789* (Bloomington, IN, 1979).

U. Dann, *Hanover and Great Britain: Diplomacy and Survival, 1740–1760* (Leicester, 1991).

H. Delbrück, *Die Strategie des Perikles, erläutert durch die Strategie Friedrichs des Grossen. Mit einem Anhang über Thukydides und Kleon* (Berlin, 1890).

Id., *Erinnerungen, Aufsätze und Reden* (Berlin, 1902).

Id., *Geschichte der Kriegskunst* (4 vols, Hamburg new ed. 2000 [1st 1900–20]).

Id., *Historische und politische Aufsätze* (Berlin, 2nd ed. 1907).

Id., *Das Leben des Feldmarschalls Grafen Neidhardt von Gneisenau* (2 vols, Berlin, 3rd ed. 1908).

Id., *Vor und nach dem Weltkrieg: Politische und historische Aufsätze, 1902–1925* (Berlin, 1926).

K. Demeter, *Das deutsche Offizierskorps in Gesellschaft und Staat, 1650–1945* (Frankfurt, 1963).

P. G. M. Dickson, *Finance and Government under Maria Theresa, 1740–1780* (2 vols, Oxford, 1987).

C. Dipper, *Deutsche Geschichte, 1648–1789* (Frankfurt, 1991).

P. F. Doran, *Andrew Mitchell and Prussia's Diplomatic Relations during the Seven Years' War* (New York, 1986).

A. Dorpalen, *German History in Marxist Perspective: The East German Approach* (London, 1967).

J. G. Droysen, *Geschichte der preussischen Politik* (14 vols, Leipzig, 1855–86).

H. Duchhardt, *Gleichgewicht der Kräfte, Convénance, europäisches Konzert: Friedenskongresse und Friedensschlüsse vom Zeitalter Ludwigs XIV. bis zum Wiener Kongress* (Darmstadt, 1976).

Id., *Deutsche Verfassungsgeschichte, 1495–1806* (Stuttgart, 1991).

C. Duffy, *The Army of Frederick the Great* (London, 1974).

Id., *Fire and Stone: The Science of Fortress Warfare, 1660–1860* (Newton Abbot, 1975).

Id., *The Army of Maria Theresa: The Armed Forces of Imperial Austria, 1740–1780* (London, 1977).

Id., *Siege Warfare: The Fortress in the Early Modern World, 1494–1660* (London, repr. 1996).

Id., *Prussia's Glory: Rossbach and Leuthen 1757* (Chicago, 2003).

M. Egremont, *Forgotten Land; Journeys among the Ghosts of East Prussia* (London, 2011).

H.-P. Ehni, *Bollwerk Preussen?: Preussen-Regierung, Reich-Länder-Problem und Sozialdemokratie, 1928–1932* (Bonn, 1975).

B. Faulenbach, *Ideologie des deutschen Weges: Die deutsche Geschichte in der Historiographie zwischen Kaiserreich und Nationalsozialismus* (Munich, 1980).

J. Fest, *Der Untergang: Hitler und das Ende des Dritten Reiches: Eine historische Skizze* (Reinbek, 2002).

S. Fiedler, *Grundriss der Militär- und Kriegsgeschichte, i, Die stehenden Heere im Zeitalter des Absolutismus* (Munich, 1972).

C. R. L. Fletcher, *Gustavus Adolphus and the Struggle of Protestantism for Existence* (London, 1890).

H. von Freytag-Loringhoven, *König Friedrich als Kriegsherr und Heerführer* (Berlin, 1912) (= *Beiheft zum Militär-Wochenblatt* 2/3).

G. Friedrich, *Fontanes preussische Welt: Armee-Dynastie-Staat* (Herford, 1988).

A. Gat, *A History of Military Thought: From the Enlightenment to the Cold War* (Oxford, 2001).

R. Gerba, *Feldzüge des Prinzen Eugen von Savoyen*, xix, *Polnischer Thronfolgekrieg: Feldzug 1733 und 1734* (Vienna, 1891).

P. Gerber, *Die Schlacht bei Leuthen* (Berlin, 1901).

D. Gerhard, *England und der Aufstieg Russlands* (Berlin, 1933).

P. Geyl, *Willem IV en Engeland tot 1748 (Vrede van Aken)* (The Hague, 1924).

F. Gilbert, *Johann Gustav Droysen und die preussisch-deutsche Frage* (Munich, 1931).

L. H. Gipson, *Zones of International Friction: North America, south of the Great Lakes Region, 1748–1754* (New York, 1937).

W. D. Godsey, *The Sinews of Habsburg Power: Lower Austria in a Fiscal-Military State, 1650–1820* (Oxford, 2018).

W. Görlitz, *Der deutsche Generalstab: Geschichte und Gestalt, 1657–1945* (Frankfurt, s.a. [1953]).

A. von der Goltz, *Hindenburg: Power, Myth, and the Rise of the Nazis* (Oxford, 2009).

D. Goslich, *Die Schlacht bei Kolin am 18. Juni 1757* (Berlin, 1911).

G. Graf, *Gottesbild und Politik: Eine Studie zur Frömmigkeit in Preussen während der Befreiungskriege, 1813–1915* (Göttingen, 1993).

O. Groehler, *Die Kriege Friedrichs II.* (Berlin, 6th ed. 1990).

Grosser Generalstab, Kriegsgeschichtliche Abteilung, *Die Kriege Friedrichs des Grossen*, ser. 1, *Der Erste Schlesische Krieg, 1740–1742* (3 vols, Berlin, 1890–3).

Id., *Die Kriege Friedrichs des Grossen*, ser. 2, *Der Zweite Schlesische Krieg, 1744–1745* (3 vols, Berlin, 1895).

Id., *Die Kriege Friedrichs des Grossen*, ser. 3, *Der Siebenjährige Krieg, 1756–1763* (13 vols, Berlin, 1901–14).

C. Grünhagen, *Schlesien unter Friedrich dem Grossen* (2 vols, Wolfenbüttel, repr. 2014 [1st 1889]).

M. Grünzig, *Für Deutschtum und Vaterland: Die Potsdamer Garnisonskirche im 20. Jahrhundert* (Berlin, 2017).

R. Hanke, *Brühl und das Renversement des Alliances: Die antipreussische Politik des Dresdener Hofes, 1744–1756* (Berlin, 2006).

H. Hantsch, *Die Entwicklung Österreich-Ungarns zur Grossmacht* (Freiburg, 1933).

W. Hardtwig, *Geschichtskultur und Wissenschaft* (Munich, 1990).

W. O. Henderson, *Studies in the Economic Policy of Frederick the Great* (London, 1968).

C. Hinrichs, *Preussen als historisches Problem: Gesammelte Aufsätze*, ed. G. Oestreich (Berlin, 1964).

O. Hintze, *Die Hohenzollern und ihr Werk: Funfhundert Jahre vaterländische Geschichte* (Berlin, 1915).

Id., *Staat und Verfassung: Gesammelte Abhandlungen zur Allgemeinen Verfassungsgeschichte*, ed. by G. Oestreich (Göttingen, 2nd ed. 1962).

Id., *Regierung und Verwaltung: Gesammelte Abhandlungen zur Staats-, Rechts-, und Sozialgeschichte Preussens*, ed. by G. Oestreich (Göttingen, 2nd ed. 1967).

M. Hochedlinger, *Austria's Wars of Emergence: War, State and Society in the Habsburg Monarchy, 1683–1797* (London, 2003).

Id., *Thron und Gewehr: Das Problem der Heeresergänzung und der Militarisierung der Habsburger Monarchie im Zeitalter des aufgeklärten Absolutismus, 1740–1790* (Graz, 2021).

H. H. Hofmann, *Der Hitlerputsch: Krisenjahre deutscher Geschichte, 1920–1924* (Munich, 1961).

R. Höhn, *Scharnhorsts Vermächtnis* (Bonn, 1952).

W. Hubatsch, *Frederick the Great: Absolutism and Administration* (London, repr. 1975).

E. Hübner, *Staatspolitik und Familieninteressen in der russischen Aussenpolitik, 1741–1773* (Neumünster, 1984).

D. J. Hughes, *The King's Finest: A Social and Bureaucratic Profile of Prussia's General Officers, 1871–1914* (Westport, CT, 1987).

M. Hughes, *Nationalism and Society: Germany, 1800–1945* (London, 1988).

C. W. Ingrao, *The Hessian Mercenary State: Ideas, Institutions and Reform under Frederick II* (Cambridge, 1987).

M. Jähns, *Geschichte der Kriegswissenschaften, vornehmlich in Deutschland* (3 vols, Munich and Leipzig, 1883–1901).

C. Jany, *Geschichte der Königlich Preussischen Armee bis zum Jahre 1807* (3 vols, Berlin, 1928–29).

J. T. Johnson, *Ideology, Reason and the Limitation of War: Religious and Secular Concepts, 1200–1740* (Princeton, NJ, 1975).

A. Jones, *The Art of War in the Western World* (Oxford, 1989 (pb)).

L. Just, *Um die Westgrenze des alten Reiches: Vorträge und Aufsätze* (Cologne, 1941).

E. Kaeber, *Die Idee des europäischen Gleichgewichts in der publizistischen Literatur vom 16. bis zum 18. Jahrhundert* (Hildesheim, repr. 1971 [1st 1907]).

H. H. Kaplan, *Russia and the Outbreak of the Seven Years' War* (Berkeley, CA, 1968).

C. Keisch and M. U. Riemann-Reyher (eds), *Adolph Menzel, 1815–1905: Between Romanticism and Impressionism* (New Haven, CT, 1996).

L. Kennett, *The French Armies in the Seven Years' War: A Study in Military Organization and Administration* (Durham, NC, 1967).

E. Kessel, *Quellen und Untersuchungen zur Schlacht bei Torgau* (Berlin, 1937).

M. Kitchen, *The German Officer Corps, 1890–1914* (Oxford, 1968).

Id., *The Silent Dictatorship: The Politics of the German High Command under Hindenburg and Ludendorff, 1916–1918* (New York, 1976).

A. Kitschke, *The Peace Church in Potsdam-Sanssouci* (Passau, 2011).

G. Kley, *Friedrich Polack (1835–1915): Der Pestalozzi der Eichsfelder* (Bad Langensalza, 2021).

C. M. Klinkert, *Nassau in het nieuws: Nieuwsprenten van Maurits van Nassaus militaire ondernemingen uit de periode 1590–1600* (Zutphen, 2005).

A. Kloppert, *Der Schlesische Feldzug von 1762* (Bonn, 1988).

R. Knoetel and W. Friedrich, *Der Alte Fritz in fünfzig Bildern für Jung und Alt* (Dortmund, repr. 3rd ed. 1986 [1st 1905]).

J. Koch, *Von Helden und Opfern: Kulturgeschichte des deutschen Kriegsgedenkens* (Darmstadt, 2013).

G. Korff (ed.), *Preussen: Versuch einer Bilanz* (Reinbek, 1981).

A. Kossert, *Ostpreussen: Geschichte und Mythos* (Munich, 2007 (pb)).

S. Kracauer, *From Caligari to Hitler: A Psychological History of German Film* (Princeton, NJ, 1947).

K.-H. Krill, *Die Rankerenaissance: Max Lenz und Erich Marcks: Ein Beitrag zum historisch-politischen Denken in Deutschland* (Berlin, 1962).

A. Kuhle, *Die preussische Kriegstheorie um 1800 und ihre Suche nach dynamischen Gleichgewichten* (Berlin, 2018).

J. Kunisch, *Das Mirakel des Hauses Brandenburg: Studien zum Verhältnis von Kabinettspolitik und Kriegsführung im Zeitalter des Siebenjährigen Krieges* (Munich, 1978).

Id., *Fürst—Gesellschaft—Krieg: Studien zur bellizistischen Disposition der absoluten Fürstenstaaten* (Cologne and Vienna, 1992).

Id., *Friedrich der Grosse in seiner Zeit: Essays* (Munich, 2008).

M. Kutz, *Realitätsflucht und Aggression im deutschen Militär* (Baden Baden, 1990).

R. F. Lacher, *"Friedrich unser Held": Gleim und sein König* (Göttingen, 2017).

G. Lammel, *Zwischen Legende und Wahrheit: Bilderfolgen zur brandenburgisch-preussischen Geschichte* (Münster, 1997).

E. Lange, *Die Soldaten Friedrich des Grossen* (Leipzig, 1853).

S. Lange, *Hans Delbrück und der Strategiestreit: Kriegführung und Kriegsgeschichte in der Kontroverse, 1879–1914* (Freiburg, 1995).

D. Langewische, *Liberalismus in Deutschland* (Frankfurt, 1988).

J. P. LeDonne, *The Russian Empire and the World, 1700–1917: The Geopolitics of Expansion and Containment* (Oxford, 1997).

M. Lehmann, *Friedrich der Grosse und der Ursprung des siebenjährigen Krieges* (Leipzig, 1894).

M. Lenz, *Kleine historische Schriften, ii, Von Luther bis Marx* (Munich, 1922).

U. Liedtke, *Ich bin Komponist: Friedrich II. als Musiker* (Berlin, 2012).

R. Lodge, *Great Britain and Prussia in the Eighteenth Century* (Oxford, 1923).

Id., *Studies in Eighteenth-Century Diplomacy, 1740–1748* (London, 1930).

P. A. Lorge, *The Asian Military Revolution: From Gunpowder to the Bomb* (Cambridge, 2008).

E. Ludendorff, *Kriegführung und Politik* (Berlin, 2nd ed. 1922).

Id., *Der totale Krieg* (Munich, 1933).

R. Lüdicke, *Die Preussischen Kultusminister, ihre Beamten im ersten Jahrhundert des Ministeriums, 1817–1917* (Stuttgart and Berlin, 1918).

H. Mackowski, *Das Friedrich-Denkmal nach den Entwürfen Schinkels und Rauchs* (Berlin, 1894).

T. Mann, *Friedrich und die grosse Koalition* (Frankfurt, 1915).

W. Mediger, *Moskaus Weg nach Europa: Der Aufstieg Russlands zum europäischen Machtstaat im Zeitalter Friedrich des Grossen* (Braunschweig, 1952).

F. Meinecke, *Die deutsche Katastrophe* (Wiesbaden, 1946).

G. Mendelssohn Bartholdy, *Der König: Friedrich der Grosse in seinen Briefen und Erlassen, sowie in zeitgenössischen Berichten und Anekdoten* (Ebenhausen bei München, 1912).

K. Merckle, *Das Denkmal Friedrichs des Grossen in Berlin: Aktenmässige Geschichte und Beschreibung des Monuments* (Berlin, 1894).

R. Meyer, *Die Neutralitätsverhandlungen des Kurfürstentums Hannover beim Ausbruch des Siebenjährigen Krieges* (Kiel, 1912).

R. Middleton, *The Bells of Victory: The Pitt-Newcastle Ministry and the Conduct of the Seven Years' War, 1757–1762* (Cambridge, 1985).

Militärgeschichtliches Forschungsamt (ed.), *Deutsche Militärgeschichte, 1648–1939* (6 vols, Munich, 1983).

I. Mittenzwei, *Preussen nach dem Siebenjährigen Krieg: Auseinandersetzung zwischen Bürgertum und Staat in der Wirtschaftspolitik* (East Berlin, 1979).

K. and S. Möbius, *Prussian Army Soldiers and the Seven Years' War: The Psychology of Honour* (London, 2019).

A. Moeller van den Bruck, *Preussischer Stil* (Berlin, 1916).

W. von Molo, *Der Grosse Fritz im Krieg* (Stuttgart, 1917).

Id., *Fridericus* (Munich, 1918).

Id., *Das Fridericus-Rex-Buch* (Berlin, 1923).

Id., *Vom alten Fritz: Vier Erzählungen aus dem leben des grossen Königs* (Nuremberg, 1924).

Müller, *Die Elemente der Staatskunst: Sechsunddreissig Vorlesungen* (Berlin, 1936 [1st 1808–9]).

K. Müller, *Das Kaiserliche Gesandtschaftswesen im Jahrhundert nach dem Westfälischen Frieden* (Bonn, 1976).

R. Müller, *Die Armee August des Starken: Das sächsische Heer von 1730 bis 1733* (East Berlin, 1984).

J. Muth, *Flucht aus dem militärischen Alltag: Ursachen und individuelle Ausprägung der Desertion in der Armee Friedrichs des Grossen* (Freiburg, 2003).

G. Nekrasov, *Rol' Rossii v evropeiskoi mezhdunarodnoi politike 1725–1739 gg.* (Moscow, 1976).

T. Nipperdey, *Deutsche Geschichte, 1800–1866: Bürgerwelt und starker Staat* (Munich, 1987).

C. Nolan, *The Allure of Battle A History of How Wars Have Been Won and Lost* (Oxford, 2017).

P. Nora, *Les Lieux de Mémoire* (3 vols, Paris, 1984).

G. Oestreich, *Geist und Gestalt des frühmodernen Staates* (Berlin, 1969).

S. Oredsson, *Gustav Adolf, Sverige och Trettioåriga kriget: Historieskrivning och kult* (Lund, 1992).

D. Orlow, *Weimar Prussia, 1918–1925: The Unlikely Rock of Democracy* (Pittsburgh, PA, 1986).

G. Otruba, *Die Wirtschaftspolitik Maria Theresias* (Vienna, 1963).

P. Paret, *York and the Era of Prussian Reforms, 1807–1815* (Princeton, NJ, 1966).

Id., and *The Cognitive Challenge of War: Prussia 1806* (Princeton, NJ, 2009).

G. Parker, *The Military Revolution: Military Innovation and the Rise of the West, 1500–1800. The Lees Knowles Lectures 1984* (Cambridge, 1988).

D. Parrott, *The Business of War: Military Enterprise and Military Revolution in Early Modern Europe* (Cambridge, 2012).

F. Polack, *Zweihundert Jahre preussisches Königtum: Volks- und Jugendschrift zur zweihundertjährigen Jubelfeier des preussischen Königtums* (Berlin, s.a. [1901]).

H. Count Praschma, *Das Kürassier-Regiment von Driesen (Westfalen) Nr. 4, 1717–1900* (Münster, 1901).

R. S. Quimby, *The Background to Napoleonic Warfare: The Theory of Military Tactics in Eighteenth-Century France* (New York, 1957).

L. von Ranke, *Der Ursprung des Siebenjährigen Krieges* (Leipzig, 1871).

M. Raschke, *Der politisierende Generalstab: Die friderizianischen Kriege in der amtlichen deutschen Militärgeschichtsschreibung, 1890–1914* (Freiburg, 1993).

F. Ratzel, *Politische Geographie* (Munich, 3rd ed. 1925).

K. von Raumer, *Die Zerstörung der Pfalz von 1689 im Zusammenhang der französischen Rheinpolitik* (Munich, 1930).

O. Redlich, *Das Werden einer Grossmacht: Österreich von 1700 bis 1740* (Brno and Vienna, 3rd ed. 1942).

T. Rehtwisch, *Leuthen: Blätter der Erinnerung an den grossen König und das Jahr 1757* (Leipzig, 1907).

J. C. Riley, *The Seven Years' War and the Old Regime in France: The Economic and Financial Toll* (Princeton, NJ, 1986).

G. Ritter, *Staatskunst und Kriegshandwerk: Das Problem des "Militarismus" in Deutschland, ii, Die Hauptmächte Europas und das Wilhelminische Reich* (Munich, 1960).

Id., *The Schlieffen Plan: Critique of a Myth* (London, 1958).

M. Roberts, *The Military Revolution, 1560–1660* (Belfast, 1956).

Id., *Splendid Isolation, 1763–1780* (Reading, 1970) (= *Stenton Lecture 1969*).

A. L. Rochau, *Grundsätze der Realpolitik*, ed. H.-U. Wehler (Berlin, 1972 [1st 1853]).

K. A. Roider, *Austria's Eastern Question, 1700–1790* (Princeton, NJ, 1982).

H. Rosenberg, *Bureaucracy, Aristocracy and Autonomy: The Prussian Experience, 1660–1815* (Cambridge, MA, 1958).

M. von Salisch, *Treue Deserteure: Das Kursächsische Militär und der Siebenjährige Krieg* (Munich, 2008).

E. M. Satow, *Frederick the Great and the Silesian Loan* (London, 1907).

M. Sautai, *Les préliminaires de la guerre de la Succession d'Autriche* (Paris, 1907).

R. Savory, *His Britannic Majesty's Army in Germany during the Seven Years' War* (Oxford, 1966).

L. von Scharfenort, *Die Königlich-Preussische Kriegsakademie* (Berlin, 1910).

K. Scheel, *Der Tag von Potsdam* (Berlin, 1996).

A. Schiller, *Die Schlacht bei Leuthen: Zur 150-jährigen Erinnerung an die Schlacht bei Leuthen und an die Einweihung des Denksteines auf dem Schlachtfelde am 5. Dezember 1907 durch seine Majestät Kaiser Wilhelm II* (Schweidnitz, 1907).

L. Schilling, *Kaunitz und das Renversement des alliances: Studien zur aussenpolitischen Konzeption Wenzel Antons von Kaunitz* (Berlin, 1994).

A. Schindling, *Die Anfänge des immerwährenden Reichstages zu Regensburg* (Mainz, 1991).

H. Schleier, *Die bürgerliche Geschichtsschreibung der Weimarer Republik* (East Berlin, 1975).

M. Schlenke, *England und das friderizianische Preussen, 1740–1763: Ein Beitrag zum Verhältnis von Politik und Öffentlicher Meinung im England des 18. Jahrhunderts* (Freiburg, 1963).

A. von Schlieffen, *Friedrich der Grosse* (Berlin, 1912) (= supplement no. 1 to the *Vierteljahreshefte für Truppenführung und Heereskunde*).

F. J. Schmidt, K. Molinski, and S. Mette, *Hans Delbrück: Der Historiker and Politiker* (Berlin, 1928).

J. Schmidt, *Die Geschichte des Genie-Gedankens in der deutschen Literatur, Philosophie und Politik, 1750–1945* (2 vols, Darmstadt, 1985).

R. Schnur, *Der Rheinbund von 1658 in der deutschen Verfassungsgeschichte* (Bonn, 1955).

H.-J. Schoeps, *Das andere Preussen* (Stuttgart, 1952).

P. W. Schroeder, *The Transformation of European Politics, 1763–1847* (Oxford, 1994).

H. Schulze, *Otto Braun oder Preussens demokratische Sendung* (Frankfurt, 1977).

U. Schulze, *Die Beziehungen zwischen Kursachsen und Friedrich dem Grossen nach dem Siebenjährigen Krieg bis zum Bayerischen Erbfolgekrieg* (Jena, 1930).

W. Schulze, *Landesdefension und Staatsbildung: Studien zum Kriegswesen des innerösterreichischen Territorialstaats (1564–1619)* (Vienna, 1973).

T. Schwark, *Lübecks Stadtmilitär im 17. und 18. Jahrhundert: Untersuchungen zur Sozialgeschichte einer reichsstädtischen Berufsgruppe* (Lübeck, 1990).

K. W. Schweizer, *England, Prussia and the Seven Years' War* (Lewiston, NY, 1989).

Id., *Frederick the Great, William Pitt, and Lord Bute: The Anglo-Prussian Alliance, 1756–1763* (New York, 1991).

B. Schwertfeger, *Die grossen Erzieher des deutschen Heeres: Aus der Geschichte der Kriegsakademie* (Potsdam, 1936).

H. M. Scott, *The Emergence of the Eastern Powers, 1756–1775* (Cambridge, 2001).

D. E. Showalter, *The Wars of Frederick the Great* (London, 1996).

D. Siemens, *Stormtroopers: A New History of Hitler's Brownshirts* (New Haven, CT, 2017).

B. Simms, *The Struggle for Mastery in Germany, 1779–1850* (London, 1998).

S. Skalweit, *Frankreich und Friedrich der Grosse: Der Aufstieg Preussens in der öffentlichen Meinung des "Ancien Régime"* (Bonn, 1952).

K. Sontheimer, *Thomas Mann und die Deutschen* (Frankfurt, 1965 (pb)).

Id., *Antidemokratisches Denken in der Weimarer Republik: Die politischen Ideen des deutschen Nationalismus zwischen 1918 und 1933* (Munich, 3rd ed. 1992).

H. Stabenau, *Die Schlacht bei Soor* (Frankfurt, 1901).

C. B. Stevens, *Russia's Wars of Emergence, 1460–1730* (Harlow, 2007).

S. D. Stirk, *The Prussian Spirit: A Survey of German Literature and Politics* (London, s.a. [1941]).

H. Strachan, *European Armies and the Conduct of War* (London, 1983 (pb)).

Id., *The Direction of War: Contemporary Strategy in Historical Perspective* (Cambridge, 2013).

W. Stribny, *Die Russlandpolitik Friedrich des Grossen, 1764–1786* (Würzburg, 1966).

J. L. Sutton, *The King's Honor and the King's Cardinal: The War of the Polish Succession* (Lexington, KT, 1980).

F. A. J. Szabo, *The Seven Years' War in Europe, 1756–1763* (Abingdon, repr. 2013).

A. von Taysen, *Miscellaneen zur Geschichte König Friedrich des Grossen* (Berlin, 1878).

Id., *Zur Beurteilung des Siebenjährigen Krieges* (Berlin, 1882).

A. Thimme, *Hans Delbrück als Kritiker der wilhelminischen Epoche* (Düsseldorf, 1953).

Id., *Flucht in den Mythos: Die Deutschnationale Volkspartei und die Niederlage von 1918* (Göttingen, 1969).

L. Freiherr von Thüna, *Die Würzburger Hilfstruppen im Dienste Österreichs 1756–1763: Ein Beitrag zur Geschichte des Siebenjährigen Krieges. Nach archivalischen Quellen* (Würzburg, 1893).

H. von Treitschke, *Deutsche Geschichte im 19. Jahrhundert* (5 vols, Berlin, 1879–94).

Id., *Historische und Politische Aufsätze* (Leipzig, 4th ed. 1920).

H. Trevor-Roper, *The Last Days of Hitler* (London, rev. ed. 1965 (pb)).

H. Trierenberg, *Reisewege zu historischen Stätten in Niederschlesien* (Dülmen, 1996).

US Army Center of Military History, *Military Improvisation during the Russian Campaign* (Washington, DC, repr. 1986).

A. Unzer, *Die Konvention von Klein-Schnellendorf (9. Oktober 1741)* (Frankfurt, 1889).

G. Vogler and K. Vetter, *Preussen: Von den Anfängen bis zur Reichsgründung* (East Berlin, 1970), 81–126.

R. Waddington, *Louis XV et le Renversement des Alliances* (Paris, 1896).

Id., *La Guerre de Sept Ans: Historie Diplomatique et Militaire* (5 vols, Paris, 1899–1914).

F. Wagner, *Kaiser Karl VII und die grossen Mächte, 1740–1745* (Stuttgart, 1938).

J. L. Wallach, *Das Dogma der Vernichtungsschlacht: Die Lehren von Clausewitz und Schlieffen und ihre Wirkungen in zwei Weltkriegen* (Frankfurt, 1967).

M. Weber, *Das Verhältnis Schlesiens zum alten Reich in der Frühen Neuzeit* (Cologne, 1992).

H. Weczerka, *Handbuch der Historischen Stätten: Schlesien* (Stuttgart, 1977).

H.-U. Wehler, *Deutsche Gesellschaftsgeschichte, iii, Von der "Deutschen Doppelrevolution" bis zum Beginn des Ersten Weltkrieges, 1849–1914* (Frankfurt, 1995).

G. de Werd, *Schenkenschanz, "de sleutel van den hollandschen tuin"* (Cleves, 1996), 96–103.

W. von Wersebe, *Geschichte der Hannoverschen Armee* (Hanover, 1928).

J. Whaley, *Germany and the Holy Roman Empire* (2 vols, Oxford, 2013 (pb)).

A. M. Wilson, *French Foreign Policy during the Administration of Cardinal Fleury* (Cambridge, MA, 1938).

P. H. Wilson, *German Armies, War and German Politics, 1648–1806* (London, 1998).

Id., *The Holy Roman Empire: A Thousand Years of European History* (London, 2016).

Id., *Lützen* (Oxford, 2018).

M. Winter, *Untertanengeist durch Militärpflicht: Das preussische Kantonsystem in brandenburgischen Städten im 18. Jahrhundert* (Bielefeld, 2005).

A. Wirtgen, *Die preussischen Handfeuerwaffen: Modelle und Manufaktur, 1700–1806* (2 vols, Osnabrück, 1976).

U. W. Wolf, *Preussen Glanz und Gloria im Film: Die berühmten deutschen Tonfilme über Preussens glorreiche Vergangenheit* (Munich, 1981).

G. Wollstein, *Das "Grossdeutschland" der Paulskirche: Nationale Ziele in der bürgerlichen Revolution 1848/49* (Düsseldorf, 1977).

E. Wormsbächer, *Daniel Nikolaus Chodowiecki (1726–1804): Erklärungen und Erläuterungen zu seinen Radierungen* (Hanover, 1988).

K. Zernack, *Polen und Russland: Zwei Wege in der europäischen Geschichte* (Berlin, 1994).

T. Zuber, *Inventing the Schlieffen Plan: German War Planning, 1871–1914* (Oxford, 2006).

Articles in Learned Journals and Chapters in Edited Volumes

D. Albers, 'Nordwestdeutschland als Kriegsschauplatz im Siebenjährigen Krieg', *Niedersächsisches Jahrbuch* xv (1938), 142–81.

J. C. Allmayer-Beck, 'Wandlungen im Heerwesen zur Zeit Maria Theresias', Heeresgeschichtliches Museum (ed.), *Maria Theresia: Beiträge zur Geschichte des Heerwesens ihrer Zeit* (Graz, 1967), 7–24.

Id., 'Das Heerwesen in Österreich und Preussen', R. A. Kann and F. E. Prinz (eds), *Deutschland und Österreich: Ein bilaterales Geschichtsbuch* (Vienna and Munich, 1980), 490–521.

M. L. Anderson, 'The Kulturkampf and the Course of German History', *Central European History* xix, 1 (1986), 86–115.

J. Angelow, 'Friedenskirche und Grabmal Friedrich Wilhelms IV.: Monarchie und Armee in der Revolution von 1848', B. R. Kroener and H. Ostertag (eds), *Potsdam: Staat, Armee, Residenz in der preussisch-deutschen Militärgeschichte* (Berlin, 1993), 377–92.

H. Bagger, 'The Role of the Baltic in Russian Foreign Policy, 1721–1773', H. Ragsdale (ed.), *Imperial Russian Foreign Policy* (Cambridge, 1993), 36–74.

R. N. Bain, 'Russia und Anne and Elizabeth', A. W. Ward, G. W. Prothero, and S. Leathes (eds), *The Cambridge Modern History*, vi, *The Eighteenth Century* (Cambridge, 1909), 301–28.

T. M. Barker, 'Military Nobility: The Daun Family and the Evolution of the Austrian Officer Corps', id., *Army, Aristocracy and Monarchy: Essays on War, Society and Government in Austria, 1618–1780* (Boulder, CO, 1980), 128–46.

D. Bartetzko, 'Unter dem Berufe des Kriegerischen—Ein Missverständnis: Arthur Moeller van den Brucks preussischer Stil', P. Bahners and G. Roellecke (eds), *Preussische Stile: Ein Staat als Kunststück* (Stuttgart, 2001), 380–90.

P. Baumgart, 'Schlesien', J. Ziechmann (ed.), *Panorama der Fridericianischen Zeit: Friedrich der Grosse und seine Epoche—ein Handbuch* (Bremen, 1985), 705–15.

Id., 'Schlesien als eigenständige Provinz im altpreussischen Staat (1740–1806)', N. Conrads (ed.), *Deutsche Geschichte im Osten*, iii, *Schlesien* (Berlin, 1994), 346–465.

W. Baumgart, 'Der Ausbruch des Siebenjährigen Kriegs: Zum gegenwärtigen Forschungsstand', *Militärgeschichtliche Mitteilungen* xi (1972), 157–65.

C. Becker, 'Über die finanziellen Aufwendungen Kurköln sim Siebenjährigen Kriege für den Reichskrieg gegen Friedrich den Grossen', *Annalen des Historischen Vereins für den Niederrhein* xcii (1912), 72–91.

Id., 'Die Erlebnisse der kurkölnischen Truppen im Verbande der Reichsarmee während des Siebenjährigen Krieges', ibid. xci (1914), 63–108.

Id., 'Von Kurkölns Beziehungen zu Frankreich und seiner wirtschaftlichen Lage im Siebenjährigen Kriege', ibid. c (1917), 43–119.

A. Beer, 'Die Staatsschulden und die Ordnung des Staatshaushalts unter Maria Theresia', *Archiv für Österreichische Geschichte* lxxxii (1894), 1–135.

H.-W. Bergerhausen, 'Nur ein Stück Papier?: Die Garantieerklärung für die österreichisch-preussischen Friedensverträge von 1742 und 1745', H. Neuhaus and B. Stollberg-Rillinger (eds), *Menschen und Strukturen in der Geschichte Alteuropas: Festschrift für Johannes Kunisch zur Vollendung seines 65. Lebensjahres* (Berlin, 2002), 267–78.

F. von Bernhardi, 'Die Elemente des modernen Krieges', *Beiheft zum Militär-Wochenblatt* no. 9 (1898), 430–53.

Id., 'Über angriffsweise Kriegführung', ibid., no. 4 (1905), 125–52.

L. Beutin, 'Die Wirkungen des Siebenjährigen Kriegs auf die Volkswirtschaft Preussens', *Vierteljahresschrift für Sozial- und Wirtschaftsgeschichte* xxvi, 2 (1933), 209–43.

J. Black, 'Anglo-French Relations in the Mid-Eighteenth Century, 1740–1756', *Francia* xlii, 2 (1990), 45–79.

Id., 'The Hanoverian Nexus: Walpole and the Electorate', B. Simms and T. Riotte (eds), *The Hanoverian Dimension in British History, 1714–1837* (Cambridge, 2007), 18–19 [10–27].

Id., 'Strategic Culture and the Seven Years' War', W. Murray, R. H. Sinnreich, and J. Lacey (eds), *The Shaping of Grand Strategy: Politics, Diplomacy and War* (Cambridge, 2011), 63–78.

Id., 'Eighteenth-Century Warfare in a Global Perspective', A. S. Burns (ed.), *The Changing Face of Old Regime Warfare: Essays in Honour of Christopher Duffy* (Warwick, 2022), 21–35.

H. Bleckwenn, 'Bauernfreiheit durch Wehrpflicht—ein neues Bild der altpreussischen Armee', Militärgeschichtliches Forschungsamt (ed.), *Friedrich der Grosse und das Militärwesen seiner Zeit* (Bonn, 1987), 55–72.

K. D. Bracher, 'Preussen und die deutsche Demokratie', M. Schlenke (ed.), *Preussen: Beiträge zu einer politischen Kultur* (Reinbek, 1981), 295–311.

M. Braubach, 'Kurfürst Joseph Clemens von Köln als Vermittler zwischen Versailles und Wien', *Annalen des Historischen Vereins für den Niederrhein* cxlviii (1948), 228–38.

Id., 'Politik und Kriegsführung am Niederrhein während des Siebenjährigen Krieges', *Düsseldorfer Jahrbuch* xlviii (1956), 65–103.

R. Browning, 'The Duke of Newcastle and the Imperial Election Plan, 1749–1754', *Journal of British Studies* i, 1 (1967), 28–67.

Id., 'The British Orientation of Austrian Foreign Policy, 1749–1754', *Central European History* i, 3 (1968), 299–323.

H.-W. Büchsel, 'Oberschlesien im Brennpunkt der Grossen Politik', *Forschungen zur Brandenburgisch-Preussischen Geschichte* xli (1939), 83–102.

J. Burkhardt, 'Geschichte als Argument in der Habsburgisch-Französischen Diplomatie: Der Wandel des frühneuzeitlichen Geschichtsbewusstseins in seiner Beduetung für die Diplomatische Revolution von 1756', R. Babel (ed.), *Frankreich im Europäischen Staatssystem der Frühen Neuzeit* (Sigmaringen, 1995), 191–217.

O. Büsch, 'Die Militarisierung von Staat und Gesellschaft im alten Preussen', M. Schlenke (ed.), *Preussen: Beiträge zu einer politischen Kultur* (Reinbek, 1981), 45–60.

Id., 'Militärwesen und Militarisierung', W. Treue (ed.), *Preussens grosser König: Lebenswerk Friedrichs des Grossen* (Freiburg, 1986), 92–100.

F. L. Carsten, 'Potsdam in historischer Sicht', B. R. Kroener and H. Ostertag (eds), *Potsdam: Staat, Armee, Residenz in der preussische-deutschen Militärgeschichte* (Berlin, 1993), 19–30.

T. R. Clayton, 'The Duke of Newcastle, the Earl of Halifax, and the American Origins of the Seven Years' War', *Historical Journal* xxiii, 4 (1981), 571–603.

R. Conrad, 'Auf dem Schlachtfelde von Leuthen: Zur Erinnerung an die Schlacht am 5. Dezember 1757', *Schlesische Heimatblätter: Zeitschrift für Schlesische Kultur* (1907–8), 87–91.

G. A. Craig, 'Delbrück: The Military Historian', id., *War, Politics, Diplomacy* (London, 1966), 59–87.

K. Cramer, 'The Cult of Gustavus Adolphus: Protestant Identity and German Nationalism', H. Walser Smith (ed.), *Protestants, Catholics and Jews in Germany, 1800–1914* (Oxford, 2001), 97–120.

E. Daniels, 'The Seven Years' War', A. W. Ward, G. W. Prothero, and S. Leathes (eds), *The Cambridge Modern History*, vi, *The Eighteenth Century* (Cambridge, 1909), 251–300.

H. Delbrück, 'Carl von Clausewitz', *Zeitschrift für Preussische Geschichte und Landeskunde* xv, 2 (1878), 217–31.

Id., 'Carl von Clausewitz: Über das Fortschreiten und den Stillstand der kriegerischen Begebenheiten', ibid. iv, 3 (1878), 233–41.

Id., review of 'Das militärische Testament Friedrich des Grossen', ibid. xvi, 1 (1879), 27–32.

W. Deist, 'Hans Delbrück: Militärhistoriker und Publizist', *Militärgeschichtliche Zeitschrift* lvii, 2 (1998), 371–84.

[E.] von Deutelmoser, 'Die Gefechtsaufklärung Friedrichs des Grossen im Siebenjährigen Kriege', *Vierteljahresheft für Truppenführung und Heereskunde* viii, 2 (1911), 194–210.

P. G. M. Dickson, 'English Negotiations with Austria, 1737–1752', A. Whiteman (ed.), *Essays in Eighteenth-Century History, Presented to Dame Lucy Sutherland* (Oxford, 1973), 81–112.

E. Dovifat, 'Die Publizistik der Weimarer Zeit: Presse, Rundfunk, Film', L. Reinisch (ed.), *Die Zeit ohne Eigenschaften: Eine Bilanz der Zwanziger Jahre* (Stuttgart, 1961), 119–38.

H. Duchhardt, 'Die Absolutismusdebatte: Eine Antikritik', *Historische Zeitschrift* cclxxv, 3 (2002), 323–31.

G. Eckhardt, 'Der junge Menzel in Sanssouci', K. Thiele (ed.), *Staatliche Museen zu Berlin: Forschungen und Berichte* 26 ([East] Berlin, 1987), 251–8.

J. H. Elliot, 'A Europe of Composite Monarchies', *Past & Present*, no. 137 (1992), 48–71.

F. Escher, 'Die brandenburgisch-preussische Residenz und Hauptstadt im 17. und 18. Jahrhundert', W. Ribbe (ed.), *Geschichte Berlins* (2 vols, Munich, 1987), 343–406.

H. Feld, 'Potsdam gegen Weimar oder Wie Otto Gebühr den Siebenjährigen Krieg gewann', A. Marquardt (ed.), *Preussen im Film* (Reinbek, 1981), 68–73.

E. Fehrenbach, 'Die Ideologisierung des Krieges und die Radikalisierung der Französischen Revolution', D. Langenwiesche (ed.), *Revolution und Krieg: Zur Dynamic historischen Wandels seit dem 18. Jahrhundert* (Paderborn, 1989), 57–66.

S. Fiedler, 'Die taktische Entwicklung der Armee unter Friedrich dem Grossen', Wehrgeschichliches Museum Schloss Rastatt (ed.), *Die Bewaffnung und Ausrüstung der Armee Friedrich des Grossen: Eine Dokumentation* (Rastatt, 1986), 15–31.

H. Fleischhacker, 'Porträt Petters III.', *Jahrbücher für die Geschichte Osteuropas*, n.s. v (1957), 127–89.

S. Förster, 'Der deutsche Generalstab und die Illusion des kurzen Krieges, 1871–1914: Metakritik eines Mythos', *Militärgeschichtliche Mitteilungen* liv, 1 (1995), 61–95.

L. and M. Frey, 'A Question of Empire: Leopold I and the War of Spanish Succession, 1701–1705', *Austrian History Yearbook* xiv (1978), 56–72.

H. von Freytag-Loringhoven, 'Theorie und Praxis bei König Friedrich, Napoleon und Moltke', *Vierteljahreshefte für Truppenführung und Heereskunde* vi, 1 (1909), 28–47.

Id., 'König Friedrich als Kriegsherr und Heerführer', *Beiheft zum Militär-Wochenblatt* no. 2/3 (1912), 25–37.

R.-P. Fuchs, 'The Supreme Court of the Holy Roman Empire: The State of Research and the Outlook', *Sixteenth Century Journal* xxxiv, 1 (2003), 9–27.

H. Funke, 'Potsdamer Notizen', *Die Neue Gesellschaft/Frankfurter Hefte* xxxviii, 10 (1991), 874–6.

W. Gembruch, 'Prinz Heinrich von Preussen, Bruder Friedrich des Grossen', J. Kunisch (ed.), *Persönlichkeiten im Umfeld Friedrich des Grossen* (Cologne and Vienna, 1988), 89–120.

C. von der Goltz, 'Antikritik zu Delbrücks Rezension von Adalbert von Tayssens "Das Militärische Testament Friedrich des Grossen"', *Zeitschrift für preussische Geschichte und Landeskunde* xvi, 2 (1879), 292–304.

H. M. Green, 'Adolf Stoecker: Portrait of an Antisemite', *Politics & Policy* xxxi, 1 (2003), 106–29.

G. P. Gross, 'There was a Schlieffen Plan: Neue Quellen', id., H. Ehlert and M. Epkenhans (eds), *Der Schlieffen Plan: Analysen und Dokumente* (Paderborn, 2006), 117–60.

P.-M. Hahn, 'Aristokratisierung und Professionalisierung: Der Aufstieg der Obristen zu einer militärischen und höfischen Elite in Brandenburg-Preussen, 1650–1725', *Forschungen zur Brandenburgisch-Preussischen Geschichte* n.s. i (1991), 161–208.

I. Harrison, 'Alter Kämpfer im Widerstand: Graf Helldorff, die NS-Bewegung und Opposition gegen Hitler', *Vierteljahresheft für Zeitgeschichte* xlv, 3 (1997), 385–424.

F.-W. Henning, 'Die preussische Thesaurierungspolitik im 18. Jahrhundert', I. Bog, G. Franz, K.-H. Kaufhold, H. Kellenbenz, and W. Zorn (eds), *Wirtschaftliche und Soziale Strukturen im saekularen Wandel: Festschrift für Wilhelm Abel zum 70. Geburtstag* (2 vols, Hanover, 1974), ii, 399–416.

O. Herrmann, 'Von Mollwitz bis Chotusitz: Ein Beitrag zur Taktik Friedrich des Grossen', *Forschungen zur Brandenburgisch-Preussischen Geschichte* vii, 2 (1894), 13–61.

Id., 'Zur Schlacht von Zorndorf', *Forschungen zur Brandenburgisch-Preussischen Geschichte* xxiv (1911), 547–66.

P. Higgonet, 'The Origins of the Seven Years' War', *Journal of Modern History* xl, 1 (1968), 57–90.

A. Hillgruber, 'Hans Delbrück', H.-U. Wehler (ed.), *Deutsche Historiker IV* (Göttingen, 1972), 40–52.

O. Hintze, 'Delbrück, Clausewitz und die Strategie Friedrichs des Grossen: Eine Erwiderung', *Forschungen zur Brandenburgisch-Preussischen Geschichte* xxxiii, 1 (1921), 131–77.

M. Hobohm, 'Delbrück, Clausewitz und die Kritik des Weltkrieges', *Preussische Jahrbücher* clxxxi, 2 (1920), 202–32.

M. Hochedlinger, 'Mars Ennobled: The Ascent of the Military and the Creation of a Military Nobility in Mid-Eighteenth-Century Austria', *German History* xvii, 2 (1999), 141–76.

Id., 'The Habsburg Monarchy: From "Military-Fiscal State" to "Militarization"', C. Storrs (ed.), *The Fiscal-Military State in Eighteenth-Century Europe: Essays in Honour of P. G. M. Dickson* (Farnham, 2009), 55–95.

Id., 'Das stehende Heer', id., P. Maťa and T. Winkelbauer (eds), *Verwaltungsgeschichte der Habsburgermonarchie in der frühen Neuzeit* (2 vols, Vienna, 2019), 655–763.

H. O. Horch, 'Judenbilder in der realistischen Erzählliteratur: Jüdische Gestalten bei Gustav Freytag, Fritz Reuter, Berthold Auerbach und Wilhelm Raabe', H. A. Strauss and C. Hoffmann (eds), *Juden und Judentum in der Literatur* (Munich, 1985), 140–71.

D. B. Horn, 'The Cabinet Controversy on Subsidy Treaties in Time of Peace, 1749–1750', *English Historical Review* xliii, 3 (1930), 463–6.

Id., 'The Diplomatic Revolution', J. O. Lindsay (ed.), *The New Cambridge Modern History*, vii, *The Old Regime* (Cambridge, 1957), 440–64.

Id., 'The Duke of Newcastle and the Origins of the Diplomatic Revolution', J. H. Elliott and H. G. Koenigsberger (eds), *The Diversity of History: Essays in Honour of Sir Herbert Butterfield* (London, 1970), 245–68.

L. Hüttl, 'Die bayerischen Erbansprüche auf Böhmen, Ungarn und Österreich in der frühen Neuzeit', F. Seibt (ed.), *Die böhmischen Länder zwischen Ost und West: Festschrift für Karl Bosl* (Munich, 1983), 7–88.

C. W. Ingrao, 'The Pragmatic Sanction and the Theresian Succession', W. J. McGill (ed.), *The Habsburg Dominions under Maria Theresa* (Washington, PA, 1980), 3–18.

Id., 'Habsburg Strategy and Geopolitics during the Eighteenth Century', G. Rothenberg (ed.), *East Central European Society and War in the Pre-Revolutionary Eighteenth Century* (Boulder, CO, 1982), 49–66.

M. Jähns, 'Die Kriegskunst als Kunst' [1874], id., *Geschichtliche Aufsätze*, ed. K. Koetschau (Berlin, 1903), 97–130.

G. Jordan and N. Rogers, 'Admirals as Heroes: Patriotism and Liberty in Hanoverian England', *Journal of British Studies* xxviii, 3 (1989), 201–22.

I. Kállay, 'Die Staatsrechtliche Stellung Ungarns un des Landtags unter Maria Theresia', G. Mraz and G. Schlag (eds), *Maria Theresia als Königin von Ungarn* (Eisenstadt, 1980), 22–9.

W. van Kampen, 'Das "preussische Beispiel" als Propaganda und politisches Lebensbedürfnis: Anmerkungen zur Authentizität und Instrumentalisierung von Geschichte im Preussenfilm', A. Marquardt (ed.), *Preussen im Film* (Reinbek, 1981), 164–77.

J. H. L. Keep, 'Die russische Armee im Siebenjährigen Krieg', B. R. Kroener (ed.), *Europa im Zeitalter Friedrichs des Grossen* (Munich, 1989), 133–70.

R. Keibel, 'Die schräge Schlachtordnung in den beiden ersten Kriegen Friedrichs des Grossen', *Forschungen zur Brandenburgisch-Preussischen Geschichte* xiv, 1 (1901), 95–139.

C. Keisch, 'Adolph Menzels "Ansprache Friedrich des Grossen vor der Schlacht bei Leuthen"', K. Thiele (ed.), *Staatliche Museen zu Berlin: Forschungen und Berichte* 26 ([East] Berlin, 1987), 259–82.

E. Kehrt, 'Das ganze Erbe soll es sein: Die Erweiterung des Erbe- und Traditions-verständnisses im Geschichtsbild der SED', id. and H. von Löwis, *Griff nach der deutschen Geschichte:: Erbaneignung und Traditionspflege in der DDR* (Paderborn, 1988), 128–43.

E. von Kessel, 'Zum Problem des Wandels des Krieges', *Wehr und Wissen* xx, 4 (1939), 100–10.

A. Kilb, 'Der Mann aus Marmor: Friedrich der Grosse als Heldenfigur in den Filmen der Weimarer Republik und des Nationalsozialismus', A. Dorgerloh and M. Becker (eds), *Preussen aus Celluloid: Friederich II. im Film* (Berlin, 2011), 17–29.

G. Klingenstein, 'Kaunitz contra Bartenstein: Zur Geschichte der Staatskanzlei in den Jahren 1749–1753', H. Fichtenau and E. Zöllner (eds), *Beiträge zur neueren Geschichte Österreichs* (Vienna, 1974), 243–63.

R. Koser, 'Vor und nach der Schlacht von Leuthen: Die Parchwitzer Rede und der Abend im Schloss Lissa', *Forschungen zur Brandenburgisch-Preussischen Geschichte* i (1888), 288–94.

Id., 'Der preussische Staatsschatz von 1740–1756', *Forschungen zur Brandenburgisch-Preussischen Geschichte* iv, (1891), 529–51.

Id., 'Zum Ursprung des Siebenjährigen Krieges', *Historische Zeitschrift* lxxiv, 1 (1895), 69–85.

Id., 'Zur Geschichte des preussischen Feldzugplanes vom Frührjahr 1757', *Historische Zeitschrift* xcii, 1 (1904), 71–4.

R. Koser, 'Die preussische Kriegsführung im Siebenjährigen Krieg', ibid. xcii, 2 (1904), 239–73.

B. R. Kroener, '"Nun danket alles Gott": Der Choral von Leuthen und Friedrich der Grosse als protestantischer Held. Die Produktion politischer Mythen im 19. und 20. Jahrhundert', G. Krumeich and H. Lehmann (eds), *"Gott mit uns": Nation, Religion und Gewalt im 19. und frühen 20. Jahrhundert* (Göttingen, 2000), 103–34.

Id., 'Herrschaftsverdichtung als Kriegsursache: Wirtschaft und Rüstung der europäischen Grossmächte im Siebenjährigen Krieg', B. Wegener (ed.), *Wie Kriege entstehen: Zum historischen Hintergrund von Staatenkonflikten* (Paderborn, 2000), 145–74.

J. Kunisch, 'Der Ausgang des Siebenjährigen Kriegs: Ein Beitrag zum Verhältnis von Kabinettspolitik und Kriegsführung im Zeitalter des Absolutismus', *Zeitschrift für Historische Forschung* ii, 2 (1975), 173–222.

Id., 'La guerre c'est moi?: Zum Problem der Staatenkonflikte im Zeitalter des Absolutismus', *Zeitschrift für Historische Forschung* xiv (1987), 407–38.

Id., 'Die grosse Allianz der Gegner Preussen sim Siebenjährigen Krieg', B. R. Kroener (ed.), *Europa im Zeitalter Friedrichs des Grossen: Wirtschaft, Gesellschaft, Kriege* (Munich, 1989), 79–97.

Id., 'Der Aufstieg neuer Grossmächte im 18. Jahrhundert und die Aufteilung der Machtsphären in Ostmitteleuropa', G. Klingenstein and F. A. J. Szabo (eds),

Staatskanzler Wenzel Anton von Kaunitz-Rietberg, 1711–1794: Neue Perspektiven zur Politik und Kultur der europäischen Aufklärung (Graz, 1996), 70–90.

G. Küntzel, 'Die Westminster Konvention', *Forschungen zur Brandenburgisch-Preussischen Geschichte* ix (1897), 541–69.

Id., 'Friedrich der Grosse am Ausgang des Siebenjährigen Krieges und sein Bündnis mit Russland', ibid. xiii (1901), 75–122.

C. Lepp, 'Protestanten feiern ihre Nation: Die kulturprotestantischen Ursprünge des Sedanstages', *Historisches Jahrbuch* cxviii (1998), 201–22.

G. Lind, 'The Making of the Neutrality Convention of 1756: France and the Scandinavian Alliance', *Scandinavian Journal of History* viii, 2 (1983), 171–92.

J. Luh, 'Early Modern Military Revolution: The German Perspective', J. Black (ed.), *Global Military Transformation: Change and Continuity, 1450–1800* (Rome, 2023), 205–24.

J. A. Lynch II, 'The Grand Strategy and the *Grand Siècle*: Learning from the Wars of Louis XIV', W. Murray, R. H. Sinnreich, and J. Lacey (eds), *The Shaping of Grand Strategy: Politics, Diplomacy and War* (Cambridge, 2011), 34–62.

F. Mankartz, 'Die Marke Friedrich: Der preussische König im zeitgenössischen Bild', Stiftung Preussische Schlösser und Gärten (ed.), *Friederisico: Friedrich der Grosse* (Munich, 2012), 204–23.

P. Mansel, 'Monarchy, Uniform and the Rise of the *Frac*, 1760–1813', *Past & Present* cxvi (1982), 103–22.

P. Maťa, 'Die Habsburgermonarchie', id., M. Hochedlinger and T. Winkelbauer (eds), *Verwaltungsgeschichte der Habsburgermonarchie in der frühen Neuzeit* (2 vols, Vienna, 2019), i, 29–62.

W. Maurenbrecher, 'Die Politik Friedrich des Grossen (I)', *Preussische Jahrbücher* xxvii, 5 (1871), 543–65.

W. J. McGill, 'The Roots of Policy: Kaunitz in Italy and the Netherlands, 1742–1746', *Central European History* i, 2 (1968), 131–49.

Id., 'Wenzel Anton von Kaunitz-Rietberg and the Conference of Aix-la-Chappelle, 1748', *Duquesne Review* xiv, 2 (1969), 154–69.

Id., 'The Roots of Policy: Kaunitz in Vienna and Versailles', *Journal of Modern History* xlii, 2 (1971), 228–44.

J. R. McIntyre, 'The Raid on Berlin, 1757', *Journal of the Seven Years' War Association* xxii, 3 (2019), 20–42.

W. Mediger, 'Russland und die Ostsee im 18. Jahrhundert', *Jahrbücher für die Geschichte Osteuropas* n.s. xvi (1968), 85–103.

Id., 'Hastenbeck und Zeven: Der Eintritt Hannovers in den Siebenjährigen Krieg', *Niedersächsisches Jahrbuch für Landesgeschichte* lvi (1984), 137–66.

E. Melton, 'The Prussian Junkers, 1600–1786', H. M. Scott (ed.), *The European Nobilities in the Seventeenth and Eighteenth Centuries* (2 vols, London, 1995), ii, 71–109.

M. Messerschmidt, 'Aussenpolitik und Kriegsvorbereitung', Militärgeschichtliches Forschungsamt (ed.), *Das Deutsche Reich und der zweite Weltkrieg* (6 vols, Stuttgart, 1979), i, 535–701.

Id., 'Nachwirkung Friedrichs II. in Preussen-Deutschland', B. R. Kroener (ed.), *Europa im Zeitalter Friedrichs des Grossen: Wirtschaft, Gesellschaft, Kriege* (Munich, 1989), 269–88.

I. Mittenzwei, 'Die zwei Gesichter Preussens', *Deutschland-Archiv* xvi, 2 (1983), 214–18.

Id., 'Das unerwünschte Erbe: Preussen und die DDR', *Preussen Jahr-Buch: Ein Almanach* (Berlin, 2001), 136–9.

K. and S. Möbius, '"They imbibed their hatred of the French with their mother's milk...": The Battle of Rossbach and Mid-18th Century Gallophobia', *Journal of the Seven Years' War Association* xxiii, 2 (2019/20), 4–26.

W. Mock, 'The Function of "Race" in Imperialist Ideologies: The Example of Joseph Chamberlain', P. M. Kennedy and A. J. Nicholls (eds), *Nationalist and Racialist Movements in Britain and Germany before the First World War* (London, 1981), 190–203.

W. J. Mommsen, 'Der Geist von 1914:: Das Programm eines politischen "Sonderwegs" der Deutschen', id., *Der autoritäre Nationalstaat: Verfassung, Gesellschaft und Kultur des deutschen Kaiserreichs* (Munich, 1990), 407–21.

K.-J. Müller, 'Deutsche Militär-Elite in der Vorgeschichte des Zweiten Weltkrieges', M. Brozsat (ed.), *Die deutschen Elite und der Weg in den Zweiten Weltkrieg* (Munich, 1989), 226–90.

Id., 'Der Tag von Potsdam und das Verhältnis der preussisch-deutschen Militär-Elite zum Nationalsozialismus', B. R. Kroener and H. Ostertag (eds), *Potsdam: Staat, Armee, Residenz in der preussisch-deutschen Militärgeschichte* (Berlin, 1993), 435–50.

M. J. Müller, 'Russland und der Siebenjährige Krieg: Beitrag zu einer Kontroverse', *Jahrbuch für die Geschichte Osteuropas* xxviii (1980), 198–219.

L. Näf, 'Carl Heinrich Graun: Te Deum', CD booklet (CPO 777 158–2), 5–7.

W. Neugebauer, 'Brandenburg im absolutistischen Staat: Das 17. und 18. Jahrhundert', I. Materna and W. Ribbe (eds), *Brandenburgische Geschichte* (Berlin, 1995), 291–394.

H. Neuhaus, 'Das Problem der militärischen Exekutive in der Spätphase des alten Reiches', J. Kunisch (ed.), *Staatsverfassung und Heeresverfassung in der europäischen Geschichte in der frühen Neuzeit* (Berlin, 1986), 297–346.

Id., 'Reichskreise und Reichskriege in der Frühen Neuzeit', H. Wüst (ed.), *Reichskreis und Territorium: Die Herrschaft über der Herrschaft: Supraterritoriale Tendenzen in Politik, Kultur, Wirtschaft und Gesellschaft* (Stuttgart, 2000), 71–86.

T. Nicklas, 'Die Schlacht bei Rossbach (1757) zwischen Wahrnehmung und Deutung', *Forschungen zur Brandenburgischen und Preussischen Geschichte*, n.s. xii (2002), 35–51.

T. Nipperdey, 'Nationalidee und Nationaldenkmal in Deutschland im 19. Jahrhundert', id., *Kann Geschichte ojektiv sein?: Historische Essays*, ed. P. Nolte (Munich, 2013), 105–60.

R. Pares, 'American versus Continental Warfare', *English Historical Review* li, 203 (1936), 429–65.

P. Paret, 'Jena and Auerstedt', id., *Understanding War: Essays on Clausewitz and the History of Military Power* (Princeton, NJ, 1992), 85–92.

W. Petter, 'Hans-Karl von Winterfeldt als General der friderizianischen Armee', J. Kunisch (ed.), *Persönlichkeiten im Umfeld Friedrichs des Grossen* (Cologne and Vienna, 1988), 59–87.

B. Pilske, 'Vermittlung der Geschichte in den Medien zur Zeit Anton von Werners', D. Bartmann (ed.), *Anton von Werner: Geschichte in Bildern* (Munich, 1993), 163–73.

R. Pommerin, 'Bündnispolitik und Mächtesystem: Österreich und der Aufstieg Russlands im 18. Jahrhundert', J. Kunisch (ed.), *Expansion und Gleichgewicht: Studien zur europäischen Mächtepolitik des ancien régime* (Berlin, 1986), 113–64.

Id. and L. Schilling, 'Denkschrift des Grafen Kaunitz zur mächtepolitischen Konstellation mach dem Aachener Frieden von 1748', ibid., 165–239.

H. F. Potempa, '"Und kommt der grosse Friedrich…": Die Reichsarmee im Siebenjährigen Krieg', E. Birk, T. Loch, and P.A. Popp (eds), *Wie Friedrich "der Grosse" wurde* (Freiburg, 2012), 64–9.

V. Press, 'Österreichische Grossmachtbildung und Reichsverfassung: Zur Kaiserlichen Stellung nach 1648', *Mitteilungen des Institutes für Österreichische Geschichte* xcviii, 1–2 (1990), 131–54.

U. Raulff, 'Politik als Passion: Hans Delbrück und der Krieg in der Geschichte', Delbrück, *Kriegskunst* I (1878), ix–xlvi.

H. Regel, 'Die Fridericus-Filme der Weimarer Republik', A. Marquardt (ed.), *Preussen im Film* (Reinbek, 1981), 124–34.

O. Regele, 'Die Schuld des Grafen Reinhard Wilhelm von Neipperg am Belgrader Frieden, 1739, und an der Niederlage bei Mollwitz, 1741', *Mitteilungen des Österreichischen Staatsarchivs* vii (1954), 373–98.

W. G. Rödel, 'Eine geheime französische Initiative als Auslöser für das Renversement des Alliances?', J. Kunisch (ed.), *Expansion und Gleichgewicht: Studien zur europäischen Mächtepolitik des ancien régime* (Berlin, 1986), 98–112.

M. Rohrschneider, 'Leopold I. von Anhalt-Dessau. Die oranische Heeresreform und die Reorganisation der preussischen Armee unter Friedrich Wilhelm I.', P. Baumgart, B. R. Kroener, and H. Stübig (eds), *Die Preussische Armee: Zwischen Ancien Régime und Reichsgründung* (Paderborn, 2008), 45–72.

K. A. Roider, 'Perils of Eighteenth-Century Peacemaking: Austria and the Treaty of Belgrade', *Central European History* v, 2 (1972), 195–207.

J. H. Rose, 'Frederick the Great and England (I) and (II)', *English Historical Review* xxix, 113 (1914), 79–93 and 114 (1914), 257–75.

J. Rüsen, 'Johann Gustav Droysen', H.-U. Wehler (ed.), *Deutsche Historiker II* (Göttingen, 1971), 7–23.

F. Schellack, 'Sedan- und Kaisergeburtsfeste', D. Düding, P. Friedemann, and P. Münch (eds), *Öffentliche Festkultur: Politisches Fest in Deutschland von der Aufklärung bis zum ersten Weltkrieg* (Reinbek, 1988), 278–97.

T. Schieder, 'Macht und Recht: Der Ursprung der Eroberung Schlesiens durch König Friedrich II. von Preussen', *Hamburger Jahrbuch für Wirtschafts- und Gesellschaftspolitik* xxiv (1979), 235–91.

L. Schilling, 'Der Wiener Hof und Sachsen-Polen, 1697–1764', Verein für sächsische Landesgeschichte (ed.), *Sachsen-Polen zwischen 1697 und 1765* (Dresden, 1998), 119–36.

A. Schindling, 'Der Westfälische Frieden und der Reichstag', H. Weber (ed.), *Politische Ordnungen und Soziale Kräfte im Alten Reich* (Wiesbaden, 1980), 113–54.

Id. Schindling, 'Kurbrandenburg im System des Reiches während der zweiten Hälfte des 17. Jahrhunderts', O. Hauser (ed.), *Preussen, Europa und das Reich* (Cologne and Vienna, 1987), 32–64.

H. Schleier, 'Hans Delbrück: Ein politischer Historiker zwischen Preussen-Legende, amtlicher Militärgeschichtsschreibung und historischer Realität', G. Seeber (ed.), *Gestalten der Bismarckzeit* (East Berlin, 1978), 378–403.

A. von Schlieffen, 'Cannae (I)', *Vierteljahreshefte für Truppenführung und Heereskunde* vi, 4 (1909), 527–572; 'Cannae (II)', ibid. vii, 1 (1910), 11–30, (III), ibid. vii, 2 (1910), 196–232, (IV), ibid. vii, 4 (1910), 485–521, (V), ibid. viii, 3 (1911), 355–64, (VI), ibid. viii, 4 (1911), 523–45, (VII), ibid. ix, 2 (1912), 185–214, and (VIII), ibid. x, 1 (1913), 1–41.

Id., 'Der Feldherr' [1909], id., *Cannae*, ed. H. von Freytag-Loringhoven (Berlin, 1925), 264–72.

V. Schmidtchen, 'Der Einfluss der Technik auf die Kriegsführung zur Zeit Friedrich des Grossen', Militärgeschichtliches Forschungsamt (ed.), *Friedrich der Grosse und das Militärwesen seiner Zeit* (Herford, 1987), 121–42.

H. Schnitter, 'Die Schlacht bei Torgau 1760', *Militärgeschichtliche Mitteilungen* xviii (1979), 216–24.

H.-J. Schoeps, 'Die preussischen Konservativen', G. K. Kaltenbrunner (ed.), *Rekonstruktion des Konservatismus* (Bern, 3rd ed. 1978), 180–8.

W. Schulze, 'Das Ständewesen in den Erblanden der Habsburger Monarchie bis 1740: Vom dualistische Ständestaat zum organisch-föderativen Absolutismus', P. Baumgart and J. Schmädeke (eds), *Ständetum und Staatsbildung in Brandenburg-Preussen* (Berlin, 1983), 263–79.

K. W. Schweizer, 'William Pitt, Lord Bute and the Peace Negotiations with France, May-September 1761', *Albion* xiii, 2 (1981), 262–75.

[B.] Schwertfeger, 'Die Strategie Friedrichs des Grossen im Siebenjährigen Kriege', *Beiheft zum Militär-Wochenblatt* no. 2 (1913), 39–62.

H. M. Scott, 'Frederick the Great and the Administration of Prussian Diplomacy', R. Oresko, G. C. Gibbs, and H. M. Scott (eds), *Royal and Republican Sovereignty in Early Modern Europe: Essays in Memory of Ragnhild Hatton* (Cambridge, 1997), 501–26.

Id., 'Hanover in Mid-Eighteenth-Century Franco-British Geopolitics', B. Simms and T. Riotte (eds), *The Hanoverian Dimension in British History, 1714–1837* (Cambridge, 2007), 275–300.

D. E. Showalter, 'The Retaming of Bellona: Prussia and the Institutionalization of the Napoleonic Legacy, 1815–1876', *MA* xliv, 2 (1976), 57–63.

Id., 'Hubertusburg to Auerstädt: The Prussian Army in Decline', *German History* xii, 3 (1994), 308–33.

F. Spenser, 'The Anglo-Prussian Breach of 1762', *English Historical Review* xli, 1 (1956), 100–12.

W. Stratmann, 'Die Militärreform der Oranier—Wurzeln, Umsetzung und Rezeption', H. J. Vogt, H.-J. Giersberg, and A. W. Vliegenhart (eds), *Onder den Oranje Boom: Niederländische Kunst und Kultur im 17. und 18. Jahrhundert an den deutschen Fürstenhöfen* (Munich, 1999), 77–105.

R. Taverneaux, 'La Lorraine, les Habsbourg et l'Europe', id., J.-P. Bled and E. Faucher (eds), *Les Habsbourg et la Lorraine* (Nancy, 1988), 11–28.

A. von Taysen, 'Das militärische Testament Friedrich des Grossen', in Königlich-Preussische Archiv-Verwaltung (ed.), *Miscellaneen zur Geschichte König Friedrich des Grossen* (Berlin, 1878), 110–204.

R. von Thadden, 'Kirche im Schatten des Staates?: Zur Problematik der evangelischen Kirche in der preussischen Geschichte', H.-J. Puhle and H.-U. Wehler (eds), *Preussen im Rückblick* (Göttingen, 1980), 146–75.

V. Veltzke, 'Das brandenburgisch-preussische Herrscherbild: Kontinuität und Wandel', id. (ed.), *Macht und Dienst: Zur Darstellung des brandenburgisch-preussischen Herrscherhauses in Gemälde und Graphik, 1650–1900* (Minden, 1993), 7–9.

Id., 'Herrscher und Haus in Beispielen der Ölmalerei', ibid., 11–48.

T. Vial, 'Schleiermacher and the State', J. Mariña (ed.), *The Cambridge Companion to Friedrich Schleiermacher* (Cambridge, 2005), 269–85.

H. Weber, 'Frankreich, Münster und Kurtrier, 1692–1693', K. Repgen and S. Skalweit (eds), *Spiegel der Geschichte: Festgabe für Max Braubach zum 10. April 1964* (Münster, 1964), 501–49.

A. Werner, 'Die Verbotsschlaufe: Der Schriftsteller Walter von Molo, der "Fridericus"-Film von 1936 und die Zensur', A. Dorgerloh and M. Becker (eds), *Preussen aus Celluloid: Friederich II. im Film* (Berlin, 2011), 111–22.

H. Wilderotter, 'Das widerspenstige Erbe', *Preussen JahrBuch: Ein Almanach* (Berlin, 2001), 140–3.

B. Williams, 'Carteret and the So-Called Treaty of Hanau', *English Historical Review* xliv, 4 (1934), 684–7.

J. Willms, 'Posthume Zeitgenossenschaft: Anmerkungen zur rezeption Friedrichs II von Preussen', *Aus Politik und Zeitgeschichte* no. B20–21 (1986), 27–38.

P. Wilson, 'Violence and Rejection of Authority on Eighteenth-Century Germany: The Case of the Swabian Mutiny in 1757', *German History* xii, 1 (1994), 1–26.

Id., 'The German "Soldier Trade" of the Seventeenth and Eighteenth-Centuries: A Reassessment', *International History Review* xviii, 4 (1996), 757–92.

Id., 'Social Militarization in Eighteenth-Century Germany', *German History* xviii, 1 (2000), 1–39.

Id., 'Prussia's Relations with the Holy Roman Empire, 1740–1786', *Historical Journal* li, 2 (2008), 337–71.

Id., 'The Württemberg Army in the Seven Years' War', A. S. Burns (ed.), *The Changing Face of Old Regime Warfare: Essays in Honour of Christopher Duffy* (Warwick, 2022), 69–99.

R. A. Wines, 'The Imperial Circles: Princely Diplomacy and Imperial Reform, 1681–1714', *Journal of Modern History* xxxix, 1 (1967), 1–29.

R. Wirtgen, 'Das Feldgeschützmaterial der preussischen Artillerie zwischen 1740 und 1786', E. H. Schmidt and A. Wirtgen (eds), *Die Bewaffnung und Ausrüstung der Armee Friedrichs des Grossen* (Rastatt, 1986), 51–69.

H. von Zwiedeneck-Südenhorst, 'Die Anerkennung der pragmatischen Sanktion durch das Deutsche Reich', *Mitteilungen des Instituts für Österreichische Geschichte* xvi (1894), 276–341.

INDEX